The Spirit of Sociology

A Reader

Ron Matson
Wichita State University

PEARSON

Boston   New York   San Francisco
Mexico City   Montreal   Toronto   London   Madrid   Munich   Paris
Hong Kong   Singapore   Tokyo   Cape Town   Sydney

Senior Editor: Jeff Lasser
Series Editorial Assistant: Sara Owen
Senior *Marketing Manager:* Krista Groshong
Editorial-Production Service: Omegatype Typography, Inc.
Composition and Prepress Buyer: Linda Cox
Manufacturing Buyer: JoAnne Sweeney
Cover Administrator: Linda Knowles
Electronic Composition: Omegatype Typography, Inc.

For related titles and support materials, visit our
online catalog at www.ablongman.com.

Library of Congress Cataloging-in-Publication Data

The spirit of sociology : a reader / [edited by] Ron Matson.
    p. cm.
    Includes bibliographical references.
    ISBN 0-205-40446-4 (alk. paper)
    1. Sociology. 2. Applied sociology. 3. United States—Social
conditions—1980– I. Matson, Ronald R. (Ronald Robert)

HM585.S67 2005
301—dc22

                                    2004047832

Printed in the United States of America

10 9 8 7 6 5 4 3 2 1   09 08 07 06 05 04

This book is dedicated with heartfelt gratitude to
Linda
and the kids,
Sarah, Nick, Angie, and Jennifer

Contents

Can you imagine how our own culture would look if an anthropologist came along?

Topic 4 **Socialization 83**

look back and see how their childhood, class-based socialization experiences have affected them?

are "gendered" by the structures they manifest. Lorber is able to show us the reality of gender inside us, around us, and the processes whereby we come to "do" gender without being aware of our performance. The metaphor "night to his day" examines the complementary roles of men and women.

It can be said that the first wisdom of sociology is this—things are not what they seem. This too is a deceptively simple statement. It ceases to be simple after a while. Social reality turns out to have many layers of meaning. The discovery of each new layer changes the perception of the whole. Anthropologists use the term "culture shock" to describe the impact of a totally new culture upon a newcomer. In an extreme instance such shock will be experienced by the Western explorer who is told, halfway through dinner, that he is eating the nice old lady he had been chatting with the previous day—a shock with predictable physiological if not moral consequences. Most explorers no longer encounter cannibalism in their travels today. However, the first encounters with polygamy or with puberty rites or even with the way some nations drive their automobiles can be quite a shock to an American visitor. With the shock may go not only disapproval or disgust but a sense of excitement that things can *really* be that different from what they are at home. To some extent, at least, this is the excitement of any first travel abroad. The experience of sociological discovery could be described as "culture shock" minus geographical displacement In other words, the sociologist travels at home— with shocking results. He is unlikely to find that he is eating a nice old lady for dinner. But the discovery, for instance, that his own church has considerable money invested in the missile industry or that a few blocks from his home there are people who engage in cultic orgies may not be drastically different in emotional impact. Yet we would not want to imply that sociological discoveries are always or even usually outrageous to moral sentiment. Not at all. What they have in common with exploration in distant lands, however, is the sudden illumination of new and unsuspected facets of human existence in society. This is the excitement and . . . the humanistic justification of sociology.

People who like to avoid shocking discoveries, who prefer to believe that society is just what they were taught in Sunday School, who like the safety of the rules and the maxims of what Alfred Schuetz has called the "world-taken-for-granted," should stay away from sociology. People who feel no temptation before closed doors, who have no curiosity about human beings, who are content to admire scenery without wondering about the people who live in those houses on the other side of that river, should probably also stay away from sociology. They will find it unpleasant or, at any rate, unrewarding. People who are interested in human beings only if they can change, convert or reform them should also be warned, for they will find sociology much less useful than they hoped. And people whose interest is mainly in their own conceptual constructions will do just as well to turn to the study of little white mice. Sociology will be satisfying, in the long run, only to those who can think of nothing more entrancing than to watch men and to understand things human.

It may now be clear that we have, albeit deliberately, understated the case in the title of this chapter. To be sure, sociology is an individual pastime in the sense that it interests some men and bores others. Some like to observe human beings, others to experiment with mice. The world is big enough to hold all kinds and there is no logical priority for one interest as against another. But the word "pastime" is weak in describing what we mean. Sociology is more like a passion. The sociological perspective is more like a demon that possesses one, that drives one compellingly, again and again, to the questions that are its own. An introduction to sociology is, therefore, an invitation to a very special kind of passion.

Study Questions

1. What personal qualities does Berger argue will make for a good sociologist?
2. Why might we be shocked as sociology reveals its understanding of the world?

Reading 2
The Sociological Imagination

C. Wright Mills

Nowadays men often feel that their private lives are a series of traps. They sense that within their everyday worlds, they cannot overcome their troubles, and in this feeling, they are often quite correct: What ordinary men are directly aware of and what they try to do are bounded by the private orbits in which they live; their visions and their powers are limited to the close-up scenes of job, family, neighborhood; in other milieux, they move vicariously and remain spectators. And the more aware they become, however vaguely, of ambitions and of threats which transcend their immediate locales, the more trapped they seem to feel.

Underlying this sense of being trapped are seemingly impersonal changes in the very structure of continent-wide societies. The facts of contemporary history are also facts about the success and the failure of individual men and women. When a society is industrialized, a peasant becomes a worker; a feudal lord is liquidated or becomes a businessman. When classes rise or fall, a man is employed or unemployed; when the rate of investment goes up or down, a man takes new heart or goes broke. When wars happen, an insurance salesman becomes a rocket launcher; a store clerk, a radar man; a wife lives alone; a child grows up without a father. Neither the life of an individual nor the history of a society can be understood without understanding both.

Yet men do not usually define the troubles they endure in terms of historical change and institutional contradiction. The well-being they enjoy, they do not usually impute to the big ups and downs of the societies in which they live. Seldom aware of the intricate connection between the patterns of their own lives and the course of world history, ordinary men do not usually know what this connection means for the kinds of men they are becoming and for the kinds of history-making in which they might take part. They do not possess the quality of mind essential to grasp the interplay of man and society, of biography and history, of self and world. They cannot cope with their personal troubles in such ways as to control the structural transformations that usually lie behind them.

Surely it is no wonder. In what period have so many men been so totally exposed at so fast a pace to such earthquakes of change? That Americans have not known such catastrophic changes as have the men and women of other societies is due to historical facts that are now quickly becoming "merely history." The history that now affects every man is world history. Within this scene and this period, in the course of a single generation, one sixth of mankind is transformed from all that is feudal and backward into all that is modern, advanced, and fearful. Political colonies are freed; new and less visible forms of imperialism installed. Revolutions occur; men feel the intimate grip of new kinds of authority. Totalitarian societies rise, and are smashed to bits—or succeed fabulously. After two centuries of ascendancy, capitalism is shown up as only one way to make society into an industrial apparatus. After two centuries of hope, even formal democracy is restricted to a quite small portion of mankind. Everywhere in the underdeveloped world, ancient ways of life are broken up and vague expectations become urgent demands. Everywhere in the overdeveloped world, the means of authority and of violence become total in scope and bureaucratic in form. Humanity itself now lies before us, the super-nation at either pole concentrating its most co-ordinated and massive efforts upon the preparation of World War Three.

The very shaping of history now outpaces the ability of men to orient themselves in accordance with cherished values. And which values? Even when they do not panic, men often sense that older ways of feeling and thinking have collapsed and that newer beginnings are ambiguous to the point of moral stasis. Is it any wonder that ordinary men feel they cannot cope with the larger worlds with which they are so suddenly confronted? That they cannot understand the meaning of their epoch for their own lives? That—in defense of selfhood—they become morally insensible, trying to remain altogether private men? Is it any wonder that they come to be possessed by a sense of the trap?

It is not only information that they need—in this Age of Fact, information often dominates their attention and overwhelms their capacities to assimilate it. It is not only the skills of reason that they need—although their struggles to acquire these often exhaust their limited moral energy.

What they need, and what they feel they need, is a quality of mind that will help them to use information and to develop reason in order to achieve lucid summations of what is going on in the world and of

Consider marriage. Inside a marriage a man and a woman may experience personal troubles, but when the divorce rate during the first four years of marriage is 250 out of every 1,000 attempts, this is an indication of a structural issue having to do with the institutions of marriage and the family and other institutions that bear upon them.

Or consider the metropolis—the horrible, beautiful, ugly, magnificent sprawl of the great city. For many upper-class people, the personal solution to 'the problem of the city' is to have an apartment with private garage under it in the heart of the city, and forty miles out, a house by Henry Hill, garden by Garrett Eckbo, on a hundred acres of private land. In these two controlled environments—with a small staff at each end and a private helicopter connection—most people could solve many of the problems of personal milieux caused by the facts of the city. But all this, however splendid, does not solve the public issues that the structural fact of the city poses. What should be done with this wonderful monstrosity? Break it all up into scattered units, combining residence and work? Refurbish it as it stands? Or, after evacuation, dynamite it and build new cities according to new plans in new places? What should those plans be? And who is to decide and to accomplish whatever choice is made? These are structural issues; to confront them and to solve them requires us to consider political and economic issues that affect innumerable milieux.

In so far as an economy is so arranged that slumps occur, the problem of unemployment becomes incapable of personal solution. In so far as war is inherent in the nation-state system and in the uneven industrialization of the world, the ordinary individual in his restricted milieu will be powerless—with or without psychiatric aid—to solve the troubles this system or lack of system imposes upon him. In so far as the family as an institution turns women into darling little slaves and men into their chief providers and unweaned dependents, the problem of a satisfactory marriage remains incapable of purely private solution. In so far as the overdeveloped megalopolis and the overdeveloped automobile are built-in features of the overdeveloped society, the issues of urban living will not be solved by personal ingenuity and private wealth.

What we experience in various and specific milieux, I have noted, is often caused by structural changes. Accordingly, to understand the changes of many personal milieux we are required to look beyond them. And the number and variety of such structural changes increase as the institutions within which we live become more embracing and more intricately connected with one another. To be aware of the idea of social structure and to use it with sensibility is to be capable of tracing such linkages among a great variety of milieux. To be able to do that is to possess the sociological imagination.

3

What are the major issues for publics and the key troubles of private individuals in our time? To formulate issues and troubles, we must ask what values are cherished yet threatened, and what values are cherished and supported, by the characterizing trends of our period. In the case both of threat and of support we must ask what salient contradictions of structure may be involved.

When people cherish some set of values and do not feel any threat to them, they experience *well-being* When they cherish values but *do* feel them to be threatened, they experience a crisis—either as a personal trouble or as a public issue. And if all their values seem involved, they feel the total threat of panic.

But suppose people are neither aware of any cherished values nor experience any threat? That is the experience of *indifference*, which, if it seems to involve all their values, becomes apathy. Suppose, finally, they are unaware of any cherished values, but still are very much aware of a threat? That is the experience of *uneasiness*, of anxiety, which, if it is total enough, becomes a deadly unspecified malaise.

Ours is a time of uneasiness and indifference—not yet formulated in such ways as to permit the work of reason and the play of sensibility. Instead of troubles—defined in terms of values and threats—there is often the misery of vague uneasiness; instead of explicit issues there is often merely the beat feeling that all is somehow not right. Neither the values threatened nor whatever threatens them has been stated; in short, they have not been carried to the point of decision. Much less have they been formulated as problems of social science.

In the 'thirties there was little doubt—except among certain deluded business circles that there was an economic issue which was also a pack of personal troubles. In these arguments about "the crisis of capitalism," the formulations of Marx and the many unacknowledged re-formulations of his work probably set the leading terms of the issue, and some men came to understand their personal troubles in these terms. The values threatened were plain to see and cherished by all; the structural contra-

Step #2: "OK, I'm Interested, But is There a Future for Me in Sociology?"

It is the *extremely* rare student who comes out of high school with their mind made up to study sociology in college. The number is something like 3 out of every 10,000 (Howery, 1985). Yikes! If it were not for the requirements most colleges impose on students you would find a lot of academic sociologists roaming the streets. . . .

What I am suggesting, is it could happen to you; you could choose to major in sociology. It has happened to others. The question is, how should you respond? What type of questions should you ask? How does one go about pursuing sociology as a major? Is there a future in sociology? This choice, making sociology your major, or part of a double major, is a critical choice, and should not be made lightly. . . .

In my experience once the typical student decides on sociology there develops a sense of energy and anticipation about the future. But the future is as much on the collective minds of parents as it is on the mind of the son or daughter. At some point the student tells Mom and Dad what their interests are and what their decision is. And, Mom and Dad do what good parents should do; they test the decision. Recently I had lunch with a parent of [a] junior sociology major who is interested in a career in criminal justice. This parent and I have had several in-depth discussions about his son. At one point the father said, "The bottom line is, will my son be able to get a job when he graduates? By that time we will have spent $60,000 on his education. That's quite an investment. We want to make sure he has a future." Such sentiment is valid and is to be expected. . . .

Now back to the question regarding the future. The short answer is, yes, there is a future. And it is a future which is bright and growing brighter as time passes. It is bright because people with vision have begun to take the central and universal ideas of sociology and have begun looking for ways to put them into action. This effort in itself is neither new nor unique. Many other disciplines have been doing this for decades or centuries. Some have been doing this for years, but with tools and concepts derived from sociology. Marketing experts, political pollsters, etc., have been employing basic survey research techniques and statistical procedures developed over time in sociology for very practical purposes. It is also the case that sociology has developed and given birth to whole new disciplines such as criminal justice/criminology, gerontology, women's studies, black studies, demography, and social work. Each of these has put the discipline to work in very specific ways. Now sociology as a discipline, and sociologists as a profession are asserting their collective strengths. And, we find that more and more these strengths are finding expression and applications outside the classroom. . . .

In 1988 the U.S. Office of Personal Management established a position-classification standard for sociology. This means that the federal government officially recognizes the specific contributions which sociology can make. The standard for "Sociology GS-184" begins with the following statement:

> This series includes positions which involve professional work requiring a knowledge of sociology and sociological methods specifically related to the establishment, validation, interpretation, and application of knowledge about social processes. Sociologists study specialized areas such as: changes in the character, size, distribution, and composition of the population: social mechanisms for enforcing compliance with widely accepted norms and for controlling deviance; social phenomena having to do with human health and disease; the structure and operation of organizations; and the complex interrelationship of the individual and society.
>
> Sociologists are concerned primarily with the study of patterns of group and organizational behavior, social interaction, and social situations in which interaction occurs. The emphasis is on the patterns of behavior that are characteristic of social groups, organizations, institutions, and nations. Some sociologists perform sociological research, others apply sociological principles and findings, and some perform a combination of both kinds of work.

Based on this standard five specializations are recommended, including demography, law and social control, medical sociology, organizational analysis, and social psychology. In addition the standard advises prospective applicants that sociology is appropriate education for work in other areas such as but not limited to:

GS-020	Community Planning Series
GS-101	Social Work Series
GS-131	International Relations Series
GS-135	Foreign Agricultural Affairs Series
GS-140	Manpower Research and Analysis Series
GS-142	Manpower Development Series
GS-160	Civil Rights Analysis Series
GS-185	Social Work Series
GS-230	Employee Relations Series
GS-685	Public Health Program Specialist Series
GS-696	Consumer Safety Series
GS-1150	Industrial Specialist Series

W. I. Thomas, Herbert Blumer, Everett Hughes, and Erving Goffman, who taught or studied at the University of Chicago between 1910 and 1960. Because it originated at the University of Chicago, symbolic interactionism is sometimes referred to as the Chicago School.

Symbolic interactionism is based on five core ideas. First, it assumes that human beings act in terms of the meanings they assign to objects in their environment. (Interactionists define the term object very broadly to include material things, events, symbols, actions, and other people and groups.) Using slightly different terminology to make the same point, interactionists maintain that people's conduct is powerfully influenced by their definition of the situation. This assumption can be clarified by contrasting it to a rudimentary model of social action advanced by a psychological perspective known as behaviorism. The behaviorist approach characterizes conduct as a response to objective stimuli, and suggests that human behavior resembles a series of stimulus-response chains:

stimulus ————————> response.

Rejecting the notion that individuals respond directly to an objective stimulus, interactionists insist that people interpret, or assign meanings to, the stimulus before they act:

stimulus ————> interpretation ————> response.

Athletes' reactions to coaches criticisms, for instance, depends largely on whether they interpret that criticism as a constructive attempt to improve their play or as a malicious attack on their character.

Even when a definition of the situation is demonstrably false, it can still exert a powerful effect on behavior. As W. I. Thomas once said, "A situation defined as real is real in its consequences." Many adults, for example, perceive Halloween as filled with potential danger, and believe that their young children are vulnerable to sadistic strangers dispensing drug-tainted candy or apples laced with razor blades. The belief that such acts of Halloween sadism are widespread is, in fact, an urban legend with virtually no factual basis (Best and Horiuchi 1985). Nevertheless, millions of parents are convinced that the threat is genuine and, acting in terms of their definition of the situation, continue to inspect their children's treats for signs of tampering.

Symbolic interactionism's second assumption asserts that social action typically involves making a series of adjustments and readjustments as an individual's interpretation of the situation changes. Interactionists reject the notion that behavior is the unmediated product of a variable or cause. Instead, they view action as something that is continually being built up, modified, re-directed, and transformed (Blumer 1969). People's initial definition of the situation is always subject to change, and as they redefine the situation their conduct changes accordingly. Effective teachers, for example, routinely interpret students' comments, facial expressions, and other gestures to determine whether the subject matter is being communicated clearly. They rely on this feedback to define and re-define the unfolding classroom situation and to make corresponding adjustments in their presentations. When students look confused, they may introduce a familiar example; if students' attention should wander, the instructors may call on them; and if students are visibly upset, they may ask to meet privately with them after class.

Third, interactionists assume that the meanings imputed to an object are socially constructed (Berger and Luckmann 1966). Meanings do not, in other words, simply reflect a quality or essence built into the very nature of an object. Other than its size and color, the cloth used to make handkerchiefs is virtually identical to that used to produce American flags. Though handkerchiefs and flags are sewn from the same physical material, the meanings attached to these two objects differ in dramatic ways. Rather than being intrinsic to an object, then, meanings are attributed to it by individuals, groups, and communities.

Elaborating this logic, some interactionists treat the self as an object whose meanings are socially constructed. In other words, the kind of person you assume yourself to be, and that others take you to be, mirror the meanings that individuals and groups have assigned to you. If, from a young age, family members, friends, and teachers have said you were "brilliant" and have acted toward you in a manner consistent with that characterization, then one assumption you are likely to make about yourself—one meaning that you are likely to assign to yourself—is that you are a highly intelligent person.

Fourth, symbolic interactionism holds that in modern, heterogeneous societies, different groups often assign divergent meanings to the "same" object. Contemporary societies contain a wide variety of groups (e.g., occupational, religious, age-based, racial and ethnic groups). Since group members interact and communicate frequently with one another, they tend to develop a common "universe of discourse" (Mead 1934) or "war of all against all." According to one prominent functionalist, the relative stability of American society over the last two hundred years (the Civil War being a glaring exception) is largely attributable to the continuing consensus on the values of achievement and liberty (Lipset 1979).

Fifth, functionalism asserts that deviance and conflict arise from social strains, or contradictions within an institution or between institutions. That is, the primary source of contention and crime are inconsistencies inherent in the social system itself. In an influential essay, Robert Merton (1938) contends that in American society everyone, regardless of his or her station in life, is encouraged to pursue the American Dream. At the same time, however, the institutional means (e.g., a quality education and well-connected friends or acquaintances on the job market) for attaining success are not equally distributed: middle- and upper-class people are, in general, much more likely to have access to these institutional means than are working-class people. Confronted with this contradiction between a cultural goal (i.e., success) and the institutional means (e.g., a quality education) to achieve it, some individuals and groups will turn to crime (e.g., selling drugs). Note that in Merton's terms, crime often involves using "innovative," illegal means to realize a cultural goal prized both by criminals and law-abiding citizens. Under certain conditions, the same contradiction between cultural goals and institutional means can prompt widespread rebellion, with various groups replacing established cultural goals and the standard, institutional means with radically different values and means.

The Conflict Perspective

Like functionalism, the conflict perspective is a macrosociological approach that examines the emergence, persistence, and transformation of long-standing practices, institutions, and societies. Karl Marx, whose work first appeared in the mid-nineteenth century, is usually credited with crystallizing the key principles of this approach. Max Weber, an early twentieth-century German sociologist, is also recognized as a founding figure of conflict sociology. Leading contemporary conflict theorists include William Chambliss, Randall Collins, Ralf Dahrendorf, William Domhoff, and C. Wright Mills.

The conflict perspective rejects the functionalist notion that societies can be accurately portrayed as problem-solving entities. It also disputes the complementary idea that long-standing practices and institutions represent reasonably satisfactory answers to problems and as such contribute to a society's general welfare. Conflict sociologists embrace a very different orienting assumption: societies are arenas in which groups with fundamentally antagonistic interests struggle against one another. Different theorists within this tradition differ in terms of which particular groups and struggles they emphasize. Marx, for instance, highlights the conflicts between social classes, while Weber focuses on competing status groups (e.g., racial, ethnic, religious, age-based, etc.) and Dahrendorf and Collins draw attention to the battles between those who have authority and those subject to that authority. Despite disagreements about which groups and struggles are most important, all conflict sociologists believe that the interests that divide groups (whether classes, status groups, and so on) are built into the very fabric of a social order; these opposing interests are not readily negotiated, compromised, or resolved, nor can they be wished away or papered-over.

Second, conflicts among classes, status groups, and between those exercising authority and those subject to it supply the energy and the motivation for constructing and maintaining (as well as challenging and transforming) practices and institutions. Platt's (1977) well-known study of the origins of the juvenile court, for example, contends that this institution was created (in 1899) by social and economic elites and was employed to target and control the children of working-class immigrants residing in large cities. Conflict sociologists argue that today the nation's newly constructed maximum security prisons are, in practice, reserved predominantly for young, minority males raised in inner-city areas where good jobs are scarce (Chambliss 1999). On the other hand, white-collar, middle-class criminals, if they receive a prison sentence at all, are rarely housed in these types of facilities.

Third, the conflict perspective characterizes on-going practices and institutions as structures of domination that promote the interests of a relatively powerful, superordinate group while subverting the interests of relatively powerless, subordinate groups, even though the latter are usually much larger, numerically, than the powerful elites. Consequently, this perspective's orienting question is: which group's interests are served by a specific practice or institution? Kozol's (1991) investigation of how public schools are funded found that schools located in well-to-do suburban areas receive substantially more support than inner-city schools, which often lack textbooks, desks, and even serviceable plumbing. Far from enabling students from economically disadvantaged backgrounds to compete fairly on a level playing field, the current school system simply reflects and reproduces existing class inequalities. Fourth, the conflict perspective reconceptualizes what functionalism terms values as ideologies. The primary purpose of an ideology is to protect and promote the distinctive interests of a particular class (or status or authority group). This legitimating purpose is best served when the ideology is presented in universal terms; when its ideas are stated as if they apply to everyone equally. According to the conflict approach, achievement and equal opportunity are most accurately viewed not as widely shared values but as a dominant ideology that operates to preserve (and reproduce) existing systems of inequality. In essence, the ideology of achievement and equal opportunity asserts that individuals and groups with great wealth, prestige, and power are rightfully entitled to these rewards because they have sacrificed, worked hard, and/or displayed exceptional talent. This ideology also explains why many people have few or none of these rewards: they are lazy, unwilling to make the sacrifices necessary for success, and/or lack the requisite talent. This ideology justifies the unequal distribution of social rewards by referring to individuals' character and moral virtues (or lack thereof). At the same time, it draws attention away from the structural inequities that largely explain why members of some groups are much more likely to "succeed" than are members of other groups.

Fifth, the conflict approach holds that significant social change usually reflects the efforts of groups mobilizing to advance their collective interests, often at the expense of other groups' interests. In this regard, proponents of conflict sociology question the functionalist claim that the substantial financial rewards enjoyed by physicians are due to the fact that medical doctors perform tasks that are, objectively, of great functional importance to society. Physicians' impressive incomes are more persuasively explained, conflict sociologists contend, with the observation that the American medical profession has established, in effect, a monopoly on the provision of health care (Starr 1982). Prior to 1850, this monopoly did not exist, and physicians were poorly paid and given little esteem. After the Civil War, however, doctors began to organize in earnest, and by the late nineteenth century they secured legislation prohibiting other groups and individuals from providing health care. The exclusion of competitors paved the way for a remarkable surge in doctors' income and a parallel rise in their prestige.

References

Berger, Peter and Thomas Luckmann. 1966. *The Social Construction of Reality.* New York: Doubleday.

Best, Joel and Gerald Horiuchi. 1985. "The Razor Blade in the Apple: The Social Construction of Urban Legends." *Social Problems* 32: 488–499.

Blumer, Herbert. 1969. *Symbolic Interactionism.* Englewood Cliffs: Prentice-Hall.

Chambliss, William J. 1999. *Power, Politics, and Crime.* Boulder: Westview Press.

Collins, Randall. 1981. "On the Microfoundations of Macrosociology." *American Journal of Sociology* 86: 984–1014.

Davis, Kingsley and Wilbert E. Moore. 1945. "Some Principles of Stratification." *American Sociological Review* 10: 242–249.

Gusfield, Joseph R. 1963. *Symbolic Crusade.* Urbana: University of Illinois Press.

Kozol, Jonathan. 1991. *Savage Inequalities.* New York: HarperCollins.

Lipset, Seymour M. 1979. *The First New Nation.* New York: W. W. Norton.

Mead, George H. 1934. *Mind, Self and Society.* Edited by Charles W. Morris. Chicago: University of Chicago Press.

Merton, Robert K. 1938. "Social Structure and Anomie." *American Societal Review* 3: 672–682.

———. 1968. *Social Theory and Social Structure.* Enlarged edition. New York: Free Press.

Parsons, Talcott. 1977. *The Evolution of Society.* Edited and with an Introduction by Jackson Toby. Englewood Cliffs: Prentice-Hall.

Platt, Anthony M. 1977. *The Child Savers.* 2nd edition. Chicago: University of Chicago Press.

Starr, Paul. 1982. *The Social Transformation of American Medicine.* Cambridge: Harvard University Press.

Study Questions

1. Distinguish the main qualities of symbolic interaction, functionalism, and conflict theories.

2. What are the main terms you can identify that belong to each of the three theoretical perspectives? Make a list of each.

Reading 5

Tell Them Who I Am

The Lives of Homeless Women

Elliot Liebow

This is a participant observer study of single, homeless women in emergency shelters in a small city just outside Washington, D.C. In participant observation, the researcher tries to participate as fully as possible in the life of the people being studied. Of course, there are obvious and severe limits to how well a man with a home and family can put himself in the place of homeless women. One simply goes where they go, gets to know them over time as best one can, and tries very hard to see the world from their perspective.

It is often said that, in participant observation studies, the researcher is the research instrument. So is it here. Everything reported about the women in this study has been selected by me and filtered through me, so it is important that I tell you something about myself and my prejudices as well as how this study came about. Indeed, I feel obliged to tell you more than is seemly and more than you may want to know, but these are things that the women themselves knew about me and that had an important if unknown influence on my relationship with them.

In a real sense, I backed into this study, which took shape, more or less, as I went along. In 1984, I learned that I had cancer and a very limited life expectancy. I did not want to spend my last months on the 12th floor of a government office building, so at 58 I retired on disability from my job of 20-some years as an anthropologist with the National Institute of Mental Health.

I looked well, felt well, and had a lot of time on my hands, so I became a volunteer at a soup kitchen that had recently opened. I worked there one night a week. In the early part of the evening, I helped serve food or just sat around with the men and women who had come there, usually eating with them. In case of trouble, I tried to keep the peace. Later I went upstairs to "the counselor's office," where I met with people who needed assistance in getting shelter for the night. For the next hour or so, I called around to the various shelters in the county or in downtown Washington, D.C., trying to locate and reserve sleeping space for the men and women who needed it.

I enjoyed the work and the people at the soup kitchen, but this was only one night a week, so I became a volunteer at The Refuge, an emergency shelter for homeless women. This, too, was one night a week, from 6:30 to 10:00, and involved sleeping overnight twice a month. I picked this shelter because I had visited there briefly the year before and liked the feel of it. Here, along with three other volunteers, my job was to help prepare the food (usually just heat the main dishes and make a salad); help serve the food; distribute towels, soap, and other sundries on request; socialize with the women; keep order; and keep a daily log that included the names of all the women present and their time of arrival.

Almost immediately, I found myself enjoying the company of the women. I was awed by the enormous effort that most of them made to secure the most elementary necessities and decencies of life that the rest of us take for granted. And I was especially struck by their sense of humor, so at odds with any self-pity—the ability to step back and laugh at oneself, however wryly. One evening, soon after I started working at the shelter, several of us remained at the table to talk after finishing dinner. Pauline turned to me and said, in a stage whisper, making sure that Hilda would hear her, "Hilda has a Ph.D."

Hilda laughed. "No," she said, "I don't have a Ph.D., but I do have a bachelor's degree in biology." She paused, then began again. "You know," she said, "all my life I wanted to be an MD and now, at the age of 54, I finally made it. I'm a Manic Depressive."

Seduced by the courage and the humor of the women, and by the pleasure of their company, I started going to the shelter four and sometimes five days a week. (For the first two years, I also kept my one-night-a-week job with the soup kitchen.) Probably because it was something I was trained to do, or perhaps out of plain habit, I decided to take notes.

"Listen," I said at the dinner table one evening, after getting permission to do a study from the shelter director. "I want your permission to take notes. I want to go home at night and write down what I can remember about the things you say and do. Maybe I'll write a book about homeless women."

Most of the dozen or so women there nodded their heads or simply shrugged. All except Regina. Her acceptance was conditional. "Only if you promise not to publish before I do," she said. Believing that neither one of us, for different reasons, would ever publish anything in the future, I readily agreed.[1] . . .

It is difficult to be precise about how I was perceived by the women. I am 6'1" and weigh about 175 pounds. I had a lot of white hair but was otherwise nondescript. I dressed casually, often in corduroy pants, shirt, and cardigan. The fact that I was Jewish did not seem to matter much one way or another so far as I could tell.

Most of the women probably liked having me around. Male companionship was generally in short supply and the women often made a fuss about the few male volunteers. I would guess that there were as many women who actively sought me out as there were women who avoided me. The fact that I had written a book that was available at the library (three or four women took the trouble to read it) enhanced my legitimacy in their eyes.[2]

Principally, I think, the women saw me as an important resource. I had money and a car, and by undertaking to write a book, I had made it my business to be with them. I routinely lent out $2, $5, $10 or even $20 on request to the handful who asked. I told them I had set aside a certain amount as a revolving fund and I could only keep lending money if they kept returning it. This worked fairly well.

There were a few women, of course, who would never be in a position to return the money, and this made for a problem. It would have been patronizing simply to make a gift of the money; they wanted to be borrowers, not beggars, and I was just as eager as they to avoid a demeaning panhandler/donor relationship. But I did not want them to be embarrassed or to avoid me simply because they couldn't repay a loan, nor did I want to shut them off from borrowing more. My solution was to reassure these women I had no immediate need for the money and could wait indefinitely for repayment.

Some of the women would perhaps characterize me as a friend, but I am not certain how deep or steadfast this sense of friendship might be. One day, Regina and I were talking about her upcoming trial about two months away. I had already agreed to accompany her to the courtroom and serve as an advisor, but Regina wanted further reassurance.

"You will be there, won't you?" she said.

As a way of noting the profundity that nothing in life is certain, I said, jokingly, "It's not up to me, it's up to The Man Upstairs."

"Well," she said, "if you die before the trial, you will ask one of your friends to help me, won't you?" I looked hard at her to see if she was joking, too. She wasn't. She was simply putting first things first.

One or two of the women did say something like "If you weren't married, would you give me a run for my money?" Neither "yes" nor "no" was a suitable response, but it usually sufficed for me to say (and mean), "I think you are a very nice person."

I tried to make myself available for driving people to Social Services, a job interview, a clinic or hospital, a cemetery, to someone's house, to another shelter, to help them move their belongings, or on other personal errands. With my consent, several women used my name as a personal reference for jobs or housing, and a few used my home as a mailing address for income tax refunds or other business.

Several of the women got to know my two daughters, both of whom came to The Refuge a few evenings each during the winters. One daughter was engaged to be married and her fiancé also came a few times. These visits helped strengthen my ties to those women who knew my daughters by face and name. They could ask me how my wife, Harriet, or Elisabeth and Jessica and Eric were doing, and my subsequent participation in discussions about family or child-rearing was much more personal and immediate as a result.

It is difficult to exaggerate the importance of this kind of familiarity. It is essential, I believe, in this kind of study—a participant observer kind of study—that relationships be as symmetrical as possible, that there be a quid pro quo; the women needed to know as much about me as I knew about them.

My association with the women was most intense during the winter of 1984–85, all of 1986, much of 1987, and the winter of 1987–88. Thereafter, I slackened off, partly for health reasons and partly because I had already collected more notes than I knew what to do with.[3] I continued to go to the shelters intermittently, and several of the women called me regularly at home. It was also at this time that I started playing around with the notes to see how I might eventually make sense of them.

In general, I have tried to avoid labeling any of the women as "mentally ill," "alcoholic," "drug addicted," or any other characterization that is commonly used to describe—or, worse, to explain—the homeless person. Judgments such as these are almost always made against a background of homelessness. If the same person were seen in another setting, the judgment might be altogether different. Like you, I know people who drink, people who do drugs, and bosses who have tantrums and treat their subordinates like dirt. They all have good jobs. Were they to become homeless, some of them would surely also become "alcoholics," "addicts," or "mentally ill." Similarly, if some of the homeless women who are now so labeled were to be magically transported to a more usual and acceptable setting, some of them—not all, of course—would shed their labels and take their places with the rest of us somewhere on the spectrum of normality.

The reader may be puzzled by the short shrift given here to mental illness. This was no oversight. I have no training as a mental health professional so it is not always clear to me who is mentally ill and who is not. There were always some women who acted crazy or whom most considered crazy, and the women themselves often agreed with the public at large that many homeless people are mentally ill.

From the beginning, however, I paid little attention to mental illness, partly because I had difficulty recognizing it, and partly for other reasons. Sometimes mental illness seemed to be a "now-you-see-it, now-you-don't" phenomenon; some of the women were fine when their public assistance checks arrived, but became increasingly "symptomatic" as the month progressed and their money (security?) diminished, coming full circle when the next check arrived.[4] Others had good or bad days or weeks but with no obvious pattern or periodicity, although one woman linked her down period to her menstrual cycle. With a little patience on my part, almost all the women with mental or emotional problems were eventually and repeatedly accessible. Even on "bad" days, perhaps especially on "bad" days, these women sometimes said things that seemed to come, uncensored, from the depths of their emotional lives.

It seems to me that those women who may have been mentally ill (or alcoholic or drug addicted) by one or another standard were homeless for exactly the same proximal reason that everyone else was homeless: they had no place to live. Similarly, their greatest need of the moment was the same as everyone else's: to be assured of a safe, warm place to sleep at night, one or more hot meals a day, and the presence, if not the companionship, of fellow human beings. Given this perspective and my purposes, which and how many of the women were mentally ill was not a critical issue.

Whatever one's view of mental illness, it is probably true that the more one gets to know about a person, the easier it is to put oneself in that person's place or to understand his or her viewpoint, and the less reason one has for thinking of that person or treating that person as mentally ill.[5]

This perspective—indeed, participant observation itself—raises the age-old problem of whether anyone can understand another or put oneself in another's place. Many thoughtful people believe that a sane person cannot know what it is to be crazy, that a white man cannot understand a black man, a Jew cannot see through the eyes of a Christian, a man through the eyes of a woman, and so forth in both directions. In an important sense, of course, and to a degree, this is certainly true; in another sense, and to a degree, it is surely false, because the logical extension of such a view is that no one can know another, that only John Jones can know John Jones, in which case social life would be impossible.[6]

I do not mean that a man with a home and family can see and feel the world as homeless women see and feel it. I do mean, however, that it is reasonable and useful to try to do so. Trying to put oneself in the place of the other lies at the heart of the social contract and of social life itself.

In the early months, I sometimes tried to get Betty or one of the other women to see things as I saw them. One night Betty waited half an hour in back of the library for a bus that never came. She was convinced this was deliberate and personal abuse on the part of the Metro system. Metro was out to get her, she said. "But how did Metro know you were waiting for a bus at that time?" I asked. Betty shook her head in pity of me. "Well for Christ's sake, Elliot, I was there on the street, right there in public, in the open! How could they not see me waiting for that damn bus?"

Fairly quickly, I learned not to argue with Betty but simply to relax and marvel at her end-of-the-month ingenuity. ("End-of-the-month" because that's when her public assistance money ran out and when she was most bitter at the way the world was treating her. At that time, a $10 or $20 loan could dramatically reduce or even eliminate her paranoid thoughts.) Once, when her food stamps had not come, even two days after Judy had received hers, Betty dryly observed that this was further proof that Richman County was trying to rid itself of homeless women. "They give Judy Tootie her food stamps so she'll eat herself to death

[Judy weighed 300 pounds]. They won't give me mine so I'll starve to death." She got no argument from me. I had learned to go with the flow. Sometimes I annoyed or even angered some of the women. When Louise told me that some of the women were following her around all day and harassing her, I asked her why they did these things. "You're just like the state's attorney," she said, "always asking for reasons. Whenever I tell him that someone assaulted me, he always asks me why they did it. People with criminal minds don't need a reason to do something. That's what makes them criminals."

I think of Betty and Louise and many of the other women as friends. As a friend, I owe them friendship. Perhaps I also owe them something because I have so much and they have so little, but I do not feel under any special obligation to them as research subjects. Indeed, I do not think of them as "research subjects." Since they knew what I was trying to do and allowed me to do it, they could just as well be considered collaborators in what might fairly be seen as a cooperative enterprise.

Notes

1 Let the record show that now, some seven-plus years later, I have her permission to go ahead.

2 *Tally's Corner: A Study of Negro Streetcorner Men.*

3 For the same reason, I stopped taking life histories. After the women had known me for a few months, I took about 20 life histories on tape, often at the request of the women themselves and over a period of two years or so. Some of these lasted several hours over two or three sessions and I found myself accumulating more information than I could handle.

4 Many schizophrenics are completely lucid for long periods of time, and their thoughts and behavior are completely indistinguishable from those of normals. Even Bleuler . . . asserted that there were certain very important cognitive processes . . . that were frequently identical among schizophrenics and normals. *In many important respects, then, an insane person may be completely sane"* (emphasis added). Morris Rosenberg, "A Symbolic Interactionist View of Psychosis," *Journal of Health and Social Behavior*, 25, no. 3 (September 1984), p. 291.

5 In a symbolic interactionist view, "insanity is not a matter of . . . impaired functioning or social maladjustment. . . . It is unequivocally an interactional concept that is distinguished by an *observer's* inability to take the role of the actor" (emphasis in original). Rosenberg, "A Symbolic Interactionist View," p. 291.

6 Those who romanticize history and heroes are especially likely to close their minds to the possibility of people "understanding" one another. Allan Bloom, who does not let his brilliance get in the way of drawing wrong conclusions, is one such person. After separating "thinkers" from "doers," he argues that the thinker cannot understand the doer, then proceeds to a spectacular nonsequitur: "Does one not have to be akin to

Caesar to understand him? To say that one does not have to be Caesar to understand him is equivalent to saying that one does not have to be anything to understand everything." *The Closing of the American Mind*, p. 303.

Study Questions

1. What sort of personal relationships did Liebow have with the members of his study sample?

2. How are Liebow's relationships both helpful and harmful to his research?

Reading 6
Theory, Practice, and Sociology

Howard M. Rebach and John G. Bruhn

During the course of the twentieth century, the population of the world increased from less than 2 billion to about 6 billion people. With this increase has come increasing demands on the world's resources, global warming and increasing pollution of our environment, and the potential for shortages of food and fuel and fouling of air and water. The world carries into the twenty-first century the social problems of the twentieth: ethnic conflict, the growth and centralization of corporate power, an increasing gulf between the haves and have-nots, all problems that threaten the existence of democratic institutions in both the developed part of the world as well as the developing nations. If the world's citizens are to address these problems, we will need a combination of scientific knowledge, wisdom, and activism. We contend that well-trained sociological practitioners can and should take their place among those working on solutions. . . .

Clinical Sociology *Is* Sociology

Of interest to those of us who call ourselves "clinical sociologists," another question has been raised: Why do sociologists who are interested in applying the theories, principles, concepts, and methods of the field have to be marginalized by their peers (Turner, 1998)? As Turner (1998:250) pointed out, "the early founders of sociology all had a vision of using sociology." Straus (1985) is another who held that sociology is eminently practical. Straus asked, if sociology is not to be used to make sense out of life, what is its purpose? Why, then, "do sociologists debate who is and who is not a real sociologist, dismissing those who apply or practice sociology as clinicians without accepted credentials and theoretical rules of thumb" (Turner, 1998:252; Babbie *et al.*, 1998).

Babbie (1994) pointed out that sociology involves the study of human beings. More specifically, it is the study of the interactions and relations among human beings. Society is a living laboratory. Sociology provides the opportunity to study the constant process of social change and its continuous effects on human behavior; a moving picture that never stops. Some sociologists have prided themselves as being observers and social critics who remain value free and noninvolved with their subjects. But of what use is it to observe, document, and discuss human issues and problems? Of what use is it to seek to develop theory, if one never acts to apply principles, concepts, and research findings to guide change to achieve positive outcomes? Bystanders are criticized for not being involved. It might appear that they do not care to take on the risks of involvement. As the world becomes smaller and more complex, problems multiply. The intertwining of cultures, values, and behaviors increases the chances of conflict and decreases the predictability of human behavior. This would seem to be a superb natural laboratory for sociologists to develop and test theories, gather new facts, refine methodologies, as well as evaluate the impact of interventions. Indeed, rather than question the value, viability, and usefulness of sociology, it should be gaining preeminence and sociologists should be increasingly called on to be active practitioners. However, there appears to be an inverse relationship between the increase in social problems and mainstream sociology's involvement in them.

Many years ago, Street and Weinstein (1975:65) expressed the view that for sociology to be of any use to publics besides other sociologists, it must "contribute sufficiently to our understanding of how social institutions come into being, operate, change, and affect the people who deal with them." They contended that "sociological knowledge is too important to be monopolized by professors," that it is not for an elite but should genuinely serve the human condition.

Clinical sociology *is* sociology. Clinical sociologists do the same things that other sociologists do—they theorize, conceptualize, observe, test, evaluate, teach, do research, and become involved in professional and community service. What clinical sociologists do that other sociologists do not we call *intervention*, active involvement in various social systems with the goal of positive social change. When they intervene, clinical sociologists are referred to by their colleagues as *clinicians*, and seen as therapists much like psychologists and social workers. Indeed, some clinical sociologists do have additional credentials as mediators, marriage and family therapists or counselors, organizational or management consultants, policy experts, and so on. These additional credentials do not detract from their sociological training, but build on it. In-depth interviewing, focus group techniques, case histories, biographies and autobiographies, and the like are all techniques that can be added to the usual sociological armamentarium. Clinical sociologists become involved in problems firsthand, but remain well aware of the ethics of involvement and the limits of their intervention. The clinical sociologist also is ready to work with other disciplines as it becomes apparent that most problems are more complex than the knowledge base of any single discipline. As Wirth (1931/1982) held, "any single scientific viewpoint was inadequate to solve behavioral problems" (Larson, 1990). Thus, clinical sociologists put their sociological knowledge and skills into action. They become involved in society's problems as professionals and as citizens.

A variety of pressures from outside sociology have also encouraged the activities of applied and clinical practitioners, especially the growing intensity of social problems, the downsizing of applied programs in general in universities, and declining enrollments in sociology. Sociology is finding it difficult to compete as a career choice in a high-salaried, hands-on job market. By the same token, clinical sociology is undergoing its own developmental transitions (Robinette, 1992). As scholars of social change, sociologists are now challenged to deal with social change in their own discipline; in particular, how to plan and direct change to maximize its positive benefits.

The Maturity of Clinical Sociology

Foote (1996) pointed to certain "frontiers" or new directions for development in sociological practice. One of these new directions is for clinical sociologists to convince our sociological colleagues as well as others that clinical sociology is not fixed at the microlevel. This is what Church (1991) meant when he noted that clinical sociology should not be just another mental health profession. Not all interventions require "fixing" a person or situation. As Foote stated, individuals who have been downsized or otherwise lose their job do not need therapy, they need a job, a livelihood! Foote went on to note that it is the reciprocal relationships between people that should be the focus of clinical sociological interventions. That is not to say that individually focused interventions are unnecessary, but clinical sociology is not just "fixing" individuals who are in trouble.

Another frontier concerns the perception that clinical sociology deals with qualitative and descriptive data. For some reason clinical sociologists are perceived by some sociologists as using (and perhaps overusing) the interview or case approach. In this way clinical sociology has become stereotyped as a helping specialty much like social work, clinical psychology, and counseling. The implication here is that descriptive data are less rigorous or less scientific. One of the assets of sociology is its variety of methodologies. It is rare that sociologists focus all of their efforts around one method, but rather call on a combination of skills as a situation warrants. It is rare, even among clinical sociologists in full-time practice in an area like marriage and family, that only one approach is used. Clinical sociologists also make use of survey data, archival data, and the full range of quantitative techniques. It is the responsibility of clinical sociologists to help to minimize the perceptions of the polarization of the methodologies and levels of their practice.

A third frontier is that of identity and status. As specializations in sociology and new organizations have been formed—and often shunned by mainstream sociologists—there are concerns of how specialists will be perceived and treated. One of the ways to control membership in organizations is to have strict rules of entry. Certification is one such rule. Clinical sociologists have established certification as an important credential to provide identity and status. Certification can serve useful purposes and enhance professionalization. On the other hand, certification can exclude possible valuable colleagues who, for various reasons, do not wish to undergo the steps leading to certification. Clinical sociology needs to guard against becoming an exclusive club thereby alienating fellow sociologists and other colleagues in related disciplines. Clinical sociology should not compete with other professionals by one-upping credentials for membership. Indeed, the societal problems of today call for more collaboration rather than elitism.

A fourth frontier for clinical sociology is to establish more effective means of sharing experiences and results of interventions with others in and outside of the field. Academicians have annual meetings, journals, newsletters, interest groups, and the like, to provide for information exchange and collegial bonding. Clinical sociologists do too. However, the majority of clinical sociologists are not in academic positions and their rewards do not come from writing papers to obtain tenure, so there is little incentive to write and see the results of one's work disseminated. The work of clinical sociologists often yields a report that in turn might lead to a policy or an organizational innovation. Sharing the process of how change came about is often more useful than the outcome itself. Clinical sociologists need to be more creative in finding ways to share what they do with peers and colleagues.

A fifth, and final, frontier is that sociologists need to do a better job of integrating knowledge and practice. Typically in sociology programs graduates are imbued with theory and often cannot see or are not given the opportunity to experience its applications. Wang Yang-ming (1472–1529) put it succinctly when he said

> knowledge is the beginning of practice; doing is the completion of knowing. Men of the present, however, make knowledge and action two different things and go not forth to practice, because they hold that one must first have knowledge before one is able to practice.

Perhaps this is where sociology could follow the teaching model of many professions, namely, providing real opportunities to apply the theory that is taught in the classroom.

Thus, we ask the question: Why a "clinical" sociology? Why promote an emphasis on application and sociological practice? In our opinion, it is good for the discipline and there is a societal need. The discipline benefits from a healthy and visible clinical sociology. This touches on the need for and benefit of a societal referent. Biology and chemistry as pure sciences have societal referents in closely allied practice professions: medicine, pharmacology, sanitation, engineering, and so on. Ultimately, for sociology to grow and prosper, for the store of knowledge to grow, society—and its various decision makers—must support sociology. For this to take place, sociology has to be seen as useful; that it has something practical to offer society.

Also, as a practical matter, any discipline remains viable if it regularly attracts new entrants who can see a recognized and accepted, interesting and rewarding career path before them. It must attract talented young people who seek meaningful work, with an accepted role in society, and they can grow and develop and make a living. As van de Vall (1992) noted, in discussing sociological practice, "In the cost–benefit world of modern Academe, university departments are required to attract minimal numbers of students. Today's freshmen are less attracted by abstract notions of scholarship, however, than by the concrete perspective of a professional career."

The opportunity for sociological practice with the chance to address real social problems presents a challenge that can attract young people. van de Vall wrote that in Holland graduates trained in sociological practice have career options in policy work, organizational consultation, or a host of general applications.

Indeed, a common query from undergraduates is, "What can I do with a degree in sociology?" Classically, graduate education and on to teaching sociology was seen as the primary career path. But as Dotzler and Koppel (1999) reported, while this model may still be the perception, it may no longer give an accurate picture of what sociologists do:

> Recent data from the NSF survey of Ph.D. sociologists, however, reveal that . . . less than one-half of all sociologists—45.8%—teach sociology. The majority of our colleagues spend their days managing and administering, conducting applied or basic research, . . . and engaging in a wide range of tasks that are divergent from the traditional image.

The data showed that about 27% (3300) of sociologists do not work for educational institutions, about 20% of whom are self-employed. Another 17% are employed as "sociologist"—researchers, policy experts, planners, and the like (Dotzler & Koppel, 1999). Moreover, as the data showed, a large proportion of academic sociologists spend a significant part of their time also doing sociological work dealing with clients in applied research, advising on policy and programs, and so on. In other fields such as economics, biology, physics, and psychology, "practice" is valued. Entrants and students are taught and encouraged to take roles where they apply the knowledge base and skills of the field. To quote Dotzler and Koppel again, "Sociology appears to be special in its adherence to a traditional image, despite its destroying and ultimately disempowering effects."

We agree with Dotzler and Koppel that disparaging practice is not good for the discipline of sociology. We also note that others—criminal justice, social workers, management analysts, policy scientists, public and private administrators, and even journalists—are "doing" sociology but often do not have the depth and rigor of sociological grounding that goes with graduate education in sociology. . . .

The emergence and persistence of clinical sociology and sociological practice attest that many of us see the relevance of sociology and feel a strong need to apply the tools and perspectives of the field in the public arena.

We recall Albion Small's (1896/1985) challenge:

> I would have American scholars, especially in the social sciences, declare their independence of do-nothing traditions. I would have them repeal the law of custom which bars marriage of thought and action. I would have them become more profoundly and sympathetically scholarly by enriching the wisdom which comes from knowing with the larger wisdom which comes from doing. I would have them advance from knowledge of facts to knowledge of forces, and from knowledge of forces to control of forces in the interest of more complete social and personal life.

An active clinical sociology can also serve society. When people—and decision makers—see others acting in a particular way, the tendency is to attribute that action to some characteristics of the individual without reference to the social context. The tendency of many observers is to attribute social problems to bad or flawed individuals. One important role we can play is to elaborate a social structural and cultural view. We contend that application of sociological perspectives, theory, research findings, and skills for problem solving and positive social change takes us back to the beginnings of sociology.

References

Babbie, E. (1994). *The sociological spirit* (2nd ed.). Belmont, CA: Wadsworth.

Babbie, E., Cicourel, A., & Perlstadt, H. (1998). Commentary on Turner. *Sociological Perspectives*, 41(2), 259–271.

Church, N. (1991). The effects of social change on clinical practice. In H. M. Rebach and J. G. Bruhn (Eds.), *Handbook of clinical sociology* (pp. 125–139). New York: Plenum Press.

Dotzler, R. J., & Koppel, R. (1999). What sociologists do and where they do it—the NSF survey on sociologists' work activities and workplaces. *Sociological Practice: A Journal of Clinical and Applied Sociology*, 1, 71–84.

Foote, N. N. (1996). Frontiers in sociological practice. *Clinical Sociology Review*, 14, 1–13.

Larson, C. J. (1990). Applied/practical sociological theory: Problems and issues. *Sociological Practice Review*, 1, 8–18.

Robinette, P. D. (1992). Sociological practice's mid-life crisis. *Clinical Sociology Review*, 10, 21–36.

Small, A. (1896/1985). Scholarship and social agitation. *The American Journal of Sociology*, 1, 564–582. Reprinted in *Clinical Sociology Review*, 3, 25–38.

Straus, R. A. (1985). *Using sociology: An introduction from the clinical perspective*. Bayside, NY: General Hall.

Street, D. P., & Weinstein, E. A. (1975). Prologue: Problems and prospects of applied sociology. *The American Sociologist*, 10, 65–72.

Turner, J. H. (1998). Must sociological theory and sociological practice be so far apart? A polemical answer. *Sociological Perspectives*, 41, 243–258.

van de Vall, M. (1992). Sociological practice in modern policymaking: Supply and demand. *Sociological Practice Review*, 3, 272–276.

Wang Yang-ming, 1472–1529, Chinese philosopher, *Works of Wang-yang-ming*. Translated by Henke. As cited in *The choice is always ours*, edited by D. B. Phillips *et al.* Jove Publications, 1975.

Wirth, L. (1931/1982). Sociology and clinical procedure. *American Journal of Sociology*, 37, 49–66. Reprinted in *Clinical Sociology Review*, 1, 7–22.

Study Questions

1. What is the historical evidence that sociological practice or clinical sociology was destined to be a central part of the discipline?

2. What are the frontiers or "new directions" that sociological practice must address?

PART TWO

The Organization of Society

Topic 3
Culture

It has been said that culture is to people as water is to fish: it is the last thing we would recognize about our social environment unless we were outside this milieu. As the fish might be gasping for air, persons might be gasping for social sustenance, for a commonly understood way to act and communicate with others. As long as people grow up inside a society and culture and learn all the values, norms (rules), behaviors, and language as they age, the culture will come to be viewed as only natural, as something taken for granted. In this circumstance, we are acculturated and the culture is understood as something we do each day that requires no conscious thought, no real decisions, just "doing what comes naturally." Clearly, if we were to wake up tomorrow and be in another culture where we did not know the values, norms, or language, we would quickly come to appreciate how much we depend on culture and how much culture shapes our lives.

Kendall (2004, p. 43) defines culture as "the knowledge, language, values, customs, and material objects that are passed from person to person and from one generation to the next in a human group or society." According to this definition, culture is the repository of accumulated knowledge, of the language spoken by the members of the culture, of the values, beliefs, and customs—even material objects—that we inherit socially from previous generations. Where would we be without culture? How would we communicate? What rules would need to be followed to keep order and create patterns in the society? Stop and think about all the assumptions people make regarding customs of meeting one another, of rules to guide moving traffic, or social activities centering around a meal. As long as the assumptions are commonly shared, we can anticipate what will happen next, what others will do in response to us and us to them. Without the cultural guides, these every-day occurrences might come to a standstill—moments of silence filled with awkward feelings, traffic that is grid-locked, and continual embarrassment over missed cues to act or speak. Appreciating culture as an elemental, organizing principle of social life brings us closer to an important dimension of the sociological imagination.

Culture is the crucible of social life. Each of us is born out of it, and each of us lives our social lives through it. The values, beliefs, norms, and customs tell us what we can and cannot do or think, and how we are to behave. Culture is a paradox, both prison and playground. As a prison, we are tied by the many rules that tell us we must go to school, work, meet our obligations to family, and so on. As a playground, culture is the medium through which we develop our social and physical skills, the vehicle for our self-actualization and development. Learning to live a balanced and happy life inside the paradox of culture will require a lifetime of effort and learning.

Topic 3: Culture includes readings from Barry Glassner, "The Culture of Fear," Horace Miner, "Body Ritual Among the Nacerima," and Mitch Albom's discussion with Morrie Schwartz entitled "We Talk about Our Culture." From Glassner we will learn that popular media (popular culture) creates a sentiment of fear among the population. He adds that it might be the media are using information that is more inflammatory than accurate. In the piece by Miner, we are taking a look at a most unusual culture where people have equally unusual habits. I wonder how an anthropologist, in search of objectivity, might describe our own society. Morrie Schwartz, a Brandeis sociologist, is dying while the entire world is getting his final lessons, and one of his students writes to tell the narrative in a popular book, *Tuesdays with Morrie.* Morrie gives us some thought-provoking insights about culture in this brief but emotional excerpt. How might we go about "creating our own culture"?

Reference

Diana Kendall, from *Sociology in Our Times: The Essentials* (4th ed.). Belmont, CA: Wadsworth, a division of Thomson Learning, 2004.

Reading 7

The Culture of Fear
Why Americans Fear the Wrong Things

Barry Glassner

Why are so many fears in the air, and so many of them unfounded? Why, as crime rates plunged throughout the 1990s, did two-thirds of Americans believe they were soaring? How did it come about that by mid-decade 62 percent of us described ourselves as "truly desperate" about crime—almost twice as many as in the late 1980s, when crime rates were higher? Why, on a survey in 1997, when the crime rate had already fallen for a half dozen consecutive years, did more than half of us disagree with the statement "This country is finally beginning to make some progress in solving the crime problem"?[1]

In the late 1990s the number of drug users had decreased by half compared to a decade earlier; almost two-thirds of high school seniors had never used any illegal drugs, even marijuana. So why did a majority of adults rank drug abuse as the greatest danger to America's youth? Why did nine out of ten believe the drug problem is out of control, and only one in six believe the country was making progress?[2]

Give us a happy ending and we write a new disaster story. In the late 1990s the unemployment rate was below 5 percent for the first time in a quarter century. People who had been pounding the pavement for years could finally get work. Yet pundits warned of imminent economic disaster. They predicted inflation would take off, just as they had a few years earlier—also erroneously—when the unemployment rate dipped below 6 percent.[3]

We compound our worries beyond all reason. Life expectancy in the United States has doubled during the twentieth century. We are better able to cure and control diseases than any other civilization in history. Yet we hear that phenomenal numbers of us are dreadfully ill. In 1996 Bob Garfield, a magazine writer, reviewed articles about serious diseases published over the course of a year in the *Washington Post*, the *New York Times*, and *USA Today*. He learned that, in addition to 59 million Americans with heart disease, 53 million with migraines, 25 million with osteoporosis, 16 million with obesity, and 3 million with cancer, many Americans suffer from more obscure ailments such as temporomandibular joint disorders (10 million) and brain injuries (2 million). Adding up the estimates, Garfield determined that 543 million Americans are seriously sick—a shocking number in a nation of 266 million inhabitants. "Either as a society we are doomed, or someone is seriously double-dipping," he suggested.[4]

Garfield appears to have underestimated one category of patients: for psychiatric ailments his figure was 53 million. Yet when Jim Windolf, an editor of the *New York Observer*, collated estimates for maladies ranging from borderline personality disorder (10 million) and sex addiction (11 million) to less well-known conditions such as restless leg syndrome (12 million) he came up with a figure of 152 million. "But give the experts a little time," he advised. "With another new quantifiable disorder or two, everybody in the country will be officially nuts."[5]

Indeed, Windolf omitted from his estimates new-fashioned afflictions that have yet to make it into the *Diagnostic and Statistical Manual of Mental Disorders* of the American Psychiatric Association: ailments such as road rage, which afflicts more than half of Americans, according to a psychologist's testimony before a congressional hearing in 1997.[6]. . .

Killer Kids

When we are not worrying about deadly diseases we worry about homicidal strangers. Every few months for the past several years it seems we discover a new category of people to fear: government thugs in Waco, sadistic cops on Los Angeles freeways and in Brooklyn police stations, mass-murdering youths in small towns all over the country. A single anomalous event can provide us with multiple groups of people to fear. After the 1995 explosion at the federal building in Oklahoma City first we panicked about Arabs. "Knowing that the car bomb indicates Middle Eastern terrorists at work, it's safe to assume that their goal is to promote free-floating fear and a measure of anarchy, thereby disrupting American life," a *New York Post* editorial asserted. "Whatever we are doing to destroy Mideast terrorism, the chief terrorist threat against Americans, has not been working," wrote A. M. Rosenthal in the *New York Times*.[7]

When it turned out that the bombers were young white guys from middle America, two more groups instantly became spooky: right-wing radio talk show hosts who criticize the government—depicted by President Bill Clinton as "purveyors of hatred and division"—and members of militias. No group of disgruntled men was too ragtag not to warrant big, prophetic news stories.[8]. . .

The more things improve the more pessimistic we become. Violence-related deaths at the nation's schools dropped to a record low during the 1996–97 academic year (19 deaths out of 54 million children), and only one in ten public schools reported *any* serious crime. Yet *Time* and *U.S. News & World Report* both ran headlines in 1996 referring to "Teenage Time Bombs." In a nation of "Children Without Souls" (another *Time* headline that year), "America's beleaguered cities are about to be victimized by a paradigm shattering wave of ultraviolent, morally vacuous young people some call 'the superpredators,' " William Bennett, the former Secretary of Education, and John DiIulio, a criminologist, forecast in a book published in 1996.[9]

Instead of the arrival of superpredators, violence by urban youths continued to decline. So we went looking elsewhere for proof that heinous behavior by young people was "becoming increasingly more commonplace in America" (CNN). After a sixteen-year-old in Pearl, Mississippi, and a fourteen-year-old in West Paducah, Kentucky, went on shooting sprees in late 1997, killing five of their classmates and wounding twelve others, these isolated incidents were taken as evidence of "an epidemic of seemingly depraved adolescent murderers" (Geraldo Rivera). Three months later in March 1998 all sense of proportion vanished after two boys ages eleven and thirteen killed four students and a teacher in Jonesboro, Arkansas. No longer, we learned in *Time*, was it "unusual for kids to get back at the world with live ammunition." When a child psychologist on NBC's "Today" show advised parents to reassure their children that shootings at schools are rare, reporter Ann Curry corrected him. "But this is the fourth case since October," she said.[10]

Over the next couple of months young people failed to accommodate the trend hawkers. None committed mass murder. Fear of killer kids remained very much in the air nonetheless. In stories on topics such as school safety and childhood trauma, reporters recapitulated the gory details of the killings. And the news media made a point of reporting every incident in which a child was caught at school with a gun or making a death threat. In May, when a fifteen-year-old in Springfield, Oregon, did open fire in a cafeteria filled with students, killing two and wounding twenty-three others, the event felt like a continuation of a "disturbing trend" (*New York Times*). The day after the shooting, on National Public Radio's "All Things Considered," the criminologist Vincent Schiraldi tried to explain that the recent string of incidents did not constitute a trend, that youth homicide rates had declined by 30 percent in recent years, and more than three times as many people were killed by lightning than by violence at schools. But the show's host, Robert Siegel, interrupted him. "You're saying these are just anomalous events?" he asked, audibly peeved. The criminologist reiterated that *anomalous* is precisely the right word to describe the events, and he called it "a grave mistake" to imagine otherwise. . . .

Roosevelt Was Wrong

We had better learn to doubt our inflated fears before they destroy us. Valid fears have their place; they cue us to danger. False and overdrawn fears only cause hardship. . . .

I do not contend, as did President Roosevelt in 1933, that "the only thing we have to fear is fear itself." My point is that we often fear the wrong things. In the 1990s middle-income and poorer Americans should have worried about unemployment insurance, which covered a smaller share of workers than twenty years earlier. Many of us have had friends or family out of work during economic downturns or as a result of corporate restructuring. Living in a nation with one of the largest income gaps of any industrialized country, where the bottom 40 percent of the population is worse off financially than their counterparts two decades earlier, we might also have worried about income inequality. Or poverty. During the mid- and late 1990s 5 million elderly Americans had no food in their homes, more than 20 million people used emergency food programs each year, and one in five children lived in poverty—more than a quarter million of them homeless. All told, a larger proportion of Americans were poor than three decades earlier.[11]

One of the paradoxes of a culture of fear is that serious problems remain widely ignored even though they give rise to precisely the dangers that the populace most abhors. Poverty, for example, correlates strongly with child abuse, crime, and drug abuse. Income inequality is also associated with adverse outcomes for society as a whole. The larger the gap between rich and poor in a society, the higher its overall death rates from heart disease, cancer, and murder. Some social scientists argue that extreme inequality also threatens political stability in a nation such as the United States, where we think of ourselves not as "haves and have nots" but as "haves and will haves." "Unlike the citizens of most other nations, Americans have always been united less by a shared past than by the shared dreams of a better future. If we lose that common future," the Brandeis University economist Robert Reich has suggested, "we lose the glue that holds our nation together."[12]

The combination of extreme inequality and poverty can prove explosive. In an insightful article in *U.S. News & World Report* in 1997 about militia groups reporters Mike Tharp and William Holstein noted that people's motivations for joining these groups are as much economic as ideological. The journalists argued that the disappearance of military and blue-collar jobs, along with the decline of family farming, created the conditions under which a new breed of protest groups flourished. "What distinguishes these antigovernment groups from, say, traditional conservatives who mistrust government is that their anger is fueled by direct threats to their livelihood, and they carry guns," Tharp and Holstein wrote.[13]

That last phrase alludes to a danger that by any rational calculation deserves top billing on Americans' lists of fears. So gun crazed is this nation that Burger King had to order a Baltimore franchise to stop giving away coupons from a local sporting goods store for free boxes of bullets with the purchase of guns. We have more guns *stolen* from their owners—about 300,000 annually—than many countries have gun owners. In Great Britain, Australia, and Japan, where gun ownership is severely restricted, no more than a few dozen people are killed each year by handguns. In the United States, where private citizens own a quarter-billion guns, around 15,000 people are killed, 18,000 commit suicide, and another 1,500 die accidentally from firearms. American children are twelve times more [likely] to die from gun injuries than are youngsters in other industrialized nations.[14]

Yet even after tragedies that could not have occurred except for the availability of guns, their significance is either played down or missed altogether. Had the youngsters in the celebrated schoolyard shootings of 1997–98 not had access to guns, some or all of the people they killed would be alive today. Without their firepower those boys lacked the strength, courage, and skill to commit multiple murders. Nevertheless newspapers ran editorials with titles such as "It's Not Guns, It's Killer Kids" (*Fort Worth Star-Telegram*) and "Guns Aren't the Problem" (*New York Post*), and journalists, politicians, and pundits blathered on endlessly about every imaginable cause of youthful rage, from "the psychology of violence in the South" to satanism to fights on "Jerry Springer" and simulated shooting in Nintendo games.[15]. . .

In Praise of Journalists

Any analysis of the culture of fear that ignored the news media would be patently incomplete, and of the several institutions most culpable for creating and sustaining scares the news media are arguably first among equals. They are also the most promising candidates for positive change. Yet by the same token critiques such as Stolberg's presage a crucial shortcoming in arguments that blame the media. Reporters not only spread fears, they also debunk them and criticize one another for spooking the public. A wide array of groups, including businesses, advocacy organizations, religious sects, and political parties, promote and profit from scares. News organizations are distinguished from other fear-mongering groups because they sometimes bite the scare that feeds them.

A group that raises money for research into a particular disease is not likely to negate concerns about that disease. A company that sells alarm systems is not about to call attention to the fact that crime is down. News organizations, on the other hand, periodically allay the very fears they arouse to lure audiences. Some newspapers that ran stories about child murderers, rather than treat every incident as evidence of a shocking trend, affirmed the opposite. After the schoolyard shooting in Kentucky the *New York Times* ran a sidebar alongside its feature story with the headline "Despite Recent Carnage, School Violence Is Not on Rise." Following the Jonesboro killings they ran a similar piece, this time on a recently released study showing the rarity of violent crimes in schools.[16]

Several major newspapers parted from the pack in other ways. *USA Today* and the *Washington Post*, for instance, made sure their readers knew that what should worry them is the availability of guns. *USA Today* ran news stories explaining that easy access to guns in homes accounted for increases in the number of juvenile arrests for homicide in rural areas during the 1990s. While other news outlets were respectfully quoting the mother of the thirteen-year-old Jonesboro shooter, who said she did not regret having encouraged her son to learn to fire a gun ("it's like anything else, there's some people that can drink a beer, and not become an alcoholic"), *USA Today* ran an op-ed piece proposing legal parameters for gun ownership akin to those for the use of alcohol and motor vehicles. And the paper published its own editorial in support of laws that require gun owners to lock their guns or keep them in locked containers. Adopted at that time by only fifteen states, the laws had reduced the number of deaths among children in those states by 23 percent.[17]

Morality and Marketing

Why do news organizations and their audiences find themselves drawn to one hazard rather than another? . . .

In the first half of the 1990s U.S. cities spent at least $10 billion to purge asbestos from public schools, even though removing asbestos from buildings posed a greater health hazard than leaving it in place. At a time when about one-third of the nation's schools were in need of extensive repairs the money might have been spent to renovate dilapidated buildings. But hazards posed by seeping asbestos are morally repugnant. A product that was supposed to protect children from fires might be giving them cancer. By directing our worries and dollars at asbestos we express outrage at technology and industry run afoul.[18] . . .

Within public discourse fears proliferate through a process of exchange. It is from crosscurrents of scares and counterscares that the culture of fear swells ever larger. Even as feminists disparage large classes of men, they themselves are a staple of fear mongering by conservatives. To hear conservatives tell it, feminists are not only "anti-child and anti-family" (Arianna Huffington) but through women's studies programs on college campuses they have fomented an "anti-science and anti-reason movement" (Christina Hoff Sommers).[19]

Conservatives also like to spread fears about liberals, who respond in kind. Among other pet scares, they accuse liberals of creating "children without consciences" by keeping prayer out of schools—to which liberals rejoin with warnings that right-wing extremists intend to turn youngsters into Christian soldiers.[20]

Samuel Taylor Coleridge was right when he claimed, "In politics, what begins in fear usually ends up in folly." Political activists are more inclined, though, to heed an observation from Richard Nixon: "People react to fear, not love. They don't teach that in Sunday school, but it's true." That principle, which guided the late president's political strategy throughout his career, is the sine qua non of contemporary political campaigning. Marketers of products and services ranging from car alarms to TV news programs have taken it to heart as well.[21]

The short answer to why Americans harbor so many misbegotten fears is that immense power and money await those who tap into our moral insecurities and supply us with symbolic substitutes.

Notes

1. Crime data here and throughout are from reports of the Bureau of Justice Statistics unless otherwise noted. Fear of crime: Esther Madriz, *Nothing Bad Happens to Good Girls* (Berkeley: University of California Press, 1997), ch. 1; Richard Morin, "As Crime Rate Falls, Fears Persist," *Washington Post* National Edition, 16 June 1997, p. 35; David Whitman, "Believing the Good News," *U.S. News & World Report*, 5 January 1998, pp. 45–46.

2. Eva Bertram, Morris Blachman et al., *Drug War Politics* (Berkeley: University of California Press, 1996), p. 10; Mike Males, *Scapegoat Generation* (Monroe, ME: Common Courage Press, 1996), ch. 6; Karen Peterson, "Survey: Teen Drug Use Declines," *USA Today*, 19 June 1998, p. A6; Robert Blendon and John Young, "The Public and the War on Illicit Drugs," *Journal of the American Medical Association* 279 (18 March 1998): 827–32. In presenting these statistics and others I am aware of a seeming paradox: I criticize the abuse of statistics by fearmongering politicians, journalists, and others but hand down precise-sounding numbers myself. Yet to eschew all estimates because some are used inappropriately or do not withstand scrutiny would be as foolhardy as ignoring all medical advice because some doctors are quacks. Readers can be assured I have interrogated the statistics presented here as factual. As notes throughout the book make clear, I have tried to rely on research that appears in peer-reviewed scholarly journals. Where this was not possible or sufficient, I traced numbers back to their sources, investigated the research methodology utilized to produce them, or conducted searches of the popular and scientific literature for critical commentaries and conflicting findings.

3. Bob Herbert, "Bogeyman Economics," *New York Times*, 4 April 1997, p. A15; Doug Henwood, "Alarming Drop in Unemployment," *Extra*, September 1994, pp. 16–17; Christopher Shea, "Low Inflation and Low Unemployment Spur Economists to Debate 'Natural Rate' Theory," *Chronicle of Higher Education*, 24 October 1997, p. A13.

4. Bob Garfield, "Maladies by the Millions," *USA Today*, 16 December 1996, p. A15.

5. Jim Windolf, "A Nation of Nuts," *Wall Street Journal*, 22 October 1997, p. A22.

6. Andrew Ferguson, "Road Rage," *Time*, 12 January 1998, pp. 64–68; Joe Sharkey, "You're Not Bad, You're Sick. It's in the Book," *New York Times*, 28 September 1997, pp. N1, 5.

7. Jim Naureckas, "The Jihad That Wasn't," *Extra*, July 1995, pp. 6–10, 20 (contains quotes). See also Edward Said, "A Devil Theory of Islam," *Nation*, 12 August 1996, pp. 28–32.

8. Lewis Lapham, "Seen but Not Heard," *Harper's*, July 1995, pp. 29–36 (contains Clinton quote). See also Robin Wright and Ronald Ostrow, "Illusion of Immunity Is Shat-

tered," *Los Angeles Times*, 20 April 1995, pp. A1, 18; Jack Germond and Jules Witcover, "Making the Angry White Males Angrier," column syndicated by Tribune Media Services, May 1995; and articles by James Bennet and Michael Janofsky in the *New York Times*, May 1995.

9. Statistics from "Violence and Discipline Problems in U.S. Public Schools: 1996–97," National Center on Education Statistics, U.S. Department of Education, Washington, DC, March 1998; CNN, "Early Prime," 2 December 1997; and Tamar Lewin, "Despite Recent Carnage, School Violence Is Not on Rise," *New York Times*, 3 December 1997, p. A14. Headlines: *Time*, 15 January 1996; *U.S. News & World Report*, 25 March 1996; Margaret Carlson, "Children Without Souls," *Time*, 2 December 1996, p. 70; William J. Bennett, John J. DiIulio, and John Walters, *Body Count* (New York: Simon & Schuster, 1996).

10. CNN, "Talkback Live," 2 December 1997; CNN, "The Geraldo Rivera Show," 11 December 1997; Richard Lacayo, "Toward the Root of Evil," *Time*, 6 April 1998, pp. 38–39; NBC, "Today," 25 March 1998. See also Rick Bragg, "Forgiveness, After 3 Die in Shootings in Kentucky," *New York Times*, 3 December 1997, p. A14; Maureen Downey, "Kids and Violence," 28 March 1998, *Atlanta Journal and Constitution*, p. A12.

11. "The State of America's Children," report by the Children's Defense Fund, Washington, DC, March 1998; "Blocks to Their Future," report by the National Law Center on Homelessness and Poverty, Washington, DC, September 1997; reports released in 1998 from the National Center for Children in Poverty, Columbia University, New York; Douglas Massey, "The Age of Extremes," *Demography* 33 (1996): 395–412; Trudy Lieberman, "Hunger in America," *Nation*, 30 March 1998, pp. 11–16; David Lynch, "Rich Poor World," *USA Today*, 20 September 1996, p. B1; Richard Wolf, "Good Economy Hasn't Helped the Poor," *USA Today*, 10 March 1998, p. A3; Robert Reich, "Broken Faith," *Nation*, 16 February 1998, pp. 11–17.

12. Inequality and mortality studies: Bruce Kennedy et al., "Income Distribution and Mortality," *British Medical Journal* 312 (1996): 1004–7; Ichiro Kawachi and Bruce Kennedy, "The Relationship of Income Inequality to Mortality," *Social Science and Medicine* 45 (1997): 1121–27. See also Barbara Chasin, *Inequality and Violence in the United States* (Atlantic Highlands, NJ: Humanities Press, 1997). Political stability: John Sloan, "The Reagan Presidency, Growing Inequality, and the American Dream," *Policy Studies Journal* 25 (1997): 371–86 (contains Reich quotes and "will haves" phrase). On both topics see also Philippe Bourgois, *In Search of Respect: Selling Crack in El Barrio* (Cambridge: Cambridge University Press, 1996); William J. Wilson, *When Work Disappears* (New York, Knopf, 1996); Richard Gelles, "Family Violence," *Annual Review of Sociology* 11 (1985): 347–67; Sheldon Danziger and Peter Gottschalk, *America Unequal* (Cambridge, MA: Harvard University Press, 1995); Claude Fischer et al., *Inequality by Design* (Princeton, NJ: Princeton University Press, 1996).

13. Mike Tharp and William Holstein, "Mainstreaming the Militia," *U.S. News & World Report*, 21 April 1997, pp. 24–37.

14. Burger King: "Notebooks," *New Republic*, 29 April 1996, p. 8. Statistics from the FBI's Uniform Crime Reports, Centers for Disease Control reports, and Timothy Egan, "Oregon Freeman Goes to Court," *New York Times*, 23 May 1998, pp. A1, 8.

15. Bill Thompson, "It's Not Guns, It's Killer Kids," *Fort Worth Star-Telegram*, 31 March 1998, p. 14; "Guns Aren't the Problem," *New York Post* 30 March 1998 (from *Post* Web site); "Arkansas Gov. Assails 'Culture of Violence,' " Reuters, 25 March 1998; Bo Emerson, "Violence Feeds 'Redneck,' Gun-Toting Image," *Atlanta Journal and Constitution*,

29 March 1998, p. A8; Nadya Labi, "The Hunter and the Choir Boy," *Time*, 6 April 1998, pp. 28–37; Lacayo, "Toward the Root of Evil."

16. Lewin, "More Victims and Less Sense"; Tamar Lewin, "Study Finds No Big Rise in Public-School Crimes," *New York Times*, 25 March 1998, p. A18.

17. "Licensing Can Protect," *USA Today*, 7 April 1998, p. All; Jonathan Kellerman, "Few Surprises When It Comes to Violence," *USA Today*, 27 March 1998, p. A13; Gary Fields, "Juvenile Homicide Arrest Rate on Rise in Rural USA," *USA Today*, 26 March 1998, p. A11; Karen Peterson and Glenn O'Neal, "Society More Violent, So Are Its Children," *USA Today*, 25 March 1998, p. A3; Scott Bowles, "Armed, Alienated and Adolescent," *USA Today*, 26 March 1998, p. A9. Similar suggestions about guns appear in Jonathan Alter, "Harnessing the Hysteria," *Newsweek*, 6 April 1998, p. 27.

18. Mary Douglas and Aaron Wildavsky, *Risk and Culture* (Berkeley: University of California Press, 1982), see esp. pp. 6–9; Mary Douglas, *Risk and Blame* (London: Routledge, 1992). See also Mary Douglas, *Purity and Danger* (New York: Praeger, 1966). Asbestos and schools: Peter Cary, "The Asbestos Panic Attack," *U.S. News & World Report*, 20 February 1995, pp. 61–64; Children's Defense Fund, "State of America's Children."

19. CNN, "Crossfire," 27 August 1995 (contains Huffington quote); Ruth Conniff, "Warning: Feminism Is Hazardous to Your Health," *Progressive*, April 1997, pp. 33–36 (contains Sommers quote). See also Susan Faludi, *Backlash* (New York: Crown, 1991); Deborah Rhode, "Media Images, Feminist Issues," *Signs* 20 (1995): 685–710; Paula Span, "Did Feminists Forget the Most Crucial Issues?" *Los Angeles Times*, 28 November 1996, p. E8.

20. See Katha Pollitt, "Subject to Debate," *Nation*, 26 December 1994, p. 788, and idem, 20 November 1995, p. 600.

21. Henry Nelson Coleridge, ed., *Specimens of the Table Talk of the Late Samuel Taylor Coleridge* (London: J. Murray, 1935), entry for 5 October 1930. Nixon quote cited in William Safire, *Before the Fall* (New York: Doubleday, 1975), Prologue.

Study Questions

1. What are the reasons given by Glassner that Americans are "afraid of the wrong things"?

2. Based on Glassner's analysis, what is the role of sociology in dispelling a culture of fear?

Reading 8
Body Ritual among the Nacirema

Horace Miner

The anthropologist has become so familiar with the diversity of ways in which different peoples behave in similar situations that he is not apt to be surprised by even the most exotic customs. In fact, if all of the logically possible combinations of behavior have not been found somewhere in the world, he is apt to suspect that they must be present in some yet undescribed tribe. This point has, in fact, been expressed with respect to clan organization by Murdock (1949:71). In this light, the magical beliefs and practices of the Nacirema present such unusual aspects that it seems desirable to describe them as an example of the extremes to which human behavior can go.

Professor Linton first brought the ritual of the Nacirema to the attention of anthropologists twenty years ago (1936:326), but the culture of this people is still very poorly understood. They are a North American group living in the territory between the Canadian Cree, the Yaqui and Tarahumare of Mexico, and the Carib and Arawak of the Antilles. Little is known of their origin, although tradition states that they came from the east. According to Nacirema mythology, their nation was originated by a culture hero, Notgnihsaw, who is otherwise known for two great feats of strength—the throwing of a piece of wampum across the river Pa-To-Mac and the chopping down of a cherry tree in which the Spirit of Truth resided.

Nacirema culture is characterized by a highly developed market economy which has evolved in a rich natural habitat. While much of the people's time is devoted to economic pursuits, a large part of the fruits of these labors and a considerable portion of the day are spent in ritual activity. The focus of this activity is the human body, the appearance and health of which loom as a dominant concern in the ethos of the people. While such a concern is certainly not unusual, its ceremonial aspects and associated philosophy are unique.

The fundamental belief underlying the whole system appears to be that the human body is ugly and that its natural tendency is to debility and disease. Incarcerated in such a body, man's only hope is to avert these characteristics through the use of the powerful influences of ritual and ceremony. Every household has one or more shrines devoted to this purpose. The more powerful individuals in the society have several shrines in their houses and, in fact, the opulence of a house is often referred to in terms of the number of such ritual centers it possesses. Most houses are of wattle and daub construction, but the shrine rooms of the more wealthy are walled with stone. Poorer families imitate the rich by applying pottery plaques to their shrine walls.

While each family has at least one such shrine, the rituals associated with it are not family ceremonies but are private and secret. The rites are normally only discussed with children, and then only during the period when they are being initiated into these mysteries. I was able, however, to establish sufficient rapport with the natives to examine these shrines and to have the rituals described to me.

The focal point of the shrine is a box or chest which is built into the wall. In this chest are kept the many charms and magical potions without which no native believes he could live. These preparations are secured from a variety of specialized practitioners. The most powerful of these are the medicine men, whose assistance must be rewarded with substantial gifts. However, the medicine men do not provide the curative potions for their clients, but decide what the ingredients should be and then write them down in an ancient and secret language. This writing is understood only by the medicine men and by the herbalists who, for another gift, provide the required charm.

The charm is not disposed of after it has served its purpose, but is placed in the charm-box of the household shrine. As these magical materials are specific for certain ills, and the real or imagined maladies of the people are many, the charm-box is usually full to overflowing. The magical packets are so numerous that people forget what their purposes were and fear to use them again. While the natives are very vague on this point, we can only assume that the idea in retaining all the old magical materials is that their presence in the charm-box, before which the body rituals are conducted, will in some way protect the worshipper.

Beneath the charm-box is a small font. Each day every member of the family, in succession, enters the shrine room, bows his head before the charm-box, mingles different sorts of holy water in the font, and proceeds with a brief rite of ablution. The holy waters are secured from the Water

Temple of the community, where the priests conduct elaborate ceremonies to make the liquid ritually pure.

In the hierarchy of magical practitioners, and below the medicine
men in prestige, are specialists whose designation is best translated
"holy-mouth-men." The Nacirema have an almost pathological horror of
and fascination with the mouth, the condition of which is believed to
have a supernatural influence on all social relationships. Were it not for
the rituals of the mouth, they believe that their teeth would fall out, their
gums bleed, their jaws shrink, their friends desert them, and their lovers
reject them. They also believe that a strong relationship exists between
oral and moral characteristics. For example, there is a ritual ablution of
the mouth for children which is supposed to improve their moral fiber.

The daily body ritual performed by everyone includes a mouth-rite.
Despite the fact that these people are so punctilious about care of the
mouth, this rite involves a practice which strikes the uninitiated stranger
as revolting. It was reported to me that the ritual consists of inserting a
small bundle of hog hairs into the mouth, along with certain magical
powders, and then moving the bundle in a highly formalized series of
gestures.

In addition to the private mouth-rite, the people seek out a holy-
mouth-man once or twice a year. These practitioners have an impressive
set of paraphernalia, consisting of a variety of augers, awls, probes, and
prods. The use of these objects in the exorcism of the evils of the mouth
involves almost unbelievable ritual torture of the client. The holy-mouth-
man opens the client's mouth and, using the above mentioned tools, en-
larges any holes which decay may have created in the teeth. Magical
materials are put into these holes. If there are no naturally occurring
holes in the teeth, large sections of one or more teeth are gouged out so
that the supernatural substance can be applied. In the client's view, the
purpose of these ministrations is to arrest decay and to draw friends. The
extremely sacred and traditional character of the rite is evident in the fact
that the natives return to the holy-mouth-men year after year, despite the
fact that their teeth continue to decay.

It is to be hoped that, when a thorough study of the Nacirema is
made, there will be careful inquiry into the personality structure of these
people. One has but to watch the gleam in the eye of a holy-mouth-man,
as he jabs an awl into an exposed nerve, to suspect that a certain amount
of sadism is involved. If this can be established, a very interesting pattern

emerges, for most of the population shows definite masochistic tendencies. It was to these that Professor Linton referred in discussing a distinctive part of the daily body ritual which is performed only by men. This part of the rite involves scraping and lacerating the surface of the face with a sharp instrument. Special women's rites are performed only four times during each lunar month, but what they lack in frequency is made up in barbarity. As part of this ceremony, women bake their heads in small ovens for about an hour. The theoretically interesting point is that what seems to be a preponderantly masochistic people have developed sadistic specialists.

The medicine men have an imposing temple, or *latipso*, in every community of any size. The more elaborate ceremonies required to treat very sick patients can only be performed at this temple. These ceremonies involve not only the thaumaturge but a permanent group of vestal maidens who move sedately about the temple chambers in distinctive costume and headdress.

The *latipso* ceremonies are so harsh that it is phenomenal that a fair proportion of the really sick natives who enter the temple ever recover. Small children whose indoctrination is still incomplete have been known to resist attempts to take them to the temple because "that is where you go to die." Despite this fact, sick adults are not only willing but eager to undergo the protracted ritual purification, if they can afford to do so. No matter how ill the supplicant or how grave the emergency, the guardians of many temples will not admit a client if he cannot give a rich gift to the custodian. Even after one has gained admission and survived the ceremonies, the guardians will not permit the neophyte to leave until he makes still another gift.

The supplicant entering the temple is first stripped of all his or her clothes. In every-day life the Nacirema avoids exposure of his body and its natural functions. Bathing and excretory acts are performed only in the secrecy of the household shrine, where they are ritualized as part of the body-rites. Psychological shock results from the fact that body secrecy is suddenly lost upon entry into the *latipso*. A man, whose own wife has never seen him in an excretory act, suddenly finds himself naked and assisted by a vestal maiden while he performs his natural functions into a sacred vessel. This sort of ceremonial treatment is necessitated by the fact that the excreta are used by a diviner to ascertain the course and nature of the client's sickness. Female clients, on the other hand, find their naked bodies are subjected to the scrutiny, manipulation and prodding of the medicine men. Few supplicants in the temple are well enough to do anything but lie on their hard beds. The daily ceremonies, like the rites of the holy-mouth-men, involve discomfort and torture. With ritual precision, the vestals awaken their miserable charges each dawn and roll them about on their beds of pain while performing ablutions, in the formal movements of which the maidens are highly trained. At other times they insert magic wands in the supplicant's mouth or force him to eat substances which are supposed to be healing. From time to time the medicine men come to their clients and jab magically treated needles into their flesh. The fact that these temple ceremonies may not cure, and may even kill the neophyte, in no way decreases the people's faith in the medicine men.

There remains one other kind of practitioner, known as a "listener." This witch-doctor has the power to exorcise the devils that lodge in the heads of people who have been bewitched. The Nacirema believe that parents bewitch their own children. Mothers are particularly suspected of putting a curse on children while teaching them the secret body rituals. The counter-magic of the witch-doctor is unusual in its lack of ritual. The patient simply tells the "listener" all his troubles and fears, beginning with the earliest difficulties he can remember. The memory displayed by the Nacirema in these exorcism sessions is truly remarkable. It is not uncommon for the patient to bemoan the rejection he felt upon being weaned as a babe, and a few individuals even see their troubles going back to the traumatic effects of their own birth.

In conclusion, mention must be made of certain practices which have their base in native esthetics but which depend upon the pervasive aversion to the natural body and its functions. There are ritual fasts to make fat people thin and ceremonial feasts to make thin people fat. Still other rites are used to make women's breasts larger if they are small, and smaller if they are large. General dissatisfaction with breast shape is symbolized in the fact that the ideal form is virtually outside the range of human variation. A few women afflicted with almost inhuman hyper-mammary development are so idolized that they make a handsome living by simply going from village to village and permitting the natives to stare at them for a fee.

Reference has already been made to the fact that excretory functions are ritualized, routinized, and relegated to secrecy. Natural reproductive functions are similarly distorted. Intercourse is taboo as a topic and scheduled as an act. Efforts are made to avoid pregnancy by the use of magical materials or by limiting intercourse to certain phases of the moon. Conception is actually very infrequent. When pregnant, women dress so as to hide their condition. Parturition takes place in secret, without friends or relatives to assist, and the majority of women do not nurse their infants.

Our review of the ritual life of the Nacirema has certainly shown them to be a magic-ridden people. It is hard to understand how they have managed to exist so long under the burdens which they have imposed upon themselves. But even such exotic customs as these take on real meaning when they are viewed with the insight provided by Malinowski when he wrote (1948:70):

> Looking from far and above, from our high places of safety in the developed civilization, it is easy to see all the crudity and irrelevance of magic. But without its power and guidance early man could not have mastered his practical difficulties as he has done, nor could man have advanced to the higher stages of civilization.

References Cited

Linton, Ralph
    1936   The Study of Man. New York, D. Appleton-Century Co.
Malinowski, Bronislaw
    1948   Magic, Science, and Religion. Glencoe, The Free Press.
Murdock, George P.
    1949   Social Structure. New York, The Macmillan Co.

Study Questions

1. Why would such a group have the rituals described by Miner?
2. Who are the Nacirema? Can you say for sure?

We Talk About Our Culture

Mitch Albom

"Hit him harder."

I slapped Morrie's back.

"Harder."

I slapped him again.

"Near his shoulders . . . now down lower."

Morrie, dressed in pajama bottoms, lay in bed on his side, his head flush against the pillow, his mouth open. The physical therapist was showing me how to bang loose the poison in his lungs—which he needed done regularly now, to keep it from solidifying, to keep him breathing.

"I . . . always knew . . . you wanted . . . to hit me . . ." Morrie gasped.

Yeah, I joked as I rapped my fist against the alabaster skin of his back. This is for that B you gave me sophomore year! *Whack!*

We all laughed, a nervous laughter that comes when the devil is within earshot. It would have been cute, this little scene, were it not what we all knew it was, the final calisthenics before death. Morrie's disease was now dangerously close to his surrender spot, his lungs. He had been predicting he would die from choking, and I could not imagine a more terrible way to go. Sometimes he would close his eyes and try to draw the air up into his mouth and nostrils, and it seemed as if he were trying to lift an anchor.

Outside, it was jacket weather, early October, the leaves clumped in piles on the lawns around West Newton. Morrie's physical therapist had come earlier in the day, and I usually excused myself when nurses or specialists had business with him. But as the weeks passed and our time ran down, I was increasingly less self-conscious about the physical embarrassment. I wanted to be there. I wanted to observe everything. This was not like me, but then, neither were a lot of things that had happened these last few months in Morrie's house.

So I watched the therapist work on Morrie in the bed, pounding the back of his ribs, asking if he could feel the congestion loosening within him. And when she took a break, she asked if I wanted to try it. I said yes. Morrie, his face on the pillow, gave a little smile.

"Not too hard," he said. "I'm an old man."

I drummed on his back and sides, moving around, as she instructed. I hated the idea of Morrie's lying in bed under any circumstances (his last aphorism, "When you're in bed, you're dead," rang in my ears), and curled on his side, he was so small, so withered, it was more a boy's body than a man's. I saw the paleness of his skin, the stray white hairs, the way his arms hung limp and helpless. I thought about how much time we spend trying to shape our bodies, lifting weights, crunching sit-ups, and in the end, nature takes it away from us anyhow. Beneath my fingers, I felt the loose flesh around Morrie's bones, and I thumped him hard, as instructed. The truth is, I was pounding on his back when I wanted to be hitting the walls. . . .

Morrie believed in the inherent good of people. But he also saw what they could become.

"People are only mean when they're threatened," he said later that day, "and that's what our culture does. That's what our economy does. Even people who have jobs in our economy are threatened, because they worry about losing them. And when you get threatened, you start looking out only for yourself. You start making money a god. It is all part of this culture."

He exhaled. "Which is why I don't buy into it."

I nodded at him and squeezed his hand. We held hands regularly now. This was another change for me. Things that before would have made me embarrassed or squeamish were now routinely handled. The catheter bag, connected to the tube inside him and filled with greenish waste fluid, lay by my foot near the leg of his chair. A few months earlier, it might have disgusted me; it was inconsequential now. So was the smell of the room after Morrie had used the commode. He did not have the luxury of moving from place to place, of closing a bathroom door behind him, spraying some air freshener when he left. There was his bed, there was his chair, and that was his life. If my life were squeezed into such a thimble, I doubt I could make it smell any better.

"Here's what I mean by building your own little subculture," Morrie said. "I don't mean you disregard every rule of your community. I don't go around naked, for example. I don't run through red lights. The little things, I can obey. But the big things—how we think, what we value— those you must choose yourself. You can't let anyone—or any society— determine those for you.

"Take my condition. The things I am supposed to be embarrassed about now—not being able to walk, not being able to wipe my ass, waking up some mornings wanting to cry—there is nothing innately embarrassing or shaming about them.

"It's the same for women not being thin enough, or men not being rich enough. It's just what our culture would have you believe. Don't believe it."

I asked Morrie why he hadn't moved somewhere else when he was younger.

"Where?"

I don't know. South America. New Guinea. Someplace not as selfish as America.

"Every society has its own problems," Morrie said, lifting his eyebrows, the closest he could come to a shrug. "The way to do it, I think, isn't to run away. You have to work at creating your own culture.

"Look, no matter where you live, the biggest defect we human beings have is our shortsightedness. We don't see what we could be. We should be looking at our potential, stretching ourselves into everything we can become. But if you're surrounded by people who say 'I want mine now,' you end up with a few people with everything and a military to keep the poor ones from rising up and stealing it."

Morrie looked over my shoulder to the far window. Sometimes you could hear a passing truck or a whip of the wind. He gazed for a moment at his neighbors' houses, then continued.

"The problem, Mitch, is that we don't believe we are as much alike as we are. Whites and blacks, Catholics and Protestants, men and women. If we saw each other as more alike, we might be very eager to join in one big human family in this world, and to care about that family the way we care about our own.

"But believe me, when you are dying, you see it is true. We all have the same beginning—birth—and we all have the same end—death. So how different can we be?

"Invest in the human family. Invest in people. Build a little community of those you love and who love you."

He squeezed my hand gently. I squeezed back harder. And like that carnival contest where you bang a hammer and watch the disk rise up the pole, I could almost see my body heat rise up Morrie's chest and neck into his cheeks and eyes. He smiled.

"In the beginning of life, when we are infants, we need others to survive, right? And at the end of life, when you get like me, you need others to survive, right?"

His voice dropped to a whisper. "But here's the secret: in between, we need others as well."

Study Questions

1. In following Morrie's advice, how would one go about "creating his or her own culture"?
2. What point is Morrie making about similarity between people? Why is this important in culture?

Socialization

A baby born into social life will undergo a most remarkable transformation in the first few years. From a crying, random, moving, stretching baby, this child will soon learn to sit, crawl, walk, talk, think, and react to others in patterned and predictable ways. In the span of a few months, the child will learn to think for him- or herself, express him- or herself, and develop some very sophisticated physical, intellectual, and social skills. By age four or five, this child will be able to leave the home and effectively operate at school and with other children at play, as well as many other social settings. Amazing! How does this happen?

Sociology, along with the other sciences, knows this is much more than a biological process. Socialization is the process whereby persons develop the skills to operate effectively in social life. Families are a large contributor to socialization, for it is through these early moments in our lives that we come to develop the physical and intellectual abilities that will carry us for decades to come. But as our world grows, the influence of other adults, peers, schools, and neighborhoods impinge on us and affect our socialization as well. It is through this process of socialization that we must learn to become both an individual and a member of a community, and it is through this process of socialization that what exists outside us in society will become part of our personal makeup as unique human beings.

The debate over the relative contributions of biology and social experience, *nature* and *nurture*, has been raging for nearly two centuries. Sometimes we are more ready to listen to the genetic arguments, sometimes to the social science arguments. In fact, both sets of variables affect who we are as adult human beings, but we work to refine the information in ways that make our models more accurate and more complete. For example, is our *gendered* behavior more from our genetic makeup or our social experiences? There is evidence on both sides, but the social sciences stress the data that show we are mostly human, and socialized, because of our associations with other people.

Importantly, socialization will continue for the entirety of our lives. We will be socialized in school settings, we will be socialized during our employment, and we will move to different communities and learn the social habits and patterns of this new environment as well. This socialization process enables us to learn and be effective in the new roles we adopt; at the same time, it alters our self-concepts and identities. As social beings we are in a constant state of flux as we change and adapt to the altered social circumstances life presents. If we are able to make these changes with skill and ease, we will measurably increase the equanimity in our lives. We can learn from sociology, and from understanding the process of socialization, some very important and valuable information.

The three articles for this topic, Socialization, include first, by Madonna Constantine and Sha'kema Blackmon, a study about the racial socialization experiences of "Black Adolescents." This quantitative research article shows the relationship of certain social events to the students' self-esteem. It also raises interesting questions for African-American parents and educators regarding conformity to dominant cultural norms. Second, a very important article by Kingsley Davis illustrates how the "extreme isolation" of two girls underscores the fact that children require human contact and social interaction to develop beyond the most rudimentary levels. Indeed, our humanness depends on social contact. This is case study research in the descriptive tradition. Finally, Joan Morris and Michael Grimes give us an insider's view of working class sociologists who become Ph.D.s. The contradictions inherent in jumping from one class to another can uncover problems that are both professional and personal. This is yet another glimpse of sociology from the inside and encourages the readers to wonder about the contradiction potential in their own biographies.

Reading 10

Black Adolescents' Racial Socialization Experiences

Their Relations to Home, School, and Peer Self-Esteem

Madonna G. Constantine and Sha'kema M. Blackmon

Many researchers have theorized that racism and discrimination act as developmental mediators in the lives of Black Americans across their life spans (e.g., Comer, 1989; Duncan, 1993; Fischer & Shaw, 1999; Gougis, 1986; Spencer, Swanson, & Cunningham, 1991). Among Black adolescents, in particular, developing and maintaining a healthy racial identity can be daunting in the context of current turbulent race relations in the United States (Stevenson, Reed, Bodison, & Bishop, 1997). The task of healthy racial identity development may be especially challenging for Black adolescents because they must negotiate mainstream, minority, and Black cultural and community experiences (Boykin, 1986; Boykin & Toms, 1985; Thornton, 1997). Mainstream experiences represent experiences related to the dominant culture of the United States, minority experiences may represent political and social injustices associated with being a numerical and social minority in the United States, and Black cultural and community experiences represent experiences within the African American community (Boykin, 1986; Boykin & Toms, 1985; Thornton, 1997). . . .

The link between self-esteem and academic performance among Black American adolescents may be related to how they process achievement experiences at school and in other areas of their lives. According to van Laar (2000), African American students may make two kinds of attributions about their experiences. The first type, internal attributions, cause individuals to internalize negative stigma and self-blame for lowered academic performance. In contrast, external attributions lead individuals to direct blame away from themselves and assign blame to structural barriers such as racism and discrimination (Crocker & Major, 1989; Crocker & Quinn, 1998). Thus, Black adolescents who make external attributions related to their academic performance may selectively devalue the importance of school and academic achievement in the overall context of their lives (Crocker & Quinn, 1998). Such attributions may be a primary reason that Black youth disengage their self-esteem from academically related outcomes in grade school through college (Hare, 1985; Major, Spencer, Schmader, Wolfe, & Crocker, 1998; Osbourne,1995). Further, many Black adolescents may derive a positive sense of self from their families and peers who may encourage them to derive their self-esteem from achievements outside of the academic realm. . . .

Not only may racial socialization messages be linked to Black adolescents' self-esteem at a global level, but they may also be related to these youths' self-esteem in specific areas of their lives. Because sense of self among Black American youth is complex and because the examination of global self-esteem may not provide a clear understanding of the experiences of Black adolescents, it seems important to explore specific self-esteem domains (i.e., home, school, and peer) in this population of individuals. For example, although many Black American adolescents' general sense of self is not significantly affected by lowered performance in school (e.g., Schmader et al., 2001; van Laar, 2000, 2001), it is possible that these students may have differing self-perceptions across home, school, and peer milieus (McAdoo, 1985; Smith, Walker, Fields, Brookins, & Seay, 1999).

Hence, the primary goal of this study was to examine the relationship between parental racial socialization messages and area-specific self-esteem (i.e., home, school, and peer) among Black American adolescents. Based on previous literature in the areas of academic achievement, self-esteem, and racial socialization, we hypothesized that racial socialization messages would be significantly predictive of Black adolescents' area-specific self-esteem.

Method

Participants and Procedure

The participants consisted of 115 middle-school (6th, 7th, and 8th grade) students attending a predominantly Black parochial school in the northeast region of the United States. These students were asked to participate in an anonymous study examining their personal attitudes and experiences. They completed a survey packet consisting of the Teenager Experiences of Racial Socialization Scale (TERS) (Stevenson, Cameron,

Herrero-Taylor, & Davis, 2001), the Hare General and Area-Specific Self-Esteem Scale (HGASSES) (Hare, 1996), and a brief demographic questionnaire. Informed consent was obtained from both students and their parents prior to students' participation in the study, and no incentives were provided for their participation. However, students, parents, teachers, and administrators were told that they would be given the study's results at their request. Because the surveys were administered and completed during specific class times, the return rate of surveys was high (i.e., 100%). . . .

Instrument

. . . *HGASSES.* The HGASSES (Hare, 1996) is a 30-item, 4-point, Likert-type instrument (1 = *strongly disagree* to 4 = *strongly agree*) that assesses both general self-esteem and area-specific self-esteem in the home, school, and peer domains. These domains correspond to the three HGASSES subscales, each of which consists of 10 items. The general self-esteem score is derived by computing the three subscales. . . .

Results

Table 1 provides the means and standard deviations for the study's variables, along with the interscale correlations. Prior to conducting the main analysis, a series of multivariate analyses of variance ($p = .05$) was computed to determine whether students differed by sex and ethnicity with regard to the study's variables. Results revealed no statistically significant interaction, Pillai's Trace = .18, $F(16, 204)$ =1.26, $p > .05$; or main effect differences by sex, Pillai's Trace = .12, $F(8, 101)$ = 1.70, $p > .05$; or ethnicity, Pillai's Trace = .12, $F(16, 204)$ = 0.79, $p > .05$. Hence, sex and ethnicity were not included as independent variables in the main analysis.

To examine the study's hypothesis, a multivariate multiple regression analysis was performed. This analytic procedure was chosen to control for the possible intercorrelations between the predictor and criterion variables (Haase & Ellis, 1987; Lunneborg & Abbot, 1983; Stevens, 1986). A multivariate multiple regression analysis can accommodate multiple predictor and multiple criterion variables, all of which are continuously distributed, from which follow-up tests can determine the unique contribution of each predictor variable on each criterion variable

Table 1 Means, Standard Deviations, and Intercorrelations of the Study's Variables

Variable	M	SD	1	2	3	4	5	6	7	8
Teenager Experience of Racial Socialization Scale (Stevenson, Cameron, Herrero-Taylor, & Davis, 2001)										
1. Cultural coping with antagonism subscale	24.93	5.70	—	.67***	.57***	.69***	.39***	.16	-.03	-.04
2. Cultural pride reinforcement subscale	22.94	3.20		—	.49***	.71***	.26***	.26***	.08	.20*
3. Cultural appreciation of legacy subscale	12.74	2.97			—	.64***	.35***	.24***	.04	.09
4. Cultural alertness to discrimination subscale	10.49	2.92				—	.36***	.05	-.05	-.03
5. Cultural endorsement of the mainstream subscale	7.71	1.87					—	-.09	-.31**	-.10
Hare General and Area-Specific Self-Esteem Scale (Hare, 1996)										
6. Home self-esteem subscale	33.92	5.06						—	.45***	.36***
7. School self-esteem subscale	30.41	3.93							—	.41***
8. Peer self-esteem subscale	30.20	4.29								—

$*p < .05.$ $**p < .01.$ $***p < .001.$

(Lutz & Eckert, 1994). In our study, the predictor variables were the five subscales of the TERS (i.e., cultural coping with antagonism, cultural pride reinforcement, cultural appreciation of legacy, cultural alertness to discrimination, and cultural endorsement of the mainstream). The criterion variables were the three subscales of the HGASSES (i.e., home, school, and peer self-esteem).

Results revealed that the overall proportion of variance in Black adolescents' home, school, and peer self-esteem accounted for by the five TERS subscales was statistically significant. . . . Results of [univariate] analyses revealed that the five TERS subscales accounted for significant variance in Black American youths' home self-esteem, . . . school self-esteem, . . . and peer self-esteem. . . .

Follow-up analyses were then conducted to examine the unique contribution of each of the predictor variables on the criterion variables. Results of these analyses indicated that greater cultural pride reinforcement socialization messages were related to higher peer self-esteem in Black American adolescents. . . . Conversely, higher cultural endorsement of the mainstream racial socialization messages were found to be associated with lower school self-esteem in Black youth. . . .

Discussion

The purpose of this study was to examine the relationship between parental racial socialization messages and area-specific self-esteem in Black American youth. Results revealed that cultural pride reinforcement socialization messages were positively correlated with Black adolescents' peer self-esteem. This finding may suggest that some of the racial values and practices taught by many Black American parents or caregivers are expressed and validated within Black adolescents' peer groups. Conversely, it is possible that Black youths' peer groups may reinforce their cultural pride socialization messages. Nonetheless, the potentially interdependent roles of parents and peers with regard to providing positive racial group messages seem crucial to the social success of many Black youths, and the ways in which these roles affect each other may provide Black adolescents with the skills to develop healthy self-perceptions and means for coping with racial discrimination and prejudice (Johnson, 1988). Hence, home and peer milieus that support the development of Black American youths' positive self-esteem may equip them to face a sometimes unfriendly and hostile world outside of these safe havens.

The finding that higher cultural endorsement of the mainstream racial socialization messages were negatively associated with school self-esteem may suggest that adopting more Eurocentric cultural values and behaviors (i.e., the "acting White" assumption) could serve as a detriment to Black students' academic self-efficacy in the context of predominantly Black school settings. . . . Hence, it is not surprising that some Black parents may choose to place their children in predominantly Black or Afrocentric school environments to (a) expose them to certain aspects of their culture in the context of educational settings, (b) affirm and reinforce some race-related practices and competencies with which they entered school, and (c) insulate them from racism until they have developed their own effective coping mechanisms.

In light of the aforementioned finding, it is also plausible to consider that Black adolescents who are exposed to greater cultural endorsement of the mainstream racial socialization messages may feel more comfortable in predominantly White school environments because their values may be more congruent with students matriculating in these settings. However, regardless of educational environment, the adoption of largely White cultural values or behaviors may be detrimental to some Black adolescents' self-esteem and racial identity development because it may promote the misconception that Black is inferior to White. It is also possible that this finding may be related, in part, to the ways that self-esteem generally develops among Black American youth in schools and in other institutions that may mirror cultural values associated with the dominant culture in the United States. For example, according to Crocker and Quinn (1998), Black Americans' self-esteem may be protected by directing blame away from themselves and assigning blame to structural barriers such as racism and discrimination and by devaluing domains and areas in which some members of their racial or ethnic group do not perform well historically (e.g., academics). Thus, Black American students who endorse mainstream values and behaviors, regardless of their educational setting, may evidence lower school self-esteem because they are unable or unwilling to consider the possibility that racism or discrimination could be contributing to their suboptimal academic functioning in the context of some school environments. . . .

Future investigations should continue examining racial socialization experiences and self-esteem in Black American adolescents from multiple research paradigms. For example, there is a need for longitudinal studies with Black American youth and their families to understand the specific strategies that parents may use to impart racial socialization messages and experiences to their children. Moreover, it may be important for future researchers to investigate how Black children and adolescents may process racial socialization messages in the context of home, school, and peer situations. Finally, future investigators may wish to explore how racial socialization messages may mediate the relationship between experiences of chronic racial discrimination and the development of psychological distress in African American youth.

References

Boykin, A. W. (1986). The triple quandary and the schooling of Afro-American children. In U. Neiseser (Ed.), *The school achievement of minority children: New perspectives* (pp. 57–92). London: Lawrence Erlbaum.

Boykin, A. W., & Toms, F. D. (1985). Black child socialization. In H. P. McAdoo & J. L. McAdoo (Eds.), *Black children: Social, educational, and parental environments* (pp. 33–51). London: Sage.

Comer, J. P. (1989). Racism and the education of young children. *Teachers College Record, 90*(3), 352–361.

Crocker, J., & Major, B. (1989). Social stigma and self-esteem: The self-protective properties of stigma. *Psychological Review, 96*, 608–630.

Crocker, J., & Quinn, D. (1998). Racism and self-esteem. In J. L. Eberhardt & S. T. Fiske (Eds.), *Confronting racism: The problem and the response* (pp. 169–233). London: Sage.

Duncan, G. (1993). Racism as a developmental mediator. *Educational Forum, 57*, 360–370.

Fischer, A. R., & Shaw, C. M. (1999). African Americans' mental health and perceptions of racist discrimination: The moderating effects of racial socialization experiences and self-esteem. *Journal of Counseling Psychology, 46*, 395–407.

Gougis, R. A. (1986). The effects of prejudice and stress on the academic performance of Black Americans. In U. Neiseser (Ed.), *The school achievement of minority children* (pp. 145–158). Hillsdale, NJ: Lawrence Erlbaum.

Haase, R. F., & Ellis, M. V. (1987). Multivariate analysis of variance. *Journal of Counseling Psychology, 34*, 404–413.

Hare, B. R. (1985). No place to run, no place to hide: Comparative status and future prospects of Black boys. In M. B. Spencer, G. K. Brookins, & W. R. Allen (Eds.), *Beginnings: The social and affective development of Black children* (pp. 201–214). Hillsdale, NJ: Lawrence Erlbaum.

Hare, B. R. (1996). The HARE General and Area-Specific (School, Peer and Home) Self-Esteem Scale. In R. L. Jones (Ed.), *Handbook of tests and measurements for Black populations* (Vol. 1, pp. 199–206). Richmond, CA: Cobb & Henry.

Johnson, D. J. (1988). Racial socialization strategies of parents in three Black private schools. In D. T. Slaughter & D. J. Johnson (Eds.), *Visible now: Blacks in private schools* (pp. 251–267). New York: Greenwood.

Lunneborg, C. E., & Abbott, R. D. (1983). *Elementary multivariate analysis for the behavioral sciences.* New York: North-Holland.

Lutz, J. G., & Eckert, T. L. (1994). The relationship between canonical correlation analysis and multivariate multiple regression. *Educational and Psychological Measurement, 54,* 666–675.

Major, B., Spencer, S., Schmader, T, Wolfe, C., & Crocker, J. (1998). Coping with negative stereotypes about intellectual performance: The role of psychological disengagement. *Personality & Social Psychology, 24,* 34–50.

McAdoo, H. P. (1985). Racial attitudes and self-concept of young Black children over time. In H. P. McAdoo & J. L. McAdoo (Eds.), *Black children: Social, educational, and parental, environments* (pp. 213–242). London: Sage.

Osbourne, J. W. (1995). Academics, self-esteem, and race: A look at the underlying assumptions of the disidentification hypothesis. *Personal and Social Psychology Bulletin, 21,* 449–455.

Schmader, T., Major, B., & Gramzow, R. H. (2001). Coping with ethnic stereotypes in the academic domain: Perceived injustice and psychological disengagement. *Journal of Social Issues, 57,* 93–111.

Smith, E. P., Walker, K., Fields, L., Brookins, C. C., & Seay, R. (1999). Ethnic identity and its relationship to self-esteem, perceived efficacy and prosocial attitudes in early adolescence. *Journal of Adolescence, 22,* 867–880.

Spencer, M. B., Swanson, D. P., & Cunningham, M. (1991). Ethnicity, ethnic identity, and competence formation: Adolescent transition and cultural transformation. *Journal of Negro Education, 60,* 366–387.

Stevens, J. (1986). *Applied multivariate statistics for the social sciences.* Hillsdale, NJ: Lawrence Erlbaum.

Stevenson, H. C., Cameron, R., Herrero-Taylor, T., & Davis, G. Y. (2001). *Development of the Teenage Experience of Racial Socialization Scale: Correlates of race-related socialization frequency from the perspective of Black youth.* Unpublished manuscript.

Stevenson, H. C., Reed, J., Bodison, P, & Bishop, A. (1997). Racism stress management: Racial socialization beliefs and the experience of depression and anger in African American youth. *Youth & Society, 29,* 197–222.

Thornton, M. C. (1997). Strategies of racial socialization among Black parents: Mainstream, minority, and cultural messages. In R. J. Taylor, J. S. Jackson, & L. M. Chatters (Eds.), *Family life in Black America* (pp. 201–215). Thousand Oaks, CA: Sage.

van Laar, C. (2000). The paradox of low academic achievement but high self-esteem in African American students. *Educational Psychology Review, 12,* 33–61.

van Laar, C. (2001). Declining optimism in ethnic minority students: The role of attributions and self-esteem. In F. Salili, C. Chiu, & Y. Hong (Eds.), *Student motivation: The culture and context of learning* (pp. 79–104). New York: Kluwer Academic/Plenum.

Study Questions

1. What are the relationships between self-esteem at school and the racial pride messages given by parents?
2. What cultural messages might you give your children so they have positive self-esteem and perform well in the school setting?

Reading 11

Extreme Isolation

Kingsley Davis

Early in 1940 there appeared in this *Journal* an account of a girl called Anna.[1] She had been deprived of normal contact and had received a minimum of human care for almost the whole of her first six years of life. At that time observations were not complete and the report had a tentative character. Now, however, the girl is dead, and, with more information available,[2] it is possible to give a fuller and more definitive description of the case from a sociological point of view.

Anna's death, caused by hemorrhagic jaundice, occurred on August 6, 1942. Having been born on March 1 or 6,[3] 1932, she was approximately ten and a half years of age when she died. The previous report covered her development up to the age of almost eight years; the present one recapitulates the earlier period on the basis of new evidence and then covers the last two and a half years of her life.

Early History

The first few days and weeks of Anna's life were complicated by frequent changes of domicile. It will be recalled that she was an illegitimate child, the second such child born to her mother, and that her grandfather, a widowed farmer in whose house her mother lived, strongly disapproved of this new evidence of the mother's indiscretion. This fact led to the baby's being shifted about.

Two weeks after being born in a nurse's private home, Anna was brought to the family farm, but the grandfather's antagonism was so great that she was shortly taken to the house of one of her mother's friends. At this time a local minister became interested in her and took her to his house with an idea of possible adoption. He decided against adoption, however, when he discovered that she had vaginitis. The infant was then taken to a children's home in the nearest large city. This agency found that at the age of only three weeks she was already in a miserable condition, being "terribly galled and otherwise in very bad shape." It did not regard her as a likely subject for adoption but took her in for a while anyway, hoping to benefit her. After Anna had spent nearly eight weeks in this place, the agency notified her mother to come to get her. The mother responded by sending a man and his wife to the children's home with a view to their adopting Anna, but they made such a poor impression on the agency that permission was refused. Later the mother came herself and took the child out of the home and then gave her to this couple. It was in the home of this pair that a social worker found the girl a short time thereafter. The social worker went to the mother's home and pleaded with Anna's grandfather to allow the mother to bring the child home. In spite of threats, he refused. The child, by then more than four months old, was next taken to another children's home in a near-by town. A medical examination at this time revealed that she had impetigo, vaginitis, umbilical hernia, and a skin rash.

Anna remained in this second children's home for nearly three weeks, at the end of which time she was transferred to a private foster-home. Since, however, the grandfather would not, and the mother could not, pay for the child's care, she was finally taken back as a last resort to the grandfather's house (at the age of five and a half months). There she remained, kept on the second floor in an attic-like room because her mother hesitated to incur the grandfather's wrath by bringing her downstairs.

The mother, a sturdy woman weighing about 180 pounds, did a man's work on the farm. She engaged in heavy work such as milking cows and tending hogs and had little time for her children. Sometimes she went out at night, in which case Anna was left entirely without attention. Ordinarily, it seems, Anna received only enough care to keep her barely alive. She appears to have been seldom moved from one position to another. Her clothing and bedding were filthy. She apparently had no instruction, no friendly attention.

It is little wonder that, when finally found and removed from the room in the grandfather's house at the age of nearly six years, the child could not talk, walk, or do anything that showed intelligence. She was in an extremely emaciated and undernourished condition, with skeleton-like legs and a bloated abdomen. She had been fed on virtually nothing except cow's milk during the years under her mother's care.

Anna's condition when found, and her subsequent improvement, have been described in the previous report. It now remains to say what happened to her after that.

Later History

In 1939, nearly two years after being discovered, Anna had progressed, as previously reported, to the point where she could walk, understand simple commands, feed herself, achieve some neatness, remember people, etc. But she still did not speak, and, though she was much more like a normal infant of something over one year of age in mentality, she was far from normal for her age.

On August 30, 1939, she was taken to a private home for retarded children, leaving the county home where she had been for more than a year and a half. In her new setting she made some further progress, but not a great deal. In a report of an examination made November 6 of the same year, the head of the institution pictured the child as follows:

> Anna walks about aimlessly, makes periodic rhythmic motions of her hands, and, at intervals, makes gutteral and sucking noises. She regards her hands as if she had seen them for the first time. It was impossible to hold her attention for more than a few seconds at a time—not because of distraction due to external stimuli but because of her inability to concentrate. She ignored the task in hand to gaze vacantly about the room. Speech is entirely lacking. Numerous unsuccessful attempts have been made with her in the hope of developing initial sounds. I do not believe that this failure is due to negativism or deafness but that she is not sufficiently developed to accept speech at this time. . . . The prognosis is not favorable. . . .

More than five months later, on April 25, 1940, a clinical psychologist, the late Professor Francis N. Maxfield, examined Anna and reported the following: large for her age; hearing "entirely normal"; vision apparently normal; able to climb stairs; speech in the "babbling stage" and "promise for developing intelligible speech later seems to be good." He said further that "on the Merrill-Palmer scale she made a mental score of 19 months. On the Vineland social maturity scale she made a score of 23 months."[4]

Professor Maxfield very sensibly pointed out that prognosis is difficult in such cases of isolation. "It is very difficult to take scores on tests standardized under average conditions of environment and experience," he wrote, "and interpret them in a case where environment and experience have been so unusual." With this warning he gave it as his opinion at that time that Anna would eventually "attain an adult mental level of six or seven years."[5]

The school for retarded children, on July 1, 1941, reported that Anna had reached 46 inches in height and weighed 60 pounds. She could bounce and catch a ball and was said to conform to group socialization, though as a follower rather than a leader. Toilet habits were firmly established. Food habits were normal, except that she still used a spoon as her sole implement. She could dress herself except for fastening her clothes. Most remarkable of all, she had finally begun to develop speech. She was characterized as being at about the two-year level in this regard. She could call attendants by name and bring in one when she was asked to. She had a few complete sentences to express her wants. The report concluded that there was nothing peculiar about her, except that she was feeble-minded—"probably congenital in type."[6]

A final report from the school, made on June 22, 1942, and evidently the last report before the girl's death, pictured only a slight advance over that given above. It said that Anna could follow directions, string beads, identify a few colors, build with blocks, and differentiate between attractive and unattractive pictures. She had a good sense of rhythm and loved a doll. She talked mainly in phrases but would repeat words and try to carry on a conversation. She was clean about clothing. She habitually washed her hands and brushed her teeth. She would try to help other children. She walked well and could run fairly well, though clumsily. Although easily excited, she had a pleasant disposition.

Interpretation

Such was Anna's condition just before her death. It may seem as if she had not made much progress, but one must remember the condition in which she had been found. One must recall that she had no glimmering of speech, absolutely, no ability to walk, no sense of gesture, not the least capacity to feed herself even when the food was put in front of her, and no comprehension of cleanliness. She was so apathetic that it was hard to tell whether or not she could hear. And all this at the age of nearly six years. Compared with this condition, her capacities at the time of her death seem striking indeed, though they do not amount to much more than a two-and-a-half year mental level. One conclusion therefore seems safe, namely, that her isolation prevented a considerable amount of mental development that was undoubtedly part of her capacity. Just what her original capacity was, of course, is hard to say; but her development after her period of confinement (including the ability to walk and run, to play, dress, fit into a social situation, and, above all, to speak) shows that she had at least this much capacity—capacity that never could have been realized in her original condition of isolation.

A further question is this: What would she have been like if she had received a normal upbringing from the moment of birth? A definitive answer would have been impossible in any case, but even an approximate answer is made difficult by her early death. If one assumes, as was tentatively surmised in the previous report, that it is "almost impossible for any child to learn to speak, think, and act like a normal person after a long period of early isolation," it seems likely that Anna might have had a normal or near-normal capacity, genetically speaking. On the other hand, it was pointed out that Anna represented "a marginal case [because] she was discovered before she had reached six years of age," an age "young enough to allow for some plasticity."[7] While admitting, then, that Anna's isolation *may* have been the major cause (and was certainly a minor cause) of her lack of rapid mental progress during the four and a half years following her rescue from neglect, it is necessary to entertain the hypothesis that she was congenitally deficient.

In connection with this hypothesis, one suggestive though by no means conclusive circumstance needs consideration, namely, the mentality of Anna's forebears. Information on this subject is easier to obtain, as one might guess, on the mother's than on the father's side. Anna's maternal grandmother, for example, is said to have been college educated and wished to have her children receive a good education, but her husband, Anna's stern grandfather, apparently a shrewd, hard-driving, calculating farmowner, was so penurious that her ambitions in this direction were thwarted. Under the circumstances her daughter (Anna's mother) managed, despite having to do hard work on the farm, to complete the eighth grade in a country school. Even so, however, the daughter was evidently not very smart. "A schoolmate of [Anna's mother] stated that she was retarded in school work; was very gullible at this age; and that her morals even at this time were discussed by other students." Two tests administered to her on March 4, 1938, when she was thirty-two years of age, showed that she was mentally deficient. On the Stanford Revision of the Binet-Simon Scale her performance was equivalent to that of a child of eight years, giving her an I.Q. of 50 and indicating mental deficiency of "middle-grade moron type."[8]

As to the identity of Anna's father, the most persistent theory holds that he was an old man about seventy-four years of age at the time of the girl's birth. If he was the one, there is no indication of mental or other biological deficiency, whatever one may think of his morals. However, someone else may actually have been the father.

To sum up: Anna's heredity is the kind that *might* have given rise to innate mental deficiency, though not necessarily.

Comparison with Another Case

Perhaps more to the point than speculations about Anna's ancestry would be a case for comparison. If a child could be discovered who had been isolated about the same length of time as Anna but had achieved a much quicker recovery and a greater mental development, it would be a stronger indication that Anna was deficient to start with.

Such a case does exist. It is the case of a girl found at about the same time as Anna and under strikingly similar circumstances. . . .

Born apparently one month later than Anna, the girl in question, who has been given the pseudonym Isabelle, was discovered in November, 1938, nine months after the discovery of Anna. At the time she was found she was approximately six and a half years of age. Like Anna, she was an illegitimate child and had been kept in seclusion for that reason. Her mother was a deaf-mute, having become so at the age of two, and it appears that she and Isabelle had spent most of their time together in a dark room shut off from the rest of the mother's family. As a result Isabelle had no chance to develop speech; when she communicated with her mother, it was by means of gestures. Lack of sunshine and inadequacy of diet had caused Isabelle to become rachitic. Her legs in particular were affected; they "were so bowed that as she stood erect the soles of her shoes came nearly flat together, and she got about with a skittering gait."[9] Her behavior toward strangers, especially men, was almost that of a wild animal, manifesting much fear and hostility. In lieu of speech she made only a strange croaking sound. In many ways she acted like an infant. "She was apparently utterly unaware of relationships of any kind. When presented with a ball for the first time, she held it in the palm of her hand, then reached out and stroked my face with it. Such behavior is comparable to that of a child of six months."[10] At first it was even hard to tell whether or not she could hear, so unused were her senses. Many of her actions resembled those of deaf children.

It is small wonder that, once it was established that she could hear, specialists working with her believed her to be feeble-minded. . . . "The general impression was that she was wholly uneducable and that any attempt to teach her to speak, after so long a period of silence, would meet with failure."[11]

In spite of this interpretation, the individuals in charge of Isabelle launched a systematic and skilful program of training. It seemed hopeless at first. The approach had to be through pantomime and dramatization, suitable to an infant. It required one week of intensive effort before she even made her first attempt at vocalization. Gradually she began to respond, however, and, after the first hurdles had at last been overcome, a curious thing happened. She went through the usual stages of learning characteristic of the years from one to six not only in proper succession but far more rapidly than normal. In a little over two months after her first vocalization she was putting sentences together. Nine months after that she could identify words and sentences on the printed page, could write well, could add to ten, and could retell a story after hearing it. Seven months beyond this point she had a vocabulary of 1,500–2,000 words and was asking complicated questions. Starting from an educational level of between one and three years (depending on what aspect one considers), she had reached a normal level by the time she was eight and a half years old. In short, she covered in two years the stages of learning that ordinarily require six.[12] Or, to put it another way, her I.Q. trebled in a year and a half.[13] The speed with which she reached the normal level of mental development seems analogous to the recovery of body weight in a growing child after an illness, the recovery being achieved by an extra fast rate of growth for a period after the illness until normal weight for the given age is again attained.

When the writer saw Isabelle a year and a half after her discovery, she gave him the impression of being a very bright, cheerful, energetic little girl. She spoke well, walked and ran without trouble, and sang with gusto and accuracy. Today she is over fourteen years old and has passed the sixth grade in a public school. Her teachers say that she participates in all school activities as normally as other children. Though older than her classmates, she has fortunately not physically matured too far beyond their level.[14]

Clearly the story of Isabelle's development is different from that of Anna's. In both cases there was an exceedingly low, or rather blank, intellectual level to begin with. In both cases it seemed that the girl might be congenitally feeble minded. In both a considerably higher level was reached later on. But the Ohio girl achieved a normal mentality within two years, whereas Anna was still marked inadequate at the end of four and a half years. This difference in achievement may suggest that Anna had less initial capacity. But an alternative hypothesis is possible.

One should remember that Anna never received the prolonged and expert attention that Isabelle received. The result of such attention, in the case of the Ohio girl, was to give her speech at an early stage, and her subsequent rapid development seems to have been a consequence of that. "Until Isabelle's speech and language development, she had all the characteristics of a feeble-minded child." Had Anna, who, from the standpoint of psychometric tests and early history, closely resembled this girl at the start, been given a mastery of speech at an earlier point by intensive training, her subsequent development might have been much more rapid.[15]

The hypothesis that Anna began with a sharply inferior mental capacity is therefore not established. Even if she were deficient to start with, we have no way of knowing how much so. Under ordinary conditions she might have been a dull normal or, like her mother, a moron. Even after the blight of her isolation, if she had lived to maturity, she might have finally reached virtually the full level of her capacity, whatever it may have been. That her isolation did have a profound effect upon her mentality, there can be no doubt. This is proved by the substantial degree of change during the four and a half years following her rescue.

Consideration of Isabelle's case serves to show, as Anna's case does not clearly show, that isolation up to the age of six, with failure to acquire any form of speech and hence failure to grasp nearly the whole world of cultural meaning, does not preclude the subsequent acquisition of these. Indeed, there seems to be a process of accelerated recovery in which the child goes through the mental stages at a more rapid rate than would be the case in normal development. Just what would be the maximum age at which a person could remain isolated and still retain the capacity for full cultural acquisition is hard to say. Almost certainly it would not be as high as age fifteen; it might possibly be as low as age ten. Undoubtedly various individuals would differ considerably as to the exact age.

Anna's is not an ideal case for showing the effects of extreme isolation, partly because she was possibly deficient to begin with, partly because she did not receive the best training available, and partly because she did not live long enough. Nevertheless, her case is instructive when placed in the record with numerous other cases of extreme isolation. This and the previous article about her are meant to place her in the record. It is to be hoped that other cases will be described in the scientific literature as they are discovered (as unfortunately they will be), for only in these rare cases of extreme isolation is it possible "to observe *concretely separated* two factors in the development of human personality which are always otherwise only analytically separated, the biogenic and the sociogenic factors."[16]

Notes

1. Kingsley Davis, "Extreme Social Isolation of a Child," *American Journal of Sociology*, XLV (January, 1940), 554–65.
2. Sincere appreciation is due to the officials in the Department of Welfare, Commonwealth of Pennsylvania, for their kind co-operation in making available the records concerning Anna and discussing the case frankly with the writer. Helen C. Hubbell, Florentine Hackbusch, and Eleanor Meckelnburg were particularly helpful, as was Fanny L. Matchette. Without their aid neither of the reports on Anna could have been written.
3. The records are not clear as to which day.
4. Letter to one of the state officials in charge of the case.
5. *Ibid.*
6. Progress report of the school.
7. Davis, *op. cit.*, p. 564.
8. The facts set forth here as to Anna's ancestry are taken chiefly from a report of mental tests administered to Anna's mother by psychologists at a state hospital where she was taken for this purpose after the discovery of Anna's seclusion. This excellent report was not available to the writer when the previous paper on Anna was published.
9. Maxfield, unpublished manuscript cited above.
10. Mason, *op. cit.*, p. 299.
11. Mason, *op. cit.*, p. 299.
12. *Ibid.*, pp. 300–304.
13. Maxfield, unpublished manuscript.
14. Based on a personal letter from Dr. Mason to the writer, May 13, 1946.
15. This point is suggested in a personal letter from Dr. Mason to the writer, October 22, 1946.
16. Singh and Zingg, *op. cit.*, pp. xxi–xxii, in a foreword by the writer.

Study Questions

1. Based on the research evidence in this article, how would you answer the nature versus nurture question?
2. What was the outcome for the two girls once they were found and educated?

Reading 12

Contradictions in the Childhood Socialization of Sociologists from the Working Class

Joan M. Morris and Michael D. Grimes

Early socialization within a class culture has important and long-lasting effects. Therefore, when individuals are socialized within a working-class family environment, they can expect to experience "culture shock" when they achieve upward mobility that takes them out of their class-of-origin and into the foreign terrain of middle-class culture. And, to the extent that gender and race or ethnicity manifest themselves in ways that are distinctively class-oriented, the effects of this "shock" are magnified for women, for people of color, and for the members of ethnic minorities. The focus of this paper is on the childhood socialization of a group of sociologists from working-class backgrounds—a group of people who have, by most standards, "made something" of themselves, but not necessarily in the ways their parents intended. In fact, for many of them, their successes have been accomplished in spite of what their parents taught them about what it means to be successful; their successes have also sometimes come at the expense of the approval and acceptance of their families and childhood peers.

. . . The focus of this paper is on the childhood socialization of a group of sociologists from working-class backgrounds—a group of people who have, by most standards, "made something" of themselves, but not necessarily in the ways their parents intended. In fact, as will be demonstrated below, for many of them, their successes have been accomplished in spite of what they were taught about what it means to be successful during their childhoods; their successes have also sometimes come at the expense of the approval and acceptance of their families and childhood peers. The data for the paper come from a larger study that addresses events throughout the life courses and careers of a group of forty-five sociologists from working-class backgrounds. Each participant who volunteered to be part of the study was asked to contribute three things:

responses to a set of open-ended questions; responses to a questionnaire; and a curriculum vitae. The major thesis of this paper is that early socialization within a class culture has deep and abiding effects. More specifically, when individuals are socialized within a working-class family environment, they can expect to experience "culture shock" when they achieve upward mobility that takes them out of their class-of-origin and into the foreign terrain of middle-class culture. And, to the extent that gender and race or ethnicity manifest themselves in ways that are distinctively class-oriented, the effects of this "shock" are magnified for women, for people of color, and for the members of ethnic minorities. The present analysis focuses its attention on the impacts of early socialization within working-class culture, how these experiences have influenced the careers of academics from working-class backgrounds, and the unique effects that result for women and for the members of racial and ethnic minorities from working-class backgrounds.

Learning What "Feels Right"

The first and most enduring exposure to culture occurs during childhood socialization. A number of analysts have concluded that the class location of parents is one of the most important influences on the socialization experiences of children (Kohn and Schooler 1983; Bourdieu 1984, 1986; Coleman 1990; Lareau 1989) because the parents' class location is directly linked to the nature of the resources that a family possesses and makes available to its children.

Parents may pass a variety of resources down to their children, including a range of explicit but also implicit goods, not the least of which is the cultural knowledge associated with their social class. Wright defines social class as based on three dimensions, each a type of power that is indicative of where one stands in the class structure. The three (property, skills/credentials, and organizational control) combine to produce a class system in which the hierarchy is defined according to power over oneself and others (see Wright 1985). The working-class, in Wright's model, have least power over the three dimensions, i.e., they do not own the means of production; they possess few credentials; and they have little decision-making power over their work or the work of others. Kohn and Schooler (1983) and others have found that the power relations present in one's job carry over into the home. Families who command few of the resources valued in the work world can not help also including a sense of powerlessness in the resources they pass down to their children. Bourdieu (1984, 1986) refers to family resources as the total volume of "capital" available for expropriation by a child. He argues that capital assumes three forms: economic, cultural, and social. Economic capital refers to material wealth or economic power, a form of capital "which is immediately or directly convertible into money and may be institutionalized in the form of property rights" (Bourdieu 1986:243). Cultural capital refers to a broad range of knowledge about the world within which an individual lives. This form of capital is important because it is "convertible, in certain situations, into economic capital and may be institutionalized in the form of educational qualifications (Bourdieu 1986:243). Social capital refers to the network of social connections (a social network) that can be effectively mobilized by the family for its use. It too, can be converted into economic capital under certain circumstances. Bourdieu argues that social classes can be placed on a continuum (or a set of continua) according to the level of economic or material wealth it controls, the cultural capital it possesses, and the potential benefits of its social contacts.

Bourdieu devotes most of his attention to cultural capital because he sees it as essential to the utilization of the other two forms and because of its central role in the intergenerational reproduction of social class. He argues that cultural capital may be manifested in three different ways: the embodied state, the objectified state, and institutionalized state (Bourdieu 1986:254).

The "embodied state" of cultural capital refers to the most fundamental state, that which is linked to the body, it is "external wealth converted into an integral part of the person, into a habitus . . . " (1986:245). All forms of communication in the presentation-of-self are included here, e.g., ways of speaking (vocabulary and accent), manners, posture or poise, etc. This form of capital, since it is embodied within individuals, cannot (like money or property) be transmitted by gift, bequest, purchase or exchange. This form of capital is, above all, an investment of time. . . .

Bourdieu's second type of cultural capital, objectified capital, exists in the form of material objects such as writings, paintings, etc., and as such, has some properties that are only defined in relationship to cultural capital in its embodied form. That is, the material objects can only be appreciated by those with *embodied* culture. . . .

Bourdieu's third type, the "institutionalized state" of cultural capital, is best exemplified by the academic credential. Similar to cultural capital in its embodied state, the institutionalized form of cultural capital has the same biological limits as its bearer (i.e., it can't be bequeathed, it applies only to the bearer). Cultural capital in its institutionalized state, unlike the embodied form, is more manifest. In its institutionalized form, it takes on the character of a conventional, constant, legally guaranteed value. Holding a credential means there is official recognition that one meets certain qualifications, has achieved a particular level of competence. . . .

While the participants in our study obviously posses the necessary credentials for high levels of institutionalized cultural capital, we found evidence of a lack of exposure to both "embodied" and "objectified" cultural capital. For example, we asked them to describe the cultural environment in their homes while growing up. Based on their responses, we developed a coding scheme that contained a total of eighteen indicators of cultural activities. This list included such things as: (the presence of) books, newspapers, magazines in the home; listening to music (and the type of music); visits to museums and libraries; attending movies; going to plays and concerts; taking music or dance lessons; television viewing, etc. Following Bourdieu's (1984) distinction between "high" and "low" cultural activities, we then selected a sub-set of these activities that served as a kind of index of "high" culture. This group of activities included such things as listening to classical music, taking music/dance lessons, visits to museums, attending plays and concerts, and engaging in intellectual discussions with parents or older siblings.

Our results show that a full two-thirds of our respondents had experienced *none* of these activities during their childhoods. Only two out of ten had experienced one of them; and no respondent had experienced more than three of them. In terms of gender, female respondents were no more likely to have experienced these activities than were our male respondents (though the one respondent who experienced three of them was a woman). Without identical data on this subject from a group of academics from middle-class backgrounds with which to compare findings, it is difficult to place them in a meaningful context. What we can say, however, is that these data contrast sharply with the levels of exposure to "high" culture enjoyed by our own children and those of most of our colleagues. They are also consistent with Bourdieu's (1984) conclusion that the exposure to "high" culture is directly related to the family's position in the class structure. . . .

As the work of Bourdieu, Coleman, and others makes clear, socialization in working-class homes is, in many ways, different from socialization in middle-class or upper middle-class homes. This goes beyond the level of material consumption (economic capital) the family is able to enjoy. In comparison to middle-class children, working-class children are taught a different set of values and are, themselves, valued differently. As has been well established (Kohn and Schooler 1983; Coleman 1990; Parcel and Menaghan 1994), the socialization of working-class children is heavily influenced by the occupational experiences of their parents. Parents tend to re-create components of their work environments at home; e.g., when parents work in jobs that provide little opportunity for autonomy and independent thought, they are likely to encourage their children to conform rather than to think independently. Despite the fact that most parents stress "independence" in their children; it is what they mean by it that differs. While middle-class parents may be more interested in creativity and self-determination, the primary concern of working-class parents is that their children be able to support themselves, i.e., to do a "day's work for a day's pay" and to avoid appearing weak by asking for help. To the extent that a high level of conformity is required in most working-class jobs, "independence" may come to mean just the opposite of what middle-class parents expect. In making comparisons such as these it is necessary to recognize that the differences between class cultures means there is also a lack of agreement on meanings and values—differences that may be masked by the use of similar language. . . .

Economic Capital

The U.S. working-class is a heterogeneous group in its range of material circumstances and our respondents' childhood homes were not exceptional in that regard. About one-third of respondents reported no material deprivation during their childhoods (16 respondents); another third reported they did feel a sense of material deprivation as children (15 respondents); and the remainder fell between these two extremes, reporting various experiences of relative deprivation.

The following examples are typical of those who commented on their recognition of socioeconomic differences and their disadvantaged status.

"I became aware of income differences (which is not to say class differences) around the fifth grade. Another child in my class asked me why I wore the same thing to school every day."

"I felt materially deprived after my father died. As the years after went by we became poorer and poorer. By high school, I was wearing old (my mother's) clothes, my middle brother would complain about not being able to buy new clothes. My older brother and mother would fight constantly about his giving more money to the household. The meals became smaller, but always attractively prepared."

The example below describes the sense of relative deprivation that one woman remembered feeling when she compared herself to her childhood peers.

"I was quite aware of the fact that other Jewish families often went on summer vacations . . . we never did. My father had overtime, a concept unknown to my friends, their fathers worked 9 to 5. Also, when I was in elementary school and my mother went back to work, I had to go to summer day camp. I could not go to the day camp associated with the Jewish Community Center (JCC), but had to go to Girl Scouts Camp, because it cost less. . . . We only got one present on Hanukkah, not eight. I had hand-me-down clothes, not full priced clothing from department stores."

Cultural Capital

The participants in this study provided a wealth of evidence in support of Bourdieu's statement that cultural capital is "determinant in the reproduction of social structure" (1986:254). Yet, the fact that they have failed to reproduce the class structure within which they were raised raises an important point. Cultural capital is based on values, knowledge, and meaning. The autobiographical accounts provided by our respondents show how the social structure is reinforced and usually reproduced, often in subtle, nonobvious ways by the transmission of working-class culture. Parental encouragement and expectations are perhaps the most influential, but interaction with others is also important. . . .

Encouragement and Expectations

The majority of respondents to our study reported that their parents encouraged them in their early educations. This is consistent with Laureau's

(1989) findings that both working-class and middle-class parents prepare their children for school. The main difference, however, is that working-class parents tend to leave education to the "professionals" (teachers, guidance counselors, etc.) while middle-class parents stay more involved with their children's education throughout their school years. Working-class parents often see education as the route to a better job. One respondent wrote:

> "My parents were both committed to our gaining an education so we could have 'sit-down' jobs performing 'clean' work.

To many, however, parental encouragement to "do well" in school meant to follow the rules, keep out of trouble, etc. To many working-class parents, a "good" report card was equivalent to a satisfactory evaluation at work. Getting good grades was an outward sign that you were able to fit into a system and accomplish what was expected. One respondent referred to his father's efforts to teach him "industrial discipline" in the following way:

> "He explained that I would always have a 'boss,' and that I would have to obey authority without question or reason."

And in a similar vein, a respondent talks about her parents' concern that she "do well" in school:

> ". . . this urgent need for conformity could be attributed in part to the working-class attitudes toward work. For the types of work that everyone did and that I was expected to do when I was grown, it was very necessary that one develop the 'proper' attitude toward authority."

Education was perhaps more important in minority families. Several African American respondents commented on their families' exceptional encouragement of education—encouragement at a level that was somewhat unusual for white working-class children. For example:

> "My parents, grandparents and other relatives encouraged me during the years of my early education. My maternal grandmother, with whom I spent a great deal of time when I was very young, remembered the days when it was illegal to teach blacks to read. Therefore, she was able to impress upon us the value of education. My parents were always supportive as well."

> "I was an only child and the center of a great deal of attention and favor. I was sheltered from the streets, continually watched and not allowed to play with many of the kids in the neighborhood and was sent back to the South

during the summer, a not uncommon pattern of Black Southerners. In many ways, my mother and our family always had high expectations for behavior since it was one of the ways to separate us from 'low class' people."

Pursuit of the "American Dream"

Respondents often gave accounts of parental support that were couched in the ideology of the dominant culture—the idea that one's achievements are only limited by individual ability, willingness to work, etc. In the case of childhood socialization into the working-class, this ideology is inherently contradictory. That is, the belief that individuals can "make something of themselves," and in fact, that *anyone* can make *anything* of themselves that they wish, suggests an open system, a meritocracy. However, any system within which merit would determine success would have to be based on equal access to resources, information being the most important. Working-class kids simply do not "see" the same career opportunities that middle-class kids see. Part of this is due to limited information about what is available and what the requirements are for seeking it. But some, and perhaps this is the larger issue, is due to limited aspirations. The following is a good example:

> ". . . Being a white, working class male in a stable household made me secure and comfortable. I believed in the "American Dream" which meant that I could do or be almost anything I wanted. That I didn't aspire to be a professional or manager was like not thinking that I could fly, it wasn't a possibility. I figured I was going to do some type of blue-collar work, get married, have children, and own my own house."

All children develop their career aspirations within a class-specific culture. The fact that proportionately fewer children attend college at each lower level of the socioeconomic hierarchy is no accident—and it is not entirely due to affordability factors. One of the major places in which the class system is institutionalized is the family. The family's location in the class system, in turn, determines the location and content of early educational experiences, and has a huge effect on the make-up and orientation of peer groups. Values, expectations, and aspirations are formed and reinforced through interaction with family, friends, and teachers. Thus the social-psychological effects of early socialization have deep and enduring effects on individuals' lives. The following examples illustrate some of this.

". . . I was never encouraged to think about college (by teachers) and I was even discouraged from attending college by family and friends. Their attitudes had been developed by class background. The impact was that I got a terribly late start in completing my first college class (age 24).

"None of my teachers were influential in directing my path towards higher education before I dropped out of school. In fact, just the opposite. In the 9th grade, we were tested with a battery of tests. My homeroom teacher, an English teacher whom I was crazy about, informed my mother that I was a B student and was not college material. This was ironic because two years later, while I was pregnant, I undertook testing by (a federal agency . . . my mother made me do it) and they told me that I was almost a genius. I remember her words as we were leaving the building . . . she looked at my stomach and said, 'some genius.'"

Inherent Contradictions in Parental Encouragement

Most respondents reported that their parents were interested in seeing their children "do better" than they had done. These interests were usually stated in general terms such as the following:

"Both my parents had strong upwardly mobile ambitions for themselves, but especially for their children; they strove always to "get ahead" to improve their economic condition and achieve some mobility."

Such generalized "encouragement" constitutes another contradiction to a common theme in these essays. This is something David Halle reported in his 1984 book, *America's Working Man*, the definition of manual work as the only real work, with intellectual or managerial work dismissed as not really work at all. By this definition, nonmanual workers are shamming, getting by, often not knowing what they are doing, and existing at the expense of the real workers. In response to a question concerning their parents' feelings about their work and its relative status and importance in society, the respondents repeatedly echoed this theme. One respondent said his father made a distinction between himself and those at higher levels of the socioeconomic hierarchy by referring to himself as " . . . someone who actually works for a living." Another referred to his father's "canned phrases," most of which he has forgotten but which implied that the "working man was always getting the shaft." Other examples follow.

". . . he was hostile to the 'big shots' who worked in the plant office . . ."

". . . she felt that her work was very necessary—what would all those middle-class and rich women do without people like my mother to alter and mend their clothing?—was her line. She frequently compared herself invidiously to her customers, commented that they didn't know how to thread a needle."

"Both parents felt their work was important. My dad believed the working man did the real work while managers and engineers/architects did not generally know what they were doing."

"My father would boast about how smart he was and how stupid his bosses were, I think to elevate the importance of his job."

Social Capital

Bourdieu's third form of capital is social capital, the potential to mobilize resources to one's advantage through social ties. The clearest case of a shortage of social capital expressed by our respondents concerned access to higher education. Academics from working-class backgrounds often lack the information they need to achieve upward mobility, but this is, in large part, due to their limited access to a network of social ties with people who know the answers to their questions. For the members of working-class families who achieve mobility into professional positions, not only is it unclear how to map out a career path, but the options themselves are often as hidden as the means for finding out how to learn about them. The autobiographical essays written for this study contain numerous examples of individuals' uncertainty about the answers to important questions, but more than that, they convey the retrospective recognition that they were as ignorant about the appropriate questions to be asked as they were of whom to ask them. One respondent gave the following account of her entry into college:

"It is at this point that I became aware that both my economic and social origins provided a huge impediment to my undergraduate studies. I became aware of class for really the first time. No one was able to help me find financial aid, fill out application forms, apply for scholarships, etc. No one read my scholarship essays. No one took me to the University to check it out. No one helped me to find an apartment. Even if it had entered my parents thoughts, no one knew how to help me. I missed out on a huge chunk of financial aid because I missed the relevant deadlines. Every summer for the first three years of school, I lost 10–15 pounds for lack of food, really. I was even too stupid to apply for food stamps."

Another essayist talks about the influence of growing up in a Jewish home. Though her family was "clearly working-class," most of her parents' friends were middle-class. For her, the intersection of ethnicity and social class was somewhat positive, i.e., the influence of the Jewish subculture offset some of the limitations of working-class subculture. She attributes her parents' encouragement for her education to her ethnicity. In her words, "To them, education was the most meaningful aspect of one's life." Still, she identifies class background as an impediment to higher education:

> "In some ways my class background was an impediment to higher education, in other ways it was not. I was not aware of many options. My parents did not know much of the college scene and guidance counselors at my high school were not well versed."

The Relevance of 'Social Class' as an Issue

The popular mythology in this country is that we live in a classless society or that, since most of us are located within an amorphous middle, social class has few consequences. The study's participants reported similar attitudes for their parents. Though 81 percent of the respondents said their parents were aware of different class locations (most stated that their parents did not speak of *class* per se, but apparently recognized the existence of hierarchical arrangements in society) and of their places within the structure, nearly half said their parents saw few to no consequences for themselves. Many reported that their parents believed that most others were similar to themselves. The following examples are typical.

> "My parents, to this day, have absolutely no awareness of class and the influences of class on their place in society. As far as they are concerned, everyone is the same as them and if you are different from them, well, there is something wrong with you."

> "My parents were not significantly aware of class positions in any manner that made this clear to the children. Further, in the community we lived there were few rich people and all classes in the community participated in the same institutions (churches, schools) and lived in the same general areas. There were few families to compare one's self to and identify these as 'rich' or 'poor'.

. . . Given the pervasiveness of the dominant American ideology, it is no wonder that most of our respondents reported that their parents believed in the importance of individual achievement and self-motivation. Few respondents reported that their parents recognized any sort of systematic discrimination based on socioeconomic status or social class. In fact, in some cases, there was a certain kind of pride associated with belonging to the working-class. The following is a good example of this.

> "... I should add that being working-class in (my hometown) carried with it no shame. You were proud to be working-class. You felt yourself to be strong and to be part of a strong breed, i.e., northern working-class. (My hometown) was built on the labor of the skilled working-class and my father was part of that class."

Weighing the Effects of Race, Gender, and Class

... The effects of racial and ethnic prejudice and discrimination cross both class and gender lines. Having the experience of racial discrimination adds an important element to the equation and modifies the experience of growing up working-class. One such modification is illustrated in the following quote from an Hispanic respondent as he explains how his father instilled suspicion of the white middle-class.

> "They spoke of class only in economic terms and say the system as 'haves' versus the 'have-nots.' My Dad often told me to always watch a smiling white guy because they all cheat. He saw the haves as crooked but said he would never steal as 'most whites who are rich do.' "

The effects of the intersection of gender and class are the focus of Barker's recent (1995) paper. She defines gender as carrying implied limitations within its labels (e.g., men are "naturally" smarter than women, etc.). The negative connotations associated with femininity that are present for all academics are added to the disadvantage of class background for women from working-class families. This, coupled with the expectations that women face from working-class families (i.e., that she "owes" it to her family to remain connected and supportive) generate different results for academic women from working-class backgrounds than it does for similar men. The bottom line is that these factors combine to produce a climate within which women from working-class backgrounds find it especially challenging to perform the necessary requirements to gain entry and acquire legitimacy within primarily upper middle-class, male-dominated institutions of higher learning.

The early-childhood socialization experiences of the women in our study lend support to this. The first example illustrates the implicit preference for males in working-class families:

> "Since I was the oldest child (and only child for about nine years), I participated in ALL business and farm work: milking, field work . . . dressing turkeys, gathering and sorting and packing fruits and vegetables for sale on the routes, helping with books and often responsible for checks . . . My father often said that he had wished for a boy as his first child, but that I was [as] good as any boy would have been!"

The following is a typical scenario for girls in working-class families:

> "I was expected, as the oldest girl child, to baby-sit the younger children, clean house every week, do dishes, cook, help can food, mow the lawn, rake the leaves. Since I was a girl, it did not matter that I was in high school sports and held a part-time job, I was still expected to do my work around the house on top of everything else."

In addition to the expectation that girls will take on a larger share of domestic responsibilities, there are expectations that girls will pursue particular occupational paths. Note the following example:

> ". . . I was told that my options were nurse, teacher, nun, mommy, or secretary, and since I would ultimately be 'just' a mommy anyway, any of the others would do (except nun of course!). One distant cousin was held out as an ideal to emulate; her secretarial job was with an airline, so she got to travel—it was thought that might satisfy my craving for something more/else. There were also strong messages to never move far away (2 hours distant was considered very far), since family, relatives, etc., were the most important thing. Two of my cousins were offered complete athletic scholarships one state (about 3 hours) away, and my aunt and uncle made them turn them down because they didn't want them to move away from home. When I finally left home to go to graduate school, I felt guilty as hell!"

The effects of gender thus intensify the difficulty for women in leaving their working-class origins. Girls in working-class families are instilled with similar levels of (limited) class culture as their male peers but with the added expectations that accompany socialization into working-class womanhood.

Conclusion: Caught in the Middle

In this paper, we have begun to explore the childhood recollections of a group of sociologists from working-class backgrounds. These individuals were socialized to assume a place within the working-class and many have experienced a particular kind of angst alongside their upward class-mobility. They have experienced a form of culture shock not unlike that experienced by travelers in a foreign land. Similar to Ryan and Sackrey's metaphor of "strangers in paradise," these respondents have described how their successes have often been accompanied by ambivalence and uncertainty. In the process of "making something" of themselves, they have moved into an ambiguous "middle," no longer working-class but not comfortably middle-class either.

By considering separately the three states of cultural capital that Bourdieu defines, the source of anxiety for academics from working-class backgrounds becomes more clear. . . . Though one has acquired the requisite institutionalized capital (i.e., the degree), not having sufficient embodied capital makes it difficult to participate fully in the consumption of objectified capital and creates a sense of status inconsistency. The insecurity that accompanies the "impostor" syndrome is common as academics from working-class backgrounds try to bridge the gap between their past and present lives.

In fact, in a myriad of subtle ways, working-class culture prepares the next generation of workers to voluntarily assume their positions in the hierarchy (Willis 1977). Culture is indeed what Wuthnow refers to as the ". . . expressive dimension of social structure . . ." (1987:13). Culture offers meaning; it provides the process for internalizing the social structure and coming to see the status quo as natural, something that "feels right." Since a large part of the content of working-class culture is antithetical to scholarly pursuit, having grown up in an environment that assumes the "naturalness" of working-class values presents a conflict for intellectuals from such backgrounds. The conflict is, for many, deep and aching, lingering long after they have become, objectively, members of the middle-class. Socialization within a class culture is perhaps not as "determinant in the reproduction of the social structure" as Bourdieu implied (1983:253). It is possible to achieve upward mobility in this society; the lives of professional sociologists from working-class backgrounds attest to that. It is much more difficult, however, to "become" middle-class—to experience middle-class existence in a way that "feels right." It is this lingering difficulty that academics from working-class backgrounds experience as a feeling of being "caught in the middle."

Bibliography

Barker, J. 1995. "White Working-Class Men and Women in Academia," *Race, Gender, and Class*, 3(1):65–77.

Bourdieu, P. 1984. *Taste*. (trans. by Richard Nice). Cambridge: Harvard University Press.

———. 1986. "Forms of Capital," pp. 241–256 in John Richardson, Ed., *Handbook of Theory and Research for the Sociology of Education*. Westport, CT: Greenwood Press.

Coleman, J. S. 1988. "Social Capital in the Creation of Human Capital," *American Journal of Sociology* 94s: 95–120.

Halle, D. 1984. *America's Working Man*. Chicago: University of Chicago Press.

Kohn, M. and C. Schooler. 1983. *Work and Personality*. Norwood: Ablex.

Lareau, A. 1989. *Home Advantage: Social Class and Parental Intervention in Elementary Education*. London: Falmer Press.

Parcel, T. and E. Menaghan. 1994. *Parents' Jobs and Children's Lives*. Aldine de Gruyter.

Ryan, J. and C. Sackrey. 1984. *Strangers in Paradise: Academics from the Working Class*. Boston: South End Press.

Tokarczyk, M. and E. Fay (eds). 1993. *Working-Class Women in the Academy*. Amhurst: University of Mass. Press.

Willis, P. G. 1977. *Learning to Labor*. London: Saxon House.

Wuthnow, R. 1987. *Meaning and Moral Order*. Princeton: Princeton University Press.

Study Questions

1. What do the authors mean by "contradictions" in this article?
2. Under what circumstances could a person escape the effects of their social class and move to another with ease? Can you think of examples where this has occurred?

Topic 5
Social Structure and Social Interaction

One of the abiding dilemmas of sociology is how to simultaneously account for and explain the macro and micro influences on human behavior. It seems that as we focus the research or theoretical lens on one, the other slips from view. Bridging this gulf between the social forces of institutions and the face-to-face world of interaction is not an easy task. One world is full of large structures like government or the economy, and the other world is rich with interpersonal contact and subtle, complex connections with persons in our immediate environments. In this topic, we examine some theory and research that help us to build a bridge across the rift in the sociological landscape and illustrate the true complexities of social life.

Social structure, most sociologists agree, is the enduring patterns in society that place people into relative positions (statuses) based on important characteristics like age, income, gender, race, or ethnicity. There is even a structure based on whether one has a disability or not. The rich are in a different social class position than the poor, women in a different social position based on gender than men, and persons of color find their ethnicity and culture affecting them differently than ethnicity does for whites. New students to sociology might have one of their most difficult lessons in seeing social structure and appreciating the effects in our personal and collective lives. However, learning this lesson is the critically important dimension of a "sociological imagination." For example, knowing that your family and each classroom you attend has a structure that is set before you actually participate in them indicates that social structures exist apart from people. Parents or adults have more status (a higher position in the social structure) than children in the family, teachers a higher position than the students, and so on. Can you look at the behavior of people in your family or classroom and understand the impact of structure on behavior? Imagine the macro-social world of ethnicity, social class, or gender, and you can glimpse the large structures that have a great impact on us, almost continuously.

Social interaction is a complex, subtle process whereby people initiate and respond to one another based on commonly understood symbols. Some of the symbols are verbal, like words, and some are nonverbal, like gestures. We learn to express ourselves, respond to others, and create continuous loops of interaction in an endless number of social situations. Because we are accustomed to the meaning of the symbols and the patterns in which they occur, we do "social interaction" without thinking about it; it seems unconscious. When sociologists study this process, we discuss it as "spontaneous" and "emergent" (something that is not predetermined or set). The theory we use to study the microsocial world is "symbolic interaction," a topic covered earlier in the book. Social interaction is also an opportunity for individuals to influence social situations and affect their own and others' behaviors. If social structure feels as though it impedes our ability to be creative and spontaneous, social interaction gives us some measure of autonomy as actors in social settings. Here we are, then: human actors sandwiched between the structural influences of the macro-social world and the dynamic, creative process of social interaction in the micro-social world. Recognizing how we are affected by the world and how we affect the world will certainly enhance our understanding of human behavior and our ability to act on the world ourselves.

In Topic 5, three articles are brought to the readers as illustrations of "social structure and social interaction." First, an early French sociologist, Emile Durkheim, answers the question, "What is a social fact?" In doing so, he uses theory (constructs) to show that social facts are powerful, external social events that impact the behavior of people. This is an illustration of social structure's influence as well. Second, William Chambliss's article uses his rich qualitative study to demonstrate how social structure (social class of the boys) affects the communities' perceptions, and even the boys' future life chances as they participate in two gangs, "The Saints and the Roughnecks." Finally, nothing is more personal than interactions between marriage partners, and Lillian Rubin does an excellent job of showing how gender (a structure) affects our communication (interaction) in her applied research, "The Approach-Avoidance Dance." Structure affects behavior and the behavior reinforces, but might alter, the structure of the relationship.

Reading 13
What Is a Social Fact?

Emile Durkheim

Before beginning the search for the method appropriate to the study of social facts it is important to know what are the facts termed 'social'.

The question is all the more necessary because the term is used without much precision. It is commonly used to designate almost all the phenomena that occur within society, however little social interest of some generality they present. Yet under this heading there is, so to speak, no human occurrence that cannot be called social. Every individual drinks, sleeps, eats, or employs his reason, and society has every interest in seeing that these functions are regularly exercised. If therefore these facts were social ones, sociology would possess no subject matter peculiarly its own, and its domain would be confused with that of biology and psychology.

However, in reality there is in every society a clearly determined group of phenomena separable, because of their distinct characteristics, from those that form the subject matter of other sciences of nature.

When I perform my duties as a brother, a husband or a citizen and carry out the commitments I have entered into, I fulfill obligations which are defined in law and custom and which are external to myself and my actions. Even when they conform to my own sentiments and when I feel their reality within me, that reality does not cease to be objective, for it is not I who have prescribed these duties; I have received them through education. Moreover, how often does it happen that we are ignorant of the details of the obligations that we must assume, and that, to know them, we must consult the legal code and its authorised interpreters! Similarly the believer has discovered from birth, ready fashioned, the beliefs and practices of his religious life; if they existed before he did, it follows that they exist outside him. The system of signs that I employ to express my thoughts, the monetary system I use to pay my debts, the credit instruments I utilise in my commercial relationships, the practices I follow in my profession, etc., all function independently of the use I make of them. Considering in turn each member of society, the foregoing remarks can be repeated for each single one of them. Thus there are ways of acting, thinking and feeling which possess the remarkable property of existing outside the consciousness of the individual.

Not only are these types of behaviour and thinking external to the individual, but they are endued with a compelling and coercive power by virtue of which, whether he wishes it or not, they impose themselves upon him. Undoubtedly when I conform to them of my own free will, this coercion is not felt or felt hardly at all, since it is unnecessary. None the less it is intrinsically a characteristic of these facts; the proof of this is that it asserts itself as soon as I try to resist. If I attempt to violate the rules of law they react against me so as to forestall my action, if there is still time. Alternatively, they annul it or make my action conform to the norm if it is already accomplished but capable of being reversed; or they cause me to pay the penalty for it if it is irreparable. If purely moral rules are at stake, the public conscience restricts any act which infringes them by the surveillance it exercises over the conduct of citizens and by the special punishments it has at its disposal. In other cases the constraint is less violent; nevertheless, it does not cease to exist. If I do not conform to ordinary conventions, if in my mode of dress I pay no heed to what is customary in my country and in my social class, the laughter I provoke, the social distance at which I am kept, produce, although in a more mitigated form, the same results as any real penalty. In other cases, although it may be indirect, constraint is no less effective. I am not forced to speak French with my compatriots, nor to use the legal currency, but it is impossible for me to do otherwise. If I tried to escape the necessity, my attempt would fail miserably. As an industrialist nothing prevents me from working with the processes and methods of the previous century, but if I do I will most certainly ruin myself. Even when in fact I can struggle free from these rules and successfully break them, it is never without being forced to fight against them. Even if in the end they are overcome, they make their constraining power sufficiently felt in the resistance that they afford. There is no innovator, even a fortunate one, whose ventures do not encounter opposition of this kind.

Here, then, is a category of facts which present very special characteristics: they consist of manners of acting, thinking and feeling external to the individual, which are invested with a coercive power by virtue of which they exercise control over him. Consequently, since they consist of representations and actions, they cannot be confused with organic phenomena, nor with psychical phenomena, which have no existence save in and through the individual consciousness. Thus they constitute a new species and to them must be exclusively assigned the term *social*. It is appropriate, since it is clear that, not having the individual as their substratum, they can have none other than society, either political society in its entirety or one of the partial groups that it includes—religious denominations, political and literary schools, occupational corporations, etc. Moreover, it is for such as these alone that the term is fitting, for the word 'social' has the sole meaning of designating those phenomena which fall into none of the categories of facts already constituted and labelled. They are consequently the proper field of sociology. It is true that this word 'constraint', in terms of which we define them, is in danger of infuriating those who zealously uphold out-and-out individualism. Since they maintain that the individual is completely autonomous, it seems to them that he is diminished every time he is made aware that he is not dependent on himself alone. Yet since it is indisputable today that most of our ideas and tendencies are not developed by ourselves, but come to us from outside, they can only penetrate us by imposing themselves upon us. This is all that our definition implies. Moreover, we know that all social constraints do not necessarily exclude the individual personality.

Yet since the examples just cited (legal and moral rules, religious dogmas, financial systems, etc.) consist wholly of beliefs and practices already well established, in view of what has been said it might be maintained that no social fact can exist except where there is a well defined social organisation. But there are other facts which do not present themselves in this already crystallised form but which also possess the same objectivity and ascendancy over the individual. These are what are called social 'currents'. Thus in a public gathering the great waves of enthusiasm, indignation and pity that are produced have their seat in no one individual consciousness. They come to each one of us from outside and can sweep us along in spite of ourselves. If perhaps I abandon myself to them I may not be conscious of the pressure that they are exerting upon me, but that pressure makes its presence felt immediately I attempt to struggle against them. If an individual tries to pit himself against one of these collective manifestations, the sentiments that he is rejecting will be turned against him. Now if this external coercive power asserts itself so acutely in cases of resistance, it must be because it exists in the other instances cited above without our being conscious of it. Hence we are the victims of an illusion which leads us to believe we have ourselves produced what has been imposed upon us externally. But if the willingness with which we let ourselves be carried along disguises the pressure we have undergone, it does not eradicate it. Thus air does not cease to have weight, although we no longer feel that weight. Even when we have individually and spontaneously shared in the common emotion, the impression we have experienced is utterly different from what we would have felt if we had been alone. Once the assembly has broken up and these social influences have ceased to act upon us, and we are once more on our own, the emotions we have felt seem an alien phenomenon, one in which we no longer recognise ourselves. It is then we perceive that we have undergone the emotions much more than generated them. These emotions may even perhaps fill us with horror, so much do they go against the grain. Thus individuals who are normally perfectly harmless may, when gathered together in a crowd, let themselves be drawn into acts of atrocity. And what we assert about these transitory outbreaks likewise applies to those more lasting movements of opinion which relate to religious, political, literary and artistic matters, etc., and which are constantly being produced around us, whether throughout society or in a more limited sphere.

Moreover, this definition of a social fact can be verified by examining an experience that is characteristic. It is sufficient to observe how children are brought up. If one views the facts as they are and indeed as they have always been, it is patently obvious that all education consists of a continual effort to impose upon the child ways of seeing, thinking and acting which he himself would not have arrived at spontaneously. From his earliest years we oblige him to eat, drink and sleep at regular hours, and to observe cleanliness, calm and obedience; later we force him to learn how to be mindful of others, to respect customs and conventions, and to work, etc. If this constraint in time ceases to be felt it is because it gradually gives rise to habits, to inner tendencies which render it superfluous; but they supplant the constraint only because they are derived from it. It is true that, in Spencer's view, a rational education should shun such means and allow the child complete freedom to do what he will. Yet as this educational theory has never been put into practice among any known people, it can only be the personal expression of a *desideratum* and not a fact which can be established in contradiction to the other facts given above. What renders these latter facts particularly illuminating is that education sets out precisely with the object of creating a social being. Thus there can be seen, as in an abbreviated form, how the social being has been fashioned historically. The pressure to which the child is subjected unremittingly is the same pressure of the social environment which seeks to shape him in its own image, and in which parents and teachers are only the representatives and intermediaries.

Thus it is not the fact that they are general which can serve to characterise sociological phenomena. Thoughts to be found in the consciousness of each individual and movements which are repeated by all individuals are not for this reason social facts. If some have been content with using this characteristic in order to define them it is because they have been confused, wrongly, with what might be termed their individual incarnations. What constitutes social facts are the beliefs, tendencies and practices of the group taken collectively. But the forms that these collective states may assume when they are 'refracted' through individuals are things of a different kind. What irrefutably demonstrates this duality of kind is that these two categories of facts frequently are manifested dissociated from each other. Indeed some of these ways of acting or thinking acquire, by dint of repetition, a sort of consistency which, so to speak, separates them out, isolating them from the particular events which reflect them. Thus they assume a shape, a tangible form peculiar to them and constitute a reality *sui generis* vastly distinct from the individual facts which manifest that reality. Collective custom does not exist only in a state of immanence in the successive actions which it determines, but, by a privilege without example in the biological kingdom, expresses itself once and for all in a formula repeated by word of mouth, transmitted by education and even enshrined in the written word. Such are the origins and nature of legal and moral rules, aphorisms and popular sayings, articles of faith in which religious or political sects epitomise their beliefs, and standards of taste drawn up by literary schools, etc. None of these modes of acting and thinking are to be found wholly in the application made of them by individuals, since they can even exist without being applied at the time.

Undoubtedly this state of dissociation does not always present itself with equal distinctiveness. It is sufficient for dissociation to exist unquestionably in the numerous important instances cited, for us to prove that the social fact exists separately from its individual effects. Moreover, even when the dissociation is not immediately observable, it can often be made so with the help of certain methodological devices. Indeed it is essential to embark on such procedures if one wishes to refine out the social fact from any amalgam and so observe it in its pure state. Thus certain currents of opinion, whose intensity varies according to the time and country in which they occur, impel us, for example, towards marriage or suicide, towards higher or lower birth-rates, etc. Such currents are plainly social facts. At first sight they seem inseparable from the forms they assume in individual cases. But statistics afford us a means of isolating them. They are indeed not inaccurately represented by rates of births, marriages and suicides, that is, by the result obtained after dividing the average annual total of marriages, births, and voluntary homicides by the number of persons of an age to marry, produce children, or commit suicide. Since each one of these statistics includes without distinction all individual cases, the individual circumstances which may have played some part in producing the phenomenon cancel each other out and consequently do not contribute to determining the nature of the phenomenon. What it expresses is a certain state of the collective mind.

That is what social phenomena are when stripped of all extraneous elements. As regards their private manifestations, these do indeed having something social about them, since in part they reproduce the collective model. But to a large extent each one depends also upon the psychical and organic constitution of the individual, and on the particular circumstances in which he is placed. Therefore they are not phenomena which are in the strict sense sociological. They depend on both domains at the same time, and could be termed socio-psychical. They are of interest to the sociologist without constituting the immediate content of sociology. The same characteristic is to be found in the organisms of those mixed phenomena of nature studied in the combined sciences such as biochemistry.

It may be objected that a phenomenon can only be collective if it is common to all the members of society, or at the very least to a majority, and consequently, if it is general. This is doubtless the case, but if it is general it is because it is collective (that is, more or less obligatory); but it is very far from being collective because it is general. It is a condition of the group repeated in individuals because it imposes itself upon them. It is in each part because it is in the whole, but far from being in the whole because it is in the parts. This is supremely evident in those beliefs and practices which are handed down to us ready fashioned by previous generations. We accept and adopt them because, since they are the work of the collectivity and one that is centuries old, they are invested with a special authority that our education has taught us to recognise and respect.

It is worthy of note that the vast majority of social phenomena come to us in this way. But even when the social fact is partly due to our direct co-operation, it is no different in nature. An outburst of collective emotion in a gathering does not merely express the sum total of what individual feelings share in common, but is something of a very different order, as we have demonstrated. It is a product of shared existence, of actions and reactions called into play between the consciousnesses of individuals. If it is echoed in each one of them it is precisely by virtue of the special energy derived from its collective origins. If all hearts beat in unison, this is not as a consequence of a spontaneous, pre-established harmony; it is because one and the same force is propelling them in the same direction. Each one is borne along by the rest.

We have therefore succeeded in delineating for ourselves the exact field of sociology. It embraces one single, well defined group of phenomena. A social fact is identifiable through the power of external coercion which it exerts or is capable of exerting upon individuals. The presence of this power is in turn recognisable because of the existence of some predetermined sanction, or through the resistance that the fact opposes to any individual action that may threaten it. However, it can also be defined by ascertaining how widespread it is within the group, provided that, as noted above, one is careful to add a second essential characteristic; this is, that it exists independently of the particular forms that it may assume in the process of spreading itself within the group. In certain cases this latter criterion can even be more easily applied than the former one. The presence of constraint is easily ascertainable when it is manifested externally through some direct reaction of society, as in the case of law, morality, beliefs, customs and even fashions. But when constraint is merely indirect, as with that exerted by an economic organisation, it is not always so clearly discernible. Generality combined with objectivity may then be easier to establish. Moreover, this second definition is simply another formulation of the first one: if a mode of behaviour existing outside the consciousnesses of individuals becomes general, it can only do so by exerting pressure upon them.

However, one may well ask whether this definition is complete. Indeed the facts which have provided us with its basis are all *ways of functioning:* they are 'physiological' in nature. But there are also collective *ways of being,* namely, social facts of an 'anatomical' or morphological nature. Sociology cannot dissociate itself from what concerns the substratum of collective life. Yet the number and nature of the elementary parts which constitute society, the way in which they are articulated, the degree of co-alescence they have attained, the distribution of population over the earth's surface, the extent and nature of the network of communications, the design of dwellings, etc., do not at first sight seem relatable to ways of acting, feeling or thinking.

Yet, first and foremost, these various phenomena present the same characteristic which has served us in defining the others. These ways of being impose themselves upon the individual just as do the ways of act-ing we have dealt with. In fact, when we wish to learn how a society is divided up politically, in what its divisions consist and the degree of sol-idarity that exists between them, it is not through physical inspection and geographical observation that we may come to find this out: such di-visions are social, although they may have some physical basis. It is only through public law that we can study such political organisation, because this law is what determines its nature, just as it determines our domestic and civic relationships. The organisation is no less a form of compulsion. If the population clusters together in our cities instead of being scattered over the rural areas, it is because there exists a trend of opinion, a col-lective drive which imposes this concentration upon individuals. We can no more choose the design of our houses than the cut of our clothes—at least, the one is as much obligatory as the other. The communication net-work forcibly prescribes the direction of internal migrations or commer-cial exchanges, etc., and even their intensity. Consequently, at the most there are grounds for adding one further category to the list of phenom-ena already enumerated as bearing the distinctive stamp of a social fact. But as that enumeration was in no wise strictly exhaustive, this addition would not be indispensable.

Moreover, it does not even serve a purpose, for these ways of being are only ways of acting that have been consolidated. A society's political structure is only the way in which its various component segments have become accustomed to living with each other. If relationships between them are traditionally close, the segments tend to merge together; if the contrary, they tend to remain distinct. The type of dwelling imposed upon us is merely the way in which everyone around us and, in part, previous generations, have customarily built their houses. The communication network is only the channel which has been cut by the regular current of commerce and migrations, etc., flowing in the same direction. Doubtless if phenomena of a morphological kind were the only ones that displayed this rigidity, it might be thought that they constituted a separate species. But a legal rule is no less permanent an arrangement than an architectural style, and yet it is a 'physiological' fact. A simple moral maxim is certainly more malleable, yet it is cast in forms much more rigid than a mere professional custom or fashion. Thus there exists a whole range of gradations which, without any break in continuity, join the most clearly delineated structural facts to those free currents of social life which are not yet caught in any definite mould. This therefore signifies that the differences between them concern only the degree to which they have become consolidated. Both are forms of life at varying stages of crystallisation. It would undoubtedly be advantageous to reserve the term 'morphological' for those social facts which relate to the social substratum, but only on condition that one is aware that they are of the same nature as the others. Our definition will therefore subsume all that has to be defined if it states:

> *A social fact is any way of acting, whether fixed or not, capable of exerting over the individual an external constraint;*

or:

> *which is general over the whole of a given society whilst having an existence of its own, independent of its individual manifestations.*

Study Questions

1. What does the construct "social fact" do for sociology as a science?
2. How would you explain the power of social facts to control the behavior of individuals?

Reading 14

The Saints and the Roughnecks

William J. Chambliss

Eight promising young men—children of good, stable, white upper-middle-class families, active in school affairs, good pre-college students—were some of the most delinquent boys at Hanibal High School. While community residents and parents knew that these boys occasionally sowed a few wild oats, they were totally unaware that sowing wild oats completely occupied the daily routine of these young men. The Saints were constantly occupied with truancy, drinking, wild driving, petty theft and vandalism. Yet not one was officially arrested for any misdeed during the two years I observed them.

This record was particularly surprising in light of my observations during the same two years of another gang of Hanibal High School students, six lower-class white boys known as the Roughnecks. The Roughnecks were constantly in trouble with police and community even though their rate of delinquency was about equal with that of the Saints. What was the cause of this disparity? the result? The following consideration of the activities, social class and community perceptions of both gangs may provide some answers.

The Saints from Monday to Friday

The Saints' principal daily concern was with getting out of school as early as possible. The boys managed to get out of school with minimum danger that they would be accused of playing hookey through an elaborate procedure for obtaining "legitimate" release from class. The most common procedure was for one boy to obtain the release of another by fabricating a meeting of some committee, program or recognized club. Charles might raise his hand in his 9:00 chemistry class and asked to be excused—a euphemism for going to the bathroom. Charles would go to Ed's math class and inform the teacher that Ed was needed for a 9:30 rehearsal of the drama club play. The math teacher would recognize Ed and Charles as "good students" involved in numerous school activities and would permit Ed to leave at 9:30. Charles would return to his class, and Ed would go to Tom's English class to obtain his release. Tom would engineer Charles' escape. The strategy would continue until as many of the Saints as possible were freed. After a stealthy trip to the car (which had been parked in a strategic spot), the boys were off for a day of fun. . . .

Having escaped from the concrete corridors the boys usually went either to a pool hall on the other (lower-class) side of town or to a cafe in the suburbs. Both places were out of the way of people the boys were likely to know (family or school officials), and both provided a source of entertainment. The pool hall entertainment was the generally rough atmosphere, the occasional hustler, the sometimes drunk proprietor and, of course, the game of pool. The cafe's entertainment was provided by the owner. The boys would "accidentally" knock a glass on the floor or spill cola on the counter—not all the time, but enough to be sporting. They would also bend spoons, put salt in sugar bowls and generally tease whoever was working in the cafe. The owner had opened the cafe recently and was dependent on the boys' business which was, in fact, substantial since between the horsing around and the teasing they bought food and drinks.

The Saints on Weekends

On weekends the automobile was even more critical than during the week, for on weekends the Saints went to Big Town—a large city with a population of over a million 25 miles from Hanibal. Every Friday and Saturday night most of the Saints would meet between 8:00 and 8:30 and would go into Big Town. Big Town activities included drinking heavily in taverns or nightclubs, driving drunkenly through the streets, and committing acts of vandalism and playing pranks.

By midnight on Fridays and Saturdays the Saints were usually thoroughly high, and one or two of them were often so drunk they had to be carried to the cars. Then the boys drove around town, calling obscenities to women and girls; occasionally trying (unsuccessfully so far as I could tell) to pick girls up; and driving recklessly through red lights and at high speeds with their lights out. Occasionally they played "chicken." One boy would climb out the back window of the car and across the roof to the driver's side of the car while the car was moving at high speed (between 40 and 50 miles an hour); then the driver would move over and the boy who had just crawled across the car roof would take the driver's seat.

Searching for "fair game" for a prank was the boys' principal activity after they left the tavern. The boys would drive alongside a foot patrolman and ask directions to some street. If the policeman leaned on the car in the course of answering the question, the driver would speed away, causing him to lose his balance. The Saints were careful to play this prank only in an area where they were not going to spend much time and where they could quickly disappear around a corner to avoid having their license plate number taken.

Construction sites and road repair areas were the special province of the Saints' mischief. A soon-to-be-repaired hole in the road inevitably invited the Saints to remove lanterns and wooden barricades and put them in the car, leaving the hole unprotected. The boys would find a safe vantage point and wait for an unsuspecting motorist to drive into the hole. Often, though not always, the boys would go up to the motorist and commiserate with him about the dreadful way the city protected its citizenry. . . .

Through all the pranks, drinking and reckless driving the boys managed miraculously to avoid being stopped by police. Only twice in two years was I aware that they had been stopped by a Big City policeman. Once was for speeding (which they did every time they drove whether they were drunk or sober), and the driver managed to convince the policeman that it was simply an error. The second time they were stopped they had just left a nightclub and were walking through an alley. . . .

The boys had a spirit of frivolity and fun about their escapades. They did not view what they were engaged in as "delinquency," though it surely was by any reasonable definition of that word. They simply viewed themselves as having a little fun and who, they would ask, was really hurt by it? The answer had to be no one, although this fact remains one of the most difficult things to explain about the gang's behavior. Unlikely though it seems, in two years of drinking, driving, carousing and vandalism no one was seriously injured as a result of the Saints' activities.

The Saints in School

The Saints were highly successful in school. The average grade for the group was "B," with two of the boys having close to a straight "A" average. Almost all of the boys were popular and many of them held offices in the school. One of the boys was vice-president of the student body one year. Six of the boys played on athletic teams.

At the end of their senior year, the student body selected ten seniors for special recognition as the "school wheels"; four of the ten were Saints. Teachers and school officials saw no problem with any of these boys and anticipated that they would all "make something of themselves."

How the boys managed to maintain this impression is surprising in view of their actual behavior while in school. Their technique for covering truancy was so successful that teachers did not even realize that the boys were absent from school much of the time. Occasionally, of course, the system would backfire and then the boy was on his own. A boy who was caught would be most contrite, would plead guilty and ask for mercy. He inevitably got the mercy he sought.

Cheating on examinations was rampant, even to the point of orally communicating answers to exams as well as looking at one another's papers. Since none of the group studied, and since they were primarily dependent on one another for help, it is surprising that grades were so high. Teachers contributed to the deception in their admitted inclination to give these boys (and presumably others like them) the benefit of the doubt. When asked how the boys did in school, and when pressed on specific examinations, teachers might admit that they were disappointed in John's performance, but would quickly add that they "knew that he was capable of doing better," so John was given a higher grade than he had actually earned. How often this happened is impossible to know. During the time that I observed the group, I never saw any of the boys take homework home. Teachers may have been "understanding" very regularly. . . .

The Police and the Saints

The local police saw the Saints as good boys who were among the leaders of the youth in the community. Rarely, the boys might be stopped in town for speeding or for running a stop sign. When this happened the boys were always polite, contrite and pled for mercy. As in school, they received the mercy they asked for. None ever received a ticket or was taken into the precinct by the local police.

The situation in Big City, where the boys engaged in most of their delinquency, was only slightly different. The police there did not know the boys at all, although occasionally the boys were stopped by a patrolman. Once they were caught taking a lantern from a construction site. Another time they were stopped for running a stop sign, and on several occasions they were stopped for speeding. Their behavior was as before: contrite, polite and penitent. The urban police, like the local police, accepted their demeanor as sincere. More important, the urban police were convinced that these were good boys just out for a lark.

The Roughnecks

Hanibal townspeople never perceived the Saints' high level of delinquency. The Saints were good boys who just went in for an occasional prank. After all, they were well dressed, well mannered and had nice cars. The Roughnecks were a different story. Although the two gangs of boys were the same age, and both groups engaged in an equal amount of wild-oat sowing, everyone agreed that the not-so-well-dressed, not-so-well-mannered, not-so-rich boys were heading for trouble. Townspeople would say, "You can see the gang members at the drugstore, night after night, leaning against the storefront (sometimes drunk) or slouching around inside buying cokes, reading magazines, and probably stealing old Mr. Wall blind. When they are outside and girls walk by, even respectable girls, these boys make suggestive remarks. Sometimes their remarks are downright lewd."

From the community's viewpoint, the real indication that these kids were in for trouble was that they were constantly involved with the police. Some of them had been picked up for stealing, mostly small stuff, of course, "but still it's stealing small stuff that leads to big time crimes." "Too bad," people said. "Too bad that these boys couldn't behave like the other kids in town; stay out of trouble, be polite to adults, and look to their future."

The community's impression of the degree to which this group of six boys (ranging in age from 16 to 19) engaged in delinquency was somewhat distorted. In some ways the gang was more delinquent than the community thought; in other ways they were less.

The fighting activities of the group were fairly readily and accurately perceived by almost everyone. At least once a month, the boys would get into some sort of fight, although most fights were scraps between members of the group or involved only one member of the group and some peripheral hanger-on. Only three times in the period of observation did the group fight together: once against a gang from across town, once against two blacks and once against a group of boys from another school. For the first two fights the group went out "looking for trouble"—and they found it both times. The third fight followed a football game and began spontaneously with an argument on the football field between one of the Roughnecks and a member of the opposition's football team.

Jack had a particular propensity for fighting and was involved in most of the brawls. He was a prime mover of the escalation of arguments into fights.

More serious than fighting, had the community been aware of it, was theft. Although almost everyone was aware that the boys occasionally stole things, they did not realize the extent of the activity. Petty stealing was a frequent event for the Roughnecks. Sometimes they stole as a group and coordinated their efforts; other times they stole in pairs. Rarely did they steal alone.

The thefts ranged from very small things like paperback books, comics and ballpoint pens to expensive items like watches. The nature of the thefts varied from time to time. The gang would go through a period of systematically shoplifting items from automobiles or school lockers. Types of thievery varied with the whim of the gang. Some forms of thievery were more profitable than others, but all thefts were for profit, not just thrills.

Roughnecks siphoned gasoline from cars as often as they had access to an automobile, which was not very often. Unlike the Saints, who owned their own cars, the Roughnecks would have to borrow their parents' cars, an event which occurred only eight or nine times a year. The boys claimed to have stolen cars for joy rides from time to time. . . .

The Roughnecks, then, engaged mainly in three types of delinquency: theft, drinking and fighting. Although community members perceived that this gang of kids was delinquent, they mistakenly believed that their illegal activities were primarily drinking, fighting and being a nuisance to passersby. Drinking was limited among the gang members, although it did occur, and theft was much more prevalent than anyone realized. . . .

There was a high level of mutual distrust and dislike between the Roughnecks and the police. The boys felt very strongly that the police were unfair and corrupt. Some evidence existed that the boys were correct in their perception.

The main source of the boys' dislike for the police undoubtedly stemmed from the fact that the police would sporadically harass the group. From the standpoint of the boys, these acts of occasional enforcement of the law were whimsical and uncalled for. It made no sense to them, for example, that the police would come to the corner occasionally and threaten them with arrest for loitering when the night before the boys had been out siphoning gasoline from cars and the police had been nowhere in sight. To the boys, the police were stupid on the one hand, for not being where they should have been and catching the boys in a serious offense, and unfair on the other hand, for trumping up "loitering" charges against them.

From the viewpoint of the police, the situation was quite different. They knew, with all the confidence necessary to be a policeman, that these boys were engaged in criminal activities. They knew this partly from occasionally catching them, mostly from circumstantial evidence ("the boys were around when those tires were slashed"), and partly because the police shared the view of the community in general that this was a bad bunch of boys. The best the police could hope to do was to be sensitive to the fact that these boys were engaged in illegal acts and arrest them whenever there was some evidence that they had been involved. Whether or not the boys had in fact committed a particular act in a particular way was not especially important. The police had a broader view: their job was to stamp out these kids' crimes; the tactics were not as important as the end result.

Over the period that the group was under observation, each member was arrested at least once. Several of the boys were arrested a number of times and spent at least one night in jail. While most were never taken to court, two of the boys were sentenced to six months' incarceration in boys' schools.

The Roughnecks in School

The Roughnecks' behavior in school was not particularly disruptive. During school hours they did not all hang around together, but tended instead to spend most of their time with one or two other members of the gang who were their special buddies. Although every member of the gang attempted to avoid school as much as possible, they were not particularly successful and most of them attended school with surprising regularity. They considered school a burden—something to be gotten through with a minimum of conflict. If they were "bugged" by a particular teacher, it could lead to trouble. One of the boys, Al, once threatened to beat up a teacher and, according to the other boys, the teacher hid under a desk to escape him.

Teachers saw the boys the way the general community did, as heading for trouble, as being uninterested in making something of themselves. Some were also seen as being incapable of meeting the academic standards of the school. Most of the teachers expressed concern for this group of boys and were willing to pass them despite poor performance, in the belief that failing them would only aggravate the problem.

The group of boys had a grade point average just slightly above "C." No one in the group failed either grade, and no one had better than a "C" average. They were very consistent in their achievement or, at least, the teachers were consistent in their perception of the boys' achievement.

Two of the boys were good football players. Herb was acknowledged to be the best player in the school and Jack was almost as good. Both boys were criticized for their failure to abide by training rules, for refusing to come to practice as often as they should, and for not playing their best during practice. What they lacked in sportsmanship they made up for in skill, apparently, and played every game no matter how poorly they had performed in practice or how many practice sessions they had missed.

Two Questions

Why did the community, the school and the police react to the Saints as though they were good, upstanding, nondelinquent youths with bright futures but to the Roughnecks as though they were tough, young criminals who were headed for trouble? Why did the Roughnecks and the Saints in fact have quite different careers after high school—careers which, by and large, lived up to the expectations of the community?

The most obvious explanation for the differences in the community's and law enforcement agencies' reactions to the two gangs is that one group of boys was "more delinquent" than the other. Which group was more delinquent? The answer to this question will determine in part how we explain the differential responses to these groups by the members of the community and, particularly, by law enforcement and school officials.

In sheer number of illegal acts, the Saints were the more delinquent. They were truant from school for at least part of the day almost every day of the week. In addition, their drinking and vandalism occurred with surprising regularity. The Roughnecks, in contrast, engaged sporadically in delinquent episodes. While these episodes were frequent, they certainly did not occur on a daily or even a weekly basis.

The difference in frequency of offenses was probably caused by the Roughnecks' inability to obtain liquor and to manipulate legitimate excuses from school. Since the Roughnecks had less money than the Saints, and teachers carefully supervised their school activities, the Roughnecks' hearts may have been as black as the Saints', but their misdeeds were not nearly as frequent.

There are really no clear-cut criteria by which to measure qualitative differences in antisocial behavior. The most important dimension of the difference is generally referred to as the "seriousness" of the offenses.

If seriousness encompasses the relative economic costs of delinquent acts, then some assessment can be made. The Roughnecks probably stole an average of about $5.00 worth of goods a week. Some weeks the figure was considerably higher, but these times must be balanced against long periods when almost nothing was stolen.

The Saints were more continuously engaged in delinquency but their acts were not for the most part costly to property. Only their vandalism and occasional theft of gasoline would so qualify. Perhaps once or twice a month they would siphon a tankful of gas. The other costly items were street signs, construction lanterns and the like. All of these acts combined probably did not quite average $5.00 a week, partly because much of the stolen equipment was abandoned and presumably could be recovered. The difference in cost of stolen property between the two groups was trivial, but the Roughnecks probably had a slightly more expensive set of activities than did the Saints.

Another meaning of seriousness is the potential threat of physical harm to members of the community and to the boys themselves. The Roughnecks were more prone to physical violence; they not only welcomed an opportunity to fight; they went seeking it. In addition, they fought among themselves frequently. Although the fighting never included deadly weapons, it was still a menace, however minor, to the physical safety of those involved.

The Saints never fought. They avoided physical conflict both inside and outside the group. At the same time, though, the Saints frequently endangered their own and other people's lives. They did so almost every time they drove a car, especially if they had been drinking. Sober, their driving was risky; under the influence of alcohol it was horrendous. In addition, the Saints endangered the lives of others with their pranks. Street excavations left unmarked were a very serious hazard.

Evaluating the relative seriousness of the two gangs' activities is difficult. The community reacted as though the behavior of the Roughnecks was a problem, and they reacted as though the behavior of the Saints was not. But the members of the community were ignorant of the array of delinquent acts that characterized the Saints' behavior. Although concerned citizens were unaware of much of the Roughnecks' behavior as well, they were much better informed about the Roughnecks' involvement in delinquency than they were about the Saints'.

Visibility

Differential treatment of the two gangs resulted in part because one gang was infinitely more visible than the other. This differential visibility was a direct function of the economic standing of the families. The Saints had access to automobiles and were able to remove themselves from the sight of the community. In as routine a decision as to where to go to have a milkshake after school, the Saints stayed away from the mainstream of community life. Lacking transportation, the Roughnecks could not make it to the edge of town. The center of town was the only practical place for them to meet since their homes were scattered throughout the town and any noncentral meeting place put an undue hardship on some members. Through necessity the Roughnecks congregated in a crowded area where everyone in the community passed frequently, including teachers and law enforcement officers. They could easily see the Roughnecks hanging around the drugstore.

The Roughnecks, of course, made themselves even more visible by making remarks to passersby and by occasionally getting into fights on the corner. Meanwhile, just as regularly, the Saints were either at the cafe on one edge of town or in the pool hall at the other edge of town. Without any particular realization that they were making themselves inconspicuous, the Saints were able to hide their time-wasting. Not only were they removed from the mainstream of traffic, but they were almost always inside a building.

On their escapades the Saints were also relatively invisible, since they left Hanibal and travelled to Big City. Here, too, they were mobile, roaming the city, rarely going to the same area twice.

Demeanor

To the notion of visibility must be added the difference in the responses of group members to outside intervention with their activities. If one of the Saints was confronted with an accusing policeman, even if he felt he was truly innocent of a wrongdoing, his demeanor was apologetic and penitent. A Roughneck's attitude was almost the polar opposite. When confronted with a threatening adult authority, even one who tried to be pleasant, the Roughneck's hostility and disdain were clearly observable. Sometimes he might attempt to put up a veneer of respect, but it was thin and was not accepted as sincere by the authority.

School was no different from the community at large. The Saints could manipulate the system by feigning compliance with the school norms. The availability of cars at school meant that once free from the immediate sight of the teacher, the boys could disappear rapidly. And this escape was well enough planned that no administrator or teacher was nearby when the boys left. A Roughneck who wished to escape for a few hours was in a bind. If it were possible to get free from class, downtown was still a mile away, and even if he arrived there, he was still very visible. Truancy for the Roughnecks meant almost certain detection, while the Saints enjoyed almost complete immunity from sanctions.

Bias

Community members were not aware of the transgressions of the Saints. Even if the Saints had been less discreet, their favorite delinquencies would have been perceived as less serious than those of the Roughnecks.

In the eyes of the police and school officials, a boy who drinks in an alley and stands intoxicated on the street corner is committing a more serious offense than is a boy who drinks to inebriation in a nightclub or a tavern and drives around afterwards in a car. Similarly, a boy who steals a wallet from a store will be viewed as having committed a more serious offense than a boy who steals a lantern from a construction site.

Perceptual bias also operates with respect to the demeanor of the boys in the two groups when they are confronted by adults. It is not simply that adults dislike the posture affected by boys of the Roughneck ilk; more important is the conviction that the posture adopted by the Roughnecks is an indication of their devotion and commitment to deviance as a way of life. The posture becomes a cue, just as the type of the offense is a cue, to the degree to which the known transgressions are indicators of the youths' potential for other problems.

Visibility, demeanor and bias are surface variables which explain the day-to-day operations of the police. Why do these surface variables operate as they do? Why did the police choose to disregard the Saints' delinquencies while breathing down the backs of the Roughnecks?

The answer lies in the class structure of American society and the control of legal institutions by those at the top of the class structure. Obviously, no representative of the upper class drew up the operational chart for the police which led them to look in the ghettoes and on street corners—which led them to see the demeanor of lower-class youth as troublesome and that of upper-middle-class youth as tolerable. Rather, the procedures simply developed from experience—experience with irate and influential upper-middle-class parents insisting that their son's vandalism was simply a prank and his drunkenness only a momentary "sowing of wild oats"—experience with cooperative or indifferent, powerless, lower-class parents who acquiesced to the laws' definition of their son's behavior.

Adult Careers of the Saints and the Roughnecks

The community's confidence in the potential of the Saints and the Roughnecks apparently was justified. If anything, the community members underestimated the degree to which these youngsters would turn out "good" or "bad."

Seven of the eight members of the Saints went on to college immediately after high school. Five of the boys graduated from college in four years. The sixth one finished college after two years in the army, and the seventh spent four years in the air force before returning to college and receiving a B.A. degree. Of these seven college graduates, three went on for advanced degrees. One finished law school and is now active in state politics, one finished medical school and is practicing near Hanibal, and one boy is now working for a Ph.D. The other four college graduates entered submanagerial, managerial or executive training positions with larger firms.

The only Saint who did not complete college was Jerry. Jerry had failed to graduate from high school with the other Saints. During his second senior year, after the other Saints had gone on to college, Jerry began to hang around with what several teachers described as a "rough crowd"—the gang that was heir apparent to the Roughnecks. At the end of his second senior year, when he did graduate from high school, Jerry took a job as a used-car salesman, got married and quickly had a child. Although he made several abortive attempts to go to college by attending night school, when I last saw him (ten years after high school) Jerry was unemployed and had been living on unemployment for almost a year. His wife worked as a waitress.

Some of the Roughnecks have lived up to community expectations. A number of them were headed for trouble. A few were not.

Jack and Herb were the athletes among the Roughnecks and their athletic prowess paid off handsomely. Both boys received unsolicited athletic scholarships to college. After Herb received his scholarship (near the end of his senior year), he apparently did an about-face. His demeanor became very similar to that of the Saints. Although he remained a member in good standing of the Roughnecks, he stopped participating in most activities and did not hang on the corner as often.

Jack did not change. If anything, he became more prone to fighting. He even made excuses for accepting the scholarship. He told the other gang members that the school had guaranteed him a "C" average if he would come to play football—an idea that seems far-fetched, even in this day of highly competitive recruiting.

During the summer after graduation from high school, Jack attempted suicide by jumping from a tall building. The jump would certainly have killed most people trying it, but Jack survived. He entered college in the fall and played four years of football. He and Herb graduated in four years, and both are teaching and coaching in high schools. They are married and have stable families. If anything, Jack appears to have a more prestigious position in the community than does Herb, though both are well respected and secure in their positions.

Two of the boys never finished high school. Tommy left at the end of his junior year and went to another state. That summer he was arrested and placed on probation on a manslaughter charge. Three years later he was arrested for murder; he pleaded guilty to second degree murder and is serving a 30-year sentence in the state penitentiary.

Al, the other boy who did not finish high school, also left the state in his senior year. He is serving a life sentence in a state penitentiary for first degree murder.

Wes is a small-time gambler. He finished high school and "bummed around." After several years he made contact with a bookmaker who employed him as a runner. Later he acquired his own area and has been working it ever since. His position among the bookmakers is almost identical to the position he had in the gang; he is always around but no one is really aware of him. He makes no trouble and he does not get into any. Steady, reliable, capable of keeping his mouth closed, he plays the game by the rules, even though the game is an illegal one.

That leaves only Ron. Some of his former friends reported that they had heard he was "driving a truck up north," but no one could provide any concrete information.

Reinforcement

The community responded to the Roughnecks as boys in trouble, and the boys agreed with that perception. Their pattern of deviancy was reinforced, and breaking away from it became increasingly unlikely. Once the boys acquired an image of themselves as deviants, they selected new friends who affirmed that self-image. As that self-conception became more firmly entrenched, they also became willing to try new and more extreme deviances. With their growing alienation came freer expression of disrespect and hostility for representatives of the legitimate society. This disrespect increased the community's negativism, perpetuating the entire process of commitment to deviance. Lack of a commitment to deviance works the same way. In either case, the process will perpetuate itself unless some event (like a scholarship to college or a sudden failure) external to the established relationship intervenes. For two of the Roughnecks (Herb and Jack), receiving college athletic scholarships created new relations and culminated in a break with the established pattern of deviance. In the case of one of the Saints (Jerry), his parents' divorce and his failing to graduate from high school changed some of his other relations. Being held back in school for a year and losing his place among the Saints had sufficient impact on Jerry to alter his self-image and virtually to assure that he would not go on to college as his peers did. Although the experiments of life can rarely be reversed, it seems likely in view of the behavior of the other boys who did not enjoy this special treatment by the school that Jerry, too, would have "become something" had he graduated as anticipated. For Herb and Jack outside intervention worked to their advantage; for Jerry it was his undoing.

Selective perception and labelling—finding, processing and punishing some kinds of criminality and not others—means that visible, poor, nonmobile, outspoken, undiplomatic "tough" kids will be noticed, whether their actions are seriously delinquent or not. Other kids, who have established a reputation for being bright (even though underachieving), disciplined and involved in respectable activities, who are mobile and monied, will be invisible when they deviate from sanctioned activities. They'll sow their wild oats—perhaps even wider and thicker than their lower-class cohorts—but they won't be noticed. When it's time to leave adolescence most will follow the expected path, settling into the ways of the middle class, remembering fondly the delinquent but unnoticed fling of their youth. The Roughnecks and others like them may turn around, too. It is more likely that their noticeable deviance will have been so reinforced by police and community that their lives will be effectively channelled into careers consistent with their adolescent background.

Study Questions

1. Using the concepts from the article, can you illustrate the effects of social class on the community's definition of the boys?
2. How does the idea of "self-fulfilling prophesy" relate to Chambliss's research?

The Approach-Avoidance Dance

Men, Women, and Intimacy

Lillian B. Rubin

For one human being to love another, that is perhaps the most difficult of all our tasks, the ultimate, the last test and proof, the work for which all other work is but preparation.

—Rainer Maria Rilke

Intimacy. We hunger for it, but we also fear it. We come close to a loved one, then we back off. A teacher I had once described this as the "go away a little closer" message. I call it the approach-avoidance dance.

The conventional wisdom says that women want intimacy, men resist it. And I have plenty of material that would *seem* to support that view. Whether in my research interviews, in my clinical hours, or in the ordinary course of my life, I hear the same story told repeatedly. "He doesn't talk to me," says a woman. "I don't know what she wants me to talk about," says a man. "I want to know what he's feeling," she tells me. "I'm not feeling anything," he insists. "Who can feel nothing?" she cries. "I can," he shouts. As the heat rises, so does the wall between them. Defensive and angry, they retreat—stalemated by their inability to understand each other.

Women complain to each other all the time about not being able to talk to their men about the things that matter most to them—about what they themselves are thinking and feeling, about what goes on in the hearts and minds of the men they're relating to. And men, less able to expose themselves and their conflicts—those within themselves or those with the women in their lives—either turn silent or take cover by holding women up to derision. It's one of the norms of male camaraderie to poke fun at women, to complain laughingly about the mystery of their minds, wonderingly about their ways. Even Freud did it when, in exasperation, he asked mockingly, "What do women want? Dear God, what do they want?"

But it's not a joke—not for the women, not for the men who like to pretend it is.

> The whole goddamn business of what you're calling intimacy bugs the hell out of me. I never know what you women mean when you talk about it. Karen complains that I don't talk to her, but it's not talk she wants, it's some other damn thing, only I don't know what the hell it is. Feelings, she keeps asking for. So what am I supposed to do if I don't have any to give her or to talk about just because she decides it's time to talk about feelings? Tell me, will you; maybe we can get some peace around here.

The expression of such conflicts would seem to validate the common understandings that suggest that women want and need intimacy more than men do—that the issue belongs to women alone; that, if left to themselves, men would not suffer it. But things are not always what they seem. And I wonder: "If men would renounce intimacy, what is their stake in relationships with women?"

Some would say that men need women to tend to their daily needs—to prepare their meals, clean their houses, wash their clothes, rear their children—so that they can be free to attend to life's larger problems. And, given the traditional structure of roles in the family, it has certainly worked that way most of the time. But, if that were all men seek, why is it that, even when they're not relating to women, so much of their lives is spent in search of a relationship with another, so much agony experienced when it's not available?

These are difficult issues to talk about—even to think about—because the subject of intimacy isn't just complicated, it's slippery as well. Ask yourself: What is intimacy? What words come to mind, what thoughts?

It's an idea that excites our imagination, a word that seems larger than life to most of us. It lures us, beckoning us with a power we're unable to resist. And, just because it's so seductive, it frightens us as well—seeming sometimes to be some mysterious force from outside ourselves that, if we let it, could sweep us away.

But what is it we fear?

Asked what intimacy is, most of us—men and women—struggle to say something sensible, something that we can connect with the real experience of our lives. "Intimacy is knowing there's someone who cares about the children as much as you do." "Intimacy is a history of shared experience." "It's sitting there having a cup of coffee together and watching the eleven-o'clock news." "It's knowing you care about the same things." "It's knowing she'll always understand." "It's him sitting in the hospital for hours at a time when I was sick." "It's knowing he cares when I'm hurting." "It's standing by me when I was out of work." "It's seeing each other at our worst." "It's sitting across the breakfast table." "It's talking when you're in the bathroom." "It's knowing we'll begin and end each day together."

These seem the obvious things—the things we expect when we commit our lives to one another in a marriage, when we decide to have children together. And they're not to be dismissed as inconsequential. They make up the daily experience of our lives together, setting the tone for a relationship in important and powerful ways. It's sharing such commonplace, everyday events that determines the temper and the texture of life, that keeps us living together even when other aspects of the relationship seem less than perfect. Knowing someone is there, is constant, and can be counted on in just the ways these thoughts express provides the background of emotional security and stability we look for when we enter a marriage. Certainly a marriage and the people in it will be tested and judged quite differently in an unusual situation or in a crisis. But how often does life present us with circumstances and events that are so out of the range of ordinary experience?

These ways in which a relationship feels intimate on a daily basis are only one part of what we mean by intimacy, however—the part that's most obvious, the part that doesn't awaken our fears. At a lecture where I spoke of these issues recently, one man commented also, "Intimacy is putting aside the masks we wear in the rest of our lives." A murmur of assent ran through the audience of a hundred or so. Intuitively we say "yes." Yet this is the very issue that also complicates our intimate relationships.

On the one hand, it's reassuring to be able to put away the public persona—to believe we can be loved for who we *really* are, that we can show our shadow side without fear, that our vulnerabilities will not be counted against us. "The most important thing is to feel I'm accepted just the way I am," people will say.

But there's another side. For, when we show ourselves thus without the masks, we also become anxious and fearful. "Is it possible that someone could love the *real* me?" we're likely to ask. Not the most promising question for the further development of intimacy, since it suggests that, whatever else another might do or feel, it's we who have trouble loving ourselves. Unfortunately, such misgivings are not usually experienced consciously. We're aware only that our discomfort has risen, that we feel a need to get away. For the person who has seen the "real me" is also the one who reflects back to us an image that's usually not wholly to our liking. We get angry at that, first at ourselves for not living up to our own expectations, then at the other, who becomes for us the mirror of our self-doubts—a displacement of hostility that serves intimacy poorly.

There's yet another level—one that's further below the surface of consciousness, therefore, one that's much more difficult for us to grasp, let alone to talk about. I'm referring to the differences in the ways in which women and men deal with their inner emotional lives—differences that create barriers between us that can be high indeed. It's here that we see how those early childhood experiences of separation and individuation—the psychological tasks that were required of us in order to separate from mother, to distinguish ourselves as autonomous persons, to internalize a firm sense of gender identity—take their toll on our intimate relationships.

Stop a woman in mid-sentence with the question, "What are you feeling right now?" and you might have to wait a bit while she reruns the mental tape to capture the moment just passed. But, more than likely, she'll be able to do it successfully. More than likely, she'll think for a while and come up with an answer.

The same is not true of a man. For him, a similar question usually will bring a sense of wonderment that one would even ask it, followed quickly by an uncomprehending and puzzled response. "What do you mean?" he'll ask. "I was just talking," he'll say.

I've seen it most clearly in the clinical setting where the task is to get to the feeling level—or, as one of my male patients said when he came into therapy, to "hook up the head and the gut." Repeatedly when therapy begins, I find myself having to teach a man how to monitor his internal states—how to attend to his thoughts and feelings, how to bring them into consciousness. In the early stages of our work, it's a common experience to say to a man, "How does that feel?", and to see a blank look come over his face. Over and over, I find myself listening as a man speaks with calm reason about a situation which I know must be fraught with pain. "How do you feel about that?" I'll ask. "I've just been telling you," he's likely to reply. "No," I'll say, "you've told me what happened, not how you *feel* about it." Frustrated, he might well respond, "You sound just like my wife."

It would be easy to write off such dialogues as the problems of men in therapy, of those who happen to be having some particular emotional difficulties. But it's not so, as any woman who has lived with a man will attest. Time and again women complain: "I can't get him to verbalize his feelings." "He talks, but it's always intellectualizing." "He's so closed off from what he's feeling, I don't know how he lives that way." "If there's one thing that will eventually ruin this marriage, it's the fact that he can't talk about what's going on inside him." "I have to work like hell to get anything out of him that resembles a feeling that's something besides anger. That I get plenty of—me and the kids, we all get his anger. Anything else is damn hard to come by with him." One woman talked eloquently about her husband's anguish over his inability to get problems in his work life resolved. When I asked how she knew about his pain, she answered:

> I pull for it, I pull hard, and sometimes I can get something from him. But it'll be late at night in the dark—you know, when we're in bed and I can't look at him while he's talking and he doesn't have to look at me. Otherwise, he's just defensive and puts on what I call his bear act, where he makes his warning, go-away faces, and he can't be reached or penetrated at all.

To a woman, the world men live in seems a lonely one—a world in which their fears of exposing their sadness and pain, their anxiety about allowing their vulnerability to show, even to a woman they love, is so deeply rooted inside them that, most often, they can only allow it to happen "late at night in the dark."

Yet, if we listen to what men say, we will hear their insistence that they *do* speak of what's inside them, *do* share their thoughts and feelings with the women they love. "I tell her, but she's never satisfied," they complain. "No matter how much I say, it's never enough," they grumble.

From both sides, the complaints have merit. The problem lies not in what men don't say, however, but in what's not there—in what, quite simply, happens so far out of consciousness that it's not within their reach. For men have integrated all too well the lessons of their childhood—the experiences that taught them to repress and deny their inner thoughts, wishes, needs, and fears; indeed, not even to notice them. It's real, therefore, that the kind of inner thoughts and feelings that are readily accessible to a woman generally are unavailable to a man. When he says, "I don't know what I'm feeling," he isn't necessarily being intransigent and withholding. More than likely, he speaks the truth.

Partly that's a result of the ways in which boys are trained to camouflage their feelings under cover of an exterior of calm, strength, and rationality. Fears are not manly. Fantasies are not rational. Emotions, above all, are not for the strong, the sane, the adult. Women suffer them, not men—women, who are more like children with what seems like their never-ending preoccupation with their emotional life. But the training takes so well because of their early childhood experience when, as very young boys, they had to shift their identification from mother to father and sever themselves from their earliest emotional connection. Put the two together and it does seem like suffering to men to have to experience that emotional side of themselves, to have to give it voice.

This is the single most dispiriting dilemma of relations between women and men. He complains, "She's so emotional, there's no point in talking to her." She protests, "It's him you can't talk to, he's always so darned rational." He says, "Even when I tell her nothing's the matter, she won't quit." She says, "How can I believe him when I can see with my own eyes that something's wrong?" He says, "Okay, so something's wrong! What good will it do to tell her?" She cries, "What are we married for? What do you need me for, just to wash your socks?"

These differences in the psychology of women and men are born of a complex interaction between society and the individual. At the broadest social level is the rending of thought and feeling that is such a fundamental part of Western thought. Thought, defined as the ultimate good, has been assigned to men; feeling, considered at best a problem, has fallen to women.

So firmly fixed have these ideas been that, until recently, few thought to question them. For they were built into the structure of psychological thought as if they spoke to an eternal, natural, and scientific truth. Thus, even such a great and innovative thinker as Carl Jung wrote, "The woman is increasingly aware that love alone can give her her full stature, just as the man begins to discern that spirit alone can endow his life with its highest meaning. Fundamentally, therefore, both seek a psychic relation one to the other, because love needs the spirit, and the spirit love, for their fulfillment."[1]

For a woman, "love"; for a man, "spirit"—each expected to complete the other by bringing to the relationship the missing half. In German, the word that is translated here as spirit is *Geist.* But *The New Cassell's German Dictionary* shows that another primary meaning of *Geist* is "mind, intellect, intelligence, wit, imagination, sense of reason." And, given the context of these words, it seems reasonable that *Geist* for Jung referred to a man's highest essence—his mind. There's no ambiguity about a woman's calling, however. It's love.

Intuitively, women try to heal the split that these definitions of male and female have foisted upon us.

> I can't stand that he's so damned unemotional and expects me to be the same. He lives in his head all the time, and he acts like anything that's emotional isn't worth dealing with.

Cognitively, even women often share the belief that the rational side, which seems to come so naturally to men, is the more mature, the more desirable.

> I know I'm too emotional, and it causes problems between us. He can't stand it when I get emotional like that. It turns him right off.

Her husband agrees that she's "too emotional" and complains:

> Sometimes she's like a child who's out to test her parents. I have to be careful when she's like that not to let her rile me up because otherwise all hell would break loose. You just can't reason with her when she gets like that.

It's the rational-man-hysterical-woman script, played out again and again by two people whose emotional repertoire is so limited that they have few real options. As the interaction between them continues, she reaches for the strongest tools she has, the mode she's most comfortable and familiar with: She becomes progressively more emotional and expressive. He falls back on his best weapons: He becomes more rational, more determinedly reasonable. She cries for him to attend to her feelings, whatever they may be. He tells her coolly, with a kind of clenched-teeth reasonableness, that it's silly for her to feel that way, that she's just being emotional. And of course she is. But that dismissive word "just" is the last straw. She gets so upset that she does, in fact, seem hysterical. He gets so bewildered by the whole interaction that his only recourse is to build the wall of reason even higher. All of which makes things measurably worse for both of them.

> The more I try to be cool and calm her the worse it gets. I swear, I can't figure her out. I'll keep trying to tell her not to get so excited, but there's nothing I

can do. Anything I say just makes it worse. So then I try to keep quiet, but . . . wow, the explosion is like crazy, just nuts.

And by then it *is* a wild exchange that any outsider would agree was "just nuts." But it's not just her response that's off, it's his as well—their conflict resting in the fact that we equate the emotional with the nonrational.

This notion, shared by both women and men, is a product of the fact that they were born and reared in this culture. But there's also a difference between them in their capacity to apprehend the *logic* of emotions— a difference born in their early childhood experiences in the family, when boys had to repress so much of their emotional side and girls could permit theirs to flower. . . .

It should be understood: Commitment itself is not a problem for a man; he's good at that. He can spend a lifetime living in the same family, working at the same job—even one he hates. And he's not without an inner emotional life. But when a relationship requires the sustained verbal expression of that inner life and the full range of feelings that accompany it, then it becomes burdensome for him. He can act out anger and frustration inside the family, it's true. But ask him to express his sadness, his fear, his dependency—all those feelings that would expose his vulnerability to himself or to another—and he's likely to close down as if under some compulsion to protect himself.

All requests for such intimacy are difficult for a man, but they become especially complex and troublesome in relations with women. It's another of those paradoxes. For, to the degree that it's possible for him to be emotionally open with anyone, it is with a woman—a tribute to the power of the childhood experience with mother. Yet it's that same early experience and his need to repress it that raises his ambivalence and generates his resistance.

He moves close, wanting to share some part of himself with her, trying to do so, perhaps even yearning to experience again the bliss of the infant's connection with a woman. She responds, woman style—wanting to touch him just a little more deeply, to know what he's thinking, feeling, fearing, wanting. And the fear closes in—the fear of finding himself again in the grip of a powerful woman, of allowing her admittance only to be betrayed and abandoned once again, of being overwhelmed by denied desires.

So he withdraws.

It's not in consciousness that all this goes on. He knows, of course, that he's distinctly uncomfortable when pressed by a woman for more intimacy in the relationship, but he doesn't know why. And, very often, his behavior doesn't please him any more than it pleases her. But he can't seem to help it.

That's his side of the ambivalence that leads to the approach-avoidance dance we see so often in relations between men and women.

Note

1. Carl Gustav Jung, *Contributions to Analytical Psychology* (New York: Harcourt, Brace & Co., 1928), p. 185.

Study Questions

1. How does the gender structure in marriage affect communication for these married couples?
2. What is the "approach-avoidance dance" as presented by Rubin? How could we change and improve these relationships?

Topic 6
Social Groups

To many, sociology is about social groups. Groups play an immensely important part in social life. Groups are elements embedded in larger social structures, and group membership determines much of our identity as individuals. In many ways, groups are key links between the individual and the larger society. A tee shirt slogan found around many sociology conventions reads, "Sociologists do it in groups," and this sentiment simply underscores the perceived importance of groups to sociology. The idea of "social groups" may seem simple at first, but there are many types of groups and the study of social groups will illustrate how crucial groups are to the creation and maintenance of society.

Sociology likes to typify groups based on a distinction between those that are "primary" and those that are "secondary." Primary and secondary groups rest along a continuum that distinguishes these polar opposites on several criteria. Primary groups are smaller, depend on face-to-face interaction, and have strong identification of the members with the groups. Examples of this type would include one's family or peer group. At the opposite end of the continuum are secondary groups, which have attributes including that they are larger, they depend on indirect communication, and the members identify rather weakly with the group. Examples here would include a city or a large corporation. There are other groups that have both primary and secondary group characteristics, like a fraternity or sorority or perhaps a small church. It is important to note that even within large, complex secondary groups are small, primary groups; cities are composed of neighborhoods and families, and corporations are made up of personal, primary work groups or teams.

Another dimension of social groups is the formal-informal dimension. Bureaucracies are large and formal groups: they have a hierarchy and rules that create the organization and channels of communication for its members. At the same time, there are lots of informal groups, such as a peer group, whose activities are largely free of hierarchy and formal rules. Groups, formal or informal, provide an organizing principle in social life, and while we might believe some of them create problems for us (bureaucracies, for instance, might dehumanize us personally), they are critical to the smooth operation of large numbers of people. Many universities are prime examples of formal, bureaucratic groups. In these same settings, however, we can find many informal activities among students and faculty that are critical to the survival of the group. Again, as we see, social life is lived along a continuum that includes diverse structures and activities, and groups point this out once more.

As the Internet emerged during the past 20 years, new "communities" or "groups" have taken shape as well. This will be discussed in more depth later, in Topic 15, but it merits discussion in our "Social Groups" topic, because people who "meet," "chat," and support one another around a multitude of issues are performing functions much like more traditional, non-cyberspace groups. Sometimes cyber-acquaintances move on to face-to-face meetings and form relationships that may even end in marriage. Sociology will be very interested in whether cyber-groups and -communities can enrich or replace social groups as we knew them before the Internet.

The three readings in this section include a work by James Quinn, which shows how the 1% motorcycle groups sustain their respective groups through time and survive by adapting to changing group structures as well as a changing society. This reading points to the adaptability of groups and the necessity of change to survival. Second, Donald Kraybill talks about the struggle of a religious group, the Amish, and how they have managed to maintain their members and beliefs through resisting change in a society that changes very rapidly. But the author poses the question to us at the same time: are the Amish becoming more modern even as they resist the ways of the larger society? Finally, Joel Best gives us a sociological birds-eye view of why sociology itself is a potential "social problem." Indeed, sociology has been criticized by others, but not nearly so much as we criticize ourselves.

Angels, Bandidos, Outlaws, and Pagans

The Evolution of Organized Crime among the Big Four 1% Motorcycle Clubs

James F. Quinn

Introduction

The Hell's Angels, Bandidos, Outlaws, and Pagans are the largest, and most consistently radical of all 1% clubs. Within the subculture they are known as the "Big Four" clubs. They are also deeply involved in both organized crime and internecine violence (Barger 2000:37, Rosenberg 1980; Wolf 1991:268, 272). . . .

The idea that some 1% M.C.s [motorcycle clubs] are heavily involved in organized crime has been widely accepted by law enforcement for decades (Barger 2000:214–252; Clark 1981; Clark and O'Neill 1981a, 1981b, 1981c, 1981d; Clawson 1983; Davis 1982; Domey 1996; Draffen 1998; Frisman 1981; Hell's Angels 1979; Hell's Angels Shift Gears 1973; Linder 1981; O'Brien 1997; Royal Canadian Mounted Police (R.C.M.P.) 1980, 1987; Wood 1979). One Bureau of Alcohol, Tobacco, and Firearms (A.T.F.) agent (in Clawson, 1983:4) referred to the Big Four clubs as "priority A.T.F. investigation targets" describing them as "the largest—and best armed—criminal organizations in the nation." He asserted that they specialized in narcotics, prostitution, and murder while a former Bandido linked topless bars to that club's finances (Clawson 1983:4). More recently, the U.S. Attorney General described the Hell's Angels as one of the most notorious crime cartels in the nation (O'Brien 1997). Canadian authorities have linked biker gangs to the drug trade, prostitution, smuggling, auto theft, extortion, and other rackets (Nickerson 1998). . . .

Past Inquiries into the 1% Subculture

. . . Thompson stressed the fact that bikers are "very respectful of power" and "intensely aware of belonging, of being able to depend on each other" (1966:101). They conceive of themselves as modern outlaws (Barger 2000:7) and their identities are closely tied to both their bikes and their clubs (Wolf 1991:31–32, 126). Much of their behavior and attitudes can be traced to their desire to uphold this image (Barger 2000:9, 21–22, 39, 254–255). Both Montgomery (1976, 1977) and Watson (1980, 1982) use status frustration to explain this fascination with power. Reynolds (1967), a former officer of the San Francisco Hell's Angels and Barger (2000) a national leader from the Oakland, California chapter, implicitly support this view: Bikers are outsiders both by choice and by socialization. Their response to this marginalization mixes extremes of retreatism, rebellion, and innovation in combinations that vary across groups, regions, and time periods. Thompson cogently describes 1%ers as:

> urban outlaws with a rural ethic and a new, improvised style of self-preservation. Their image of themselves derives mainly from celluloid . . . [movies and television] have taught them most of what they know about the society they live in (1966:332).

Wolf (1991) concurs that bikers are products of technological urban society who adhere to their own version of a wild west ethic and are driven by a sense of alienation and anomie (see also, Barger 2000:21). These writers believe that social trends that threaten lower class white men drive the growth of the biker subculture. In the 1960s, such anomic trends consisted of the civil rights movement and anti-Vietnam protests (e.g., Barger 2000:119–124). More recently they have resulted from various threats to the economic viability of factory workers. Club membership helps resolve the stress created by such threats by creating an alternative elite in which bikers can attain supremacy (Wolf 1991:340–341).

Like Barger (2000) and Reynolds (1967), Wolf (1991) insists that individual bikers see themselves as loners and define their organizations as mutual protection associations of like-minded isolates. Their bonds to one another and their clubs are intensified by the rejection of the mainstream society as well as by constant, intense interaction. Their loyalty to one another is almost as intense as the distrust of the outside world that guides their impression management (Barger 2000:39; Wolf 1991:37).

The extremes to which bikers go to establish and maintain their public image as dangerous, unpredictable, and outrageous is a product of status frustration that also functions as a method of exercising power. It provides them with a marketable commodity that allows them to obtain both legal (e.g., concert security) and illegal (e.g., debt collector for loan sharks) employment (Wolf 1991:266). They also enjoy "freaking out the citizens"[1] (Berger, 2000:74, 157; Wolf, 1991:116, 120; Thompson, 1966:149, 256) whenever feasible. Reynolds (1967) proudly described himself and his "brothers" as "the most illiterate, degenerate bastards that ever walked the face of the earth" (1967:97). Watson more cogently claims that bikers deliberately present themselves as bitter and dangerous outlaws with nothing to lose. However, this image is more commodity than reality. Many 1%ers have families, most hold normal jobs, and virtually all have much to lose despite their episodic recklessness (Barger 2000:33; Thompson 1966:73–75; Wolf 1991:257–265).

The primacy of brotherhood, the joys of motorcycling, and respect for mechanical skills are the central values of the subculture. Barger devotes a full chapter of his autobiography (2000:49–65) to his experiences and opinions of various aspects of the construction and modification of Harley-Davidson motorcycles over the last 40 years. Watson lists five characteristics that define a righteous biker:

1. Owns and rides a bike (Harley-Davidson)
2. Has an appreciation for, and skill with, the mechanical aspects of bikes
3. Has a lifestyle in the biker subculture and treats other righteous bikers as bro's
4. Fits the general cultural model of masculine in outlook, behavior, and sexual orientation
5. Is free in the sense of "outrageous" nonconformity to worldly values while conforming to [this] lifestyle (Watson 1982:334).

Wolf's lengthier and more recent analysis confirms the priority of these values within the subculture (1991:82). "Righteous," in biker society, is the functional equivalent of "outrageous" in conventional society. The concept also includes nearly unconditional loyalty to Harley-Davidson motorcycles, one's club, and one's "brothers.". . .

Organized Crime in Big Four Motorcycle Clubs

Organized crime, be it at the chapter or club level, is a central source of income for some of these groups and has played a significant role in the development of the subculture (Clark 1981; Clawson 1983; Domey 1996; Frisman 1981; O'Brien 1997). The emergence of the Big Four clubs is at least partially attributable to the combination of retreatism and rebellion occurring in the socially isolated 1% subculture that creates a sense of entitlement and criminal pride (Walters 1990; Yochelson and Samenow 1976). However, these traits can motivate deep criminal involvements or act as a rationale to avoid them depending on interpersonal and regional contingencies.

One critical contingency is the degree to which club leadership alternates between periods of growth and retrenchment, guided respectively by radical and conservative interpretations of core biker values. Conservative bikers are reluctant to employ economic innovations within the organization while radicals focus much time and effort on them. Thus, it is the mode of adaptation to strain chosen by an individual biker that determines his orientation. Radicalism tends to increase in popularity during anomic periods, which are also associated with subcultural growth. This is largely due to the intensity of the interclub rivalries engendered by such widespread expansion. Prolongation of such periods within a club or region creates demands on the membership that encourage organized crime.

It is difficult to set a single precise time line for these changes because they proceeded at varying rates within different segments of different clubs. Such a discussion must account for both regional and club-specific variations because bikers' opportunity structures are regional in scope. Nor is this development steady within a single club or region; groups will often progress toward greater organization for a period of months or years and then regress, wholly or partly, for an equal period. Nonetheless, a few generalities can be noted at the regional and club level. The Hells' Angels moved the most rapidly with clearly organized operations coming to light by the mid-1970s (Hell's Angels shift gear 1973; *Newsweek* 1975). In the northeast and midwest, Pagan and Outlaw enmeshment in sophisticated enterprises began a few years later and became evident to the authorities by the early 1980s (Clawson 1983; Frisman 1981; Kerre and Vogt 1981; Linder 1981; Organized crime

1980). Developments in the southeast lagged a year or two behind those in the rest of the nation (Miami News 1983).

This pattern of trends being initiated on the west coast and being adopted in the industrial midwest and northeast before finally spilling over to the south is generally typical of the subculture. For example, the Angels set the tone for the subculture from their San Francisco bay area base in the 1950s. This tone, in modified form, was quickly adopted by the then-Chicago-based Outlaws[2] and the Pagans in the northeast. The Texas-based Bandidos did not emerge until 1966 (Barger 2000:37; Alabama/Mississippi Chapter of the Bandidos MCs.) . . .

The Hell's Angels emerged as the hegemonic power in California by the mid-1960s era chronicled by Thompson (1966), Reynolds (1967), and von Hoffman (1968). Their hegemony seems best attributed to (1) the extremism of their tactics and solidarity (Barger 2000:35–37, 141, 146; Reynolds 1967; Thompson 1966), and (2) their deliberate and prolonged efforts to build a well-integrated, international scale organization (Barger 2000:103, 254; Clawson 1983; Elfman 1982; Mellgren 1996; Thompson 1966). The intensity of these early struggles cemented the Angels into a cohesive group in precisely the manner described by group conflict theory (Vold 1980).

Fueled by media glorification of the early Hell's Angels (whose chapters were autonomous and sometimes even unknown to one another [Barger 2000:27–31]) and the anomie of affluence, many other 1% MCs. arose throughout the continent. The Pagans, Grim Reapers, Devil's Disciples, and Satan's Slaves originated in the 1950s but their memberships expanded most rapidly between 1965 and 1975 (Barger 2000:35). This anomic era of civil rights activity and anti-military sentiments posed major status threats to young, working class whites. Demographically, this is precisely the modal background of 1% club members (Danner and Silverman 1986; Thompson 1966:196; Wolf 1991:30). Rampant drug use and sexual liberation added to the anomie and contributed to the emerging norms of the biker subculture (von Hoffman 1968). . . .

Club Expansion

Exemplary of the link between organized criminality and violence is the bitter war between the Hell's Angels and Bandidos that is currently plaguing Scandinavia. The Bandidos have very close ties with the Outlaws and are determined to break Angel hegemony in Northwestern Europe. This situation is exemplary of the expansionist mode of thought. These hostilities have involved military ordinance as well as automatic weapons: At one point the Angels launched a grenade at a jail holding an enemy leader (Ibrahim 1997). Other attacks have occurred at the Copenhagen airport and on the streets of a resort town as well as at clubhouses and homes (Andersson 1997; Ibrahim 1997; Moseley 1997).

While such extremes of violent bravado are typical of expansionist radicalism (Quinn 1987), the development of organized crime is quite evident to Scandinavian authorities. "We don't call them bikers," said a spokesman for Stockholm County Police. "We call them criminal gangs. As far as Scandinavia goes, we believe the bikes are only a camouflage" (Andersson 1997:7). The manner in which the war is being fought is only slightly more extreme than what occurred in the U.S. in the 1970s. This would seem to reflect the growing sophistication of these groups and the increased ease with which military ordinance can be obtained by their organizations. Similar hostilities now plague the Quebec area (Nickerson 1998).

Retrenchment

The biker leaders who inspired and led the interclub wars of the 1970s were selected for their toughness and reckless "class." This helped individual clubs to establish effective reputations within their own local saloon societies. As these leaders were driven to ever more outrageous exhibitions of these focal concerns, many were eliminated by police, rival clubs, other saloon society actors, or their own recklessness (Quinn 1987; Thompson 1966:82–86, 148, 220). By the late 1970s local police and federal investigations began to expose the involvement of many 1% M.Cs. in drug trafficking, theft, extortion, and prostitution rings (Clark and O'Neill 1981a, 1981b, 1981c, 1981d; Clawson 1983; Frisman 1981; Hell's Angels shift gear 1973; Linder 1981; Wood 1979).

The demise of these club and chapter leaders often brought biker purists into power. They had survived the era of expansion by relying on smartness instead of toughness and immediately sought to rid their groups of what they felt to be less than righteous bikers. This new cohort of leaders feared the subculture's demise through the disintegration of subcultural values, mutual annihilation, and police efforts. Thus, immediate paramilitary supremacy was often devalued in favor of quietude and retreatism in order to restore the subculture's core values and facilitate criminal enterprises. This leadership was more utilitarian than that of the previous era and generally more conciliatory than its predecessors toward both rival clubs and the mainstream culture (Beissert 1988). Some clubs did not undergo changes in role occupants but had leaders who changed with the demands of the era. When entire clubs shifted to such neoconservativism, subcultural idealism and retreatism became the hallmarks of the clubs' persona. Where radicals retained power, as in the Big Four clubs, retrenchment was motivated by the desire to increase profits from criminal enterprises and retain subcultural status by adhering to subcultural values. . . .

As the scale of their drug, theft, prostitution, and other enterprises grew throughout the 1970s, peace became more valuable to the Big Four clubs than the constant publicity which had fueled their growth and inspired these organized criminal operations. In fact, several of the Big Four clubs have made deliberate efforts to present a positive image to the mainstream society (Harper 1982; Marlowe 1983) and even publicly contributed to charity (Bread 1985). This trend was facilitated by the firmness with which the outlaw biker's public image had been established in the public mind by various mass media (Barger 2000:67, 150–155). . . .

Each club has an inner circle of members who are much more aware of the extent and details of the club's criminal operations and profits than rank and file members. Some of these club officials feel less pressure to hold a job or hustle as do their "brothers" (Do the Bandidos 1981). Rank and filers are generally on the hustle constantly—meaning that they work sporadically, sponsor or pressure their female associates into prostitution, steal and sell motorcycles, and so forth. Increasingly, however, such hustles can be at least coordinated with, if not directly subsidized by, group criminal endeavors.

Rank and file members of Big Four clubs do not seem to object to the profiteering of their leaders whose lives are wholly devoted to club business. Core members may conceal the magnitude of club profits from rank and filers but adhere to their own consensus on their division. These core members are also the bikers most constantly and seriously in danger of arrest by police or assassination by rivals. Much of the skimmed money is redistributed as loans or gifts, or indirectly through donations to the club or chapter (e.g., alcohol or drugs, a new or refurbished pick-me-up truck, a pool table for the clubhouse). The loyalty of rank and filers to their officers is thus maintained through ties of gratitude and indebtedness (Sahlins 1963). . . .

Conclusion

It should not be inferred that illegal business operations are the central function of any 1% M.C. Devotion to Harley-Davidson motorcycles and a powerful sense of camaraderie are the central motivations to subcultural participation for all currently active club bikers. Indeed, most 1% clubs are led by conservatives who avoid serious criminality and seek only to be left alone to ride and party with their "brothers." However, radicals lead the Big Four clubs and many of their members are deeply involved in drugs, prostitution, racketeering, stolen goods, extortion, and violence. It is the development of these organizations that has been the focus of this sketch of the subculture's evolution.

Anomic conditions that especially affected lower middle class white men gave birth to the outlaw motorcycle subculture. These clubs provide an outlet for the status frustration of their members that is facilitated by their isolation from the mainstream. The forces that lead men to join these groups are exacerbated by the intensity of their internal dynamics and the social isolation of the subculture. Because of their intense pride, loyalty, and bravado, these clubs are fiercely competitive and intergroup conflicts are inevitable. The intensity of these conflicts is extreme enough to create a siege mentality that further deepens members' isolation from extra-club sources. Isolation intensifies bonding processes while creating a world view and emotional tone that encourage violence.

Radical leaders of large clubs became seriously involved in organized crime to finance interclub warfare as the subculture expanded. These activities, along with the violence of interclub conflict, increased legal scrutiny which ultimately led to retrenchment in conservative biker norms. However, the profits and power provided by the criminal activity became a goal unto themselves within some clubs. In part this transition also marks the counterculture's tendency to drift toward accommodation with the mainstream. This is most clearly seen in the seeking of positive publicity for 1% clubs and the subculture as a whole. It can also be discerned in the lower profile kept by most modern 1% clubs in the U.S. today.

Notes

1. Anyone who is not a 1% biker, or affiliated with a club (e.g., ol' lady, friend of the club), is defined as a "citizen." The result is a stratified world view consisting of righteous bikers, their associates, and citizens.
2. The Outlaws recently relocated their national headquarters from Chicago to Detroit.

References

Alabama/Mississippi Chapter, Bandidos Motorcycle Club home page [On-line]. Available: www.freetown.com/ParadiseValley/DeerGlen/1013.

Andersson, Martha. 1997, March 4. "Police Out En Masse During Hell's Angels Gathering in Sweden." *Christian Science Monitor*, p. 7.

Barger, Ralph "Sonny," with Keith and Kent Zimmerman. 2000. *Hell's Angel.* New York: HarperCollins.

Beissert, Wayne. 1988, October 25. "Hell's Angels Act Heavenly During Ky. Firearms Trial." *USA Today*, p. A3.

"Bread . . . because under the leather is a heart." 1985, January 25. *Baton Rouge Morning Advocate*, p. A3.

Clark, Robin. 1981, October 14. "Police Warned of Biker Gangs' Training, Tactics." *Charlotte Observer*, B1.

Clark, Robin, and T. O'Neill. 1981a, August 16. "Carolina Clubs Run on Drugs, Sex, Violence." *Charlotte Observer.*

Clark, Robin, and T. O'Neill. 1981b, August 17. "Biker's Survival Code Based on Bloodshed." *Charlotte Observer.*

Clark, Robin, and T. O'Neill. 1981c, August 18. "Shadowy Businesses Revolve Around Drugs, Theft." *Charlotte Observer.*

Clark, Robin, and T. O'Neill. 1981d, August 19. "Those Who Join." *Charlotte Observer.*

Clawson, Paul. 1983, March 30. "Ex-Hell's Angel Tells Senators About Corrupt Police; Describes Drug Trafficking by Bikers." *Narcotics Control Digest*, 13(7):2–5.

Danner, T. A., and Silverman, I. J. 1986. "Characteristics of Incarcerated Outlaw Bikers as Compared to Nonbiker Inmates." *Journal of Crime and Justice* 9:43–70.

Davis, James R. 1982. *Street Gangs.* Dubuque, Iowa: Kendall-Hunt.

Domey, Gregory. 1996, September 6. "15 Held in Hell's Angels Drug Bust." *Boston Globe*, B1.

"Do the Bandidos fit their Name?" 1981, November 23. *Newsweek*, p. 49.

Draffen, Duayne. 1998, April 8. "Members of Motorcycle Gang Are Charged in Extortion Case." *New York Times*, p. B5.

"Elfman Opgepakt bij Inval Angels." 1982, September 24. *Volkskrant.*

"Fallen Angels." 1973, January 8. *Newsweek*, p. 25.

Frisman, P. 1981, July 22. "Hell's Angel Focus of Extortion Trial." *Hartford Courant.*

Harper, Timothy. 1982, August 15. "Ski Resort Town Ready for Visit from the 1982-Model Hell's Angels." *Miami Herald,* p. 14A.

"Hell's Angels Shift Gear into Fifth Speed Mobsters." 1973, July 1. *New Orleans Times-Picayune,* section 1, p. 20.

"Hell's Angels: Some Wheelers may be Dealers." 1979, July 2. *Time Magazine,* p. 34.

Ibrahim, Youssef. 1997, March 3. "Sweden's Courteous Police Spoil a Hell's Angels Clubhouse Party." *New York Times,* p. Al.

Kerre, Rich, and Henry T. Vogt. 1981, March 10. "Cycle Gangs on Move Here, Police Say." *St. Louis Globe-Democrat.*

Linder, L. 1981, March 26. "Gun Shells Breaking Up the Old Gang." *Miami Herald,* p. 25-A.

Marlowe, Jon. 1983, May 17. "The Hell's Angels Take a Bath." *Miami News,* p. 3C.

Mellgren, Doug. 1996, August 4. "Bloody Biker Battles Shatter Scandinavian Serenity." *Dallas Morning News,* p. 1-A.

Montgomery, Randall. 1976. "The Outlaw Motorcycle Subculture." *Canadian Journal of Criminology* pp. 332–342.

Montgomery, Randall. 1977. "The Outlaw Motorcycle Subculture II." *Canadian Journal of Criminology* pp. 356–361.

Moseley, Ray. 1997, July 3. "Biker War Revving up in Denmark—Guns, Grenades Rattle Usually Peaceful Land." *Chicago Tribune,* p. 1.

Nickerson, Colin. 1998, November 6. "Hells Angels Roar at Center of Violent Quebec Drug War." *Boston Globe,* p. A-1.

O'Brien, John. 1997, February 17. "Drug Crackdown on Hell's Angels Launched." *Chicago Tribune,* p. 2C-1.

"Organized Crime Threat Seen in Motorcycle Gangs." 1980, July 27. *Indianapolis Star,* B2.

"Outlaw Gang is Finished, U.S. Says After Verdict." 1983, April 2. *Miami News,* p. 9-A.

Quinn, James F. 1987. "Sex Roles and Hedonism Among Members of 'Outlaw' Motorcycle Clubs." *Deviant Behavior* 8(1): 47–63.

Reynolds, Frank (as told to M. McClure). 1967. *Freewheelin' Frank.* London: New English Library.

Rosenberg, Beth. 1980, July 24. "Outlaw Cycle Gangs are Crime Kingpins, Congressman Claims." *Miami Herald,* p. 23A.

Royal Canadian Mounted Police. 1980. "Outlaw Motorcycle Gangs." R.C.M.P. Gazette 42:10.

Royal Canadian Mounted Police. 1982. "Outlaw Motorcycle Gangs." R.C.M.P. Gazette 49:5.

Sahlins, Marshall. 1963. "Poor Man, Rich Man, Big Man, Chief." *Comparative Studies in Society and History* 5:285–303.

Thompson, Hunter. 1966. *Hell's Angels.* New York: Random House.

Vold, George B, 1980. *Theories of Deviance.* In "Group Conflict Theory as Explanation of Crime." Pp. 300–311 edited by Stuart H. Traub & Craig B. Little. Itasca, IL: F.E. Peacock.

von Hoffman, Nicholas. 1968. *We Are The People Our Parents Warned Us About.* New York: Quadrangle.

Walters, G. O. 1990. *The Criminal Lifestyle.* Beverly Hills, CA: Sage.

Watson, J. Mark. 1980. "Outlaw Motorcyclists as an Outgrowth of Lower Class Values." *Deviant Behavior* 4:31–48.

Watson, J. Mark. 1982. "Righteousness on Two Wheels." *Sociological Spectrum* 2:333–349.

Wolf, Daniel R. 1991. *The Rebels: A Brotherhood of Outlaw Bikers*. Toronto: University of Toronto Press.

Wood, J. 1979, October 31. "The Criminal Organization Statute the Hell's Angels Hate." *San Francisco Examiner*.

Yochelson, Samuel and Samenow, Stanton. 1976. *The Criminal Personality, volume 1: Profile for Change*. New York: Jason Aronson.

Study Questions

1. In the last forty years of the "Big Four," what has happened to alter the groups' activities?
2. How do the "1%" operate as organized criminal groups?

Reading 17
The Amish

Donald B. Kraybill

Modern Amish?

Booming machine shops in some Amish settlements hold sophisticated manufacturing equipment powered by air and hydraulic pressure. Some Amish craftsmen use the latest fiberglass techniques to manufacture horse-drawn carriages. Hundreds of Amish-owned microenterprises place entrepreneurs in direct relation with the outside world on a daily basis. Successful Amish dairy farms in the more progressive settlements are efficient operations that use feed supplements, vitamins, fertilizers, insecticides, chemical preservatives, artificial insemination, and state-of-the-art veterinary practices. Professional farm consultants advise Amish farmers in some settlements about their use of pesticides, fertilizers, and seed selection. New Amish homes in the more progressive settlements tout up-to-date bathroom facilities, modern kitchens with lovely cabinets, formica, vinyl floor coverings, and the latest gas stoves and refrigerators. In spite of cherished stereotypes, some Amish are embracing certain aspects of modernity.

Modernization, however, varies considerably from settlement to settlement across North America. Among the more conservative Amish groups, refrigerators and indoor bathrooms are taboo. Cows are milked by hand and hay balers are not pulled in fields. It is reasonable to hypothesize that Amish adaptation to modern life directly varies with the population density of non-Amish who live in the same geographical area. In other words, innovative Amish behavior appears highly correlated with urbanization. Amish settlements in more isolated rural areas are, generally speaking, more resistant to modernizing influences.[1] Settlements such as the one near Lancaster, Pennsylvania, situated in the midst of a rapidly urbanizing region, are quite progressive in their use of technology and openness to the outside world.

The Amish do indeed cling to older customs in their church services, in their attitudes toward education, and in their rejection of individualism. The lack of electricity in their homes blocks the door to microwave ovens, air conditioners, toasters, doorbells, televisions, clothes dryers, and blow dryers. But does a rejection of high school education, cars, and public-utility-line electricity mean that the Amish are a premodern folk society? The unusual mixture of progress and tradition abounding in Amish society poses interesting questions about the meaning of modernization. How have the Amish responded to the pressures of modernity? What strategies have they employed to cope with modern life in the twentieth century? They have drifted along with the stream of progress in some areas of their culture but have staunchly and successfully resisted it in others. . . .

Dimensions of Modernity

To what extent have the features of modernity penetrated Amish life—their organizational structure as well as their cultural consciousness? The facets of modernity identified by social analysts are legion. The following, somewhat arbitrarily selected dimensions of modernity are not exhaustive nor do they follow a causal sequence.[2] Typically underscored by sociologists, these factors do, however, distinguish modern worlds from nonmodern ones. After a brief discussion of each dimension, we will explore the ways in which the Amish have grappled with it.

Modern societies by and large are highly *specialized*. In nonmodern societies social functions from cradle to grave—birth, work, play, education, worship, friendship, and death—revolve around the home. They often, in fact, occur in the home. In advanced societies such social activities "grow up" and leave home, and as they depart, they split into specialized spheres. These cradle-to-grave functions eventually become lodged in specialized institutions—birthing centers, fitness spas, day care centers, schools, grooming salons, factories, hospitals, golf courses, hospices, and funeral homes. It is in these sharply differentiated settings that experts deliver their highly specialized services. The automobile and mass transit enable modern folks to spend their days shuttling from site to site to both deliver and receive such services. The imprint of structural differentiation and functional specialization is thus stamped across the face of modern life.

The degree to which specialization has shaped Amish life varies of course among Amish settlements, but without exception the Amish world is clearly less differentiated than modern society. The rejection of high school and the primacy given to agriculture have minimized occupational specialization. As Amish families move from farms to microenterprises as well as into factory work in some settlements, the degree of occupational specialization will likely increase. It will undoubtedly remain low as long as high school and college remain taboo. Terminating education at eighth grade effectively deters members from pursuing professional jobs. The relatively low degree of occupational specialization has also minimized social class differences and contributed to the relative homogeneity of the Amish social structure. The rising numbers of Amish microenterprises in some settlements may over time encourage the emergence of a three-tier class structure consisting of farm owners, business entrepreneurs, and day laborers. . . .

The pluralism of modern life means that many individuals face many views of reality—a bewildering array of beliefs and opinions. The common sentiments of traditional cultures dissolve in the streams of pluralism. The wide assortment of ideas and clashing lifestyles focuses the stark relativity of modernity since "it all depends" on who you are, on where you're from, and on your point of view. The religious beliefs of individuals become especially fragile and vulnerable to change as discrepant world views collide in the public media of mass society.

At both structural and cultural levels the Amish have remained aloof from the pluralism of modern life. Their theological stance of separation from the world has in many ways insulated them from the forces of diversity afoot in the modern world. The Amish community does interact with the surrounding society, tapping the use of professional services—medicine, dentistry, and law. Moreover, they are frequently buying and selling supplies and services for personal use as well as for business purposes. The practice of endogamy, the use of the dialect, the prohibition on membership in public organizations, the taboo on political involvement, and the rejection of mass media are among many of the factors that help to preserve the cultural boundaries that separate the Amish from the winds of pluralism. All of these factors impede structural assimilation and preserve the homogeneity of Amish life.

More importantly, Amish parochial schools bridle interaction with outsiders—both peers and teachers—and restrict consciousness. Amish children do not study science or critical thinking, nor are they exposed to the relativity and diversity so pervasive in higher education today. The Amish rejection of mass media, especially television, severely limits their exposure to the smorgasbord of modern values. The tight plausibility structure embodied in th Amish community thus helps to hold the forces of pluralism at bay. . . .

In contrast to the discontinuities of modern culture, Amish societies exude continuity. Social relationships are more likely to be primary, local, enduring, and stable. The rejection of automobile ownership, bicycles, and air travel places limits on Amish mobility. To be sure, the Amish do travel in hired motor vehicles and in public busses and trains, but, all things considered, the amount of mobility is relatively low. The rejection of college and consequently of professional work enables young adults to live in their childhood communities, which increases the longevity of social ties with family, neighborhood, and place. Parents teach occupational skills to their children.

Amish schools are a supreme example of continuity. Children often walk to school, where they may have the same teacher for all eight grades. The teacher, responsible for some thirty students, may relate to only a dozen households, since many families have several children in attendance. Such continuity contrasts starkly with modern education, where children may have dozens of teachers in a few years and teachers relate to hundreds of families. . . .

The Amish commitment to a rational mentality that calculates means and ends has grown as their farming enterprises expand and as they enter the larger world of commerce via cottage industries. Although Amish entrepreneurs engage in planning to keep their businesses afloat, there is, however, decidedly less planning activity among the Amish than typically found in modern life. The absence of artificial means of family planning, career planning, and time management reflects a less rationalized approach to life—a greater willingness to yield to nature and destiny. The rejection of science and critical thinking in Amish schools, the taboo on theological training for ordained leaders, and the lack of a formal theology attenuate the level of rationality in the collective consciousness.

The tentacles of bureaucracy have barely touched Amish society. Their social architecture is remarkably decentralized, small, and informal. A central national office, with an executive director and professional staff have never developed. Church districts are organized as a loose federation in each settlement, and there is little centralized or formal coordination between settlements. The decentralized character of Amish society fosters diversity in the struggle with modernity. Different settlements and different church districts even within affiliations adapt at different paces and in different directions. The *Ordnung*, the body of policies regulating the life of the community, is generally not written down but is a fluid, dynamic set of understandings. The hierarchial, formal, rationalized structure of modern bureaucracy has simply not developed in Amish society. . . .

The . . . traits of modernity encourage *individuation*—the widely heralded triumph of modern culture. The modernizing process unhooks individuals from the confining grip of custom and encourages individualism to flourish. In traditional societies, individuals for the most part are under the tight thumb of kin, tribe, and village. Modern culture with its ideology of individual rights, liberties, privileges, and freedoms celebrates the individual as the supreme social reality. To question the rights of an individual has become a cardinal and unforgivable sin. The personal résumé is, of course, the ultimate document of individuation, and one that is missing in Amish files. Modern individuals are free to pursue careers and seek personal fulfillment, but they also carry the responsibility to succeed—"to make it"—a responsibility that entails the fear of failure.

The subordination of the individual to the community is the fundamental key that unlocks many of the riddles and puzzles of Amish life and sharply distinguishes their culture from modern ways. *Gelassenheit*, submitting and yielding to higher authorities—parents, teachers, leaders, and God—structures Amish values, symbols, personality, rituals, and social organization. Personal submission clashes with modern individualism and its concomitants of self-achievement, self-expression, and self-fulfillment. By contrast, the Amish vocabulary of obedience, simplicity, humility, and the posture of kneeling—for baptism, prayer, confession, and ordination—reflect a premodern understanding of the individual. Clothing, for instance, is used in modern life as a tool of self-expression. In Amish life, uniform dress serves as a badge of group identity and loyalty as well as a symbol of self-surrender to community priorities. The taboo on photography, publicity, jewelry, and other forms of personal adornment bridles an individualism that otherwise might foster pride and arrogance. The Amish rejection of individualism—that supremely cherished value of modern culture—reflects the heartbeat of a counterculture that has not absorbed modern ways. . . .

The Amish have made collective choices. But many of these decisions have been reactive responses to choices imposed on them by modern life. The Amish have been less likely to be proactive—deliberately initiating choices, for such initiatives parallel the modern impulse to plan, order, and control one's environment. The Amish have made collective choices not to be modern. They have rejected higher education. But in many other cases they have surely conceded to modernity by accepting the use of modern forms of technology.

Their collective decisions, however, have restricted individual choice. Individuals are not free to wear what they want, to aspire to professional occupations, to own a car, or to buy a television set. This does not necessarily mean that Amish folks are dour and unhappy. A variety of evidence suggests that they are as happy and satisfied, if not more so, than many "homeless" moderns. The range of occupational options and lifestyle choices available to the individual in Amish society is of course quite narrow. And although a restricted range of choices may suffocate the modern spirit of freedom, it also removes the burden of incessant decision making with its concomitant guilt, stress, and anxiety from the shoulders of many Amish persons.

The Great Separator

. . . The hallmark of Amish culture has been its highly integrated community where all the bits and pieces of social life, from birth to death, are gathered into a single system. To avoid the fragmentation that accompanies modernity, the Amish have separated themselves from the modern world. In order to stay whole, to preserve their community, they have separated themselves from modernity—the greatest separator of all. The Amish impulse to remain separate from the great separator has become a significant strategy in their cultural survival.

Seen in this light it is not surprising that a fundamental tenet of Amish religion is separation from the world—a belief that sprouted in the seedbed of European persecution and is legitimated today with references to the scriptures. This linkage between the fragmentation of modern life and the integration of Amish society unlocks many of the Amish riddles. For only by being a separate people are they able to preserve the integrity of their tightly knit community. Many of the seemingly odd Amish practices that often perplex outside observers are in fact social devices that shield their subculture from the divisive pressures of modernity that threaten to tear their corporate life asunder.

Endnote

1. A competing explanation to this hypothesis is the fact that some of the smaller, more rural Amish settlements are also newer. These are sometimes made up of families who want to maintain a more traditional Ordnung and have sought more rural isolated areas where they can continue in farming. Consequently a self-selection factor may complicate what otherwise appears to be an inverse relationship between urbanization and traditional Amish practices.
2. As Berger (1977) and Kraybill (1990) have shown, the various features of modernity are highly interrelated and not easily separated into discrete categories for causal analysis.

References

Berger, Peter. 1977. *Facing Up to Modernity.* New York: Basic Books.

Kraybill, Donald B. 1990. "Modernity and Modernization," *Anabaptist-Mennonite Identities in Ferment.* Occasional papers no. 14, pp. 91–101. Elkhart, IN: Institute of Mennonite Studies.

Study Questions

1. What attributes distinguish the Amish as a cohesive group?
2. Based on what you have read in the Kraybill research, what would you predict for the future of the Amish? Will they prosper or slowly lose their community?

Reading 18
Killing the Messenger
The Social Problems
of Sociology

Joel Best

One hundred years ago, in 1902, President Theodore Roosevelt hoped to avert a coal strike by establishing an arbitration commission. The miners, of course, insisted that any commission include a representative of labor, while the mine operators sought to block any labor appointment by specifying the qualifications of the various commissioners. However, they agreed that one commissioner should be "a man of prominence, eminent as a sociologist." Roosevelt broke the log-jam by appointing Edgar E. Clark, chief of the Railway Conductors Union, to fill the sociology slot, on the grounds that anyone in his position must have "thought and studied deeply on social questions." The maneuver succeeded and TR's biographer, Edmund Morris (2001:166–169), reports: "to the end of his days, [Roosevelt] could rejoice with falsetto giggles at 'the eminent sociologist.'"

This revealing tale offers several lessons for contemporary sociologists, but I want to focus on its comic aspect: for one of the greatest U.S. presidents, the term "sociologist" was funny, the punch line for a favorite anecdote.

Is there something funny about sociology? Peter L. Berger begins his *Invitation to Sociology* (1963:1) with the observation that: "There are very few jokes about sociologists." This perhaps misses the point. In our culture, sociology is rarely taken seriously; when sociologists are recognized, they often become figures of fun. We've all heard the aphorism that a sociologist is someone who needs a grant to find a house of ill repute, although we're no longer sure just who said it—H. L. Mencken? James T. Farrell? Dismissive comments abound. P. J. O'Rourke (2001) says that "sociology is journalism without news." A British journalist calls it "the ology everyone loves to hate" (Rayment 1991). Diane Bjorklund (2001:24), after reviewing more than 80 twentieth-century novels featuring sociologists as characters, notes that: ". . . in almost none of these novels is the sociologist a particularly admirable or even sympathetic character. There are virtually no positive comments made about sociologists." In our culture, the sociologist is almost never a hero, but rather a villain or a fool.

Popular discourse frequently criticizes sociologists and, by extension, sociology. For sociologists of social problems, of course, the assorted jokes and put-downs can be understood as claims, as arguments that there is something wrong with sociology that demands correction. That is, even though sociology never receives its own chapter in our thick, four-color social problems textbooks, sociology is—when people bother to pay attention to it—frequently constructed as a social problem.[1] My goal in this article is to explore some of these constructions of sociology as a social problem, to analyze this claimsmaking and try to explain why it is so common. I begin with the rhetoric of critics who are not sociologists, but then I want to turn to critiques from within, to sociologists' attacks on, if not the entire discipline, at least one another.

Sociology as a Social Problem

When non-sociologists criticize sociology, their indictments tend to center on three themes.[2] The first of these, of course, is that sociology lacks substance. Sociology, we are told, is nothing more than common sense; it is trivial, "the scientific study of the obvious."[3] Further, it is confused and probably mistaken. One of Iris Murdoch's (1983:165) characters "was a sociologist; he had got into an intellectual muddle early on in life and never managed to get out." A Harvard economist observed, "Economics is all about how people make choices. Sociology is all about why they don't have any choices to make" (Duesenberry 1960:233), while an Indian-born economist "explained his personal theory of reincarnation . . . : 'If you are a good economist, . . . you are reborn as a physicist. But if you are an evil, wicked economist, you are reborn as a sociologist' " (Krugman 1994).

Closely-related is the second complaint, that sociologists cannot communicate what they do know, that they write in impenetrable, obfuscating jargon. Howard S. Becker (1986:1) notes ". . . everyone knows that sociologists write very badly, so that literary types can make jokes about bad writing just by saying 'sociology,' the way vaudeville comedians used to get a laugh just by saying 'Peoria' or 'Cucamonga.' " "What is it about sociology," Russell Baker (1990) asks, "that instantly bogs us down in fens of jargon." One popular answer is that sociology's complicated language is designed to conceal and compensate for its modest substance. The authoritative *Dictionary of Modern English Usage* suggests: "Sociology is a new science concerning itself with . . . the ordinary affairs of ordinary people. This seems to engender in those who write about it a feeling that the lack of any abstruseness in their subject demands a compensatory abstruseness in their language"—this from the entry on "Sociologese" (Fowler 1965:570).[4]

The third indictment, of course, is that sociology is just ideology, only thinly and disingenuously disguised as science, that it is the domain of "knee-jerk liberals" and irresponsible radicals who would coddle criminals while blaming society. Here critics range from those who naively conflate socialists with sociologists, to more sophisticated indictments of sociology as deeply implicated in what are seen as academia's disturbing turns toward feminism, multiculturalism, postmodernism, and political correctness (e.g., Goodman 2000; Petersen 1970).

In short, non-sociologists suspect that there isn't much to sociology, beyond a lot of unnecessarily complicated verbiage designed to give false authority to leftist politics. While we may take pride in some of our opponents—after all, being denounced by anti-intellectual ignoramuses may enhance our own sense of self-worth—we are hurt, disappointed, and defensive about the low regard for sociology in other circles. Joan Huber's (1995) warning that university administrators value disciplinary centrality, quality of faculty, and quality of students—and see sociology as falling short on all three criteria—is worrisome. While proposals to eliminate sociology graduate programs or even departments haven't been all that common, they have aroused considerable concern.[5] And there is the sense that relatively few sociologists become genuine public intellectuals, that we get less than our share of op-ed pieces and "Booknotes" interviews.[6] Even the people we'd like to have like us don't seem to care for us much.

Sociologists are more than a little sensitive about their discipline's social standing. Our shaky reputation has an extensive history, and has led a long line of sociologists to defensiveness. I remember my professor, Arnold M. Rose, describing one of his professors—I think it was Louis Wirth—deconstructing a joke.[7] The joke went like this: A physicist, a psychologist, and a sociologist are walking down an alley, and they come upon a dead man's body. The physicist stops and declares, "Aha! This is a mass weighing 150 pounds, and it is not in motion." The psychologist stops and says, "No—it's a dead person." But the sociologist just keeps on walking because he's looking for a group. Since Peter Berger complains that there aren't any jokes about sociologists, I guess we ought to be grateful for this one. But, according to Rose, Wirth used to correct this joke for his students, and explain that it was the sociologist who would know enough to check the man's pockets, to open his wallet and find the identifying information that could locate him within the larger society. Wirth's rebuttal—and all those introductory classes over the decades that have begun with bold declarations that sociology is more than just common sense—do not strike me as the reactions of a profession completely confident of its own worth.

Claims within Sociology

But, of course, the critiques outsiders have leveled against sociology are nothing compared to our history of intradisciplinary bloodletting. There is a long, cranky tradition of sociologists denouncing one another, of challenging the worth of each other's contributions. Landmark statements in this vein include Robert Lynd's *Knowledge for What?* (1939), Pitriam Sorokin's *Fads and Foibles in Modern Sociology* (1956), C. Wright Mills's *The Sociological Imagination* (1959), Alvin Gouldner's *The Coming Crisis of Western Sociology* (1970), and Irving Louis Horowitz's *The Decomposition of Sociology* (1993). Stephen Cole's recent collection, *What's Wrong with Sociology?* (2001), features an all-star line-up of contributors who, if not angry, are at least troubled. This list only scratches the surface; a full bibliography of contentious, or at least self-conscious, sociology obviously would be much longer. Sociologists, then, routinely construct at least some forms of sociology as problematic.

Sociologists' critiques of one another tend to parallel those of non-sociologists. There are doubts about substance. These often take the form of critiques—ranging from dismissive asides to book-length polemics—of rival theories, methodologies, or even epistemologies. The list of targets has included—and this list is by no means comprehensive—functionalism, conflict theory, ethnomethodology, feminism, rational choice theory, postmodernism, symbolic interactionism, path analysis, advocacy research, sponsored research, qualitative sociology, quantitative sociology, and positivism. We can at least suspect that there is no form of sociological analysis that has not been denounced by some sociologists. These critiques often take few prisoners; they depict their targets not as merely flawed or wrong-headed, but as intellectually and even morally bankrupt. In comparison, outsiders' charges that sociology seems trivial or obvious appear tolerant, even generous. It is no wonder that, in recent years, senior sociologists have worried that our discipline lacks a "core."

Similarly, sociological critics often echo charges about jargon and "sociologese." In his presidential address to the American Sociological Association, Alfred McClung Lee (1976:929) spoke of the "jargonized superficiality and quantophrenia of the A.S.A. periodicals." And, of course, C. Wright Mills (1959:25–33, 217–220) warned against "socspeak"; his dissection of the difficult prose of Talcott Parsons became a classic in its own right. We have a surprisingly large literature encouraging sociologists to write in clearer, more accessible prose.[8] At the same time, methodological developments have led to the presentation of research findings in ever more arcane terms. Thirty years ago, it was not uncommon for anthologies aimed at introductory students to reprint articles from the *American Sociological Review* and the *American Journal of Sociology*; very often, the tables in those articles featured percentages or perhaps a chi-square test of significance. Today, vastly increased computing power and sophisticated, easily mastered software packages allow analysts to present elaborate tables based on ordinary least-squares regression, log-linear regression, and other techniques that few first-year undergraduates can hope to understand, so that it becomes much harder to assign students to read actual sociological research articles. Nor is this methodological distancing found only among quantitative sorts; qualitative analysts increasingly claim to have new, improved methods that they catalog in thick manuals describing varieties of ethnography, interviewing, and interpretation.

And, of course, sociologists do not hesitate to criticize one another's ideological stances. If non-sociologists tend to worry that sociology has a leftist bias, sociologists are more likely to attack one another for being reactionary, conservative, or politically incorrect, or at least for being pawns of powerful elites and the institutions they control. At the same time, there are counterclaims that these critics on the left are blinded by ideology. The bitterness of the rhetoric obscures the larger context within which this intradisciplinary debate occurs. Academics are more liberal than most

Americans, and sociology consistently ranks among academia's most liberal disciplines. There are few conservatives among sociologists; in fact, many of the sociologists most often accused of "conservatism" were active in socialist causes as students and even advocated what was considered radical sociology when they entered the profession (Lipset 2001). What appear to be ideological gulfs within sociology must strike outsiders as intramural fissures.

There are, in short, plenty of claims that construct sociology as a social problem. Outsiders suspect that sociologists are pompous, vacuous, ideological wolves, hiding behind scientists' sheepskins. In contrast, those within the discipline are more likely to charge their brethren with being sheep, whose wooly thoughts are easily shorn by their masters and used to cloak injustice in false legitimacy. Typically, our discussions focus on these charges; we debate whether sociology in fact matches the critics' descriptions, just as traditional social problems analysis focuses on social conditions. But adopting a constructionist approach (see Spector and Kitsuse 1977) and redirecting our attention to the process of making claims about social problems offers different insights on the problem of sociology.

The Context for Claims about Sociology

Sociology's contentious history is filled with principled disagreements about the logic of inquiry, the nature of science, and the sociologist's responsibilities to such higher values as morality, truth, equality, and justice. Needless to say, proponents of various intellectual, theoretical, methodological, and political causes contrast their own principles with the inconsistent, unsound, flawed stances of their opponents. Typically, both our most bitter polemics and our most carefully reasoned analyses of sociological theory either affirm or challenge such principles. . . .

There are two familiar temptations to which sociologists are constantly prone. The first is the temptation of method. Its logic is familiar: methodological care is required to make our evidence convincing; therefore, we must devise operational definitions and research designs, choose samples, and apply analytic techniques—usually statistical measures—that represent the highest standards of methodological rigor. The more carefully the sociologist adheres to these standards, the more compelling the methods. I call this a temptation because it becomes easy to lose sight of other considerations, so that analysts forget real-world—as opposed to statistical—significance, or so that they come to communicate their findings in language and calculations that only a few can understand. These are trade-offs that, if not inherent in the enthusiastic pursuit of methodological rigor, are at least very common.

The second temptation, of course, is that of theory. Here, the sociologist assembles airy castles of ideas, connecting concepts in creative ways, so that nearly all seems explicable, albeit in the abstract. There is terrific variety among these theoretical perspectives: some are structural, others are cognitive; some deductive, others inductive; some invoke objectivity, others celebrate ideology; and so on. But, again, as theories advance, there is the need for careful precision in articulating ideas, ideas so nicely defined as to require a special vocabulary that, once more, is understood only by a few. Here, the temptation is to drift off into a theoretical world bounded, if not by tautology, at least by this shared language. Once more, the notion of trade-off seems applicable; the more elaborate and elegant the theory, the fewer those who understand and appreciate it, and the greater the distance between the theoretical and real worlds. . . .

Just the Messengers

. . . We are also comforted by the notion that we are punished because we boldly speak the truth, if sociologists are attacked, it is only because we are messengers bearing bad news. Some years ago, the graduate students at Southern Illinois University at Carbondale produced a t-shirt featuring "The Top Ten Reasons to Study Sociology at SIUC." The list included: "You learn unpopular explanations for everything."[9] More formal versions of this account appear when sociologists try to respond to our critics. Thus, Bjorklund (2001:36) explains fiction's harsh portraits of sociologists: "Novelists and sociologists are competitors in a sense; they are both trying to explain human behavior in what are often very different ways"; and Herbert Gans (1989:1) suggests that "the majority of the literary community still believes that only it can analyze society."[10]. . .

Moreover, we can point to sociology that's had an impact, particularly in shaping how Americans view social problems. Perhaps the single most influential sociological work of the past century was Gunnar Myrdal's *An American Dilemma* (1944). That book documented the nature and effects of racism, articulated contradictions in American culture, and provided an intellectual foundation for thinking about the emerging civil rights movement. Other sociological work has at least been widely disseminated. Gans's (1997) list of 53 sociological best-sellers from the second half of the twentieth century includes several other volumes on racial issues, including two C. Wright Mills Award winners (*Tally's Corner* and *The Truly Disadvantaged*); virtually all of the titles on his list address one or more social problems. Sometimes, our message does get through.

What Works? Not Being Part of the Problem

Perhaps sociology cannot escape being labeled a social problem. Still, some sociologists become influential beyond the narrow bounds of their particular disciplinary arenas, even if no sociological work can hope to achieve universal acclaim within, let alone outside, sociology. This raises a question: what can sociologists do to avoid being part of the social problems of sociology? Can understanding the claimsmaking process help us craft solutions?

I'd like to offer three suggestions. The first is familiar: we really ought to watch our language. Sociologists should not simply write to and for one another. Our jargon is one of the principal clubs outsiders use to beat up sociologists, and we love to denounce one another's pompous, awkward language. Clear writing is a prerequisite for reaching a large audience. As Gans (1997:133) notes, "just about all of [sociology's best-sellers] are jargon-free; whatever their other virtues, they are written in a language that at least educated readers can understand." Even if one doesn't aspire to the best-seller list, gaining recognition from sociologists outside one's home arena requires making oneself—one's methods and theoretical questions—understandable. The cost of dazzling one's in-group with a masterful command of its esoteric vocabulary is almost always the loss of everyone else's attention. Your brilliance just becomes part of their construction of sociology as a social problem.

My second suggestion is that we need to remember the importance of evidence. When outsiders do turn to sociologists, it is because they expect—or at least hope—that we actually know things about the real world, things that not everyone else knows. Our authority, our legitimacy does not reside in the purity of our outrage, the elegant complexity of our theories, the sophistication of our statistical techniques, or the moral correctness of our politics. Those postures may play to admiring audiences within a particular arena, but they rarely have much appeal beyond its borders; in fact, as we have seen, they are precisely the stuff of which anti-sociological claims are made. . . .

This leads to my third suggestion. Sociologists need to acknowledge complexity. Inevitably, our theories emphasize particular arguments—that society is fundamentally organized around consensus, or around conflicting interests, or whatever. These can be helpful guides to spotting interesting features of the world, but they should not be treated as complete descriptions of social life. Obviously, every social system features both consensus (if only because social interaction requires shared understandings) and conflict (if only because resources are never sufficient to sate demand). It is one thing to insist that a particular perspective can add something to our understanding, but quite another to imply that no other approach has merit.

Aversion to complexity is hardly limited to sociology. Simplistic, melodramatic portraits of heroes and villains characterize our popular culture, but also much journalism. Our culture usually delivers, and we come to expect—and even want—simple stories. Don't give us a lot of contradictory findings, just tell us: Does coffee cause cancer, or doesn't it? Should all women over 40 years of age have annual mammograms, or not? Has welfare reform been a success, or a failure?

It seems to me that public discourse could tolerate a little more complexity; sociology has much to contribute in this regard—if only we can bring ourselves to accept complexity. Life offers relatively few clear-cut choices between good and evil, but lots and lots of trade-offs. Building a bridge or implementing a childhood vaccination program both have risks and costs, but then so do doing without the bridge and not vaccinating children. . . .

Sociologists' reluctance to talk about progress (Best 2001a) is partly rooted in our difficulties with complexity. If our counterparts a century ago now seem too optimistic and insufficiently critical, many of our colleagues today appear to view almost any change with suspicion. Some sociologists offer nostalgic sketches of a better past, while glossing over the details—the shorter life expectancies, lower standards of living, limited education, and brutal, institutionalized inequalities. Obviously, this world isn't perfect, but neither was that one, and I don't think we ought to pretend that perfection is likely, or even possible. History rarely offers the clear choices of melodrama. Change always has a price. But sociology offers some tools for understanding those trade-offs. Instead of pretending they don't exist, we can try to understand them, and help others toward that understanding. I have suggested that sociologists often are charged with being biased. This is usually understood in terms of political ideology; that is, critics argue that sociologists' claims can be discounted because they represent some political faction. Within our discipline, these charges in turn lead to now predictable debates about whether objectivity is possible or even desirable. My suggestion is intended to circumvent this arguing. If sociologists can respect—even embrace—complexity, if they can avoid melodramatic simplicity and do justice to the ambiguities inherent in social life, we are far less likely to be caricatured as mere ideologues. . . .

Even though it has never been a particularly prestigious discipline, sociology has been remarkably influential (Best 2001b; Merton and Wolfe 1995). It is easy to point to sociological concepts that have made their way, not just into other disciplines, but into the larger culture; charisma, self-fulfilling prophecy, peer group, status symbol, role model, even significant other—you heard it here first! Our success at disseminating these ideas is due to a simple fact: the sociological perspective is a useful way to think about the world. That is, it often helps to focus on the ways people influence one another.

Sociologists seem to spend an awful lot of time jostling with one another, declaring not just which side we're on, but which epistemology commands our loyalty. I am not arguing that this is completely misguided. Ours is a diverse discipline, organized around many different arenas, and most of us spend most of our time talking to other members in the one or two arenas we frequent. This is probably inevitable given our numbers, and desirable as a way of encouraging intellectual activity. Naturally, we can expect rivalries between these arenas, as we struggle for—for what?

These rivalries should not be treated as holy wars. Most often, we are struggling to be heard—to affect students, place papers in journals, perhaps influence the direction of social policy. In gaining those things, what we have to say—the usefulness of our ideas for understanding the world around us—is almost certainly more important than our cleverness at denouncing others. The substantive ideas, the evidence, and the clarity of our presentations matter. The enduring importance of Mills's (1959)

The Sociological Imagination was in its articulation of the link between private troubles and public issues, not in the demolition of the prose of Parsons.

I happen to believe in the sociological perspective's value. It is a perspective built on relativism, built on the recognition that people understand the world differently. One of the most basic lessons we teach our students is to doubt their own taken-for-granted assumptions, to avoid ethnocentrism and seek to understand and appreciate others' cultures and social structures. It couldn't hurt for us to take those lessons to heart, to construct sociology as a perspective, rather than a problem.

Notes

1. My analysis falls within a constructionist subgenre that examines claims that identify problematic features of relatively mundane, everyday life. At least for some determined claimsmakers, sociology is a social problem, just as some claim meat (Maurer 1995), toys (Best 1998), and drowsiness (Kroll-Smith 2000) are public problems. For introductions to the constructionist approach, see Spector and Kitsuse (1977) or Loseke (2003). I am aware that, in writing this article, I, too, am constructing some sociological work as problematic.
2. I will ignore other, less common charges, such as two mentioned by Neil Smelser (1992:56), that social science research "is of no use to the government," and "is basically unscientific."
3. My colleague Frank Scarpitti assures me that this quote comes from *Time* magazine in the 1950s, although I have been unable to track down a citation. Doubts about sociology in turn raise questions about sociologists. Thus, according to Robert D. Leighninger, Jr., the sociology section in Blackwell's bookstore once featured a sign: "Studies of people who don't need to be studied by people who do." For other dismissive portraits of sociologists, see Bjorklund (2001).
4. Again: ". . . sociologists are clothing a paucity of thought in a smokescreen of verbiage or putting a Prussian helmet, greatcoat, and cavalry boots on a pip-squeak of an idea, the object being intimidation rather than elucidation" (Middleton 1975:59).
5. Recent writings on sociology's precarious relation to the larger society include Gans (1989) and the essays collected in Cole (2001), Erikson (1997), and Halliday and Janowitz (1992).
6. This impression may be somewhat mistaken. Richard Posner's (2001) analysis of 546 public intellectuals identifies 37 sociologists (6.8 percent), a number which is fewer than that of historians (57), political scientists (46), or economists (45), but greater than the numbers of psychologists (15) or anthropologists (5). However, he found only two sociologists ranked among the top 100 public intellectuals in number of media citations.
7. Both Rose and Wirth were among the 21 people who met to organize SSSP (Abbott 1999:78).
8. For example, see Becker (1986) or the newsletter *Writing Sociology* (published from 1993–1997).

9. Other items on the list pointed to sociology's incoherent image: "I thought I was signing up for social work"; "We don't have to learn any math . . . do we?"; "Your parents will have a [sic] heart attack thinking you're a socialist"; and "It has fewer big words than philosophy." This reminds us that students are another set of claimsmakers with considerable exposure to sociology. Casual observation, at least, suggests that many students leave their courses unconvinced of sociology's worth.

10. Such arguments cut both ways. Sociologists have largely ignored—or even attacked—some of the most prominent journalists who have favored a sociological perspective, such as Tom Wolfe and Vance Packard (Best 2001c; Nelson 1978). The vigor with which sociologists denounce "pop sociology" stands in marked contrast with natural scientists' many-faceted efforts to encourage popular understanding of developments in their disciplines. Instead, sociologists periodically establish magazines that they hope will be read by non-sociologists, although the writing and editing often remain restricted to those in the profession.

References

Abbott, Andrew
    1999   *Department and Discipline: Chicago Sociology at One Hundred.* Chicago: University of Chicago Press.
Baker, Russell
    1990   "Kindly toward arithmetic." *New York Times* (December 15):A27.
Becker, Howard S.
    1986   *Writing for Social Scientists.* Chicago: University of Chicago Press.
Berger, Peter L.
    1963   *Invitation to Sociology.* Garden City, NY: Doubleday Anchor.
Best, Joel
    1998   "Too much fun: Toys as social problems and the interpretation of culture." *Symbolic Interaction* 21:197–212.
    2001a   "Social progress and social problems: Toward a sociology of gloom." *Sociological Quarterly* 42:1–12.
    2001b   "Giving it away: Ironies of sociology's place in academia." *American Sociologist* 32:107–113.
    2001c   " 'Status! Yes!': Tom Wolfe as a sociological thinker." *American Sociologist* 32:5–22.
Bjorklund, Diane
    2001   "Sociologists as characters in twentieth century novels." *American Sociologist* 32:23–41.
Cole, Stephen, ed.
    2001   *What's Wrong with Sociology?* New Brunswick, NJ: Transaction.
Duesenberry, James S.
    1960   "Comment." In *Demographic and Economic Change in Developed Countries,* 231–239. (National Bureau of Economic Research). Princeton: Princeton University Press.
Erikson, Kai, ed.
    1997   *Sociological Visions.* Lanham, MD: Rowman and Littlefield.

Fowler, H. W.
    1965   "Sociologese." In *A Dictionary of Modern English Usage*, 2nd ed. (revised by Sir Ernest Gowers), 569–570. Oxford, England: Clarendon Press.

Gans, Herbert J.
    1989   "Sociology in America: The discipline and the public." *American Sociological Review* 54:1–16.
    1997   "Best-Sellers by sociologists: An exploratory study." *Contemporary Sociology* 26:131–135.

Goodman, Walter
    2000   "Sociologists to the barricades." *New York Times* (August 19):B7.

Gouldner, Alvin W.
    1970   *The Coming Crisis of Western Sociology.* New York: Basic Books.

Halliday, Terence C., and Morris Janowitz, eds.
    1992   *Sociology and Its Publics: The Forms and Fates of Disciplinary Organization.* Chicago: University of Chicago Press.

Horowitz, Irving Louis
    1993   *The Decomposition of Sociology.* New York: Oxford University Press.

Huber, Joan
    1995   "Institutional perspectives on sociology." *American Journal of Sociology* 101:194–216.

Kroll-Smith, Steve
    2000   "The social production of the 'drowsy person.'" *Perspectives on Social Problems* 12:89–109.

Krugman, Paul
    1994   *Peddling Prosperity: Economic Sense and Nonsense in the Age of Diminished Expectations.* New York: Norton.

Lee, Alfred McClung
    1976   "Sociology for whom?" *American Sociological Review* 41:925–936.

Lipset, Seymour Martin
    2001   "The state of American sociology." In *What's Wrong with Sociology?*, Stephen Cole, ed., 247–270. New Brunswick, NJ: Transaction.

Loseke, Donileen R.
    2003   *Thinking about Social Problems*, 2nd ed. Hawthorne, NY: Aldine de Gruyter.

Lynd, Robert S.
    1939   *Knowledge for What? The Place of Social Science in American Culture.* Princeton, NJ: Princeton University Press.

Maurer, Donna
    1995   "Meat as a social problem." In *Eating Agendas: Food and Nutrition as Social Problems*, Donna Maurer and Jeffrey Sobal, eds., 143–163. Hawthorne, NY: Aldine de Gruyter.

Merton, Robert K., and Alan Wolfe
    1995   "The cultural and social incorporation of sociological knowledge." *American Sociologist* 26:15–39.

Middleton, Thomas H.
    1975   "Talk of sociology." *Saturday Review* 2 (May 3):59.

Mills, C. Wright
    1959   *The Sociological Imagination.* New York: Oxford University Press.

Morris, Edmund
    2001   *Theodore Rex.* New York: Random House.

Murdoch, Iris
    1983   *The Philosopher's Pupil.* New York: Viking.
Myrdal, Gunnar
    1944   *An American Dilemma.* New York: Harper & Row.
Nelson, Michael
    1978   "What's wrong with sociology." *Washington Monthly* 10:42–49.
O'Rourke, P. J.
    2001   *The CEO of the Sofa.* New York: Atlantic Monthly Press.
Petersen, William
    1970   "Sociologists of the world, ignite." *National Review* 26 (December 20):1460.
Posner, Richard A.
    2001   *Public Intellectuals: A Study of Decline.* Cambridge, MA: Harvard University
            Press.
Rayment, Tim
    1991   "40 Years of the 'ology' we all love to hate." *Sunday [London] Times* (Febru-
            ary 17).
Smelser, Neil J.
    1992   "External influences on sociology." In *Sociology and Its Publics,* Terence C.
            Halliday and Morris Janowitz, eds., 43–59. Chicago: University of Chicago
            Press.
Sorokin, Pitirim A.
    1956   *Fads and Foibles in Modern Sociology.* Chicago: Regnery.
Spector, Malcolm, and John I. Kitsuse
    1977   *Constructing Social Problems.* Menlo Park, CA: Cummings.

Study Questions

1. Why might sociology be considered a "social problem"?
2. What two "temptations" do sociologists have, according to Best?

Topic 7

Deviance and Social Control

When sociologists examine deviance, it is understood that as a cultural universal, all societies have some form of deviance. Since it is an ever-present part of social groups, there are many ways to explain it (theories) and many different examples of it (research). Norms, or rules that guide behavior, are an important reference for understanding deviance, which is a violation of societal or group norms. On closer examination, however, it is not only rule violation that determines deviance, but it is just as important to know who made the rules and who enforces them. Social control, institutions and agencies in large societies that attempt to create order, is exercised by the police, courts, and corrections, for example. On a smaller scale, when a group has its rules (norms) violated, it can exercise informal controls on group members through disapproval or ostracism. Students of sociology are often drawn to the discipline because it provides a glimpse of life that is hidden from the view of people who live lives of greater conformity. It should be obvious, however, that the most conforming person still engages in some deviance, and the most deviant person is conforming in most circumstances.

Deviant activities in any society, and the careers of deviant persons, are very diverse. Of course, crime and delinquency are violations of formal norms (laws), but there are many other types of rules for behavior that don't reach the threshold of legal infractions. What about behaviors like mental illness, alcohol use/abuse, extreme facial and body disfigurations, certain persons with eating disorders, the non-working, homeless populations, and so on? Some would find these circumstances to be most "deviant," while others may not. Because it is left to "local standards" to determine what is pornographic, where is pornography in the list of deviant activities? Because of the diversity of such activities, and the responses of different people to such activities and persons, there is no way to create a list of deviant behaviors that applies to any society at any point in time. Sometimes deviance occurs in reputable organizations like corporations, religious institutions, and governments. Even police departments and lawyers can engage in deviance. Deviance cuts across all persons and structures in society.

Deviance is also relative and changeable. Time alone can change deviance—even a short span of time, such as a few years or a decade.

Terrorism, a recent realization in the United States, was redefined in a matter of a few days. Different settings can lead to different definitions of deviance. Midtown Manhattan, New York, has activities and behaviors tolerated that would never be excused in many other towns and cities across the United States. So, rural and urban settings seem to have their relative definitions of deviance. Situations, too, redefine deviance. Taking a human life on the streets of our communities might be murder and punishable by the death of the perpetrator. If you are given a government-issue uniform and rifle and deployed to another country to fight, taking human lives in this situation would be called patriotism and the "perpetrators" might become heroes. There is enormous importance in who defines deviance for a society or group, so much so that sociology can view the definition as more important than the act itself. If we are to fully understand deviance in a society, we must know that it is "relative," that defining and enforcing the rules and laws can tell much about social life in this culture.

The first of the three articles in the deviance topic is by DeAnn Gauthier and Craig Forsyth, and here is a chance to examine the behavior of a set of "groupies," the rodeo circuit's "buckle bunnies." Women, in this case, desire the companionship of men who compete for prize money in different events. The second article is by A. Ayres Boswell and Joan Spade; they look at "rape culture" as an artifact of fraternity organization and activities on college campuses. Their research identifies some of the variables responsible for safe and unsafe environments for women. Violence is a topic that must be addressed as a masculine gender issue, of which this is one example. The third and final article is by D. L. Rosenhan, a professional psychologist, who, with some colleagues, admitted himself to a mental institution and used this personal experience to examine "sanity in insane places." This article shows how researchers can "go native" and discover how social control maintains definitions of deviance and controls the behaviors of its residents—insane or not.

Reading 19

Buckle Bunnies

Groupies of the Rodeo Circuit

DeAnn K. Gauthier and Craig J. Forsyth

Introduction

The rodeo attracts many people who want to see the epitome of the Old West when roping calves and taming wild horses was part of everyday life on the ranch. Fans play an important part in the rodeo cowboy's life on the road. Among these fans are women that those around the rodeo circuit call "buckle bunnies." They are essentially cowboy groupies, who purposefully seek encounters with contestants who have proven successful in their particular rodeo event(s) (Carroll 1985; Morris 1993; Stern and Stern 1992). An easy identification system exists whereby bunnies can quickly locate their "winners" via his wearing of the winning belt buckle—hence the term "buckle bunny." These women come into contact with the cowboys at the rodeo, or in the hotels and bars where the cowboys stay. Once identified, bunnies offer the cowboys many different things, such as a ride to a rodeo, a place to sleep, a shower, or many times, just sex. There is little research on buckle bunnies, but literature does exist on rock star groupies and high profile sports groupies.

Methodology

Data for this study were gathered through interviews and observation. Subjects were identified by a key informant. Additional subjects were identified via snowball sampling, in which each subject suggest other subjects (Babbie 1998). The Internet also provided data about the rodeo. Interviews were conducted at the homes of rodeo cowboys, rodeos, and bars and hotels. Thirty-eight interviews were conducted with individuals who currently compete on the rodeo circuit at the college, amateur, or professional levels. Seven interviews were conducted with former professional cowboys. Eight wives of rodeo cowboys were also interviewed. Twelve single women who follow the rodeo and one rodeo promoter were also interviewed. The data presented here are part of a larger occupational study of the rodeo cowboy. The intent of this article is to describe the interaction between buckle bunnies and rodeo cowboys.

Groupies

"Groupie" is a term usually used to refer to a young woman who follows rock groups around on tours. The popular San Francisco-based group of the 1960s, The Grateful Dead, attracted a large contingent of traveling fans numbering in the thousands from all over the world. These fans were given the name "Deadheads." Being a Deadhead was a master status in the eyes of the Grateful Dead. Deadheads traveled at their own expense to see the band and they invested a great deal of time and money into their traveling. . . .

The groupie subculture also surrounds professional athletics, with each sport having specific names for these women (Elson 1991). Baseball players refer to these girls as "Annies" and hockey players call them "puck bunnies." The girls who follow athletes around and wait for them at bars or hotels all want to become an "acquaintance" of the athlete. Many athletes find these women very appealing because "it is easy sex" with no expectations following the encounter. These women make themselves readily available to the athletes. . . .

Groupies who follow athletes can be innocent teenagers who just want to catch a glimpse of their favorite star (Oller 1998), but most are between the ages of 18 and 25. They are seeking money, attention, and status from being associated with high-profile athletes. These women rarely approach the athletes on the court or field. They often become acquainted with the hotels where the teams are staying or the popular after-game hang-outs. Many of the same people are seen from town to town and they are very straightforward about their intentions (Elson 1991; Oller 1998).

Buckle Bunnies

As the wife of one cowboy commented:

There's a lot of them [buckle bunnies] . . . at the bigger rodeos. If you were in one certain area for a while . . . you'd see a lot of the same groupies. It's just like in any sport. You have it in professional football. Girls who like athletes. [In] hockey [they] call them puck bunnies. I guess it is the ruggedness of a cowboy that they like.

Bunnies come from a variety of backgrounds, but the majority have some family association with the rodeo. In the past, bunnies wore a distinct style of revealing Western attire. This is still true in some cases, depending on the location of the rodeo.

> It all depends on where you go. The ones down in the circuit I was in . . . wore the tightest pants they could get in, the latest style Western shirts . . . Roper boots and a buckle. Most of the time it was a buckle from some cowboy.

Several cowboys stated that these girls are getting away from the Western attire. As one steer wrestler stated:

> Not a lot of people dress the rodeo part unless they're at the rodeo. A lot of the girls are doing the same thing. They're wearing Levi's, Girbaud's, Guess, something like that. They don't look the part they used to, but you can still pick them out pretty easy.

Today, "picking them out" seems to depend in large part on the bunnies' lack of attire: "real skimpy shirts," "tank tops," "slutty," or as one interviewee put it, "They wear clothes so you can see their boobs."

Motivations behind bunny behavior seem multifaceted. One primary motivation is the atmosphere of excitement surrounding the rodeo and the cowboys. Bunnies admit to being physically attracted to cowboys in general, although looks are not the main motivation. One interviewee said:

> I'm attracted to them, but they have to be successful in their event.

. . . Buckle bunnies are likely to frequent the host hotel of the major rodeos. The host hotels usually send out papers so the contestants will know where to stay for these rodeos, including the Cheyenne Frontier Days, Denver, Houston, Fort Worth, and the National Finals Rodeo. The buckle bunnies usually find out the host hotel and try to get rooms there so they can be near the cowboys.

The most common place for the cowboys to encounter buckle bunnies is in a night club after the rodeo. This is where the majority of the buckle bunnies seek out the participants. Buckle bunnies surround the participants, waiting for them to sign an autograph, take a picture with them or to see if they can get the attention of a cowboy, each hoping she might be the favored girl of the night. As one cowboy wife notes:

> If they have a beer garden, they're there . . . a hospitality room at the hotel . . . they're there. They're everywhere the guys are socializing at.

Many times the buckle bunnies flirt with cowboys to let them know that they are interested. One cowboy told us:

> The girls kind of flirt with you, buy you a drink and they talk about rodeo. All of a sudden they pop the question on you. Who you here with? Are you going home with anybody? Do you mind if I come home with you?

Some buckle bunnies are overt and direct about their intentions:

> I've seen them ask guys if they've got a motel, or should they get one, or would they like to go back to their motel room. Some of them get off on doing guys in their campers . . . truck . . . horse trailers.

Buckle bunnies usually do not expect anything more than sex from the rodeo participants and vice versa. The majority of cowboys on the circuit are married, therefore it is even more understood by the buckle bunnies that nothing is to be expected.

> A lot of guys are married out there that they chase after . . . being with somebody who's married or just being with somebody who's going to be there for one night. They don't expect nothing from them.

A wife of a cowboy described the code of secrecy that surrounds sex with buckle bunnies on the road.

> [There is] a lot of infidelity on the road. Most of the time the guys would never let on about it. That was between them. You hope somebody would tell you if it were your husband, [but] what happens on the road stays on the road. It doesn't come back home.

Even though the cowboys enjoy the company of the buckle bunnies, many of them stated that there are negative connotations associated with them. For instance, several cowboys called these girls "whores" or "sluts." Some cowboys labeled buckle bunnies, "cut queens.". . .

As far as the sexual encounters go, these range from relatively mild flirtations to open exhibitionism. One bunny illustrates the mild form of pursuit:

> I meet cowboys at the local country bar. If I see a new bird in town I make it my business to find out who they are, buy them a drink and make them feel welcome. If they don't show an interest, I don't bother with them.

On the other hand, pursuit may be more intense, as these cowboys state:

> In Calgary, everything was different. Sex was out in the open, so to speak. The girls love cowboys and they aren't afraid to walk up to you and just ask you

if you wanted to go to their hotel room or yours. They just cut to the chase and said what they wanted.

And finally, bunnies may be so enthralled with the chase that they become exhibitionists. One typical cowboy story goes as follows:

> In Fort Worth, [a bunny wanted] oral sex in the bar. She asked, I obliged her. She told everybody to turn around and put their backs to us. She dropped to her knees. They had two girls on the dance floor who watched. She did it and then went on about her business. I went home with her that night later on. Somebody do that at the bar, you think I'm gonna let her go home by herself? What you think she gonna do by herself? The guys cheered me on. They were high-fiving me.

. . . The typical cowboy perception of the buckle bunny and who she is and what she represents is stated as follows:

> A buckle bunny . . . she's been . . . rode hard and put up wet a couple times.

The cowboys recognize that bunnies want to be able to say that they had sex with a real cowboy and, as a consequence, they expect the cowboys are the nontraditional gatekeepers of sex. Traditionally, women have been recognized as sexual game players (Ronai and Ellis 2000), but the situation seems to be somewhat reversed on the rodeo circuits. Women are seeking to acquire the "best" cowboy, whose sexual "conquest" will be viewed as a form of status attainment. One cowboy points this out by saying:

> It's a status thing for the girls . . . like being with a movie star. They brag about it.

The Rating System

To determine the "best" among cowboys, there are many ways that buckle bunnies are able to rate the rodeo participants in terms of desirability. The most obvious way is through the type of event in which the cowboy participates. Several cowboys felt that many of the buckle bunnies rated them in terms of their events.

> Some of them, all they like are bull riders, some of them, all they like are steer wrestlers.

Most of the buckle bunnies stated that they prefer rough stock riders to timed event participants. The popularity of bull riders may be because of the publicity given to this particular event. This is the only rodeo event that has its own professional rodeos set aside from the Professional Rodeo Cowboys Association (PRCA). The Professional Bullriders Association (PBR) sanctions their own bull riding events. Bull riding is considered by spectators and cowboys to be the most exciting and challenging rodeo event. . . .

Image and recognizability play important roles in the ranking of cowboy desirability.

> [Bull riding's] the most challenging event. That's who [bunnies] see on TV. They know them by face and name. That's what they want. It's always been like that.

Another way the buckle bunnies rate cowboys is using the various rodeo rankings. Buckle bunnies find rodeo participants who have excelled in their events more desirable than those who have not. As one wife stated:

> Rank and standing has something to do with who the buckle bunnies choose to be with. The ones that make more money are obviously better known because they're at the top of the rankings and they're more popular. To be with a world champion or the guy who won the Salinas Rodeo or Cheyenne is a prestigious thing.

Cowboys are aware of this use of ranking by the bunnies:

> The girls inquire about your ranking or how much money you've made, but they know. They probably get the *Pro Rodeo Sports News* and get on the Internet to check out what's going on. Most of them keep up with the standings. They're interested in the status of a cowboy.

. . . Some groups of buckle bunnies have created point systems to keep track of the cowboys with whom they have been intimate. In one such system, points were given in order of prestige of the cowboy's achievements.

> [One] group of girls had a point system. Sex had to be involved to get the points. If you had your PRCA card it was one point. If you made it to the finals it was two points. Won the world, it was three points. At the end of the year, whoever had the most points accumulated out of the group, it's like eight or 10 of them, the losers had to pay the one with the most points trip to the finals, plus their own way out there.

Although success in the event is important to the buckle bunnies, it seems to be more an issue of status than an issue of money. . . . Jackets are also marks of status. Rodeo participants who have been to the national finals usually wear their NFR jackets wherever they go.

> They give each contestant a jacket and it has their number and their name and everything on it in Las Vegas at the national finals. The night I got there,

[my husband] had won the round and they gave him a buckle, so that night afterward we were sitting down at the bar. Several girls came up to him, even while I was there and they propositioned him. They see that jacket.

I don't care who you are, if you show up at the NFR and you're not a contestant, you don't have a shot [with the bunnies]. If they can't get the jacket, they'll go after somebody else.

. . . they want the jacket. . . .

The Social Transaction

Many times, the buckle bunnies allow the cowboys to stay in their hotel rooms or at their homes so the cowboys do not have to spend another night in the truck or on the road. Cowboys often do not rent rooms of their own because they don't have enough money or because the hotel doesn't accommodate a horse trailer. Some cowboys offer to buy the women dinner if they allow them to sleep in their room and take a hot shower. If one of the guys in a group would find a woman to go home with, all of the cowboys traveling with him would follow to partake of a shower and place to sleep.

Many of the participants travel constantly and rarely go home. When they do get to stay in the same place for four or five days, they want to have fun. Buckle bunnies assist greatly in this goal.

I was at a rodeo in Oklahoma. We didn't have any place to stay, so any time one of the guys in the car would get a girl and no one else would, we would follow them to their house and that's a shower, maybe breakfast and we'd sleep. We were real young, just pro and we weren't winning hardly any money. Five days without a shower. We were scrungy. And, we went to their home and we were all sitting in the living room. I was kind of getting scared, there were three of us sitting down, and my buddy was with that other girl and there was two of them and she said, "Well, there's a couch right there," and I said, "I'll sleep on the floor," and she said, "No, you have a place to sleep in here with me." I ended up sleeping in the bed with her. The daughter was in the other room with my friend. The mother and daughter, she raised to be a buckle bunny. The next morning we got up and had pancakes and eggs. She handed me a paper with her number on it. . . .

Discussion and Conclusions

Several factors make the behavior of buckle bunnies deviant: having sex with married men, having sex in public, women initiating the sexual encounters, having sex with too many people, and the overt and utilitarian rating of sexual partners. None of these are crimes, but all fall under the heading of sins or poor taste (Smith and Pollack 2000). . . . Subcultures are, indeed, difficult for outsiders to understand. Norms of a subculture can be an antithesis to the conventional, but it is the material from which identities are constructured. The identities of the buckle bunnies emphasize a relation of unattachment, a dislocation from the confinements of work and committed relationships, and a genuine experiment with free time. It delineates the buckle bunny from others, and assists her with finding companionship with like-minded peers, enabling her to construct an identity from the symbols found in the rodeo subculture. Subculture reinforces meaningful statements about one's position relative to others. The subculture is composed of a variety of purists, those who do not quite fit in, and rebels. The attraction of the rodeo subculture is its hedonistic escape from the conventional. It offers a place to have fun and explore and expand both the traditional concepts of masculinity and femininity, but also modern roles regarding sexual pursuit. Traditional ideology maintains hegemony; it is a male-dominated culture. But what has been negotiated is a fetished image that is a twist on traditional sex roles. The new images consist of males, still dominant in a subculture that glorifies males and masculinity, but also now in possession of a role traditionally reserved for women as a group—the gatekeepers of sex. Alternatively, women are free to pursue sexually, a role traditionally denied them as adult women in mainstream U.S. culture. If one feels like a maverick, the scripts composed in this subculture are highly attractive.

References

Babbie, Earl. 1998. *The Practice of Social Research.* Belmont, CA: Wadsworth Publishing Company.

Carroll, E. Jean. 1985. *Female Difficulties.* New York: Bantom Books.

Elson, John. 1991. "The Dangerous World of Wannabes." *Time* 138(22) (Nov. 25):77, 80.

Morris, Michele. 1993. *The Cowboy Life.* New York: Fireside.

Ronai, Carol Rambo and Carolyn Ellis. 2000. "Turn-Ons for Money: Interactional Strategies of the Table Dancer." Pp. 407–426 in *Constructions of Deviance*, edited by Patricia A. Adler and Peter Adler. Belmont, CA: Wadsworth Publishing Company.

Smith, Alexander B. and Harriet Pollack. 2000. "Deviance As Crime, Sin, and Poor Taste." Pp. 19–28 in *Constructions of Deviance*, edited by Patricia A. Adler and Peter Adler. Belmont, CA: Wadsworth Publishing Company.

Stern, Jane and Michael Stern. 1992. "Raging Bulls." *The New Yorker* 68 (Sept. 14):90–103.

Study Questions

1. What are the gender patterns in the "buckle bunnies" relationships to the cowboys?
2. Why are the "buckle bunnies" considered deviant?

Reading 20

Fraternities and Collegiate Rape Culture

A. Ayres Boswell and Joan Z. Spade

Date rape and acquaintance rape on college campuses are topics of concern to both researchers and college administrators. Some estimate that 60 to 80 percent of rapes are date or acquaintance rape (Koss, Dinero, Seibel, and Cox 1988). Further, 1 out of 4 college women say they were raped or experienced an attempted rape, and 1 out of 12 college men say they forced a woman to have sexual intercourse against her will (Koss, Gidycz, and Wisniewski 1985).

Although considerable attention focuses on the incidence of rape, we know relatively little about the context or the *rape culture* surrounding date and acquaintance rape. Rape culture is a set of values and beliefs that provide an environment conducive to rape (Buchwald, Fletcher, & Roth 1993; Herman 1984). The term applies to a generic culture surrounding and promoting rape, not the specific settings in which rape is likely to occur. We believe that the specific settings also are important in defining relationships between men and women.

Some have argued that fraternities are places where rape is likely to occur on college campuses (Martin and Hummer 1989; O'Sullivan 1993; Sanday 1990) and that the students most likely to accept rape myths and be more sexually aggressive are more likely to live in fraternities and sororities, consume higher doses of alcohol and drugs, and place a higher value on social life at college (Gwartney-Gibbs and Stockard 1989; Kalof and Cargill 1991). Others suggest that sexual aggression is learned in settings such as fraternities and is not part of predispositions or preexisting attitudes (Boeringer, Shehan, and Akers 1991). To prevent further incidences of rape on college campuses, we need to understand what it is about fraternities in particular and college life in general that may contribute to the maintenance of a rape culture on college campuses.

Our approach is to identify the social contexts that link fraternities to campus rape and promote a rape culture. Instead of assuming that all fraternities provide an environment conducive to rape, we compare the interactions of men and women at fraternities identified on campus as being especially *dangerous* places for women, where the likelihood of rape is high, to those seen as *safer* places, where the perceived probability of rape occurring is lower. Prior to collecting data for our study, we found that most women students identified some fraternities as having more sexually aggressive members and a higher probability of rape. These women also considered other fraternities as relatively safe houses, where a woman could go and get drunk if she wanted to and feel secure that the fraternity men would not take advantage of her. We compared parties at houses identified as high-risk and low-risk houses as well as at two local bars frequented by college students. Our analysis provides an opportunity to examine situations and contexts that hinder or facilitate positive social relations between undergraduate men and women.

The abusive attitudes toward women that some fraternities perpetuate exist within a general culture where rape is intertwined in traditional gender scripts. Men are viewed as initiators of sex and women as either passive partners or active resisters, preventing men from touching their bodies (LaPlante, McCormick, and Brannigan 1980). Rape culture is based on the assumptions that men are aggressive and dominant whereas women are passive and acquiescent (Buchwald et al. 1993; Herman 1984). What occurs on college campuses is an extension of the portrayal of domination and aggression of men over women that exemplifies the double standard of sexual behavior in U.S. society (Barthel 1988; Kimmel 1993).

Sexually active men are positively reinforced by being referred to as "studs," whereas women who are sexually active or report enjoying sex are derogatorily labeled as "sluts" (Herman 1984; O'Sullivan 1993). These gender scripts are embodied in rape myths and stereotypes such as "She really wanted it; she just said no because she didn't want me to think she was a bad girl" (Burke, Stets, and Pirog-Good 1989; Jenkins and Dambrot 1987; Lisak and Roth 1988; Malamuth 1986; Muehlenhard and Linton 1987; Peterson and Franzese 1987). Because men's sexuality is seen as more natural, acceptable, and uncontrollable than women's sexuality, many men and women excuse acquaintance rape by affirming that men cannot control their natural urges (Miller and Marshall 1987).

Whereas some researchers explain these attitudes toward sexuality and rape using an individual or a psychological interpretation, we argue that rape has a social basis, one in which both men and women create and recreate masculine and feminine identities and relations. Based on the assumption that rape is part of the social construction of gender, we examine how men and women "do gender" on a college campus (West and Zimmerman 1987). We focus on fraternities because they have been identified as settings that encourage rape (Sanday 1990). By comparing fraternities that are viewed by women as places where there is a high risk of rape to those where women believe there is a low risk of rape as well as two local commercial bars, we seek to identify characteristics that make some social settings more likely places for the occurrence of rape.

Method

We observed social interactions between men and women at a private coeducational school in which a high percentage (49.4 percent) of students affiliate with Greek organizations. The university has an undergraduate population of approximately 4,500 students, just more than one third of whom are women; the students are primarily from upper-middle-class families. The school, which admitted only men until 1971, is highly competitive academically.

We used a variety of data collection approaches: observations of interactions between men and women at fraternity parties and bars, formal interviews, and informal conversations. The first author, a former undergraduate at this school and a graduate student at the time of the study, collected the data. She knew about the social life at the school and had established rapport and trust between herself and undergraduate students as a teaching assistant in a human sexuality course.

The process of identifying high- and low-risk fraternity houses followed Hunter's (1953) reputational approach. In our study, 40 women students identified fraternities that they considered to be high risk, or to have more sexually aggressive members and higher incidence of rape, as well as fraternities that they considered to be safe houses. The women represented all four years of undergraduate college and different living groups (sororities, residence halls, and off-campus housing). Observations focused on the four fraternities named most often by these women as high-risk houses and the four identified as low-risk houses. . . .

In addition, 50 individuals were interviewed including men from the selected fraternities, women who attended those parties, men not affiliated with fraternities, and self-identified rape victims known to the first author. The first author approached men and women by telephone or on campus and asked them to participate in interviews. The interviews included open-ended questions about gender relations on campus, attitudes about date rape, and their own experiences on campus. . . .

Results

The Settings

Fraternity Parties

We observed several differences in the quality of the interaction of men and women at parties at high-risk fraternities compared to those at low-risk houses. A typical party at a low-risk house included an equal number of women and men. The social atmosphere was friendly, with considerable interaction between women and men. Men and women danced in groups and in couples, with many of the couples kissing and displaying affection toward each other. Brothers explained that, because many of the men in these houses had girlfriends, it was normal to see couples kissing on the dance floor. Coed groups engaged in conversations at many of these houses, with women and men engaging in friendly exchanges, giving the impression that they knew each other well. Almost no cursing and yelling was observed at parties in low-risk houses; when pushing occurred, the participants apologized. Respect for women extended to the women's bathrooms, which were clean and well supplied.

At high-risk houses, parties typically had skewed gender ratios, sometimes involving more men and other times involving more women. Gender segregation also was evident at these parties, with the men on one side of a room or in the bar drinking while women gathered in another area. Men treated women differently in the high-risk houses. The women's bathrooms in the high-risk houses were filthy, including clogged toilets and vomit in the sinks. When a brother was told of the mess in the bathroom at a high-risk house, he replied, "Good, maybe some of these beer wenches will leave so there will be more beer for us."

Men attending parties at high-risk houses treated women less respectfully, engaging in jokes, conversations, and behaviors that degraded women. Men made a display of assessing women's bodies and rated them with thumbs up or thumbs down for the other men in the sight of the women. One man attending a party at a high-risk fraternity said to another, "Did you know that this week is Women's Awareness Week? I guess that means we get to abuse them more this week." Men behaved more crudely at parties at high-risk houses. At one party, a brother dropped his pants, including his underwear, while dancing in front of several women. Another brother slid across the dance floor completely naked.

The atmosphere at parties in high-risk fraternities was less friendly overall. With the exception of greetings, men and women rarely smiled or laughed and spoke to each other less often than was the case at parties in low-risk houses. The few one-on-one conversations between women and men appeared to be strictly flirtatious (lots of eye contact, touching, and very close talking). It was rare to see a group of men and women together talking. Men were openly hostile, which made the high-risk parties seem almost threatening at times. For example, there was a lot of touching, pushing, profanity, and name calling, some done by women.

Students at parties at the high-risk houses seemed self-conscious and aware of the presence of members of the opposite sex, an awareness that was sexually charged. Dancing early in the evening was usually between women. Close to midnight, the sex ratio began to balance out with the arrival of more men or more women. Couples began to dance together but in a sexual way (close dancing with lots of pelvic thrusts). Men tried to pick up women using lines such as "Want to see my fish tank?" and "Let's go upstairs so that we can talk; I can't hear what you're saying in here."

Although many of the same people who attended high-risk parties also attended low-risk parties, their behavior changed as they moved from setting to setting. Group norms differed across contexts as well. At a party that was held jointly at a low-risk house with a high-risk fraternity, the ambience was that of a party at a high-risk fraternity with heavier drinking, less dancing, and fewer conversations between women and men. The men from both high- and low-risk fraternities were very aggressive; a fight broke out, and there was pushing and shoving on the dance floor and in general.

As others have found, fraternity brothers at high-risk houses on this campus told about routinely discussing their sexual exploits at breakfast the morning after parties and sometimes at house meetings (cf. Martin and Hummer 1989; O'Sullivan 1993; Sanday 1990). During these sessions, the brothers we interviewed said that men bragged about what they did the night before with stories of sexual conquests often told by the same men, usually sophomores. The women involved in these exploits were women they did not know or knew but did not respect, or *faceless victims.* Men usually treated girlfriends with respect and did not talk about them in these storytelling sessions. Men from low-risk houses, however, did not describe similar sessions in their houses. . . .

Gender Relations

Relations between women and men are shaped by the contexts in which they meet and interact. As is the case on other college campuses, *hooking up* has replaced dating on this campus, and fraternities are places where many students hook up. Hooking up is a loosely applied term on college campuses that had different meanings for men and women on this campus.

Most men defined hooking up similarly. One man said it was something that happens

> when you are really drunk and meet up with a woman you sort of know, or possibly don't know at all and don't care about. You go home with her with the intention of getting as much sexual, physical pleasure as she'll give you, which can range anywhere from kissing to intercourse, without any strings attached.

The exception to this rule is when men hook up with women they admire. Men said they are less likely to press for sexual activity with someone they know and like because they want the relationship to continue and be based on respect.

Women's version of hooking up differed. Women said they hook up only with men they cared about and described hooking up as kissing and petting but not sexual intercourse. Many women said that hooking up was disappointing because they wanted longer-term relationships. First-year women students realized quickly that hook-ups were usually one-night stands with no strings attached, but many continued to hook up because they had few opportunities to develop relationships with men on campus. One first-year woman said that "70 percent of hook-ups never talk again and try to avoid one another, 26 percent may actually hear from them or talk to them again, and 4 percent may actually go on a date, which can lead to a relationship." Another first-year woman said,

"It was fun in the beginning. You get a lot of attention and kiss a lot of boys and think this is what college is about, but it gets tiresome fast."

Whereas first-year women get tired of the hook-up scene early on, many men do not become bored with it until their junior or senior year. As one upperclassman said, "The whole game of hooking up became really meaningless and tiresome for me during my second semester of my sophomore year, but most of my friends didn't get bored with it until the following year."

In contrast to hooking up, students also described monogamous relationships with steady partners. Some type of commitment was expected, but most people did not anticipate marriage. The term *seeing each other* was applied when people were sexually involved but free to date other people. This type of relationship involved less commitment than did one of boyfriend/girlfriend but was not considered to be a hook-up. . . .

Some fraternity brothers pressure each other to limit their time with and commitment to their girlfriends. One senior man said, "The hill [fraternities] and girlfriends don't mix." A brother described a constant battle between girlfriends and brothers over who the guy is going out with for the night, with the brothers usually winning. Brothers teased men with girlfriends with remarks such as "whipped" or "where's the ball and chain?" A brother from a high-risk house said that few brothers at his house had girlfriends; some did, but it was uncommon. One man said that from the minute he was a pledge he knew he would probably never have a girlfriend on this campus because "it was just not the norm in my house. No one has girlfriends; the guys have too much fun with [each other]."

The pressure on men to limit their commitment to girlfriends, however, was not true of all fraternities or of all men on campus. Couples attended low-risk fraternity parties together, and men in the low-risk houses went out on dates more often. A man in one low-risk house said that about 70 percent of the members of his house were involved in relationships with women, including the pledges (who were sophomores).

Treatment of Women

. . . Men said that, when together in groups with other men, they sensed a pressure to be disrespectful toward women. A first-year man's perception of the treatment of women was that "they are treated with more respect to their faces, but behind closed doors, with a group of men present, respect for women is not an issue." One senior man stated, "In general, college-aged men don't treat women their age with respect because 90 percent of them think of women as merely a means to sex." Women reinforced this perception. A first-year woman stated, "Men here are more interested in hooking up and drinking beer than they are in getting to know women as real people." Another woman said, "Men here use and abuse women."

Characteristic of rape culture, a double standard of sexual behavior for men versus women was prevalent on this campus. As one Greek senior man stated, "Women who sleep around are sluts and get bad reputations; men who do are champions and get a pat on the back from their brothers." Women also supported a double standard for sexual behavior by criticizing sexually active women. A first-year woman spoke out against women who are sexually active: "I think some girls here make it difficult for the men to respect women as a whole."

One concrete example of demeaning sexually active women on this campus is the "walk of shame." Fraternity brothers come out on the porches of their houses the night after parties and heckle women walking by. It is assumed that these women spent the night at fraternity houses and that the men they were with did not care enough about them to drive them home. Although sororities now reside in former fraternity houses, this practice continues and sometimes the victims of hecklings are sorority women on their way to study in the library. . . .

Fraternity men most often mistreated women they did not know personally. Men and women alike reported incidents in which brothers observed other brothers having sex with unknown women or women they knew only casually. A sophomore woman's experience exemplifies this anonymous state: "I don't mind if 10 guys were watching or it was videotaped. That's expected on this campus. It's the fact that he didn't apologize or even offer to drive me home that really upset me." Descriptions of sexual encounters involved the satisfaction of men by nameless women. A brother in a high-risk fraternity described a similar occurrence:

> A brother of mine was hooking up upstairs with an unattractive woman who had been pursuing him all night. He told some brothers to go outside the window and watch. Well, one thing led to another and they were almost completely naked when the woman noticed the brothers outside. She was then unwilling to go any further, so the brother went outside and yelled at the

other brothers and then closed the shades. I don't know if he scored or not, because the woman was pretty upset. But he did win the award for hooking up with the ugliest chick that weekend. . . .

Discussion and Conclusion

These findings describe the physical and normative aspects of one college campus as they relate to attitudes about and relations between men and women. Our findings suggest that an explanation emphasizing rape culture also must focus on those characteristics of the social setting that play a role in defining heterosexual relationships on college campuses (Kalof and Cargill 1991). The degradation of women as portrayed in rape culture was not found in all fraternities on this campus. Both group norms and individual behavior changed as students went from one place to another. Although individual men are the ones who rape, we found that some settings are more likely places for rape than are others. Our findings suggest that rape cannot be seen only as an isolated act and blamed on individual behavior and proclivities, whether it be alcohol consumption or attitudes. We also must consider characteristics of the settings that promote the behaviors that reinforce a rape culture.

Relations between women and men at parties in low-risk fraternities varied considerably from those in high-risk houses. Peer pressure and situational norms influenced women as well as men. Although many men in high- and low-risk houses shared similar views and attitudes about the Greek system, women on this campus, and date rape, their behaviors at fraternity parties were quite different.

Women who are at highest risk of rape are women whom fraternity brothers did not know. These women are faceless victims, nameless acquaintances—not friends. Men said their responsibility to such persons and the level of guilt they feel later if the hook-ups end in sexual intercourse are much lower if they hook up with women they do not know. In high-risk houses, brothers treated women as subordinates and kept them at a distance. Men in high-risk houses actively discouraged ongoing heterosexual relationships, routinely degraded women, and participated more fully in the hook-up scene; thus, the probability that women would become faceless victims was higher in these houses. The flirtatious nature of the parties indicated that women go to these parties looking for available men, but finding boyfriends or relationships was difficult at parties in high-risk houses. However, in the low-risk houses, where more men had long-term relationships, the women were not strangers and were less likely to become faceless victims. . . .

Although this research provides some clues to gender relations on college campuses, it raises many questions. Why do men and women participate in activities that support a rape culture when they see its injustices? What would happen if alcohol were not controlled by groups of men who admit that they disrespect women when they get together? What can be done to give men and women on college campuses more opportunities to interact responsibly and get to know each other better? These questions should be studied on other campuses with a focus on the social settings in which the incidence of rape and the attitudes that support a rape culture exist. Fraternities are social contexts that may or may not foster a rape culture. . . .

References

Barthel, D. 1988. *Putting on appearances: Gender and advertising.* Philadelphia: Temple University Press.

Boeringer, S. B., C. L. Shehan, and R. L. Akers. 1991. Social contexts and social learning in sexual coercion and aggression: Assessing the contribution of fraternity membership. *Family Relations* 40:58–64.

Buchwald, E., P. R. Fletcher, and M. Roth, eds. 1993. *Transforming a rape culture.* Minneapolis, MN: Milkweed Editions.

Burke, P., J. E. Stets, and M. A. Pirog-Good. 1989. Gender identity, self-esteem, physical abuse and sexual abuse in dating relationships. In *Violence in dating relationships: Emerging social issues,* edited by M. A. Pirog-Good and J. E. Stets. New York: Praeger.

Gwartney-Gibbs, P., and J. Stockard. 1989. Courtship aggression and mixed-sex peer groups. In *Violence in dating relationships: Emerging social issues,* edited by M. A. Pirog-Good and J. E. Stets. New York: Praeger.

Herman, D. 1984. The rape culture. In *Women: A feminist perspective,* edited by J. Freeman. Mountain View, CA: Mayfield.

Hunter, F. 1953. *Community power structure.* Chapel Hill: University of North Carolina Press.

Jenkins, M. J., and F. H. Dambrot. 1987. The attribution of date rape: Observer's attitudes and sexual experiences and the dating situation. *Journal of Applied Social Psychology* 17:875–95.

Kalof, L., and T. Cargill, 1991. Fraternity and sorority membership and gender dominance attitudes. *Sex Roles* 25:417–23.

Kimmel, M. S. 1993. Clarence, William, Iron Mike, Tailhook, Senator Packwood, Spur Posse, Magic . . . and us. In *Transforming a rape culture,* edited by E. Buchwald, P. R. Fletcher, and M. Roth. Minneapolis, MN: Milkweed Editions.

Koss, M. P., T. E. Dinero, C. A. Seibel, and S. L. Cox. 1988. Stranger and acquaintance rape: Are there differences in the victim's experience? *Psychology of Women Quarterly* 12:1–24.

Koss, M. P., C. A. Gidycz, and N. Wisniewski. 1985. The scope of rape: Incidence and prevalence of sexual aggression and victimization in a national sample of higher education students. *Journal of Consulting and Clinical Psychology* 55:162–70.

LaPlante, M. N., N. McCormick, and G. G. Brannigan. 1980. Living the sexual script: College students' views of influence in sexual encounters. *Journal of Sex Research* 16:338–55.

Lisak, D., and S. Roth. 1988. Motivational factors in nonincarcerated sexually aggressive men. *Journal of Personality and Social Psychology* 55:795–802.

Malamuth, N. 1986. Predictors of naturalistic sexual aggression. *Journal of Personality and Social Psychology* 50:953–62.

Martin, P. Y., and R. Hummer. 1989. Fraternities and rape on campus. *Gender & Society* 3:457–73.

Miller, B., and J. C. Marshall. 1987. Coercive sex on the university campus. *Journal of College Student Personnel* 28:38–47.

Muehlenhard, C. L., and M. A. Linton. 1987. Date rape and sexual aggression in dating situations: Incidence and risk factors. *Journal of Counseling Psychology* 34:186–96.

O'Sullivan, C. 1993. Fraternities and the rape culture. In *Transforming a rape culture*, edited by E. Buchwald, P. R. Fletcher, and M. Roth. Minneapolis, MN: Milkweed Editions.

Peterson, S. A., and B. Franzese. 1987. Correlates of college men's sexual abuse of women. *Journal of College Student Personnel* 28:223–28.

Sanday, P. R. 1990. *Fraternity gang rape: Sex, brotherhood, and privilege on campus.* New York: New York University Press.

West, C., and D. Zimmerman. 1987. Doing gender. *Gender & Society* 1:125–51.

Study Questions

1. List the characteristics of the social settings where women are at risk and where they are safe.

2. What is meant by "rape culture," and how is this "culture" supported by men?

Reading 21
On Being Sane in Insane Places

D. L. Rosenhan

If sanity and insanity exist, how shall we know them?

The question is neither capricious nor itself insane. However much we may be personally convinced that we can tell the normal from the abnormal, the evidence is simply not compelling. It is commonplace, for example, to read about murder trials wherein eminent psychiatrists for the defense are contradicted by equally eminent psychiatrists for the prosecution on the matter of the defendant's sanity. More generally, there are a great deal of conflicting data on the reliability, utility, and meaning of such terms as "sanity," "insanity," "mental illness," and "schizophrenia" (*1*). Finally, as early as 1934, Benedict suggested that normality and abnormality are not universal (*2*). What is viewed as normal in one culture may be seen as quite aberrant in another. Thus, notions of normality and abnormality may not be quite as accurate as people believe they are.

To raise questions regarding normality and abnormality is in no way to question the fact that some behaviors are deviant or odd. Murder is deviant. So, too, are hallucinations. Nor does raising such questions deny the existence of the personal anguish that is often associated with "mental illness." Anxiety and depression exist. Psychological suffering exists. But normality and abnormality, sanity and insanity, and the diagnoses that flow from them may be less substantive than many believe them to be.

At its heart, the question of whether the sane can be distinguished from the insane (and whether degrees of insanity can be distinguished from each other) is a simple matter: do the salient characteristics that lead to diagnoses reside in the patients themselves or in the environments and contexts in which observers find them? From Bleuler, through Kretchmer, through the formulators of the recently revised *Diagnostic and Statistical Manual* of the American Psychiatric Association, the belief has been strong that patients present symptoms, that those symptoms can be categorized, and, implicitly, that the sane are distinguishable from the insane. More recently, however, this belief has been questioned. Based in part on theoretical and anthropological considerations, but also on philosophical, legal, and therapeutic ones, the view has grown that psychological categorization of mental illness is useless at best and downright harmful, misleading, and pejorative at worst. Psychiatric diagnoses, in this view, are in the minds of the observers and are not valid summaries of characteristics displayed by the observed (3–5).

Gains can be made in deciding which of these is more nearly accurate by getting normal people (that is, people who do not have, and have never suffered, symptoms of serious psychiatric disorders) admitted to psychiatric hospitals and then determining whether they were discovered to be sane and, if so, how. If the sanity of such pseudopatients were always detected, there would be prima facie evidence that a sane individual can be distinguished from the insane context in which he is found. Normality (and presumably abnormality) is distinct enough that it can be recognized wherever it occurs, for it is carried within the person. If, on the other hand, the sanity of the pseudopatients were never discovered, serious difficulties would arise for those who support traditional modes of psychiatric diagnosis. Given that the hospital staff was not incompetent, that the pseudopatient had been behaving as sanely as he had been outside of the hospital, and that it had never been previously suggested that he belonged in a psychiatric hospital, such an unlikely outcome would support the view that psychiatric diagnosis betrays little about the patient but much about the environment in which an observer finds him.

This article describes such an experiment. Eight sane people gained secret admission to 12 different hospitals (6). Their diagnostic experiences constitute the data of the first part of this article; the remainder is devoted to a description of their experiences in psychiatric institutions. Too few psychiatrists and psychologists, even those who have worked in such hospitals, know what the experience is like. They rarely talk about it with former patients, perhaps because they distrust information coming from the previously insane. Those who have worked in psychiatric hospitals are likely to have adapted so thoroughly to the settings that they an insensitive to the impact of that experience. And while there have been occasional reports of researchers who submitted themselves to psychiatric hospitalization (7), these researchers have commonly remained in the hospitals for short periods of time, often with the knowledge of the hospital staff. It is difficult to know the extent to which they were treated like patients or like research colleagues. Nevertheless, their reports about the inside of the psychiatric hospital have been valuable. This article extends those efforts.

Pseudopatients and Their Settings

The eight pseudopatients were a varied group. One was a psychology graduate student in his 20's. The remaining seven were older and "established." Among them were three psychologists, a pediatrician, a psychiatrist, a painter, and a housewife. Three pseudopatients were women, five were men. All of them employed pseudonyms, lest their alleged diagnoses embarrass them later. Those who were in mental health professions alleged another occupation in order to avoid the special attentions that might be accorded by staff, as a matter of courtesy or caution, to ailing colleagues (8). With the exception of myself (I was the first pseudopatient and my presence was known to the hospital administrator and chief psychologist and, so far as I can tell, to them alone), the presence of pseudopatients and the nature of the research program was not known to the hospital staffs (9).

The settings were similarly varied. In order to generalize the findings, admission into a variety of hospitals was sought. The 12 hospitals in the sample were located in five different states on the East and West coasts. Some were old and shabby, some were quite new. Some were research-oriented, others not. Some had good staff-patient ratios, others were quite understaffed. Only one was a strictly private hospital. All of the others were supported by state or federal funds or, in one instance, by university funds.

After calling the hospital for an appointment, the pseudopatient arrived at the admissions office complaining that he had been hearing voices. Asked what the voices said, he replied that they were often unclear, but as far as he could tell they said "empty," "hollow," and "thud." The voices were unfamiliar and were of the same sex as the pseudopatient. The choice of these symptoms was occasioned by their apparent similarity to existential symptoms. Such symptoms are alleged to arise from painful concerns about the perceived meaninglessness of one's life. It is as if the hallucinating person were saying, "My life is empty and hollow." The choice of these symptoms was also determined by the *absence* of a single report of existential psychoses in the literature.

Beyond alleging the symptoms and falsifying name, vocation, and employment, no further alterations of person, history, or circumstances were made. The significant events of the pseudopatient's life history were presented as they had actually occurred. Relationships with parents and siblings, with spouse and children, with people at work and in school, consistent with the aforementioned exceptions, were described as they were or had been. Frustrations and upsets were described along with joys and satisfactions. These facts are important to remember. If anything, they strongly biased the subsequent results in favor of detecting sanity, since none of their histories or current behaviors were seriously pathological in any way.

Immediately upon admission to the psychiatric ward, the pseudopatient ceased simulating *any* symptoms of abnormality. In some cases, there was a brief period of mild nervousness and anxiety, since none of the pseudopatients really believed that they would be admitted so easily. Indeed, their shared fear was that they would be immediately exposed as frauds and greatly embarrassed. Moreover, many of them had never visited a psychiatric ward; even those who had, nevertheless had some genuine fears about what might happen to them. Their nervousness, then, was quite appropriate to the novelty of the hospital setting, and it abated rapidly.

Apart from that short-lived nervousness, the pseudopatient behaved on the ward as he "normally" behaved. The pseudopatient spoke to patients and staff as he might ordinarily. Because there is uncommonly little to do on a psychiatric ward, he attempted to engage others in conversation. When asked by staff how he was feeling, he indicated that he was fine, that he no longer experienced symptoms. He responded to instructions from attendants, to calls for medication (which was not swallowed), and to dining-hall instructions. Beyond such activities as were available to him on the admissions ward, he spent his time writing down his observations about the ward, its patients, and the staff. Initially these notes were written "secretly," but as it soon became clear that no one much cared, they were subsequently written on standard tablets of paper in such public places as the dayroom. No secret was made of these activities.

The pseudopatient, very much as a true psychiatric patient, entered a hospital with no foreknowledge of when he would be discharged. Each was told that he would have to get out by his own devices, essentially by convincing the staff that he was sane. The psychological stresses associated with hospitalization were considerable, and all but one of the pseudopatients desired to be discharged almost immediately after being admitted. They were, therefore, motivated not only to behave sanely, but to be paragons of cooperation. That their behavior was in no way disruptive is confirmed by nursing reports, which have been obtained on most of the patients. These reports uniformly indicate that the patients were "friendly," "cooperative," and "exhibited no abnormal indications."

The Normal Are Not Detectably Sane

Despite their public "show" of sanity, the pseudopatients were never detected. Admitted, except in one case, with a diagnosis of schizophrenia (*10*), each was discharged with a diagnosis of schizophrenia "in remission." The label "in remission" should in no way be dismissed as a formality, for at no time during any hospitalization had any question been raised about any pseudopatient's simulation. Nor are there any indications in the hospital records that the pseudopatient's status was suspect. Rather, the evidence is strong that, once labeled schizophrenic, the pseudopatient was stuck with that label. If the pseudopatient was to be discharged, he must naturally be "in remission"; but he was not sane, nor, in the institution's view, had he ever been sane.

The uniform failure to recognize sanity cannot be attributed to the quality of the hospitals, for, although there were considerable variations among them, several are considered excellent. Nor can it be alleged that there was simply not enough time to observe the pseudopatients. Length of hospitalization ranged from 7 to 52 days, with an average of 19 days. The pseudopatients were not, in fact, carefully observed, but this failure clearly speaks more to traditions within psychiatric hospitals than to lack of opportunity.

Finally, it cannot be said that the failure to recognize the pseudopatients' sanity was due to the fact that they were not behaving sanely. While there was clearly some tension present in all of them, their daily visitors could detect no serious behavioral consequences—nor, indeed, could other patients. It was quite common for the patients to "detect" the pseudopatients' sanity. During the first three hospitalizations, when accurate counts were kept, 35 of a total of 118 patients on the admissions ward voiced their suspicions, some vigorously. "You're not crazy. You're a journalist, or a professor [referring to the continual note-taking]. You're checking up on the hospital." While most of the patients were reassured by the pseudopatient's insistence that he had been sick before he came in but was fine now, some continued to believe that the pseudopatient was sane throughout his hospitalization (*11*). The fact that the patients often recognized normality when staff did not raises important questions.

Failure to detect sanity during the course of hospitalization may be due to the fact that physicians operate with a strong bias toward what statisticians call the type 2 error (*5*). This is to say that physicians are more inclined to call a healthy person sick (a false positive, type 2) than a sick person healthy (a false negative, type 1). The reasons for this are not hard to find: it is clearly more dangerous to misdiagnose illness than health. Better to err on the side of caution, to suspect illness even among the healthy.

But what holds for medicine does not hold equally well for psychiatry. Medical illnesses, while unfortunate, are not commonly pejorative. Psychiatric diagnoses, on the contrary, carry with them personal, legal, and social stigmas (*12*). It was therefore important to see whether the tendency toward diagnosing the sane insane could be reversed. The following experiment was arranged at a research and teaching hospital whose staff had heard these findings but doubted that such an error could occur in their hospital. The staff was informed that at some time during the following 3 months, one or more pseudopatients would attempt to be admitted into the psychiatric hospital. Each staff member was asked to rate each patient who presented himself at admissions or on the ward according to the likelihood that the patient was a pseudopatient. A 10-point scale was used, with a 1 and 2 reflecting high confidence that the patient was a pseudopatient.

Judgments were obtained on 193 patients who were admitted for psychiatric treatment. All staff who had had sustained contact with or primary responsibility for the patient—attendants, nurses, psychiatrists, physicians, and psychologists—were asked to make judgments. Forty-one patients were alleged, with high confidence, to be pseudopatients by at least one member of the staff. Twenty-three were considered suspect by at least one psychiatrist. Nineteen were suspected by one psychiatrist *and* one other staff member. Actually, no genuine pseudopatient (at least from my group) presented himself during this period.

The experiment is instructive. It indicates that the tendency to designate sane people as insane can be reversed when the stakes (in this case, prestige and diagnostic acumen) are high. But what can be said of the 19 people who were suspected of being "sane" by one psychiatrist and another staff member? Were these people truly "sane," or was it rather the case that in the course of avoiding the type 2 error the staff tended to make more errors of the first sort—calling the crazy "sane"? There is no way of knowing. But one thing is certain: any diagnostic process that lends itself so readily to massive errors of this sort cannot be a very reliable one.

The Stickiness of Psychodiagnostic Labels

Beyond the tendency to call the healthy sick—a tendency that accounts better for diagnostic behavior on admission than it does for such behavior after a lengthy period of exposure—the data speak to the massive role of labeling in psychiatric assessment. Having once been labeled schizophrenic, there is nothing the pseudopatient can do to overcome the tag. The tag profoundly colors others' perceptions of him and his behavior.

From one viewpoint, these data are hardly surprising, for it has long been known that elements are given meaning by the context in which they occur. Gestalt psychology made this point vigorously, and Asch (13) demonstrated that there are "central" personality traits (such as "warm" versus "cold") which are so powerful that they markedly color the meaning of other information in forming an impression of a given personality (14). "Insane," "schizophrenic," "manic-depressive," and "crazy" are probably among the most powerful of such central traits. Once a person is designated abnormal, all of his other behaviors and characteristics are colored by that label. Indeed, that label is so powerful that many of the pseudopatients' normal behaviors were overlooked entirely or profoundly misinterpreted. Some examples may clarify this issue.

Earlier I indicated that there were no changes in the pseudopatients personal history and current status beyond those of name, employment, and, where necessary, vocation. Otherwise, a veridical description of personal history and circumstances was offered. Those circumstances were not psychotic. How were they made consonant with the diagnosis of psychosis? Or were those diagnoses modified in such a way as to bring them into accord with the circumstances of the pseudopatient's life, as described by him?

As far as I can determine, diagnoses were in no way affected by the relative health of the circumstances of a pseudopatient's life. Rather, the reverse occurred: the perception of his circumstances was shaped entirely by the diagnosis. A clear example of such translation is found in the case of a pseudopatient who had had a close relationship with his mother but was rather remote from his father during his early childhood. During adolescence and beyond, however, his father became a close friend, while his relationship with his mother cooled. His present relationship with his wife was characteristically close and warm. Apart from occasional angry exchanges, friction was minimal. The children had rarely been spanked. Surely there is nothing especially pathological about such a history. Indeed, many readers may see a similar pattern in their own experiences, with no markedly deleterious consequences. Observe, however, how such a history was translated in the psychopathological context, this from the case summary prepared after the patient was discharged.

> This white 39-year-old male . . . manifests a long history of considerable ambivalence in close relationships, which begins in early childhood. A warm relationship with his mother cools during his adolescence. A distant relationship to his father is described as becoming very intense. Affective stability is absent. His attempts to control emotionality with his wife and children are punctuated by angry outbursts and, in the case of the children, spankings. And while he says that he has several good friends, one senses considerable ambivalence embedded in those relationships also. . . .

The facts of the case were unintentionally distorted by the staff to achieve consistency with a popular theory of the dynamics of a schizophrenic reaction (*15*). Nothing of an ambivalent nature had been described in relations with parents, spouse, or friends. To the extent that ambivalence could be inferred, it was probably not greater than is found in all human relationships. It is true the pseudopatient's relationships with his parents changed over time, but in the ordinary context that would hardly be remarkable—indeed, it might very well be expected. Clearly, the meaning ascribed to his verbalizations (that is, ambivalence, affective instability) was determined by the diagnosis: schizophrenia. An entirely different meaning would have been ascribed if it were known that the man was "normal."

All pseudopatients took extensive notes publicly. Under ordinary circumstances, such behavior would have raised questions in the minds of observers, as, in fact, it did among patients. Indeed, it seemed so certain that the notes would elicit suspicion that elaborate precautions were taken to remove them from the ward each day. But the precautions proved needless. The closest any staff member came to questioning these notes occurred when one pseudopatient asked his physician what kind of medication he was receiving and began to write down the response. "You needn't write it," he was told gently. "If you have trouble remembering, just ask me again."

If no questions were asked of the pseudopatients, how was their writing interpreted? Nursing records for three patients indicate that the writing was seen as an aspect of their pathological behavior. "Patient engages in writing behavior" was the daily nursing comment on one of the pseudopatients who was never questioned about his writing. Given that the patient is in the hospital, he must be psychologically disturbed. And given that he is disturbed, continuous writing must be a behavioral manifestation of that disturbance, perhaps a subset of the compulsive behaviors that are sometimes correlated with schizophrenia.

One tacit characteristic of psychiatric diagnosis is that it locates the sources of aberration within the individual and only rarely within the complex of stimuli that surrounds him. Consequently, behaviors that are stimulated by the environment are commonly misattributed to the patient's disorder. For example, one kindly nurse found a pseudopatient pacing the long hospital corridors. "Nervous, Mr. X?" she asked. "No, bored," he said.

The notes kept by pseudopatients are full of patient behaviors that were misinterpreted by well-intentioned staff. Often enough, a patient would go "berserk" because he had, wittingly or unwittingly, been mistreated by, say, an attendant. A nurse coming upon the scene would rarely inquire even cursorily into the environmental stimuli of the patient's behavior. Rather, she assumed that his upset derived from his pathology, not from his present interactions with other staff members. Occasionally, the staff might assume that the patient's family (especially when they had recently visited) or other patients had stimulated the outburst. But never were the staff found to assume that one of themselves or the structure of the hospital had anything to do with a patient's behavior. One psychiatrist pointed to a group of patients who were sitting outside the cafeteria entrance half an hour before lunchtime. To a group of young residents he indicated that such behavior was characteristic of the oral-acquisitive nature of the syndrome. It seemed not to occur to him that there were very few things to anticipate in a psychiatric hospital besides eating.

A psychiatric label has a life and an influence of its own. Once the impression has been formed that the patient is schizophrenic, the expectation is that he will continue to be schizophrenic. When a sufficient amount of time has passed, during which the patient has done nothing bizarre, he is considered to be in remission and available for discharge. But the label endures beyond discharge, with the unconfirmed expectation that he will behave as a schizophrenic again. Such labels, conferred by mental health professionals, are as influential on the patient as they are on his relatives and friends, and it should not surprise anyone that the diagnosis acts on all of them as a self-fulfilling prophecy. Eventually, the patient himself accepts the diagnosis, with all of its surplus meanings and expectations, and behaves accordingly (5).

The inferences to be made from these matters are quite simple. Much as Zigler and Phillips have demonstrated that there is enormous overlap in the symptoms presented by patients who have been variously diagnosed (16), so there is enormous overlap in the behaviors of the sane and the insane. The sane are not "sane" all of the time. We lose our tempers "for no good reason." We are occasionally depressed or anxious, again for no good reason. And we may find it difficult to get along with one or another person—again for no reason that we can specify. Similarly, the insane are not always insane. Indeed, it was the impression of the pseudopatients while living with them that they were sane for long periods of time—that the bizarre behaviors upon which their diagnoses were allegedly predicated constituted only a small fraction of their total behavior. If it makes no sense to label ourselves permanently depressed on the basis of an occasional depression, then it takes better evidence than is presently available to label all patients insane or schizophrenic on the basis of bizarre behaviors or cognitions. It seems more useful, as Mischel (17) has pointed out, to limit our discussions to *behaviors*, the stimuli that provoke them, and their correlates.

It is not known why powerful impressions of personality traits, such as "crazy" or "insane," arise. Conceivably, when the origins of and stimuli that give rise to a behavior are remote or unknown, or when the behavior strikes us as immutable, trait labels regarding the *behaver* arise. When, on the other hand, the origins and stimuli are known and available, discourse is limited to the behavior itself. Thus, I may hallucinate because I am sleeping, or I may hallucinate because I have ingested a peculiar drug. These are termed sleep-induced hallucinations, or dreams, and drug-induced hallucinations, respectively. But when the stimuli to my hallucinations are unknown, that is called craziness, or schizophrenia—as if that inference were somehow as illuminating as the others. . . .

The Consequences of Labeling and Depersonalization

Whenever the ratio of what is known to what needs to be known approaches zero, we tend to invent "knowledge" and assume that we understand more than we actually do. We seem unable to acknowledge that we simply don't know. The needs for diagnosis and remediation of behavioral and emotional problems are enormous. But rather than acknowledge that we are just embarking on understanding, we continue to label patients "schizophrenic," "manic-depressive," and "insane," as if in those words we had captured the essence of understanding. The facts of the matter are that we have known for a long time that diagnoses are often not useful or reliable, but we have nevertheless continued to use them. We now know that we cannot distinguish insanity from sanity. It is depressing to consider how that information will be used.

Not merely depressing, but frightening. How many people, one wonders, are sane but not recognized as such in our psychiatric institutions? How many have been needlessly stripped of their privileges of citizenship, from the right to vote and drive to that of handling their own accounts? How many have feigned insanity in order to avoid the criminal consequences of their behavior, and, conversely, how many would rather stand trial than live interminably in a psychiatric hospital—but are wrongly thought to be mentally ill? How many have been stigmatized by well-intentioned, but nevertheless erroneous, diagnoses? On the last point, recall again that a "type 2 error" in psychiatric diagnosis does not have the same consequences it does in medical diagnosis. A diagnosis of cancer that has been found to be in error is cause for celebration. But psychiatric diagnoses are rarely found to be in error. The label sticks, a mark of inadequacy forever.

Finally, how many patients might be "sane" outside the psychiatric hospital but seem insane in it—not because craziness resides in them, as it were, but because they are responding to a bizarre setting, one that may be unique to institutions which harbor nether people? Goffman (4) calls the process of socialization to such institutions "mortification"—an apt metaphor that includes the processes of depersonalization that have been described here. And while it is impossible to know whether the pseudopatients' responses to these processes are characteristic of all inmates—they were, after all, not real patients—it is difficult to believe that these processes of socialization to a psychiatric hospital provide useful attitudes or habits of response for living in the "real world."

Summary and Conclusions

It is clear that we cannot distinguish the sane from the insane in psychiatric hospitals. The hospital itself imposes a special environment in which the meanings of behavior can easily be misunderstood. The consequences to patients hospitalized in such an environment—the powerlessness, depersonalization, segregation, mortification, and self-labeling—seem undoubtedly countertherapeutic. . . .

I and the other pseudopatients in the psychiatric setting had distinctly negative reactions. We do not pretend to describe the subjective experiences of true patients. Theirs may be different from ours, particularly with the passage of time and the necessary process of adaptation to one's environment. But we can and do speak to the relatively more objective indices of treatment within the hospital. It could be a mistake, and a very unfortunate one, to consider that what happened to us derived from malice or stupidity on the part of the staff. Quite the contrary, our overwhelming impression of them was of people who really cared, who were committed and who were uncommonly intelligent. Where they failed, as they sometimes did painfully, it would be more accurate to attribute those failures to the environment in which they, too, found themselves than to personal callousness. Their perceptions and behavior were controlled by the situation, rather than being motivated by a malicious disposition. In a more benign environment, one that was less attached to global diagnosis, their behaviors and judgments might have been more benign and effective.

References and Notes

1. P. Ash, *J. Abnorm. Soc. Psychol.* 44, 272 (1949); A. T. Beck, *Amer. J. Psychiat.* 119, 210 (1962); A. T. Boisen, *Psychiatry* 2, 233 (1938); N. Kreitman, *J. Ment. Sci.* 107, 876 (1961); N. Kreitman, P. Sainsbury, J. Morrisey, J. Towers, J. Scrivener, *ibid.*, p. 887; H. O. Schmitt and C. P. Fonda, *J. Abnorm. Soc. Psychol.* 52, 262 (1956); W. Seaman, *J. Nerv. Ment. Dis.* 118, 541 (1953). For an analysis of these artifacts and

summaries of the disputes, see J. Zubin, *Annu. Rev. Psychol.* 18, 373 (1967); L. Phillips and J. G, Draguns, *ibid.* 22, 447 (1971).

2. R. Benedict, *J. Gen. Psychol.* 10, 59 (1934).

3. See in this regard H. Becker, *Outsiders: Studies in the Sociology of Deviance* (Free Press, New York, 1963); B. M. Braginsky, D. D. Braginsky, K. Ring, *Methods of Madness: The Mental Hospital as a Last Resort* (Holt, Rinehart & Winston, New York, 1969); G. M. Crocetti and P. V. Lemkau, *Amer. Sociol. Rev.* 30, 577 (1965); E. Goffman, *Behavior in Public Places* (Free Press, New York, 1964); R. D. Laing, *The Divided Self: A Study of Sanity and Madness* (Quadrangle, Chicago, 1960); D. L. Phillips, *Amer. Sociol. Rev.* 28, 963 (1963); T. R. Sarbin, *Psychol. Today* 6, 18 (1972); E. Schur, *Amer. J. Sociol.* 75, 309 (1969); T. Szasz, *Law, Liberty and Psychiatry* (Macmillan, New York, 1963); *The Myth of Mental Illness: Foundations of a Theory of Mental Illness* (Hoeber-Harper, New York, 1963). For a critique of some of these views, see W. R. Gove, *Amer. Sociol. Rev.* 35, 873 (1970).

4. E. Goffman, *Asylums* (Doubleday, Garden City, N.Y., 1961).

5. T. J. Scheff, *Being Mentally Ill: A Sociological Theory* (Aldine, Chicago, 1966).

6. Data from a ninth pseudopatient are not incorporated in this report because, although his sanity went undetected, he falsified aspects of his personal history, including his marital status and parental relationships. His experimental behaviors therefore were not identical to those of the other pseudopatients.

7. A. Barry, *Bellevue Is a State of Mind* (Harcourt Brace Jovanovich, New York, 1971); I. Belknap, *Human Problems of a State Mental Hospital* (McGraw-Hill, New York, 1956); W. Caudill, F. C. Redlich, H. R. Gilmore, E. B. Brody, *Amer. J. Orthopsychiat.* 22, 314 (1952); A. R. Goldman, R. H. Bohr, T. A. Steinberg, *Prof. Psychol.* 1, 427 (1970); unauthored, *Roche Report* 1 (No. 13), 8 (1971).

8. Beyond the personal difficulties that the pseudopatient is likely to experience in the hospital, there are legal and social ones that, combined, require considerable attention before entry. For example, once admitted to a psychiatric institution, it is difficult, if not impossible, to be discharged on short notice, state law to the contrary notwithstanding. I was not sensitive to these difficulties at the outset of the project, nor to the personal and situational emergencies that can arise, but later a writ of habeas corpus was prepared for each of the entering pseudopatients and an attorney was kept "on call" during every hospitalization. I am grateful to John Kaplan and Robert Bartels for legal advice and assistance in these matters.

9. However distasteful such concealment is, it was a necessary first step to examining these questions. Without concealment, there would have been no way to know how valid these experiences were; nor was there any way of knowing whether whatever detections occurred were a tribute to the diagnostic acumen of the staff or to the hospial's rumor network. Obviously, since my concerns are general ones that cut across individual hospitals and staffs, I have respected their anonymity and have eliminated clues that might lead to their identification.

10. Interestingly, of the 12 admissions, 11 were diagnosed as schizophrenic and one, with an identical symptomatology, as manic-depressive psychosis. This diagnosis has a more favorable prognosis, and it was given by the only private hospital in our sample. On the relations between social class and psychiatric diagnosis, see A. deB. Hollingshead and F. C. Redlich, *Social Class and Mental Illness: A Community Study* (Wiley, New York, 1958).

11. It is possible, of course, that patients have quite broad latitudes in diagnosis and therefore are inclined to call many people sane, even those whose behavior is patently aber-

rant. However, although we have no hard data on this matter, it was our distinct impression that this was not the case. In many instances, patients not only singled us out for attention, but came to imitate our behaviors and styles.

12. J. Cumming and E. Cumming, *Community Ment. Health* 1, 135 (1965); A. Farina and K. Ring. *J. Abnorm. Psychol.* 70, 47 (1965); H. E. Freeman and O. G. Simmons, *The Mental Patient Comes Home* (Wiley, New York, 1963); W. J. Johannsen, *Ment. Hygiene* 53, 218 (1969); A. S. Linsky, *Soc. Psychiat.* 5, 166 (1970).

13. S. E. Asch, *J. Abnorm. Soc. Psychol.* 41, 258 (1946); *Social Psychology* (Prentice-Hall, New York, 1952).

14. See also I. N. Mensh and J. Wishner, *J. Personality* 16, 188 (1947); J. Wishner, *Psychol. Rev.* 67, 96 (1960); J. S. Bruner and R. Tagiuri, in *Handbook of Social Psychology*; G. Lindzey. Ed. (Addison-Wesley, Cambridge, Mass., 1954), vol. 2, pp. 634–654; J. S. Bruner, D. Shapiro, R. Tagiuri, in *Person Perception and Interpersonal Behavior*, R. Tagiuri and L. Petrullo, Eds. (Stanford Univ. Press, Stanford, Calif., 1958), pp. 277–288.

15. For an example of a similar self-fulfilling prophecy, in this instance dealing with the "central" trait of intelligence, see R. Rosenthal and L. Jacobson, *Pygmalion in the Classroom* (Holt, Rinehart & Winston, New York, 1968).

16. E. Zigler and L. Phillips, *J. Abnorm. Soc. Psychol.* 63, 69 (1961). See also R. K. Freudenberg and J. P. Robertson, *A.M.A. Arch. Neurol. Psychiatr.* 76, 14 (1956).

17. W. Mischel, *Personality and Assessment* (Wiley, New York, 1968).

Study Questions

1. Rosenhan and his colleagues faked their way into a mental institution with symptoms. Why was this so easy?

2. If a person really was mistakenly sent to a mental hospital, what processes discussed in the article would keep them from getting out?

PART THREE

Social Inequality

Topic 8
Social Class

Social stratification systems create "layers" of people in society based on the unequal distribution of scarce rewards. Social classes are the relative position of people based on such things as income, education, and occupation. Less tangible, but no less important, is the role of prestige or how people rank the relative importance of others. This is often based on occupation; a person who owns a garbage truck and collects trash may make more money than a college professor, but the professor has more prestige. Complex measures of class tell us about the juxtaposition of persons and groups of persons based on these criteria. People who share the same position in the social stratification system comprise a social class. Social class determines a great deal about our lives, such as where we live, where we shop, the sort of car we drive, our political values, and even the colleges we attend. From the super rich to the very poor, life chances are dramatically affected by the economic and social resources available to us.

The economic dimension of life in the United States is undergoing some fascinating changes. First, it is abundantly clear that "the rich are getting richer, and the poor are getting poorer." More wealth and more income are being concentrated in fewer and fewer people at the very top of the class system. There is evidence that this is occurring throughout the world as well. From the middle-class downward in the class system, where the majority of the people are, income and assets are becoming scarcer. At the same time, large corporations are receiving benefits from local, state, and federal governments in the forms of tax breaks that some call "corporate welfare." Second, the structure of labor markets in the United States is changing as well. In the post-industrial age, there are fewer skilled labor jobs with higher wages and many more service jobs with lower wages. An $8.00 per hour job, worked for 40 hours per week and 50 weeks, would return $16,000 in wages for the year—just about the poverty line for a family of four in the United States. As we know, many people work for less that that. Hence, the standard of living of many in the United States is being affected by the transformation of labor markets in our own country.

A persistent problem in the United States, as well as the world, is poverty. Nearly one in six U.S. citizens live in economic conditions that directly affect diet, health, education, personal development, crime victimization, and so on. When we look at children, these percentages move toward one in four. Being raised in poverty, living in substandard housing, and missing needed medical care mean that life is burdened by inequalities. The economics of poverty "costs" more than the poor, as the United States creates and funds programs to relieve the circumstances of lower-class lifestyles. The poor and the near-poor struggle with everyday events (hunger, no personal transportation, illness) that the rest of the class structure rarely notice. Indeed, it may seem as though we do live in separate worlds.

The three readings in this topic are designed to look at sociological observations on poverty, the upper class, and blue-collar life. In a functionalist view of poverty, Herbert Gans analyzes what it is that makes poverty so important to the rest of social life. There actually are many reasons, "functions," to have poverty and understand who benefits from it. G. William Domhoff writes about "the upper class in America" and what institutions create and maintain it. Upper-class life is a rather closed system of relations with its own patterns, supporting structures, and family connections. Finally, a university president, John Coleman, takes a sabbatical and enters blue-collar life—quite a change in status and activity. Here, another professional uses biographical experience to produce an ethnography of the working class and let us know about the contradictions in upper-middle and blue-collar work.

Reading 22

The Positive Functions of Poverty

Herbert J. Gans

Merton (1949, p. 50) defined functions as "those observed consequences which make for the adaptation or adjustment of a given system; and dysfunctions, those observed consequences which lessen the adaptation or adjustment of the system." This definition does not specify the nature or scope of the system, but elsewhere in his classic paper "Manifest and Latent Functions," Merton indicated that social system was not a synonym for society, and that systems vary in size, requiring a functional analysis "to consider a *range* of units for which the item (or social phenomenon H.G.) has designated consequences: individuals in diverse statuses, subgroups, the larger social system and cultural systems" (1949, p. 51).

In discussing the functions of poverty, I shall identify functions for *groups* and *aggregates;* specifically, interest groups, socioeconomic classes, and other population aggregates, for example, those with shared values or similar statuses. This definitional approach is based on the assumption that almost every social system—and of course every society—is composed of groups or aggregates with different interests and values, so that, as Merton put it (1949, p. 51), "items may be functional for some individuals and subgroups and dysfunctional for others." Indeed, frequently one group's functions are another group's dysfunctions.[1] For example, the political machine analyzed by Merton was functional for the working class and business interests of the city but dysfunctional for many middle class and reform interests. Consequently, functions are defined as those observed consequences which are positive *as judged by the values of the group under analysis;* dysfunctions, as those which are negative by these values.[2] Because functions benefit the group in question and dysfunctions hurt it, I shall also describe functions and dysfunctions in the language of economic planning and systems analysis as benefits and costs.[3]. . .

In a modern heterogeneous society, few phenomena are functional or dysfunctional for the society as a whole, and most result in benefits to some groups and costs to others. Given the level of differentiation in modern society, I am even skeptical whether one can empirically identify a social system called society. Society exists, of course, but it is closer to being a very large aggregate, and when sociologists talk about society as a system, they often really mean the nation, a system which, among other things, sets up boundaries and other distinguishing characteristics between societal aggregates.

I would also argue that no social phenomenon is indispensable; it may be too powerful or too highly valued to be eliminated, but in most instances, one can suggest what Merton calls "functional alternatives" or equivalents for a social phenomena, that is, other social patterns or policies which achieve the same functions but avoid the dysfunctions.

The conventional view of American poverty is so dedicated to identifying the dysfunctions of poverty, both for the poor and the nation, that at first glance it seems inconceivable to suggest that poverty could be functional for anyone. Of course, the slum lord and the loan shark are widely known to profit from the existence of poverty; but they are popularly viewed as evil men, and their activities are, at least in part, dysfunctional for the poor. However, what is less often recognized, at least in the conventional wisdom, is that poverty also makes possible the existence or expansion of "respectable" professions and occupations, for example, penology, criminology, social work, and public health. More recently, the poor have provided jobs for professional and paraprofessional "poverty warriors," as well as journalists and social scientists, this author included, who have supplied the information demanded when public curiosity about the poor developed in the 1960s.

Clearly, then, poverty and the poor may well serve a number of functions for many nonpoor groups in American society, and I shall describe 15 sets of such functions—economic, social, cultural, and political—that seem to me most significant.

First, the existence of poverty makes sure that "dirty work" is done. Every economy has such work: physically dirty or dangerous, temporary, dead-end and underpaid, undignified, and menial jobs. These jobs can be filled by paying higher wages than for "clean" work, or by requiring people who have no other choice to do the dirty work and at low wages. In America, poverty functions to provide a low-wage labor pool that is willing—or, rather, unable to be unwilling—to perform dirty work at low cost. Indeed, this function is so important that in some Southern states, welfare payments have been cut off during the summer months when the poor are needed to work in the fields. Moreover, the debate about welfare—and about proposed substitutes such as the negative income tax and the Family Assistance Plan—has emphasized the impact of income grants on work incentive, with opponents often arguing that such grants would reduce the incentive of—actually, the pressure on—the poor to carry out the needed dirty work if the wages therefore are no larger than the income grant. Furthermore, many economic activities which involve dirty work depend heavily on the poor; restaurants, hospitals, parts of the garment industry, and industrial agriculture, among others, could not persist in their present form without their dependence on the substandard wages which they pay to their employees.

Second, the poor subsidize, directly and indirectly, many activities that benefit the affluent.[4] For one thing, they have long supported both the consumption and investment activities of the private economy by virtue of the low wages which they receive. This was openly recognized at the beginning of the Industrial Revolution, when a French writer quoted by T. H. Marshall (forthcoming, p. 7) pointed out that "to assure and maintain the prosperities of our industries, it is necessary that the workers should never acquire wealth." Examples of this kind of subsidization abound even today; for example, domestics subsidize the upper middle and upper classes, making life easier for their employers and freeing affluent women for a variety of professional, cultural, civic, or social activities. In addition, as Barry Schwartz pointed out (personal communication), the low income of the poor enables the rich to divert a higher proportion of their income to savings and investment, and thus to fuel economic growth. This, in turn, can produce higher incomes for everybody, including the poor, although it does not necessarily improve the position of the poor in the socioeconomic hierarchy, since the benefits of economic growth are also distributed unequally.

At the same time, the poor subsidize the governmental economy. Because local property and sales taxes and the ungraduated income taxes levied by many states are regressive, the poor pay a higher percentage of their income in taxes than the rest of the population, thus subsidizing the many state and local governmental programs that serve more affluent taxpayers.[5] In addition, the poor support medical innovation as patients in teaching and research hospitals, and as guinea pigs in medical experiments, subsidizing the more affluent patients who alone can afford these innovations once they are incorporated into medical practice.

Third, poverty creates jobs for a number of occupations and professions which serve the poor, or shield the rest of the population from them. As already noted, penology would be miniscule without the poor, as would the police, since the poor provide the majority of their "clients." Other activities which flourish because of the existence of poverty are the numbers game, the sale of heroin and cheap wines and liquors, pentecostal ministers, faith healers, prostitutes, pawn shops, and the peacetime army, which recruits its enlisted men mainly from among the poor.

Fourth, the poor buy goods which others do not want and thus prolong their economic usefulness, such as day-old bread, fruit and vegetables which would otherwise have to be thrown out, second-hand clothes, and deteriorating automobiles and buildings. They also provide incomes for doctors, lawyers, teachers, and others who are too old, poorly trained, or incompetent to attract more affluent clients.

In addition, the poor perform a number of social and cultural functions:

Fifth, the poor can be identified and punished as alleged or real deviants in order to uphold the legitimacy of dominant norms (Macarov 1970, pp. 31–33). The defenders of the desirability of hard work, thrift, honesty, and monogamy need people who can be accused of being lazy, spendthrift, dishonest, and promiscuous to justify these norms; and as Erikson (1964) and others following Durkheim have pointed out, the norms themselves are best legitimated by discovering violations.

Whether the poor actually violate these norms more than affluent people is still open to question. The working poor work harder and longer than high-status jobholders, and poor housewives must do more housework to keep their slum apartments clean than their middle-class peers in standard housing. The proportion of cheaters among welfare recipients is quite low and considerably lower than among income taxpayers.[6] Violent crime is higher among the poor, but the affluent commit a variety of white-collar crimes, and several studies of self-reported delinquency have concluded that middle-class youngsters are sometimes as delinquent as the poor. However, the poor are more likely to be caught when participating in deviant acts and, once caught, to be punished more often than middle-class transgressors. Moreover, they lack the political and cultural power to correct the stereotypes that affluent people hold of them, and thus continue to be thought of as lazy, spendthrift, etc., whatever the empirical evidence, by those who need living proof that deviance does not pay.[7] The actually or allegedly deviant poor have traditionally been described as undeserving and, in more recent terminology, culturally deprived or pathological.

Sixth, another group of poor, described as deserving because they are disabled or suffering from bad luck, provide the rest of the population with different emotional satisfactions; they evoke compassion, pity, and charity, thus allowing those who help them to feel that they are altruistic, moral, and practicing the Judeo-Christian ethic. The deserving poor also enable others to feel fortunate for being spared the deprivations that come with poverty.[8]

Seventh, as a converse of the fifth function described previously, the poor offer affluent people vicarious participation in the uninhibited sexual, alcoholic, and narcotic behavior in which many poor people are alleged to indulge, and which, being freed from the constraints of affluence and respectability, they are often thought to enjoy more than the middle classes. One of the popular beliefs about welfare recipients is that many are on a permanent sex-filled vacation. Although it may be true that the poor are more given to uninhibited behavior, studies by Rainwater (1970) and other observers of the lower class indicate that such behavior is as often motivated by despair as by lack of inhibition, and that it results less in pleasure than in a compulsive escape from grim reality. However, whether the poor actually have more sex and enjoy it more than affluent people is irrelevant; as long as the latter believe it to be so, they can share it vicariously and perhaps enviously when instances are reported in fictional, journalistic, or sociological and anthropological formats.

Eighth, poverty helps to guarantee the status of those who are not poor. In a stratified society, where social mobility is an especially important goal and class boundaries are fuzzy, people need to know quite urgently where they stand. As a result, the poor function as a reliable and relatively permanent measuring rod for status comparison, particularly for the working class, which must find and maintain status distinctions between itself and the poor, much as the aristocracy must find ways of distinguishing itself from the *nouveau riche.*

Ninth, the poor also assist in the upward mobility of the nonpoor, for, as Goode has pointed out (1967, p. 5), "the privileged . . . try systematically to prevent the talent of the less privileged from being recognized or developed." By being denied educational opportunities or being stereotyped as stupid or unteachable, the poor thus enable others to obtain the better jobs. Also, an unknown number of people have moved themselves or their children up in the socioeconomic hierarchy through the incomes earned from the provision of goods and services in the slums: by becoming policemen and teachers, owning "Mom and Pop" stores, or working in the various rackets that flourish in the slums.

In fact, members of almost every immigrant group have financed their upward mobility by providing retail goods and services, housing, entertainment, gambling, narcotics, etc., to later arrivals in America (or in the city), most recently to blacks, Mexicans, and Puerto Ricans. Other Americans, of both European and native origin, have financed their entry into the upper middle and upper classes by owning or managing the illegal institutions that serve the poor, as well as the legal but not respectable ones, such as slum housing.

Tenth, just as the poor contribute to the economic viability of a number of businesses and professions (see function 3 above), they also add to the social viability of noneconomic groups. For one thing, they help to keep the aristocracy busy, thus justifying its continued existence. "Society" uses the poor as clients of settlement houses and charity benefits; indeed, it must have the poor to practice its public-mindedness so as to demonstrate its superiority over the *nouveaux riches* who devote themselves to conspicuous consumption. The poor play a similar function for philanthropic enterprises at other levels of the socioeconomic hierarchy, including the mass of middle-class civic organizations and women's clubs engaged in volunteer work and fundraising in almost every American community. Doing good among the poor has traditionally helped the church to find a method of expressing religious sentiments in action; in recent years, militant church activity among and for the poor has enabled the church to hold on to its more liberal and radical members who might otherwise have dropped out of organized religion altogether.

Eleventh, the poor perform several cultural functions. They have played an unsung role in the creation of "civilization," having supplied the construction labor for many of the monuments which are often identified as the noblest expressions and examples of civilization, for example, the Egyptian pyramids, Greek temples, and medieval churches.[9] Moreover, they have helped to create a goodly share of the surplus capital that funds the artists and intellectuals who make culture, and particularly "high" culture, possible in the first place.

Twelfth, the "low" culture created for or by the poor is often adopted by the more affluent. The rich collect artifacts from extinct folk cultures (although not only from poor ones), and almost all Americans listen to the jazz, blues, spirituals, and country music which originated among the Southern poor—as well as rock, which was derived from similar sources. The protest of the poor sometimes becomes literature; in 1970, for example, poetry written by ghetto children became popular in sophisticated literary circles. The poor also serve as culture heroes and literary subjects, particularly, of course, for the Left, but the hobo, cowboy, hipster, and the mythical prostitute with a heart of gold have performed this function for a variety of groups.

Finally, the poor carry out a number of important political functions: *Thirteenth,* the poor serve as symbolic constituencies and opponents for several political groups. For example, parts of the revolutionary Left could not exist without the poor, particularly now that the working class can no longer be perceived as the vanguard of the revolution. Conversely, political groups of conservative bent need the "welfare chiselers" and others who "live off the taxpayer's hard-earned money" in order to justify their demands for reductions in welfare payments and tax relief. Moreover, the role of the poor in upholding dominant norms (see function 5 above) also has a significant political function. An economy based on the ideology of laissez faire requires a deprived population which is allegedly unwilling to work; not only does the alleged moral inferiority of the poor reduce the moral pressure on the present political economy to eliminate poverty, but redistributive alternatives can be made to look quite unattractive if those who will benefit from them most can be described as lazy, spendthrift, dishonest, and promiscuous. Thus, conservatives and classical liberals would find it difficult to justify many of their political beliefs without the poor; but then so would modern liberals and socialists who seek to eliminate poverty.

Fourteenth, the poor, being powerless, can be made to absorb the economic and political costs of change and growth in American society. During the 19th century, they did the backbreaking work that built the cities; today, they are pushed out of their neighborhoods to make room for "progress." Urban renewal projects to hold middle-class taxpayers and stores in the city and expressways to enable suburbanites to commute downtown have typically been located in poor neighborhoods, since no other group will allow itself to be displaced. For much the same reason, urban universities, hospitals, and civic centers also expand into land occupied by the poor. The major costs of the industrialization of agriculture in America have been borne by the poor, who are pushed off the land without recompense, just as in earlier centuries in Europe, they bore the brunt of the transformation of agrarian societies into industrial ones. The poor have also paid a large share of the human cost of the growth of American power overseas, for they have provided many of the foot soldiers for Vietnam and other wars.

Fifteenth, the poor have played an important role in shaping the American political process; because they vote and participate less than other groups, the political system has often been free to ignore them. This has not only made American politics more centrist than would otherwise be the case, but it has also added to the stability of the political process. If the 15% of the population below the federal "poverty line" participated fully in the political process, they would almost certainly demand better jobs and higher incomes, which would require income redistribution and would thus generate further political conflict between the haves and the have-nots. Moreover, when the poor do participate, they often provide the Democrats with a captive constituency, for they can rarely support Republicans, lack parties of their own, and thus have no other place to go politically. This, in turn, has enabled the Democrats to count on the votes of the poor, allowing the party to be more responsive to voters who might otherwise switch to the Republicans, in recent years, for example, the white working class.

I have described fifteen of the more important functions which the poor carry out in American society, enough to support the functionalist thesis that poverty survives in part because it is useful to a number of groups in society. This analysis is not intended to suggest that because it is functional, poverty *should* persist, or that it *must* persist. Whether it should persist is a normative question; whether it must, an analytic and empirical one, but the answer to both depends in part on whether the dysfunctions of poverty outweigh the functions. Obviously, poverty has many dysfunctions, mainly for the poor themselves but also for the more affluent.

Notes

1. Probably one of the few instances in which a phenomenon has the same function for two groups with different interests is when the survival of the system in which both participate is at stake. Thus, a wage increase can be functional for labor and dysfunctional for management (and consumers), but if the wage increase endangers the firm's survival, it is dysfunctional for labor as well. This assumes, however, that the firm's survival is valued by the workers, which may not always be the case, for example, when jobs are available elsewhere.

2. Merton (1949, p. 50) originally described functions and dysfunctions in terms of encouraging or hindering adaptation or adjustment to a system, although subsequently he has written that "dysfunction refers to the particular inadequacies of a particular part of the system for a designated requirement" (1961, p. 732). Since adaptation and adjustment to a system can have conservative ideological implications, Merton's later formulation and my own definitional approach make it easier to use functional analysis as an ideologically neutral or at least ideologically variable method, insofar as the researcher can decide for himself whether he supports the values of the group under analysis.

3. It should be noted, however, that there are no absolute benefits and costs just as there are no absolute functions and dysfunctions; not only are one group's benefits often another group's costs, but every group defines benefits by its own manifest and latent values, and a social scientist or planner who has determined that certain phenomena provide beneficial consequences for a group may find that the group thinks otherwise. For example, during the 1960s, advocates of racial integration discovered that a significant portion of the black community no longer considered it a benefit but saw it rather as a policy to assimilate blacks into white society and to decimate the political power of the black community.

4. Of course, the poor do not actually subsidize the affluent. Rather, by being forced to work for low wages, they enable the affluent to use the money saved in this fashion for other purposes. The concept of subsidy used here thus assumes belief in a "just wage."

5. Pechman (1969) and Herriott and Miller (1971) found that the poor pay a higher proportion of their income in taxes than any other part of the population: 50% among people earning $2,000 or less according to the latter study.

6. Most official investigations of welfare cheating have concluded that less than 5% of recipients are on the rolls illegally, while it has been estimated that about a third of the population cheats in filing income tax returns.

7. Although this paper deals with the functions of poverty for other groups, poverty has often been described as a motivating or character-building device for the poor themselves; and economic conservatives have argued that by generating the incentive to work, poverty encourages the poor to escape poverty. For an argument that work incentive is more enhanced by income than lack of it, see Gans (1971, p. 96).

8. One psychiatrist (Chernus 1967) has even proposed the fantastic hypothesis that the rich and the poor are engaged in a sadomasochistic relationship, the latter being supported financially by the former so that they can gratify their sadistic needs.

9. Although this is not a contemporary function of poverty in America, it should be noted that today these monuments serve to attract and gratify American tourists.

References

Chernus, J. 1967. "Cities: A Study in Sadomasochism." *Medical Opinion and Review* (May), pp. 104–9.

Erikson, K. T. 1964. "Notes on the Sociology of Deviance." In *The Other Side*, edited by Howard S. Becker. New York: Free Press.

Gans, H. J. 1971. "Three Ways to Solve the Welfare Problem." *New York Times Magazine*, March 7, pp. 26–27, 94–100.

Goode, W. J. 1967. "The Protection of the Inept." *American Sociological Review* 32 (February): 5–19.

Herriott, A., and H. P. Miller. 1971. "Who Paid the Taxes in 1968." Paper prepared for the National Industrial Conference Board.

Macarov, D. 1970. *Incentives to Work*. San Francisco: Jossey-Bass.

Marshall, T. H. Forthcoming. "Poverty and Inequality." Paper prepared for the American Academy of Arts and Sciences volume on poverty and stratification.

Merton, R. K. 1949. "Manifest and Latent Functions." In *Social Theory and Social Structure*. Glencoe, Ill.: Free Press.

———. 1961. "Social Problems and Sociological Theory." In *Contemporary Social Problems*, edited by R. K. Merton and R. Nisbet. New York: Harcourt Brace.

Pechman, J. A. 1969. "The Rich, the Poor, and the Taxes They Pay." *Public Interest*, no. 17 (Fall), pp. 21–43.

Rainwater, L. 1970. *Behind Ghetto Walls*. Chicago: Aldine.

Study Questions

1. In this theoretical article, what do the terms "function" and "dysfunction" mean?

2. Having read all the "functions of poverty," what would a society without the poor be like?

Reading 23

The American Upper Class

G. William Domhoff

Introduction

If there is an American upper class, it must exist not merely as a collection of families who feel comfortable with each other and tend to exclude outsiders from their social activities. It must exist as a set of interrelated social institutions. That is, there must be patterned ways of organizing the lives of its members from infancy to old age, and there must be mechanisms for socializing both the younger generation and new adult members who have risen from lower social levels. If the class is a reality, the names and faces may change somewhat over the years, but the social institutions that underlie the upper class must persist with remarkably little change over several generations.

The main purpose of this chapter will be to show that there is an upper class in this institutional, supraindividual sense. This will be accomplished through the presentation of historical, quantitative, questionnaire, and interview data that demonstrate the interconnections among a set of schools, clubs, resorts, and social activities that are the basis of the upper class. The chapter also will attempt through more anecdotal information to describe how these various social institutions provide members of the upper class with a distinctive life-style that sharply differentiates them from the rest of society. The second task is necessary because criteria for the existence of a social class include not only in-group social interaction but a unique style of life.

In addition, marriage patterns within the upper class and the continuity of upper-class families will be discussed, and the wealth, income, and occupations of its members will be examined. The result should be a clear picture of an interacting set of families and social cliques that possesses great wealth and makes up only 0.5 percent of the population. Finally, the chapter will present a lengthy list of indicators of upper-class standing that can be used to study the involvement of upper-class members in the corporate community, the policy planning network, and the government. . . .

Training the Young

From infancy through young adulthood, members of the upper class receive a distinctive education. This education begins early in life in preschools that frequently are attached to a neighborhood church of high social status. Schooling continues during the elementary years at a local private school called a day school. The adolescent years may see the student remain at day school, but there is a strong chance that at least one or two years will be spent away from home at a boarding school in a quiet rural setting. Higher education will be obtained at one of a small number of heavily endowed private universities. Harvard, Yale, Princeton, and Stanford head the list, followed by smaller Ivy League schools in the East and a handful of other small private schools in other parts of the country. Although some upper-class children may attend public high school if they live in a secluded suburban setting, or go to a state university if there is one of great esteem and tradition in their home state, the system of formal schooling is so insulated that many upper-class students never see the inside of a public school in all their years of education.

This separate educational system is important evidence for the distinctiveness of the mentality and life-style that exists within the upper class, for schools play a large role in transmitting the class structure to their students. Surveying and summarizing a great many studies on schools in general, sociologist Randall Collins concludes: "Schools primarily teach vocabulary and inflection, styles of dress, aesthetic tastes, values and manners."[1]

The training of upper-class children is not restricted to the formal school setting, however. Special classes and even tutors are a regular part of their extracurricular education. This informal education usually begins with dancing classes in the elementary years, which are seen as more important for learning proper manners and the social graces than for learning to dance. Tutoring in a foreign language may begin in the elementary years, and there are often lessons in horseback riding and music as well. The teen years find the children of the upper class in summer camps or on special travel tours, broadening their perspectives and polishing their social skills.

The linchpins in the upper-class educational system are the dozens of boarding schools that were developed in the last half of the nineteenth and the early part of the twentieth centuries, with the rise of a nationwide upper class whose members desired to insulate themselves from an inner city that was becoming populated by lower-class immigrants. Baltzell concludes that these schools became "surrogate families" that played a major role "in creating an upper-class subculture on almost a national scale in America."[2] The role of boarding schools in providing connections to other upper-class social institutions is also important. As one informant explained to Ostrander in her interview study of upper-class women: "Where I went to boarding school, there were girls from all over the country, so I know people from all over. It's helpful when you move to a new city and want to get invited into the local social clubs."[3]

Consciously molded after their older and more austere British counterparts, it is within these several hundred schools that a unique style of life is inculcated through such traditions as the initiatory hazing of beginning students, the wearing of school blazers or ties, compulsory attendance at chapel services, and participation in esoteric sports such as lacrosse, squash, and crew. Even a different language is adopted to distinguish these schools from public schools. The principal is a headmaster or rector, the teachers are sometimes called masters, and the students are in forms, not grades. Great emphasis is placed upon the building of "character." The role of the school in preparing the future leaders of America is emphasized through the speeches of the headmaster and the frequent mention of successful alumni.

There are some differences in emphasis and in the composition of the student body within even the most fashionable of boarding schools. Though most are socially exclusive and extremely expensive, a few have been open to minorities and have provided scholarships for low-income students. This more meritocratic emphasis has been especially the case with Phillips Exeter Academy and Phillip Academy (Andover, Massachusetts), which were founded in the late eighteenth century as academies to provide the necessary education for the rural populations in southeastern New Hampshire and northern Massachusetts. They became boarding schools with a focus on college preparatory courses in the first years of the twentieth century but maintained a concern for a less structured social atmosphere and a wider range of students.[4] . . .

Whatever university upper-class students attend, they tend to socialize together as members of a small number of fraternities, sororities, eating clubs, and secret societies, perpetuating to some extent the separate existence of a day or boarding school. As sociologist C. Wright Mills explained, it is not merely a matter of going to a Harvard or a Yale but to the right Harvard or Yale:

> That is why in the upper social classes, it does not by itself mean much merely to have a degree from an Ivy League college. That is assumed: the point is not Harvard, but which Harvard? By Harvard, one means Porcellian, Fly, or A.D.: by Yale, one means Zeta Psi or Fence or Delta Kappa Epsilon: by Princeton, Cottage, Tifer, Cap and Gown or Ivy.[5]

From kindergarten through college, then, schooling is very different for members of the upper class from what it is for most Americans, and it teaches them to be distinctive in many ways. In a country where education is highly valued and the overwhelming majority attend public schools, less than one student in a hundred is part of this private system that primarily benefits members of the upper class and provides one of the foundations for the old-boy and old-girl networks that will be with them throughout their lives.

Social Clubs

Just as private schools are a pervasive feature in the lives of upper-class children, so, too, are private social clubs a major point of orientation in the lives of upper-class adults. These clubs also play a role in differentiating members of the upper class from other members of society. According to Baltzell, "the club serves to place the adult members of society and their families within the social hierarchy." He quotes with approval the suggestion by historian Crane Brinton that the club "may perhaps be regarded as taking the place of those extensions of the family, such as the clan and the brotherhood, which have disappeared from advanced societies."[6] Conclusions similar to Baltzell's resulted from an interview study in Kansas City: "Ultimately, say upper-class Kansas Citians, social standing in their world reduces to one issue: where does an individual or family rank on the scale of private club memberships and informal cliques."[7]

The clubs of the upper class are many and varied, ranging from family-oriented country clubs and downtown men's and women's clubs to highly specialized clubs for yachtsmen, sportsmen, gardening enthusiasts, and fox hunters. Many families have memberships in several different types of clubs, but the days when most of the men by themselves were in a half dozen or more clubs faded before World War II. Downtown men's clubs originally were places for having lunch and dinner, and occasionally for attending an evening performance or a weekend party. But as upper-class families deserted the city for large suburban estates, a new kind of club, the country club, gradually took over some of these functions. The downtown club became almost entirely a luncheon club, a site to hold meetings, or a place to relax on a free afternoon. The country club, by contrast, became a haven for all members of the family. It offered social and sporting activities ranging from dances, parties, and banquets to golf, swimming, and tennis. Special group dinners were often arranged for all members on Thursday night, the traditional maid's night off across the United States.

Although males were the first to found formal clubs within the upper class, a parallel set of women's clubs followed closely behind. In most major cities there is at least one women's club that is similar in structure and function to the metropolitan men's clubs. Garden clubs were also formed in many of these cities. They are the major specialty clubs exclusively for women.

Sporting activities are the basis for most of the specialized clubs of the upper class. The most visible are the yachting and sailing clubs, followed by the clubs for lawn tennis or squash. The most exotic are the several dozen fox hunting clubs. They have their primary strongholds in rolling countrysides from southern Pennsylvania down into Virginia, but they exist in other parts of the country as well. Riding to hounds in pink jackets and black boots, members of the upper class sustain over 130 hunts under the banner of the Masters of Fox Hounds Association. The intricate rituals and grand feasts accompanying the event go back to the eighteenth century in the United States, including the Blessing of the Hounds by an Episcopal bishop in the eastern hunts.[8] . . .

The Debutante Season

The debutante season is a series of parties, teas, and dances, culminating in one or more grand balls. It announces the arrival of young women of the upper class into adult society with the utmost of formality and elegance. These highly expensive rituals, in which great attention is lavished on every detail of the food, decorations, and entertainment, have a long history in the upper class. Making their appearance in Philadelphia in 1748 and Charleston, South Carolina, in 1762, they vary only slightly from city to city across the country. They are a central focus of the Christmas social season just about everywhere, but in some cities debutante balls are held in the spring as well.

Dozens of people are involved in planning the private parties that most debutantes have before the grand ball. Parents, with the help of upper-class women who work as social secretaries and social consultants, spend many hours with dress designers, caterers, florists, decorators, band leaders, and champagne importers, deciding on just the right motif for their daughter's coming out. Most parties probably do not cost more than $15,000 to $25,000, but sometimes the occasion is made so extraordinary that it draws newspaper attention. In 1959 Henry Ford II spent $250,000 on a debutante party for one of his daughters, hiring a Paris designer to redo the Country Club of Detroit in an eighteenth-century chateau motif and flying in 2 million magnolia boughs from Mississippi to cover the walls of the corridor leading to the reception room. In 1965 a Texas oil and real estate family chartered a Braniff jet for a party that began in Dallas and ended with an all-night visit to the clubs in the French Quarter of New Orleans.[9]

The debutante balls themselves are usually sponsored by local social clubs. Sometimes there is an organization whose primary purpose is the selection of debutantes and the staging of the ball, such as the Saint Cecilia Society in Charleston, South Carolina, and the Allegro Club in Houston, Texas. Adding to the solemnity of the occasion, the selection of the season's debutantes is often made by the most prominent and visible upper-class males in the city, often through such secret societies as the Veiled Prophet in Saint Louis or the Mardi Gras Krewes in New Orleans. . . .

Marriage and Family Continuity

The institution of marriage is as important in the upper class as it is in any level of America society, and it does not differ greatly from other levels in its patterns and rituals. Only the exclusive site of the occasion and the lavishness of the reception distinguish upper-class marriages.

The prevailing wisdom within the upper class is that children should marry someone of their own social class. The women interviewed by Ostrander, for example, felt that marriage was difficult enough without differences in "interests" and "background," which seemed to be the code words for class in discussions of marriage. Marriages outside the class were seen as likely to end in divorce.[10]

The original purpose of the debutante season was to introduce the highly sheltered young women of the upper class to eligible marriage partners. It was an attempt to corral what Baltzell calls "the democratic whims of romantic love," which "often play havoc with class solidarity."[11] But the day when the debut could play such a role was long past even by the 1940s. The function of directing romantic love into acceptable channels was taken over by fraternities and sororities, bachelor and spinster clubs, and exclusive summer resorts. . . .

Tracing the families of the steel executives into the twentieth century, Ingham determined that they were listed in the *Social Register*, were members of the most exclusive social clubs, lived in elite neighborhoods, and sent their children to Ivy League universities. He concludes that "there has been more continuity than change among the business elites and upper classes in America," and he contrasts his results with the claims made by several generations of impressionistic historians that there has been a decline of aristocracy, the rise of a new plutocracy, or a passing of the old order.[12]

It seems likely, then, that the American upper class is a mixture of old and new members. There is both continuity and social mobility, with the newer members being assimilated into the life-style of the class through participation in the schools, clubs, and other social institutions described in this chapter. There may be some tensions between those newly arrived and those of established status, as novelists and journalists love to point out, but what they have in common soon outweighs their differences. This point is well demonstrated in the social affiliations and attitudes of highly successful Jewish businessmen, who become part of the upper class as they rise in the corporate community.[13]

The Preoccupations of the Upper Class

Members of the upper class do not spend all their time in social activities. Contrary to stereotypes, most members of the upper class are and have been hardworking people, even at the richest levels. In a study of the 90 richest men for 1950, for example, Mills found that only 26 percent were men of leisure.[14]

By far the most frequent preoccupation of men of the upper class is business and finance. This point is most clearly demonstrated through studying the occupations of boarding school alumni. A classification of the occupations of a sample of the graduates of four private schools—Saint Mark's, Groton, Hotchkiss, and Andover—for the years 1906 and 1926 showed that the most frequent occupation for all but the Andover graduates was some facet of finance and banking. Others became presidents of medium-size businesses or practiced corporation law with a large firm. Only a small handful went to work as executives for major national corporations. Andover, with a more open curriculum and a far greater number of scholarship students at the time, produced many more people who ended up in middle management, particularly in 1926, when 44 percent of the graduates were in such positions. The second area of concentration for the Andover alumni was as owners or presidents of medium-size businesses. Only 8 percent went into banking and finance, and only 4 percent into law.[15]

The business-oriented preoccupations of upper-class men is demonstrated in greater detail in a study of the careers of all those who graduated from Hotchkiss between 1940 and 1950. Using the school's alumni files, one researcher followed the careers of 228 graduates from their date of graduation until 1970. Fifty-six percent of the sample were either bankers or business executives, with 80 of the 91 businessmen serving as president, vice-president, or partner in their firms. Another 10 percent of the sample were lawyers, mostly as partners in large firms closely affiliated with the business community. Outside the world of business, the most frequent occupations of the remaining one third of the Hotchkiss graduates studied were physician (7 percent), engineer (6 percent), and public official (3 percent).[16]

Although finance, business, and law are the most typical occupations of upper-class males, there is no absence of physicians, architects, museum officials, and other professional occupations. This fact was demonstrated most systematically in Baltzell's study of the Philadelphians listed in *Who's Who in America* for 1940; 39 percent of the Philadelphia architects and physicians listed in *Who's Who* for that year were also listed in the *Social Register*, as were 35 percent of the museum officials. These figures are close to the 51 percent for lawyers and the 42 percent for businessmen, although they are far below the 75 percent for bankers, clearly the most elite profession in Philadelphia at that time.[17] . . .

The Wealth and Income of the Upper Class

Whatever the precise occupations and preoccupations of specific members of the upper class, it is obvious that members of the upper class must have a considerable amount of money to afford the tuition at private schools, the fees at country clubs, and the very high expenses of an elegant social life. Just how much they have, however, is a difficult matter to determine, for the Internal Revenue Service does not release information on individuals and most people are not willing to volunteer details on this subject.

Direct questions about a person's money are frowned upon in America, even in the upper class. One young member of the upper class in Boston told an interviewer: "Money was never talked about. I still don't know how much the family is worth. I have no idea."[18] Nor are the adult members of the upper class likely to talk about their wealth or the distribution of wealth in general. After presenting figures on the wealth distribution, an upper-class society writer notes that "I have never heard a dinner conversation in which figures such as these have been discussed."[19] Instead, she reports, any conversation concerning money is more likely to concern the outrageous starting salaries of subway drivers, policemen, and other working people. Even people with millions of dollars are likely to deny they are rich if they are asked directly. This reaction is in part genuine, for they always know someone else who has much more money and makes them feel poor by comparison. This phenomenon is well known to social psychologists from studies of other social comparisons.

In considering the distribution of wealth and income in the United States, it must be stressed that the two distributions are different matters. The wealth distribution has to do with the concentration of ownership of marketable assets, which may include "such tangible things as land, buildings, machinery, raw materials, goods in process, and animals, and such intangible things as franchises, patent rights, copyrights, and good will."[20] The income distribution, on the other hand, has to do with the percentage of wages, dividends, interest, and rents paid out each year to individuals or families at various income levels. In theory, those who own a great deal may or may not have high incomes, depending on the returns they receive from their wealth, but in reality those at the very top of the wealth distribution also tend to have the highest incomes, mostly from dividends and interest. . . .

Conclusion

The evidence in this chapter suggests that there is an interacting and intermarrying upper social stratum or social elite in America that is distinctive enough in its institutions, source and amount of income, and life-style to be called an "upper class." This upper class makes up about 0.5 percent of the population, a rough estimate that is based upon the number of students attending independent private schools, the number of listings in past *Social Registers* for several cities, and detailed interview studies in Kansas City and Boston.[21]

Not everyone in this nationwide upper class knows everyone else, but everybody knows somebody who knows someone in other areas of the country thanks to a common school experience, a summer at the same resort, or membership in the same social club. With the social institutions described in this chapter as the undergirding, the upper class at any given historical moment consists of a complex network of overlapping social circles that are knit together by the members they have in common and by the numerous signs of equal social status that emerge from a similar life-style. Viewed from the standpoint of social psychology, the upper class is made up of innumerable face-to-face small groups that are constantly changing in their composition as people move from one social setting to another.

Research work in both sociology and social psychology demonstrates that constant interaction in small-group settings leads to the social cohesion that is considered to be an important dimension of a social class.[22] This social cohesion does not in and of itself demonstrate that members of the upper class are able to agree among themselves on general issues of economic and government policy. But it is important to stress that social cohesion is one of the factors that makes it possible for policy coordination to develop. Indeed, research in social psychology demonstrates that members of socially cohesive groups are eager to reach agreement on issues of common concern to them. They are more receptive to what other members are saying, more likely to trust each other, and more willing to compromise, which are no small matters in any collection of human beings trying to get something accomplished.[23]. . .

In sociological terms, the upper class comes to serve as a "reference group." Sociologist Harold Hodges, in a discussion of his findings concerning social classes in the suburban areas south of San Francisco, expresses the power of the upper class as a reference group in the following way: "Numerically insignificant—less than one in every 500 Peninsula families is listed in the pages of the *Social Register*—the upper class is nonetheless highly influential as a 'reference group': a membership to which many aspire and which infinitely more consciously or unconsciously imitate."[24]

Exhibiting high social status, in other words, is a way of exercising power. It is a form of power rooted in fascination and enchantment. It operates by creating respect, envy, and deference in others. Considered less important than force or economic power by social scientists who regard themselves as tough-minded and realistic, its role as a method of control in modern society goes relatively unnoticed despite the fact that power was originally in the domain of the sacred and the magical.[25]

Whatever the importance that is attached to prestige and social status as mechanisms of power, this chapter has demonstrated the power of the upper class through the disproportionate amount of wealth and income that its members possess. As argued in the previous chapter, such disparities are evidence for class power if it is assumed that wealth and income are highly valued in American society. However, the case for the hypothesis that the American upper class is a ruling class will not rest solely on reference group power and inequalities in the wealth and income distributions. The following chapters will present other types of evidence for the power of this small tip of the social hierarchy.

Notes

1. Randall Collins, "Functional and Conflict Theories of Educational Stratification," *American Sociological Review* 36 (1971), p. 1010.
2. E. Digby Baltzell, *Philadelphia Gentlemen: The Making of a National Upper Class* (Glencoe, Ill.: Free Press, 1958), p. 339.
3. Susan Ostrander, "A Study of Upper Class Women" (book manuscript to be published by Temple University Press, 1984), p. 174.
4. Steven B. Levine, "The Rise of the American Boarding Schools" (senior honors thesis, Harvard University, 1978), pp. 5–6.
5. C. Wright Mills, *The Power Elite* (New York: Oxford University Press, 1956), p. 67.
6. Baltzell, *Philadelphia Gentlemen*, p. 373.
7. Richard P. Coleman and Lee Rainwater, *Social Standing in America* (New York: Basic Books, 1978), p. 144.
8. Sophy Burnham, *The Landed Gentry* (New York: G. P. Putnam's Sons, 1978).
9. Gay Pauley, "Coming-out Party: It's Back in Style," *Los Angeles Times*, March 13, 1977, section 4, p. 22; "Debs Put Party on Jet," *San Francisco Chronicle*, December 18, 1965, p. 2.

10. Ostrander, "A Study of Upper Class Women," p. 169.
11. Baltzell, *Philadelphia Gentlemen*, p. 26.
12. John Ingham, *The Iron Barons* (Westport, Conn.: Greenwood Press, 1978), pp. 230–231.
13. Richard L. Zweigenhaft and G. William Domhoff, *Jews in the Protestant Establishment* (New York: Praeger, 1982).
14. Mills, *Power Elite*, p. 108.
15. Levine, "Rise of the American Boarding Schools," pp. 128–130.
16. Christopher F. Armstrong, "Privilege and Productivity: The Cases of Two Private Schools and Their Graduates" (Ph.D. diss., University of Pennsylvania, 1974), pp. 162–163. (The second school in Armstrong's study was Putney, a much newer, smaller, and more liberal school in Vermont.)
17. Baltzell, *Philadelphia Gentlemen*, pp. 51–65.
18. Gary Tamkins, "Being Special: A Study of the Upper Class" (Ph.D. diss., Northwestern University, 1974), p. 60.
19. Burnham, *Landed Gentry*, p. 205.
20. Robert Lampman, *The Share of Top Wealth-Holders in National Wealth* (Princeton, NJ: Princeton University Press, 1962), p. 2.
21. Domhoff, *Who Rules America?* pp. 7n–8n; "Private Schools Search for a New Social Role," *National Observer*, August 26, 1968, p. 5; Coleman and Rainwater, *Social Standing in America*, p. 148. For a summary of many studies that concludes that "Capital S Society" in the United States includes "probably no more than four-tenths of one percent in large cities, and even a smaller proportion in smaller communities," see Coleman and Neugarten, *Social Status in the City*, p. 270.
22. Domhoff, *Bohemian Grove*, pp. 89–90, for a summary of this research.
23. Dorwin Cartwright and Alvin Zander, *Group Dynamics* (New York: Harper & Row, 1960), p. 89; Albert J. Lott and Bernice E. Lott, "Group Cohesiveness as Interpersonal Attraction," *Psychological Bulletin* 64 (1965): 291–296; Michael Argyle, *Social Interaction* (Chicago: Aldine, 1969), pp. 220–223.
24. Harold M. Hodges, Jr., "Peninsula People: Social Stratification in a Metropolitan Complex," in *Education and Society*, ed. Warren Kallenbach and Harold M. Hodges, Jr. (Columbus, Ohio: Merrill, 1963), p. 414.
25. See Norman O. Brown, *Life Against Death* (London: Routledge & Kegan Paul, 1959), pp. 242, 249–252, for a breathtaking argument on the roots of power in the sacred and the psychological. For one attempt to apply the argument to the class structure, see G. William Domhoff, "Historical Materialism, Cultural Determinism, and the Origin of the Ruling Classes," *Psychoanalytical Review*, no. 2 (1969). For a discussion that rightly announces itself as "the first extensive treatise on prestige as a social control system," see William J. Goode, *The Celebration of Heroes: Prestige as a Social Control System* (Berkeley, Calif.: University of California Press, 1978).

Study Questions

1. What institutions create and maintain the upper class in Domhoff's study?

2. As discussed in this selection, what is the relationship between upper-class status and power?

Reading 24

Blue-Collar Journal
A College President's Sabbatical

John R. Coleman

In the spring of 1973, I took a leave from my job as a college president. There were no strings attached. I could do whatever I chose for months on end. I had secretly known what I wanted to do if ever such a chance came along; now I had to discover whether I was serious about it.

What I wanted to do was to try my hand at manual work, for reasons more complex than I pretend to understand. I only know that, every time in recent years when I looked ahead to some time out, my thoughts turned to seeking and holding blue-collar jobs. The idea of breaking out of what I normally do and of taking up different roles for a while was so compelling that I would have felt cheated had I done anything less.

This is a record of what I did once I pulled out of the driveway of my house. The journal covers eight weeks. It omits the first week when I worked with friends of thirty years' standing, Pat and Russell Best, on their dairy farm in Ontario. That week conditioned me for physical work; thirteen hours a day in a milk shed, cow barns, and the woods have that effect. It omits the last weeks of my leave when I fulfilled a quite different dream by spending a week in Florence and a night each at Vienna's Staatsoper and at Milan's La Scala.

From the start I realized how fortunate I was in being able to get away at all, and in being able to leave without telling anyone where I was going or what I planned to do. I am divorced. I consider my children old enough and independent enough—and they consider me so—that I can disappear for some time without their having to worry about me. The college board of trustees and my administrative colleagues were trusting enough not to push me with questions about how I proposed to use the time out. And I had a paycheck going into the bank each month to meet the tuition, insurance, utility, and tax bills that found their way to the house, however far away I might be.

I did not tell anyone about what I planned to do with my sabbatical because I was afraid the response would be what part of me also said: "Jack, that's crazy." No reply to that charge would sound convincing, and I felt that my orthodoxy and my quest for respectability would take over at that point. I would probably end up using my leave to do some sort of survey of recent developments in liberal arts education, and it would no doubt be published somewhere through the help of friends in editorial posts. But it wouldn't be worth much because I'm not an original thinker on that subject. All in all, I thought, it was better to keep to myself the urge to reenter the blue-collar world for the first time since 1945. Let me see if I am willing to go where I want to go. And then let me see if I can explain it afterward. . . .

Friday, February 16, 1973   *Atlanta, Georgia*

The drive from Philadelphia to Atlanta seemed long, no matter how good the road was. I hadn't counted on Georgia's being so far from home. I was keyed up, and the miles went by as slowly as they did for my children years ago on our vacations, when, one hour after we started the all-day drive to Maine, they asked, "Are we almost there?"

The sky was still dark when I pulled out of the driveway of my campus home this morning. Even in dim light, the big old house looked inviting. I knew that I would miss its comfort and space—the books and records in the library downstairs, the paintings in the living room, the kitchen where it is fun both to cook and to talk, and the big cluttered desk in the study upstairs.

In addition to the car, I brought two hundred dollars in travelers checks with me and a gasoline credit card. The checks were to tide me over until I got a paycheck. The credit card was to let me get home even if I ran out of money for food and lodging. I had a duffel bag full of clothes, a few kitchen supplies, a box of books, a portable radio, and my camera. I also brought my social security card—I had already decided to use my own name—but nothing else. The rest of my past had to stay home. I would invent an earlier work history as I went along.

The strongest feeling today was one of freedom. Just how much freedom there was became clear as soon as I reached the main road running past the campus. I could head in any direction I chose. I stayed with my original plan and headed south, but I felt freed just in knowing that I could have changed my mind on the spot. . . .

It was 6:00 in the evening when I got into Atlanta, and time to eat. I passed up the restaurants I would ordinarily have sought out and headed for a diner on the outskirts of the downtown area. There was a copy of the morning's *Atlanta Journal* still on sale. I skipped the front pages and turned to the classified ads. The Help Wanted columns didn't look as promising as they had last month, particularly for outdoor work.

The only choices appeared to be yardman, construction worker, or general laborer. Yardman was a risky job; the weather was cold for Atlanta (18°) and work could be spotty. Just a few days of bad weather and I'd have trouble supporting myself on my earnings. Most building construction ads called for experience; I thought it would probably be better if I toughened up elsewhere before I tried to make out in that league. That left the simple classification of "laborer."

Four ads were similar. Someone was paying a lot to get clean water into, and dirty water out of, the Atlanta area. This one stood out:

"Laborers. Sewer and water line construction. Transportation furnished. Call MU 2-0736 after 7 p.m."

It was those words "after 7 P.M." that caught my eye. I had expected to use the night to build up my courage to start making calls at dawn. But here was a chance to get hired right now. Seven o'clock was drawing near; it was time to act.

I finished my hamburger and went to the telephone booth outside. I walked up and down with a dime in my hand for some time. In part, I was nervous about the work; in part, I wanted to avoid seeming too anxious by calling too soon. It was 7:05 when I dialed.

A male voice answered.

"Hello. My name is John Coleman. I'm calling about your ad for sewer laborers. Could you tell me about the job?"

"I start them at two-seventy-five an hour."

That was that. Obviously I needed more questions.

"What's the work like?"

"At this time of year it's dirty, and sloppy, and wet, and cold. It's a lousy job any way you look at it. Are you interested?"

"Yes. I'd like to try."

"What kind of work have you been doin'?"

"I've just come here from Pennsylvania. I used to be in sales. [That was true for a college president by a small stretch of the imagination.] But I got tired of it. [That would surely be true if the first statement were literally true.] So I've been working as a laborer for a while. [Completely false, except for that warm-up week on the dairy farm.]"

"Well, like I say, I start you at two-seventy-five. If you're any good, I'll move you ahead. Some of my men get three-and-a-half. Some get four."

"Do you want to meet me before you hire me?"

"No. Just come ready for work. Dress warmly. We'll supply boots when you get wet work."

"Is it a hard-hat job?"

"It's supposed to be. But I've stopped givin' them out. The men won't wear them, even though it's for their own good."

He gave me detailed instructions on how to find the job site and told me to be ready for work at 7:30 on Monday. I asked if I could start tomorrow.

"All right, if you need the money."

"I'll be there at seven-thirty. What's your name?"

"Gus Reed. R-E-E-D."

"Thank you, Mr. Reed."

That was all. I felt relieved at being hired on my first try—and without even being asked my age.

Saturday, February 17

I didn't sleep very well—partly from excitement, partly from doubts about whether I could do the day's work at 51. . . .

It was 5:45 this morning when I came down to check out at the motel desk. . . .

"Going to work?" he asked. I decided I had passed the appearance test.
"Yes."

"What do you do?"

"I'm starting today with a sewer company."

"On a cold morning like this?"

"Yes."

"You poor shit!"

It occurred to me that he could be right. . . .

There were orders to each man to start on a specified task. It was 7:50 before Gus turned to me. "Get a shovel out of the trailer and get in that ditch. Just follow the backhoe along and throw all the shit that it misses up on the bank.". . .

Gus was rather easy on me. He pointed to where the jackhammers had ripped up a road which the sewer line was to cross. The curbs on both sides of the road were left intact.

"John, take your time but shovel out that shit from under the curbs. Tunnel through from both sides so that we save the curbs."

No problem, I thought. But the six-foot-thick walls of clay there were packed hard. Sometimes I shoveled from a stooped position. Sometimes I had to kneel in the mud to get further under the curb. Either way the shovel hit the same unyielding clay with a thud. Only a small amount of dirt fell away with each try. . . .

With the tunnels under the curb done, the long ditch stretched out before me. It might not have seemed so long from the street level, and certainly wouldn't be long to anyone whizzing by in a car, but the view from the trench was of banks of mud that stretched on and on. The backhoe had moved rapidly while I was digging away at the packed clay. How many thousand shovel loads of loose dirt had it left behind for me? And would I ever catch up to that machine again?

In the work I do as college president, there are only two tasks that require doing the same thing over and over again for any sustained period of time. One is shaking hands at commencement and parents' day (a happy task); the other is signing thank-you notes to alumni contributors (a very happy task). But both the lines of people waiting to be greeted and the pile of notes waiting to be signed have definite ending points: I know when I'll be done with them. The ditch today didn't seem to have an end. As fast as I cleaned up one foot of it, the backhoe made at least one more foot of it ahead. . . .

It was 6:00 when Gus called it a day.

"John, go in that truck with all that equipment. You might as well learn where all that shit goes at night."

Everything had a neat place in the trailer. There was no way of making a mistake in stowing it for the night.

Gus and Stanley were talking down the road at some length. Or rather Gus was talking. Only the four-letter words and the strong gestures carried as far as the trailer.

At last Gus came to me. "See you Monday. This wasn't our usual work. We don't often lay lines along the highway. Usually we're over in the swampy stuff. Someday soon you'll be up to your ass in mud. Seven-thirty Monday."

I took off my coveralls before I got in my car. They were muddy enough for one clean day. . . .

I had no zest for looking for a place for the night. I had read rooming-house ads in yesterday's paper, but they were all downtown. I'm lazy enough to prefer living near the job; more than five years of stepping out of the door of a fine old home and crossing two small fields beneath the trees on the way to my office have spoiled me for commuting. I had no idea tonight where rooms could be found in the suburbs, and I was too weary to try to find out.

I remembered passing a motel this morning that advertised rooms for "$8 a day." Compared with the prices I usually paid, that seemed a steal. It was only after I registered that I realized eight dollars represented almost three hours of labor today. But at least I could now have a bath, eat, and get into bed. . . .

Sunday, April 15

These days are done. I suppose I should have unmixed emotions about going home, but I don't. No matter how restless I am to get back to my desk, I know too that some day I'll want to do again just what I've done this spring—or perhaps move to fulfill some other half-formed dream. Whatever comes, I expect to do a better job at home because I got away.

The Hasidic rabbi Zusia said, "When I shall face the celestial tribunal, I shall not be asked why I was not Abraham, Jacob, or Moses. I shall be asked why I was not Zusia."

Once, I thought I was leaving my identity behind when I set out on this leave. Now I think I may even have found some part of it along the way.

Study Questions

1. Coleman has some major adjustments to make to his new blue-collar status. What were his most difficult accommodations?
2. Which would be easier, the downward mobility of Coleman or the upward mobility of "working-class" sociologists? Give some specific reasons for your answer.

Topic 9
Race and Ethnicity

It is projected that the combined population of U.S. minority groups will outnumber whites in the next 50 years. Many rural and urban environments are already finding diversity in similar proportions. As a nation of immigrants (except for a small proportion of Native Americans), we will soon find whites, officially "white, non-Hispanics," in the numerical minority. America is very diverse, and diversity issues abound in both the structural and personal senses. How many of us understand the effects of institutionalized racism? How many of us possess the "cultural competence" to feel at ease with persons of different racial and ethnic groups?

American history is filled with examples of racial and ethnic discrimination: slavery, "separate but equal" as an educational plan struck down by *Brown vs. Topeka*, legal discrimination against members of minority groups, under-employment and under-payment of ethnic group members, the use of illegal aliens to work crops in the U.S. southwest, and many others. The ill-treatment of groups based on race or ethnicity is prevented by law in this country, and yet it persists. The formal and informal aspects of social discrimination cannot be overcome by law or in a short period of time. Persons of color have made great strides since the legal barriers were removed, but there are many more marches and many more battles to fight before full equality is achieved. Poverty, unemployment, health, and education are not equally available to all persons in the United States, and "equal" appears to be as much an ideal as a reality for minorities.

Prejudice (an attitude) and discrimination (a behavior) exist on the world stage as well as in the United States. Anti-Semitism directed against the Jews in Eastern Europe during the Third Reich in Germany accounted for six million deaths in concentration camps. More recently, we have seen "ethnic cleansing" as an outgrowth of conflicts in several parts of the world. Genocide, the extermination of an entire race or group, may seem impossible in the twenty-first century, but history would suggest otherwise. The United States, Yugoslavia, and Rwanda remind us of these possibilities. Some are quite recent.

Segregation of minorities is part of the U.S. past and present. Although we know that contact between different racial groups decreases prejudice, separation of these groups from one another and from white society persists. Busing began in the 1960s but has not solved the problem. Our communities and neighborhoods are defined by homogeneous groupings and represent both ethnic and class lines of distinction. Churches, business, and services are often tied to racial and ethnic groups with few who will cross the lines. Will we welcome different groups to our schools and our neighborhoods? Will we lead the way to cross the color lines and create dialogue between distant groups? It is easy to deny the reality of racism and discrimination when our own lives do not intersect with those who suffer the indignities each day.

The articles in Topic 9: Race and Ethnicity are presented to capture some of the diversity of American life. First, Cornel West shows a most worrisome picture of race in the current U.S. scene. Foment rests just beneath the surface and manifests in violent and predictable ways. Indeed, "race matters" in America. Second, Celia Falicov illustrates the strengths of Latino immigrant families as they leave one world behind and enter another. The research is a testimony to the courage of these families. Finally, Erika and Jay Voras's article enlists the help of a black church to work with students from a college as a way to create contact and reduce prejudice. This experiential approach actively teaches a lesson to all concerned and reminds us of the importance of personal connections in building bridges toward a future of cross-race understanding.

Reading 25
Race Matters

Cornel West

What happened in Los Angeles in April of 1992 was neither a race riot nor a class rebellion. Rather, this monumental upheaval was a multiracial, trans-class, and largely male display of justified social rage. For all its ugly, xenophobic resentment, its air of adolescent carnival, and its downright barbaric behavior, it signified the sense of powerlessness in American society. Glib attempts to reduce its meaning to the pathologies of the black underclass, the criminal actions of hoodlums, or the political revolt of the oppressed urban masses miss the mark. Of those arrested, only 36 percent were black, more than a third had full-time jobs, and most claimed to shun political affiliation. What we witnessed in Los Angeles was the consequence of a lethal linkage of economic decline, cultural decay, and political lethargy in American life. Race was the visible catalyst, not the underlying cause.

The meaning of the earthshaking events in Los Angeles is difficult to grasp because most of us remain trapped in the narrow framework of the dominant liberal and conservative views of race in America, which with its worn-out vocabulary leaves us intellectually debilitated, morally disempowered, and personally depressed. The astonishing disappearance of the event from public dialogue is testimony to just how painful and distressing a serious engagement with race is. Our truncated public discussions of race suppress the best of who and what we are as a people because they fail to confront the complexity of the issue in a candid and critical manner. The predictable pitting of liberals against conservatives, Great Society Democrats against self-help Republicans, reinforces intellectual parochialism and political paralysis.

The liberal notion that more government programs can solve racial problems is simplistic—precisely because it focuses *solely* on the economic dimension. And the conservative idea that what is needed is a change in the moral behavior of poor black urban dwellers (especially poor black men, who, they say, should stay married, support their children, and stop committing so much crime) highlights immoral actions while ignoring public responsibility for the immoral circumstances that haunt our fellow citizens.

The common denominator of these views of race is that each still sees black people as a "problem people," in the words of Dorothy I. Height, president of the National Council of Negro Women, rather than as fellow American citizens with problems. Her words echo the poignant "unasked question" of W. E. B. Du Bois, who, in *The Souls of Black Folk* (1903), wrote:

> They approach me in a half-hesitant sort of way, eye me curiously or compassionately, and then instead of saying directly, How does it feel to be a problem? they say, I know an excellent colored man in my town. . . . Do not these Southern outrages make your blood boil? At these I smile, or am interested, or reduce the boiling to a simmer, as the occasion may require. To the real question, How does it feel to be a problem? I answer seldom a word.

Nearly a century later, we confine discussions about race in America to the "problems" black people pose for whites rather than consider what this way of viewing black people reveals about us as a nation.

This paralyzing framework encourages liberals to relieve their guilty consciences by supporting public funds directed at "the problems"; but at the same time, reluctant to exercise principled criticism of black people, liberals deny them the freedom to err. Similarly, conservatives blame the "problems" on black people themselves—and thereby render black social misery invisible or unworthy of public attention.

Hence, for liberals, black people are to be "included" and "integrated" into "our" society and culture, while for conservatives they are to be "well behaved" and "worthy of acceptance" by "our" way of life. Both fail to see that the presence and predicaments of black people are neither additions to nor defections from American life, but rather *constitutive elements of that life.*

To engage in a serious discussion of race in America, we must begin not with the problems of black people but with the flaws of American society— flaws rooted in historic inequalities and longstanding cultural stereotypes. How we set up the terms for discussing racial issues shapes our perception and response to these issues. As long as black people are viewed as a "them," the burden falls on blacks to do all the "cultural" and "moral" work necessary for healthy race relations. The implication is that only certain Americans can define what it means to be American—and the rest must simply "fit in."

The emergence of strong black-nationalist sentiments among blacks, especially among young people, is a revolt against this sense of having to "fit in." The variety of black-nationalist ideologies, from the moderate views of Supreme Court Justice Clarence Thomas in his youth to those of Louis Farrakhan today, rest upon a fundamental truth: white America has been historically weak-willed in ensuring racial justice and has continued to resist fully accepting the humanity of blacks. As long as double standards and differential treatment abound—as long as the rap performer Ice-T is harshly condemned while former Los Angeles Police Chief Daryl F. Gates's antiblack comments are received in polite silence, as long as Dr. Leonard Jeffries's anti-Semitic statements are met with vitriolic outrage while presidential candidate Patrick J. Buchanan's anti-Semitism receives a genteel response—black nationalisms will thrive.

Afrocentrism, a contemporary species of black nationalism, is a gallant yet misguided attempt to define an African identity in a white society perceived to be hostile. It is gallant because it puts black doings and sufferings, not white anxieties and fears, at the center of discussion. It is misguided because—out of fear of cultural hybridization and through silence on the issue of class, retrograde views on black women, gay men, and lesbians, and a reluctance to link race to the common good—it reinforces the narrow discussions about race.

To establish a new framework, we need to begin with a frank acknowledgment of the basic humanness and Americanness of each of us. And we must acknowledge that as a people—*E Pluribus Unum*—we are on a slippery slope toward economic strife, social turmoil, and cultural chaos. If we go down, we go down together. The Los Angeles upheaval forced us to see not only that we are not connected in ways we would like to be but also, in a more profound sense, that this failure to connect binds us even more tightly together. The paradox of race in America is that our common destiny is more pronounced and imperiled precisely when our divisions are deeper. The Civil War and its legacy speak loudly here. And our divisions are growing deeper. Today, eighty-six percent of white suburban Americans live in neighborhoods that are less than 1 percent black, meaning that the prospects for the country depend largely on how its cities fare in the hands of a suburban electorate. There is no escape from our interracial interdependence, yet enforced racial hierarchy dooms us as a nation to collective paranoia and hysteria—the unmaking of any democratic order.

The verdict in the Rodney King case which sparked the incidents in Los Angeles was perceived to be wrong by the vast majority of Americans. But whites have often failed to acknowledge the widespread mistreatment of black people, especially black men, by law enforcement agencies, which helped ignite the spark. The verdict was merely the occasion for deep-seated rage to come to the surface. This rage is fed by the "silent" depression ravaging the country—in which real weekly wages of all American workers since 1973 have declined nearly 20 percent, while at the same time wealth has been upwardly distributed.

The exodus of stable industrial jobs from urban centers to cheaper labor markets here and abroad, housing policies that have created "chocolate cities and vanilla suburbs" (to use the popular musical artist George Clinton's memorable phrase), white fear of black crime, and the urban influx of poor Spanish-speaking and Asian immigrants—all have helped erode the tax base of American cities just as the federal government has cut its supports and programs. The result is unemployment, hunger, homelessness, and sickness for millions.

And a pervasive spiritual impoverishment grows. The collapse of meaning in life—the eclipse of hope and absence of love of self and others, the breakdown of family and neighborhood bonds—leads to the social deracination and cultural denudement of urban dwellers, especially children. We have created rootless, dangling people with little link to the supportive networks—family, friends, school—that sustain some sense of purpose in life. We have witnessed the collapse of the spiritual communities that in the past helped Americans face despair, disease, and death and that transmit through the generations dignity and decency, excellence and elegance.

The result is lives of what we might call "random nows," of fortuitous and fleeting moments preoccupied with "getting over"—with acquiring pleasure, property, and power by any means necessary. (This is not what Malcolm X meant by this famous phrase.) Post-modern culture is more and more a market culture dominated by gangster mentalities and self-destructive wantonness. This culture engulfs all of us—yet its impact on the disadvantaged is devastating, resulting in extreme violence in everyday life. Sexual violence against women and homicidal assaults by young black men on one another are only the most obvious signs of this empty quest for pleasure, property, and power.

Last, this rage is fueled by a political atmosphere in which images, not ideas, dominate, where politicians spend more time raising money than debating issues. The functions of parties have been displaced by public polls, and politicians behave less as thermostats that determine the climate of opinion than as thermometers registering the public mood. American politics has been rocked by an unleashing of greed among opportunistic public officials—who have followed the lead of their counterparts in the private sphere, where, as of 1989, 1 percent of the population owned 37 percent of the wealth and 10 percent of the population owned 86 percent of the wealth—leading to a profound cynicism and pessimism among the citizenry.

And given the way in which the Republican Party since 1968 has appealed to popular xenophobic images—playing the black, female, and homophobic cards to realign the electorate along race, sex, and sexual-orientation lines—it is no surprise that the notion that we are all part of one garment of destiny is discredited. Appeals to special interests rather than to public interests reinforce this polarization. The Los Angeles upheaval was an expression of utter fragmentation by a powerless citizenry that includes not just the poor but all of us.

What is to be done? How do we capture a new spirit and vision to meet the challenges of the post-industrial city, post-modern culture, and post-party politics?

First, we must admit that the most valuable sources for help, hope, and power consist of ourselves and our common history. As in the ages of Lincoln, Roosevelt, and King, we must look to new frameworks and languages to understand our multilayered crisis and overcome our deep malaise.

Second, we must focus our attention on the public square—the common good that undergirds our national and global destinies. The vitality of any public square ultimately depends on how much we *care* about the quality of our lives together. The neglect of our public infrastructure, for example—our water and sewage systems, bridges, tunnels, highways, subways, and streets—reflects not only our myopic economic policies, which impede productivity, but also the low priority we place on our common life.

The tragic plight of our children clearly reveals our deep disregard for public well-being. About one out of every five children in this country lives in poverty, including one out of every two black children and two out of every five Hispanic children. Most of our children—neglected by overburdened parents and bombarded by the market values of profit-hungry corporations—are ill-equipped to live lives of spiritual and cultural quality. Faced with these facts, how do we expect ever to constitute a vibrant society?

One essential step is some form of large-scale public intervention to ensure access to basic social goods—housing, food, health care, education, child care, and jobs. We must invigorate the common good with a mixture of government, business, and labor that does not follow any existing blueprint. After a period in which the private sphere has been sacralized and the public square gutted, the temptation is to make a fetish of the public square. We need to resist such dogmatic swings.

Last, the major challenge is to meet the need to generate new leadership. The paucity of courageous leaders—so apparent in the response to the events in Los Angeles—requires that we look beyond the same elites and voices that recycle the older frameworks. We need leaders—neither saints nor sparkling television personalities—who can situate themselves within a larger historical narrative of this country and our world, who can grasp the complex dynamics of our peoplehood and imagine a future grounded in the best of our past, yet who are attuned to the frightening obstacles that now perplex us. Our ideals of freedom, democracy, and equality must be invoked to invigorate all of us, especially the landless, propertyless, and luckless. Only a visionary leadership that can motivate "the better angels of our nature," as Lincoln said, and activate possibilities for a freer, more efficient, and stable America—only that leadership deserves cultivation and support.

This new leadership must be grounded in grass-roots organizing that highlights democratic accountability. Whoever *our* leaders will be as we approach the twenty-first century, their challenge will be to help Americans determine whether a genuine multiracial democracy can be created and sustained in an era of global economy and a moment of xenophobic frenzy.

Let us hope and pray that the vast intelligence, imagination, humor, and courage of Americans will not fail us. Either we learn a new language of empathy and compassion, or the fire this time will consume us all.

Study Questions

1. There is a threatening tone to this discussion of race. What is your assessment of "race matters" in the United States today? Do you agree with West?

2. As the economic infrastructure of U.S. cities has eroded, what impact has this had on the racial groups who reside there?

Reading 26

Ambiguous Loss

Risk and Resilience in Latino Immigrant Families

Celia Jaes Falicov

Latino immigrants, like many other immigrants, experience some degree of loss, grief and mourning. These experiences have been compared with the processes of grief and mourning precipitated by the death of loved ones (Shuval 1982; Warheit et al. 1985; Grinberg and Grinberg 1989; Volkan and Zintl 1993). Here I will argue, however, that migration loss has special characteristics that distinguish it from other kinds of losses. Compared with the clear-cut, inescapable fact of death, migration loss is both larger and smaller. It is larger because migration brings with it losses of all kinds. Gone are family members and friends who stay behind, gone is the native language, the customs, and rituals, and gone is the land itself. The ripples of these losses touch the extended kin back home and reach into the future generations born in the new land.

Yet migration loss is also smaller than death, because despite the grief and mourning occasioned by physical, cultural, and social separation, the losses are not absolutely clear, complete, and irretrievable. Everything is still alive but is just not immediately reachable or present. Unlike the finality of death, after migration it is always possible to fantasize the eventual return or a forthcoming reunion. Furthermore, immigrants seldom migrate toward a social vacuum. A relative, friend, or acquaintance usually waits on the other side to help with work and housing and to provide guidelines for the new life. A social community and ethnic neighborhood reproduce in pockets of remembrance, the sights, sounds, smells, and tastes of one's country. All of these elements create a mix of emotions—sadness and elation, loss and restitution, absence and presence—that makes grieving incomplete, postponed, ambiguous.

In this paper, I attempt to integrate concepts from family systems theory (ambiguous loss, boundary ambiguity, relational resilience) with concepts drawn from studies on migration, race, and ethnicity (familism, biculturalism, double consciousness) to deepen our understanding of the risks and resiliences that accompany migration loss for Latinos. I propose that an inclusive, "both/and" approach rather than an "either/or" approach, to the dilemmas of cultural and family continuity and change increases family resilience in the face of multiple migration losses. As we will see, however, risks arise when the experience of ambiguous loss becomes unbearable and thwarts attempts at integrating continuity with change.

Although Latinos share many similarities in the aspects of family coping with loss that are addressed in this paper, each family has a particular "ecological niche" created by combinations of nationality, ethnicity, class, education, religion, and occupation and by its individual history. Other variables that mediate the experience of migration are the degree of choice (voluntary or forced migration), proximity and accessibility to the country of origin, gender, age and generation, family form, and the degree and level of social acceptance encountered in the new environment (Falicov 1995, 1998).

Ambiguous Loss and Migration

The concept of ambiguous loss proposed by Pauline Boss (1991, 1999) describes situations in which loss is unclear, incomplete, or partial. Basing her thesis on stress theory, Boss describes two types of ambiguous loss. In one, people are physically absent but psychologically present (the family with a soldier missing in action, the noncustodial parent in divorce, the migrating relative). In the second, family members are physically present but psychologically absent (the family living with an Alzheimer's victim, the parent or spouse who is emotionally unavailable because of stress or depression).

Migration represents what Boss (1999) calls a "crossover" in that it has elements of both types of ambiguous loss. Beloved people and places are left behind, but they remain keenly present in the psyche of the immigrant. At the same time, homesickness and the stresses of adaptation may leave some family members emotionally unavailable to others. The very decision to migrate has at its core two ambiguous poles. Intense frustration with economic or political conditions compels the immigrant to move, but love of family and surroundings pull in another direction.

Dealing with Ambiguous Loss

Many internal conflicts, moods, and behaviors of immigrants can be more easily understood when seen through the lens of "ambiguous loss."

Visits to the country of origin close the gap between the immigrant and that which is psychologically present but physically absent. Phone calls, money remittances, gifts, messages, and trips back home contribute to transnational lifestyles (Rouse 1992)—and to a psychologically complex experience of presence and absence.

Leaving family members behind has pragmatic and economic justifications, but it may also ensure a powerful psychological link. It may symbolize that migration is provisional and experimental rather than permanent. Leaving a young child with the immigrant's own parents may also assuage the immigrant's guilt about leaving and offer an emotional exchange for the help of shared parenting.

Encouraging relatives and friends to migrate eases the wrenching homesickness of migration. It is a way of saying "hello again" to some of the many to whom one has bid good-byes. It also means that social networks dismantled by migration may stand a chance of being partially reconstructed in the host country.

Latino immigrants also reconstruct urban landscapes of open markets and ethnic neighborhoods that provide experiences with familiar foods, music, and language. *Recreating cultural spaces* in this manner reestablishes links with the lost land, while helping to transform the receiving cultures into more syntonic spaces (Ainslie 1998).

The long-lasting dream of returning home reinforces the gap between physical absence and psychological presence. A family may remain in a provisional limbo, unable to make settlement decisions or take full advantage of existing opportunities, paralyzed by a sort of frozen grief.

Family polarizations ensue when ambiguities overwhelm, as it were, the immigrant family's psyche. Spouses may come to represent each side of the conflict between leaving and staying, one idealizing and the other denigrating the country of origin or the "new" culture (Sluzki 1979). When such polarizations exist, they hint powerfully at denied or suppressed grief that may result in symptoms: depression or other emotional blocks to adaptation in adults, psychosomatic illness and selective mutism in children (Sluzki 1979, 1983; Grinberg and Grinberg 1989; Falicov 1998).

Generational legacies evolve when immigrant parents pass on their doubts, nostalgia, and sense of ambiguities to their children, who are sometimes recruited to one side or the other of the polarizations. Immigrant children may experience ambiguous loss themselves, but exposure to their parents' mixed emotions may significantly increase their stress.

The migration story itself can provide meaning and narrative coherence (Cohler 1991) to all life events. Experiences of success or of failure, the wife's new-found assertiveness, the ungrateful adult child—all can be readily explained: "It is because we came here." The question that will remain perennially unanswered is "How much is it migration, or is it just life challenges that would have appeared anywhere?" (Troya and Rosenberg 1999).

The construction of bicultural identities may result. The flow of people and information in a two-home, two-country lifestyle may give rise to a sense of "fitting in" in more than one place. Equally possible is the sense of not belonging in either place.

These behaviors of immigrants demonstrate the ambiguous, conflictual nature of migration losses. Yet they carry with them certain dynamic responses or "solutions" that demonstrate that people can learn to live with the ambiguity of never putting final closure to their loss. The adaptation depends on the contextual stresses that families encounter. Some are so excruciatingly oppressive that they prompt the family to repatriate. Under better circumstances, mixed feelings may be counteracted in part by building on family ties, social supports, and cultural strengths. Concepts from family systems theory and from acculturation studies can help us understand how ambiguous losses come to be tolerated and integrated in ways that strengthen families' resilience and empower their activism against social marginalization and injustice.

Dual Visions of Continuity and Change

From a family systems viewpoint, for a family to be successful in coping with family transitions, flexible attitudes toward change and flexible efforts to preserve continuity need to coexist (Hansen and Johnson 1979; Melitto 1985; Falicov 1993). Most immigrant families manage to maintain contacts with their culture of origin and to reinvent old family themes while carving out new lives. New acculturation theories reflect this dynamic balance of continuity and change, rather than the traditional "either/or" linear theory of abandoning one culture to embrace the other. Terms such as *binationalism, bilingualism, biculturalism,* and *cultural bifocality* (see Levitt, this volume) describe dual visions, ways of maintaining familiar cultural practices while making new spaces manageable, and ways of alternating language or cultural codes according to the requirements of the social context at hand (LaFramboise, Coleman, and Gerton 1993; Rouse 1992). Although there are compelling adaptational reasons for acquiring new language and cultural practices, there are equally compelling reasons for retaining cultural themes in the face of change, among them the attempt to preserve a sense of family coherence.

Relational Resilience in the Face of Loss

The concept of a "family sense of coherence" developed by Antonovsky and Sourani (1988), refers to the human struggle to perceive life as comprehensible, manageable, and meaningful. This striving for a sense of coherence (and hopefulness) is one of the key ingredients of *relational resilience*, those processes by which families cope and attempt to surmount persistent stress (Walsh 1998).

In this section, I explore immigrant families' attempts to restore meaning and purpose in life in the midst of multiple ambiguous losses. The aspects of relational resilience addressed in this discussion are family connectedness, family rituals, awareness of social marginalization, and belief or spiritual systems.

Family Connectedness

Latinos' ethnic narratives almost invariably stress familism: inclusiveness and interdependence. In family systems terms, family connectedness—the obligation to care and support one another—is a defining feature of extended family life. This cultural tendency toward family connectedness seems to withstand migration and to persist in some form for at least one or two or more generations (Suárez-Orozco and Suárez-Orozco 1995; Sabogal et al. 1987). For immigrant families, familism may be manifest in the persistence of long-distance attachments and loyalties in the face of arduous social or economic conditions, in attempts to migrate as a unit and live close to one another, and in the desire to reunify when individuals have taken up the journey alone. The family members and the ideologies of these richly joined systems make their presence felt at a psychological and a physical level.

The Psychological Presence of Extended Familism

When extended family members are far away, *la familia* may become the emotional container that holds both dreams not yet realized and lost meanings that are no longer recoverable. At the most concrete level, immigrants send remittances back home in exchange for collective caretaking of remaining family members (children and/or elders), thus reinforcing a traditional system of emotional and economic interdependence. At a more abstract level, the idea itself of three-generational family can trigger other large existential meanings, such as one's lost national identity. A study of young adults (Troya and Rosenberg 1999) who had migrated to Mexico as children with parents seeking political refuge from South America demonstrates the powerful psychological presence of absent relatives. When asked for their spontaneous images formed in response to the words *patria* ("fatherland") and *tierra* ("land"), they associated these with the street or house where the grandmother or the aunt lived, reflecting (or perhaps creating anew) deep intergenerational bonds between country and family—a psychological familism.

Other studies show that as families acculturate (Rueschenberg and Buriel 1989; Sabogal et al. 1987; Suárez-Orozco and Suárez-Orozco 1995) they learn how to behave externally in a dominant culture that values assertiveness, independence, and achievement. Yet they do not abandon internally the connectedness and interpersonal controls of many collectivistic family systems.

The Physical Presence of Extended Family

When extended family members are physically present, they play a significant role in shoring up the immigrant family. Their familism drives a concern for one another's lives, a pulling together to weather crises, a sociocentric child rearing (Harwood, Miller, and Irizarry 1995), and a closeness among adult siblings (Chavez 1985).

Multigenerational dwellings, particularly the presence of grandmothers, can be influential in terms of transfers of knowledge, cultural exposures, nurturance, and instrumental help embedded in established sociocultural practices (Garcia-Coll et al. 1996) or even as a buffer against parental neglect or abuse (Gomez 1999). However, family life is not always as rosy as it seems. The description of Latino family connectedness is sometimes taken to such extremes that stereotypical images of picturesque family life dominate while tensions and disconnectedness among extended family members simmer below, ignored or discounted. Perhaps what matters, regardless of the particular positive or negative tone of the interactions, is the sense of being part of a family group, and that in itself affords a sense of continuity in the face of ruptured attachments and the disruptions of relocation.

Cultural Family Rituals

Another interesting avenue to study family resilience in the face of ambiguous losses is through the transmission of family rituals that reaffirm family and cultural identity. Family systems theorists have long known about the power of rituals to restore continuity with a family's heritage while reinforcing family bonds and community pride (Bennett, Wolin and McAvity 1988; Imber-Black, Roberts and Whiting 1988). A good example is a clinical case of mine.

A poor, working-class, Mexican-immigrant mother was very distressed over her daughter's refusal to have a *quinceañera* party. The intensity of the mother's emotion surprised me, because the party's ritual affirmation of the girl's virginity and future availability for dating hardly applied—everybody knew the girl was sexually involved with an older boyfriend. But for the mother, the *quinceañera* was the most unforgettable (*"inolvidable,"* she said) event in a woman's life and a memory that all parents dream of bestowing upon a daughter ever since the time of her birth. To abandon this valued ritual that lends coherence to a woman's life—even when its original contents had shifted or faded—represented too much cultural discontinuity for this mother.

The enactment of life cycle rituals in the midst of cultural transformation can be construed as reflecting dual lifestyles, as being both ethnic and modern at the same time. Studies of immigrant families should include a close look at the persistence and the evolving new shapes of traditional family rituals—from routine family interactions (dinners or prayers) to celebrations of birthdays, holidays, and rites of passage or any gathering where a sense of family and national belonging is reaffirmed. Such study could help us understand not only the stable and shifting meanings of rituals but also their functions as metaphors for continuity and change.

Awareness of Social Marginalization

Although the notion of "dual vision" characterizes the incorporation of culture in the inner workings of many immigrant families, it also captures the nature of their interaction with larger external and institutional systems of the host country. The concept of "double consciousness," first described by Du Bois (1903) for African Americans, is useful here because it encompasses a perception of who one really is as a person within one's own group *and* a perception of who one is in the attributions of the larger society's story regarding the same group. Racial, ethnic, and class discriminations plague the individual stories of many Latino and Latina immigrant adults and children. One case of mine illustrates the painful awareness a Mexican family had of the gross, racist preconceptions of Latino immigrants by whites.

This family, a married couple with six children who had arrived from Oaxaca seven years ago, consulted me because a white, upper-class neighbor had accused their nine-year-old son of "molesting" her four-year-old daughter. As the Mexican boy's story unfolded, I learned that several children had been playing together in the fields when the little girl said she needed to urinate. The boy quickly pulled her panties down and held her in the upright position, but the girl ran crying home. Racism was undoubtedly part of the reaction to the boy's behavior. I recounted to the parents the alternative explanation to the "molestation," but the father responded, "I thank you but we want you to tell [the white family that you think] our son is cured and this will never happen again." When asked why should I do this, he said, "Because, when they look at us, they think 'These Mexicans are good people, *le hacen la lucha* [they struggle hard],' but if something goes wrong they suddenly see in us the faces of rapists and abusers. I promise you I will keep an eye on this boy, but please do not question their story. *No vale la pena* [It is not worth it]. It could cost us everything we worked for."

Here again is the ambiguity of gains, losses, and dual visions of immigrants. Striving for the dream of stability in a new land is riddled with pressures to subscribe to the dominant culture's story, which negatively judges dark-skinned, poor immigrants and deprives them of legal resources to fight unfair accusations. The social climate of structural exclusion and psychological violence suffered by immigrants and their children is not only detrimental to their participation in the opportunity structure but it also affects the immigrant children's sense of self, through a process of what Carola Suárez-Orozco (2000) aptly calls "social mirroring."

Indeed, most immigrants and their children are aware of the hostilities and prejudice with which they are regarded. From a psychological viewpoint, this awareness may be debilitating when internalized or denied, but it may be empowering when it helps stimulate strategic activism for social justice. Educators who stress the need for minority families' democratic participation in schools emphasize that awareness of one's own marginal status is the first step toward empowerment (Trueba 1999). Thus awareness of social injustices may create a measure of family resilience against assaults on identity.

Long-held Beliefs and Spiritual Systems

People's *belief system*, or the meaning they make of their lives and experience, is a narrative construct that helps us understand a family's ability to deal with adversity (Walsh 1998; Wright, Watson, and Bell 1996). A family's tolerance for loss and ambiguity is related to its culture's tolerance for ambiguity; fatalistic and optimistic stances are likewise embedded in culturally based systems of meaning (Boss 1999).

Some Latino cultural narratives and spiritual beliefs promote acceptance of life's adversities, tempering the need to find answers and definitive solutions to losses (Falicov 1998). Roman Catholic beliefs value acceptance of suffering, destiny, and God's will. A belief that little in life is under one's control is also related to conditions of poverty and decreased agency (Garza and Ames 1972; Comas-Díaz 1989). These beliefs should not be misconstrued as passivity, however, but as a way of marshaling one's initiative to solve what can be solved while accepting what cannot be changed—a sort of mastery of the possible.

Like other cultural and ritual practices, the old religion often takes new forms and functions in the new land. Church participation may actually help inscribe various Latino groups in dual, evolving transnational spaces. As Peggy Levitt so cogently describes in this volume, immigrants' church attendance can allow a double membership that crosses border arenas in the homeland while it grounds them locally through host country participation and even civic engagement. This balance of continuity and change may be at the core of resilient adaptations to ambiguous loss. Yet these dual visions are not always obtainable, nor is it always possible to make positive meaning out of the experience of migration. In the next sections, I describe situations where attempts to restore a sense of family coherence fail in the face of intense loss and irreparable ambiguity.

When Ambiguous Loss Becomes Unbearable

Many circumstances surrounding migration can lead to overwhelmingly problematic physical and emotional disconnections among family members. Two of these circumstances are addressed here: (1) the overlap of the consequences of migration with the impact of other life cycle transitions at any point in the life of an immigrant and (2) the short- and long-term effects of migration separations and reunifications among all family members. Both situations can be understood better by utilizing the concept of boundary ambiguity.

Boundary Ambiguity

Ambiguous loss may become problematic when it generates confusion about who is in and who is out of the family. Boss (1991) labeled this phenomenon "boundary ambiguity," a concept that is increasingly being used in family research to describe effects of family membership loss over time (Boss, Greenberg, and Pearce-McCall 1990) and that may be very helpful in illuminating migration losses. This construct encompasses the rules and definitions of family subsystems (parental, marital, sibling and other subgroups) and how they are perceived by each family group.

When Ambiguous Loss Is Compounded by Life Cycle Transitions

When nonambiguous, irretrievable losses—such as the death of a relative back home—occur in the life of an immigrant family the uncertain, provisional, and ambiguous quality of the old good-byes accentuates that loss and creates confusion about where one belongs and exactly who constitutes one's family.

A thirty-six-year-old woman consulted me for depression after her father died suddenly in Argentina. Overwhelmed by sadness and guilt at not having made the effort to see him more often and by the unbearable loneliness of not being able to participate in communal grieving, this woman asked to have a separation from her Anglo-American husband. He was the one who had brought her to this country, and she felt him to be a much less loving man than her father. Asked about her adoring father's reaction to her leaving her country twelve years ago to get married, she promptly said, "Everybody told me that for him that day was like *el velorio del angelito* [the wake of his little angel]." Now she was experiencing a great deal of confusion about where she belonged. Her husband and children, who hardly knew her father, provided little comfort. She needed the support of her family of origin, but her own shared history with them had been truncated long ago. This case illustrates the rippling effects of ambiguous loss for the immigrant, for their children, and for the family of origin left behind. This woman's eight-year-old daughter was having behavior and school difficulties that paralleled the mother's depression.

Calling Two Women "Mami"

In addition to separations between extended and nuclear family, Latino immigrants increasingly experience separations between parents and children. A father or a mother frequently migrates first, leaving children behind and planning for later reunification. Such separations complicate experiences of loss, raise issues of inclusion/exclusion, and set the stage for boundary ambiguity.

When a father or a mother migrates first, leaving the family to be reunited later, the confusion may be mild and temporary or intense and prolonged. If sufficient time passes, a family in which the father migrated first may reorganize into a single-parent household, with mother as head and substitutes performing the parental functions of the absent parent. Subsequent reunification is often stressful because family boundaries need to change yet again to allow for reentry of the absent member.

Increasingly today, mothers recruited for work make the journey north alone, leaving the children with other women in the family or social network. It is only after several years that these mothers are joined by their children, who often travel unaccompanied. Sociologist Pierrette Hondagneu-Sotelo's incisive analysis (this volume) of the changing labor demands driving these emergent transnational family forms, and of the possible new meanings of family and motherhood, provides a historical, economic, and social context for these complex and often traumatic separations and equally traumatic reunifications between mothers and children. Children are left behind with grandparents or other relatives so that an immigrant parent can face the dangers of illegal passage and the economic hardships of getting established in the new country without the added worry of having youngsters under their wing. Over time, the costs of these arrangements are significant.

The adjustments to parting and the adjustments at the time of a subsequent reunion place not only mother and child but also all the subsystems of a three-generational family (including siblings who stayed in the sending culture and those born in the receiving country) at risk for developing boundary ambiguities and concomitant individual and relational problems. Psychotherapists and social workers often encounter an immigrant child who calls two women "Mami." We know very little about the meaning of this behavior. Does it point to an attempt to deal with ambiguous loss by accepting two mothers, one here and one there? Could it represent a fluid definition of family that reflects multiple attachments and wherein "Mami" is just a generic term for significant others? Of more concern, does it signify boundary ambiguity, the beginning of divided loyalties, and confusion about who is the real mother? What makes for a successful separation and reunion? What are the consequences of separation at different ages and for various lengths of time? What transforms ambiguous loss into conflict-laden boundary ambiguity?

A recent international furor over the fate of one young Cuban immigrant highlights an extreme case of boundary ambiguity. Custody of Elián González, a six-year-old Cuban shipwreck survivor was fiercely contested by his deceased mother's relatives in Miami and by his father and grandmothers in Cuba, each side of the family (the immigrants and the nonimmigrants) claiming the right to decide where Elián belonged (Cooper Ramo 2000). At the political level, the boundary ambiguity could not be resolved because it represented the long-standing tensions between Little Havana in Miami and Havana in Cuba. Yet the symbolism of belonging goes beyond the political. At the level of migration loss, the dispute struck deep in the hearts of immigrants who have remained in perpetual mourning for the total loss of the Cuba they once knew. It is tempting to speculate that it is precisely the prohibition to visit that makes it impossible for these immigrants to lead satisfactory dual lives, recharging their emotional batteries and becoming binational or bicultural. Their ambiguous losses instead solidify into a rigid migration narrative confined to an idealization of the island's past, recreated exclusively in the space of Little Havana. The conflict over Elián González's future was magnified by these historical factors, but it illustrates what may happen in families that polarize over their efforts to keep a child close to both sides of their existential predicament.

Clinicians encounter many families from Mexico, Central America, and the Caribbean who have undergone separation and reunion with children of all ages. After a period of time following reunification, mothers often request professional help with behavior problems and defiance of their authority. Many social and psychological factors contribute to mother-child disconnections and to the development of conflict. From a family systems viewpoint, we can speculate on the family interactions that may contribute to—or help prevent—pernicious family boundary ambiguities. One factor seems to be each family member's positive or negative perceptions of the decision to migrate—that is, how much approval or disapproval there is among the adults (the biological mother and the caretaker, for example) about the decision to separate temporarily. A related outcome is the quality of the relationship between the migrating parent(s) and the temporary caretakers and whether they all try to be cooperative and inclusive at long distance.

Ongoing studies will help us learn more about how to help families strengthen their resilience in the face of the many individual and relational risks inherent in these separations, yet the separations themselves, especially if prolonged, may pose nearly insurmountable obstacles to family cohesion. Studies of the nature of the ruptured attachments among family members, the loss of shared histories, and the effects of persistent economic stress on family life may yield greater understanding of the problematic "costs of transnationalism" for immigrant families.

References

Ainslie, R. C. 1998. Cultural mourning, immigration, and engagement: Vignettes from the Mexican experience. In M. M. Suárez-Orozco (ed.), *Crossings*. Cambridge, MA: Harvard University Press, pp. 285–305.

Antonovsky, A., and Sourani, T. 1988. Family sense of coherence and family adaptation. *Journal of Marriage and the Family,* 50:79–92.

Bennett, L. A., Wolin, S. J., and McAvity, K. J. 1988. Family identity, ritual, and myth: a cultural perspective on life cycle transitions. In C. J. Falicov (ed.), *Family transitions: Continuity and change over the life cycle*. New York: Guilford Press.

Boss, P. 1991. Ambiguous loss. In F. Walsh and M. McGoldrick (eds.), *Living Beyond Loss: Death in the family*. New York: Norton.

Boss, P. 1999. *Ambiguous Loss: Learning to live with unresolved grief*. Cambridge, MA: Harvard University Press.

Boss, P., Greenberg, J. R., and Pearce-McCall, D. 1990. Measurement of boundary ambiguity in families. *Minnesota Agricultural Experiment Station Bulletin* 593:1–25.

Chavez, L. R. 1985. Households, migration, and labor market participation: The adaptation of Mexicans to life in the United States. *Urban Anthropology* 14:301–346.

Cohler, B. 1991. The life story and the study of resilience and response to adversity. *Journal of Narrative and Life History* 1:169–200.

Comas-Díaz, L. 1989. Culturally relevant issues and treatment implications for Hispanics. In D. R. Koslow and E. Salett (eds.), *Crossing cultures in mental health*. Washington, DC: Society for International Education, Training, and Research.

Cooper Ramo, J. 2000. A big battle over a little boy. *Time*, January 17.

Du Bois, W. E. B. 1903. *The souls of black folk*. Chicago: McClurg.

Falicov, C. J. 1993. Continuity and change: Lessons from immigrant families. *American Family Therapy Association Newsletter*, Spring:30–36.

Falicov, C. J. 1995. Training to think culturally: A multidimensional comparative framework. *Family Process*, 34:373–388.

Falicov, C. J. 1998. *Latino families in therapy: A guide to multicultural practice*. New York: Guilford Press.

García-Coll, C., Lamberty, G., Jenkins, R., McAdoo, H. P., Crnic, K, Wasik, B. H., and Vásquez García, H. 1996. An integrative model for the study of developmental competencies in minority children. *Child Development* 67:1891–1914.

Garza, R. T., and Ames, R. E. 1972. A comparison of Anglo and Mexican-American college students on locus of control. *Journal of Consulting and Clinical Psychology,* 42:919–922.

Gomez, M. Y. 1999. The grandmother as an enlightened witness in the Hispanic culture. *Psycheline* 3(2):15–22.

Grinberg, L., and Grinberg, R. 1989. *Psychoanalytic perspectives on migration and exile*. New Haven, CT: Yale University Press.

Harwood, R. L., Miller, J. G., and Irizarry, N. L. 1995. *Culture and attachment: Perceptions of the child in context*. New York: Guilford Press.

LaFramboise, T., Coleman, H. L., and Gerton, J. 1993. Psychological impact of biculturalism: evidence and theory. *Psychological Bulletin* 114(3):395–412.

Melitto, R. 1985. Adaptation in family systems: A development perspective. *Family Process* 24(1):89–100.

Rouse, R. 1992. Making sense of settlement: Class transformation, cultural struggle and transnationalism among Mexican immigrants in the United States. In N. G. Schiller, L.

Basch and C. Blanc-Szanton (eds.), *Towards a transnational perspective on migration*. New York: New York Academy of Sciences.

Rueschenberg, E., and Buriel, R. 1989. Mexican American family functioning and acculturation: A family systems perspective. *Hispanic Journal of Behavioral Sciences* 11(3):232–244.

Sabogal, F., Marín, G., Otero-Sabogal, R., Marín, B. V., and Perez-Stable, P. 1987. Hispanic familism and acculturation: What changes and what doesn't. *Hispanic Journal of Behavioral Sciences* 9(4):397–412.

Shuval, J. T. 1982. Migration and stress. In L. Goldberger and S. Breznitz (eds.), *Handbook of stress: Theoretical and clinical aspects*, 2nd ed. New York: Free Press, pp. 641–657.

Sluzki, C. E. 1979. Migration and family conflict. *Family Process* 18(1):79–92.

Sluzki, C. E. 1983. The sounds of silence. In C. J. Falicov (ed.), *Cultural perspectives in family therapy*. Rockville, MD: Aspen, pp. 68–77.

Suárez-Orozco, C. E. 2000. Identities under siege: Immigration stress and social mirroring among the children of immigrants. In A. Robben and M. Suárez-Orozco (eds.), *Culture under siege: Violence and trauma in interdisciplinary perspective*. Cambridge: Cambridge University Press.

Suárez-Orozco, M. M., and Suárez-Orozco, C. E. 1995. *Transformations: Immigration. family life and achievement motivation among Latino adolescents*. Stanford, CA: Stanford University Press.

Troya, E., and Rosenberg, F. 1999. "Nos fueron a México: ¿Qué nos paso a los jóvenes exiliados consureños?" *Sistemas Familiares* 15(3):79–92.

Trueba, E. T. 1999. *Latinos Unidos: From cultural diversity to the politics of solidarity*. Lanham, MD: Rowman & Littlefield.

Volkan, V. D., and Zintl, E. 1993. *Living beyond loss: The lessons of grief*. New York: Charles Scribner's Sons.

Walsh, F. 1998. *Strengthening family resilience*. New York: Guilford Press.

Warheit, G., Vega, W., Auth, J., and Meinhardt, K. 1985. Mexican-American immigration and mental health: A comparative analysis of psychosocial stress and dysfunction. In W. Vega and M. Miranda (eds.), *Stress and Hispanic mental health*. Rockville, MD: National Institutes of Health, pp. 76–109.

Wright, L. M., Watson, W. L., and Bell, J. M. 1996. *Beliefs: The heart of healing in families and illness*. New York: Basic Books.

Study Questions

1. Define and discuss "ambiguous loss" for the immigrants.
2. List the resilient qualities of the Latino families.

Reading 27

Undoing Racism in America

Help from a Black Church

Erika Vora and
Jay A. Vora

Can a Black community help reduce racism? The answer is an unequivocal yes! Our study showed that a Black church community that is supportive of and committed to helping young White college students positively changed their attitudes and behaviors toward African Americans. The purpose of this study was to investigate whether a well-planned engagement of White students with members of a Black community, in a welcoming environment, would help reduce racism and prejudice.

Racism and ethnic prejudice are major problems in our society. They are indeed our most troubling and potentially catastrophic national dilemma requiring persistent critical inquiry (Janzen, 2000; Van Dijk, 1987). Both blatant and very subtle forms of racism permeate organizational and personal levels of our society, from governmental, business, and educational institutions to our everyday interactions (Gonzalez, Houston, & Chen, 1998; Jackson, 1992; Jamieson & O'Mara, 1992; Seelye, 1993; Tjosvold, 1991). "Without the Afrocentric perspective the imposition of the European line as universal hinders cultural understanding and demeans humanity" (Asante, 1987, p.10). All of us have a responsibility to be change agents toward facilitating nonracist ways of thinking and acting. To undo racism now and for future generations, we need to be involved in this process so that our attitudes and communications will change toward racial self-acceptance without any feelings of ethnic superiority. We need to open our eyes to see the incredible potential that diversity offers, and we need to recognize the deep pain and the enormous waste of human talent that occur in everyday life where racial antagonism persists. We are challenged to create learning experiences and programs that help us recognize that our associations with diverse others enrich us and that respecting one another's racial backgrounds and ethnic groups is the key to solving our most pressing national and global problem. We need to directly confront racism by engaging our students and ourselves in self-examination of our attitudes and behaviors concerning racial diversity.

As educators, it is our quest to make our students aware of their "personal baggage" (Beane, 1990), to help them look at their personal filters, and to gently remove their ethnocentric blinders. Our educational goal for this project was to provide new opportunities for our students to understand and respond effectively to our culturally diverse nation and pluralistic world. This is not an easy task because the overwhelming majority of our students come from relatively small, homogeneous European American communities in Central Minnesota. They have had very little exposure to culturally diverse individuals, especially to those of African heritage. This lack of personal intercultural experience is supplemented by media images that are relatively negative (Davis, 1992). Rather than merely learning about a culture through the usual academic classroom endeavors, we challenged our students to get involved with an African American church community and to "walk the talk."

In this article, we would like to share an approach we adopted toward engaging students directly in culture learning by offering them an opportunity to actively participate in the activities of a culture different from their own. Because the emotional wall between Black and White folks is so huge in this country, we were especially interested in undoing racism and prejudice of European Americans toward African Americans. Therefore, our specific purpose for this experiential learning was to provide an opportunity to change the attitudes, knowledge, and behavior of our White students toward African Americans and to study the impact of this intercultural engagement to effect such a change.

Help from a Black Church

Located in a highly homogeneous, White, small Midwestern town, we searched for a variety of ways to engage our students face-to-face in a culturally diverse community and found it 75 miles away in a warm and inviting African American church. We asked the dynamic leader of this church if we could bring our White students to participate in her Sunday services. She was delighted and welcomed us graciously with open arms. Committed to making the students feel at home, she encouraged the community members to greet our students as they entered the church and to interact with them after the service. During the service, each student was recognized by name (with the help of name cards). The preacher thanked them for coming, prayed for them, and encouraged them to come back soon. During the spirited service, the preacher was leading the congregation to "come forward and hug each other." Thus, each student was hugged not only by the preacher but also by the members of the congregation. This warm and sincere embrace made a big impact on the students, for it was the first time for them to ever be hugged by a Black person. The preacher, a caring and dynamic church leader, also organized lunch events at the nearby community center and encouraged all community members to come and interact with the students and to make them feel at home. She also asked her creative choir director and good friend to teach the students a hymn or two, which they could sing together with the community members. Before leaving for their 75-mile journey home, the preacher prayed for the students' safe trip home and encouraged them again to come back soon. The members of the congregation not only greeted the students warmly and truly made all of them feel welcome, but they also waved good-bye as the students' cars were leaving for home. We could think of no better way for our students to engage with and learn about African Americans.

This open church community and our intercultural communication classes have been partners in learning, and what a rewarding and uplifting experience it has been. Our students are always welcome with open arms in this church, always encouraged to come and participate in the events that unfold during and after the services. The climate in this community is incredibly inviting, supportive, and congenial. The community knows that we are not traveling some 70 miles for religious reasons but for building human bridges of understanding and sharing across our racial divide. Over the years, the community members have built the most heartwarming and effective bridges imaginable. We sing and pray together. After the church services, we walk together to the nearby community center where we have lunch together, and thanks to the creative choir director, we learn a new song or two and sing together, swaying and making a joyful noise.

Method of Study

In this study, 510 undergraduate students participated in the activities of an African American church community and were actively engaged in creating meaningful dialogue with members of the community. The data were collected from the students enrolled in our intercultural communication classes over a period of 5 years.

Before participating in this daylong field trip to the African American church community, the students studied and discussed such concepts as cultural anxiety, functions of prejudice, stereotyping, African spirituality (Richards, 1985), and Afrocentrism (Asante, 1987). In an open and supportive classroom environment, the students were encouraged to explore the underlying reasons for their own prejudices and what each of us could do to decrease our prejudices (Vora, 1998). This was followed by an orientation to the homiletics of the Black Church (Hamlet, 1998; Richards, 1985; Stewart, 1984) and an orientation to this specific church and community.

The students drove their own cars or carpooled 75 miles to this community, leaving at 10:00 a.m. and returning about 5:00–6:00 p.m. on a Sunday. They attended the church services and actively engaged in dialogue with the members of the community at the nearby community center.

After returning home, each student was asked to anonymously respond to a 7-point Likert-type scale questionnaire seeking data on the student's changes in attitude, knowledge, and behavior toward African Americans as a result of participating in this event. In addition, the students were asked to write a brief paper describing how this intercultural field trip affected their attitudes toward African Americans, their feelings of ethnocentrism, and their intended behavioral change toward African Americans in the future.

To ensure that each student expressed his or her feelings freely, without any concern of what might be considered an expected or desirable answer, no grade was given for the written report of the experience. Every student received the same number of points for merely participating in this field trip, regardless of the content of their written papers.

The demographics of the 510 participants were 283 females and 227 males. They were all Caucasian. Four hundred forty-nine participants were between 21 and 24 years of age, and 61 participants were between 25 and 35 years of age.

Analysis and Results

Changes in Attitude

The students reported that, as a result of their participation in this experiential learning, their anxiety about interacting with African Americans in an African American community was greatly reduced, as indicated by the mean (2.06) and mode (1.00) scores on this question. They also viewed African Americans in a more positive light than they did before the field trip, as reflected by the mean (1.91) and mode (1.00) scores; their attitudes toward African Americans in general had become more positive and inclusive with mean (1.74) and mode (1.00) scores. The mode of 1.00 on each question indicated that the majority of the participants strongly agreed that their attitudes had changed positively toward African Americans. These changes in attitude had occurred relatively fast because 91% of the participants reported this to be their first time to have ever been in an African American community.

The qualitative data of the students' responses reinforced the findings of the above quantitative data. The following quotations were representative of the students' comments: . . .

I strongly believe that people can talk about this until their tongues fall off. It is not until a person experiences other cultures that they can truly say they understand that culture a little better. Man, and did I learn today, just from being in that community. My whole predisposition toward African Americans has changed from anxiety and avoidance to awareness that if I am open, and let others in, I will be the richer for it. Today I am truly rich!

To tell you the truth, I really did have a "phobia" about Black people. Now that I was there, I feel that Black people have been given an unfair chance in society. The oppression they have gone through has certainly not been done by people who have gotten to know them and knew what they were doing, but by those who, like me, have a phobia toward people they don't know. I now would question those people on how they got their stereotypes and prejudices, whether they know if they are correct, and whether they have experienced the culture and people toward which they were being racist. My own ignorance has continued too long, and I am so happy that it was not too late to bring it to an end. Thank you so much for this opportunity.

Both the quantitative and qualitative data support that the attitudes of the White students toward African Americans were favorably and significantly affected by their participation in this experiential learning. Their anxiety to interact with African Americans was reduced after this field trip. The students overwhelmingly reported that they viewed African Americans in a more positive light and that they were ashamed of their previous stereotypes and prejudices. The students reported that their attitude toward African Americans had definitely become more positive and inclusive. Occasionally, a student remarked how much there is to learn from African Americans, especially from the courage, strength, and love of the people he or she met in this community.

Change in Ethnocentrism

The all-day engagement of the White students with members in this African American community was found to have a significant but balanced effect on the students' ethnocentric views. In relation to the statement, "My ways of living and interacting with others are the best," the mean was 4.60, with a mode of 4.00 and a standard deviation of 1.36, indicating that they disagreed with the statement. Similarly, in relation to the statement, "African American ways of living and interacting with others are the best," the mean was 4.57, with a standard deviation of 1.29 and a mode of 4.00. The students' active participation in the African American community led them to believe that neither their own ways nor African American ways of living and interacting are the best. The students reported that both cultures have their own appropriateness and value.

The qualitative data supported these quantitative findings as reflected in the following quotations:

> This whole experience made me ashamed of all the superior "hoopla" that I unnecessarily went through, because of my Euro-centric way in which I was raised. This fieldtrip informed me and enlightened me. In my mind, all the way home, I began to count all of my classmates that I had in high school. Then it struck me so sad to realize that out of those 89 students, I may be the only one who will have ever experienced what I had that day. That is probably so because of the small town that I had come from, none of them have ever taken a step, such as this one, and will ever realize the difference and greatness of African American ways. This saddens me, for I have changed my views so much.

> This experience has definitely shown me that my culture is not better than the Black culture we visited. As a matter of fact, there were many aspects that I enjoyed more about the African American culture, like music, and the free spirited expression, specially [*sic*] the drums, the highly animated preacher, the call and the response. That's just great! But my way of expression is fine for me too, even though now it seems boring. As they say, "to each his own."

> I learned that the "us" can become "they" and the "they" can become "us." It all depends how we look at things. If you don't get to know another way, you will always think your own way is better. That is what I have done in relation to religion and I believed that you must pray quietly in a church. Well, today I learned that you can "make a joyful noise" and still praise the Lord, and that He probably does not care how you do it, as long as you are sincere. . . .

Discussion

The experiential activity in this study was designed to give White American students, who had very little contact with African Americans, the opportunity to get to know their African American neighbors better, and to do so in a supportive environment. The field trip was carefully designed with appropriate orientation, organized activities, and debriefing reports so that White students from highly homogeneous small towns would take the first step toward engaging in meaningful interactions with and gain respect for African Americans. It was also designed to change the students' attitudes and anxieties toward African Americans and establish a level of trust in a warm and supportive environment. The many efforts of the truly warm and inviting church leader to engage the students with the community members and to make them feel welcome and at home played a significant role in the overwhelming success of this field trip. The various engagements with members of the African American church community greatly helped the White students to recognize that they had many prejudices toward a people that they had never even met. The day's events and the active engagements of the White students with members of this truly welcoming Black community helped immensely in building a bridge toward understanding and sharing. Hence, this experiential learning adventure was a success.

The empirical evidence of this study supported the notion that a positive experience in another culture does positively impact the attitudes, understanding, and behavior of the participants. The positive experiences of the White students in this Black church community led to their positive attitudes toward African Americans. The insight gained from these findings was that, even at age 25 and beyond, a person with negative attitudes toward another culture can change these attitudes after an intensive and positive experience in that culture. This promises to be a very hopeful sign for developing intercultural understanding and mutual respect, and it gives us hope that we can indeed undo racism between Black and White folks in the United States.

The findings of this study seem to suggest that positive attitudes toward people from other cultures are also related to, and may be followed by, two other outcomes: tempering of ethnocentrism and increasing interactive behavior with individuals from other cultures. After actively participating in the Black community and engaging with its members, a large majority of the participants in this study rejected the notion that their Eurocentric ways were the best. They recognized that Afrocentric ways are equally appropriate. On the behavioral side, many of the participants indicated that they intend to interact, or already have increased their interactions, with African Americans. The experience had an uplifting effect on the participating students and shed a lot of their preconceived notions. In the words of one of the students, "It offered hope for change in many of us." Black and White folks praying together, singing, making a joyful noise together, eating, and creating meaningful dialogue created community and goodwill between them and brought them closer together. The students thoroughly enjoyed this positive experience and were thankful for the opportunity to engage in a meaningful way with members of this remarkable community. Many students reported shedding their inhibitions and desired to seek more contact with African Americans in the future.

The partnership and engagement between a predominantly White Midwestern university and a welcoming and warm African American community proved extremely successful toward helping reduce the students' intercultural anxiety, prejudice, and even racism. This unique partnership between a Black church and a White student body has turned the students' intercultural anxiety and fear into enthusiasm and excitement. Help toward undoing racism and opening cultural blinders came generously from a Black church community, and with open arms.

The implications for educators are that the traditional teacher-centered model needs to shift to a student-centered learning model, especially in relation to culture learning that involves both the cognitive and the affective domains. Positive interactions between Black folks and White folks result in positive attitudes toward one another, reduce ethnocentrism, and increase effective intercultural interactions. Furthermore, if future interactions remain positive, there would be deeper understanding of and mutual respect for one another. Because this study was designed with a careful orientation to relevant cultural concepts for a positive intercultural experience, no conclusions can be drawn about the effect of negative experiences on intercultural understanding, attitudes, and behavior.

References

Asante. M. K. (1987). *The Afrocentric idea.* Philadelphia: Temple University Press.

Beane, J. (1990). *Affect in the curriculum: Toward democracy, dignity and diversity.* New York: Teachers College Press.

Davis, N. (1992). Teaching about inequality: Student resistance, paralysis, and rage. *Teaching Sociology, 20,* 232–238.

Gonzalez, A., Houston, M., & Chen, V. (Eds.). (1998). *Our voices: Essays in culture, ethnicity, and communication.* Los Angeles: Roxbury.

Hamlet, J. (1998). The reason why we sing. In A. Gonzalez et al. (Eds.), *Our voices: Essays in culture, ethnicity, and communication* (pp. 92–97). Los Angeles: Roxbury.

Jackson, S. E. (1992). *Diversity in the workplace.* New York: The Guilford Press.

Jamieson, D., & O'Mara, J. (1992). *Managing workplace 2000: Gaining the diversity advantage.* San Francisco: Jossey-Bass.

Janzen, R. (1999). Five paradigms of ethnic relations. In L. Samovar & R. Porter (Eds.), *Intercultural communication: A reader* (9th ed.) (pp. 52–59). Belmont, CA: Wadsworth.

Richards, D. (1985). The implications of African American spirituality. In M. K. Asante & K. W. Asante (Eds.), *African culture: The rhythms of unity* (pp. 209–214). Trenton, NJ: Africa World.

Seelye, H. N. (1993). *Teaching culture: Strategies for intercultural communication.* Lincolnwood, IL: National Textbook Company.

Stewart, W. H., Sr. (1984). *Interpreting God's word in Black preaching.* Valley Forge, PA: Judson.

Tjosvold, D. (1991). *The conflict-positive organization: Stimulate diversity and create unity.* Reading, MA: Addison-Wesley.

Van Dijk, T. A. (1987). *Communicating racism: Ethnic prejudice in thought and talk.* Newbury Park, CA: Sage.

Vora, E. (1998). *Managing conflict across cultures.* Paper presented at the annual conference for public administrators. Port Elizabeth, South Africa.

Study Questions

1. How much of an impact did the visits to the Black church have on the students? Report the data.

2. Why were these experiences so "inspiring" for the students?

Topic 10
Gender

Gender is a basic, fundamental quality of social life. Each of us has been affected through socialization into gender roles and each of us has a component of gender in our identities. Recently, sociology has decided to examine gender as a social structure—something that is part of all the institutions in society. We notice strong gender patterns in the family, the economy, religion, education, the law, politics, medicine, and even in our marriages and peer groups. Everywhere we look, gender is present, in every social structure and organization, in every person. Something so elemental in society must certainly be important to understanding how society is structured and how boys and girls, and men and women, experience social life.

Sociology and the area of women's studies have shown that men and women do not have the same opportunities in society. The distribution of power in society, when it is based on gender, finds a disproportionate amount going to males. Males are privileged and females become a minority group that suffers through discrimination in nearly every area of life. Patriarchal structures, those which advantage men and disadvantage women, are typical of society. In general, men make more money in the economy, men have more power in families, marriages, religious settings, and politics, and men are benefited more than women at every turn in life. Gender stratification in society has become a heated and much studied issue as women's roles in the United States have begun to change dramatically in the past 100 years, and even more dramatically in the past 50 years.

Although it is not true that "men are from Mars and women are from Venus," television, magazines, and popular culture stress the extreme differences between the sexes. Science, in general, and sociology, specifically, does not believe that men and women are opposites. Rather, it is understood that men and women adapt to gender roles in social settings (structures) in ways that affirm gender differences and give men an advantage at the expense of women. Women in the United States do two or three times as much home labor as men and may carry as much as ninety percent of the child care responsibilities. The family, then, is a place that can be seen as oppressing women while giving men the benefits of family life with little of the labor. These same patterns of dominance and submission are enacted in every structure in society. What is to be learned from a sociological look at gender? Is equal pay and equal power something that we can expect, or is it just another ideal pursued by a minority of people who cannot affect the social structures that maintain the differences?

Men are a more recent topic in the sociology of gender. Although women comprise the minority group, men are not without their gender issues in the United States. Violence, in its many obvious and not-so-obvious forms, is part of the masculine legacy of dominance. The agreed-on cultural imperative for men to be "real men" or "traditional men" is called hegemonic masculinity. Hegemony for men carries with it problems of violence, poor health, elevated criminal activity, increased physical risk, and shorter lives—by nearly seven years compared to women. Is it really "a man's world?"

First, the piece from Judith Lorber analyzes gender as a social structure and illuminates how the "paradox of gender" brings contrary influences to society and our lives. This seminal theoretical piece has been the standard of recent discussions about gender as "social construction" and gender as "structure." Second, in a quantitative study of advertisements by Simon Davis, we learn that gender typing occurs for both men and women. A novel use of personal ads points to the reciprocal gender biases that allow men and women to be viewed as objects. Third, Beth Quinn looks at the process of "girl watching" in organizations where people work and interact. She notices that men have difficulty seeing their behaviors as sexually harassing in this very applied and interesting study.

Reading 28

"Night to His Day"
The Social Construction of Gender

Judith Lorber

Talking about gender for most people is the equivalent of fish talking about water. Gender is so much the routine ground of everyday activities that questioning its taken-for-granted assumptions and presuppositions is like thinking about whether the sun will come up.[1] Gender is so pervasive that in our society we assume it is bred into our genes. Most people find it hard to believe that gender is constantly created and re-created out of human interaction, out of social life, and is the texture and order of that social life. Yet gender, like culture, is a human production that depends on everyone constantly "doing gender" (West and Zimmerman 1987).

And everyone "does gender" without thinking about it. Today, on the subway, I saw a well-dressed man with a year-old child in a stroller. Yesterday, on a bus, I saw a man with a tiny baby in a carrier on his chest. Seeing men taking care of small children in public is increasingly common—at least in New York City. But both men were quite obviously stared at—and smiled at, approvingly. Everyone was doing gender—the men who were changing the role of fathers and the other passengers, who were applauding them silently. But there was more gendering going on that probably fewer people noticed. The baby was wearing a white crocheted cap and white clothes. You couldn't tell if it was a boy or a girl. The child in the stroller was wearing a dark blue T-shirt and dark print pants. As they started to leave the train, the father put a Yankee baseball cap on the child's head. Ah, a boy, I thought. Then I noticed the gleam of tiny earrings in the child's ears, and as they got off, I saw the little flowered sneakers and lace-trimmed socks. Not a boy after all. Gender done.

Gender is such a familiar part of daily life that it usually takes a deliberate disruption of our expectations of how women and men are supposed to act to pay attention to how it is produced. Gender signs and signals are so ubiquitous that we usually fail to note them—unless they are missing or ambiguous. Then we are uncomfortable until we have successfully placed the other person in a gender status; otherwise, we feel socially dislocated. In our society, in addition to man and woman, the status can be *transvestite* (a person who dresses in opposite-gender clothes) and *transsexual* (a person who has had sex-change surgery). Transvestites and transsexuals carefully construct their gender status by dressing, speaking, walking, gesturing in the ways prescribed for women or men—whichever they want to be taken for—and so does any "normal" person.

For the individual, gender construction starts with assignment to a sex category on the basis of what the genitalia look like at birth.[2] Then babies are dressed or adorned in a way that displays the category because parents don't want to be constantly asked whether their baby is a girl or a boy. A sex category becomes a gender status through naming, dress, and the use of other gender markers. Once a child's gender is evident, others treat those in one gender differently from those in the other, and the children respond to the different treatment by feeling different and behaving differently. As soon as they can talk, they start to refer to themselves as members of their gender. Sex doesn't come into play again until puberty, but by that time, sexual feelings and desires and practices have been shaped by gendered norms and expectations. Adolescent boys and girls approach and avoid each other in an elaborately scripted and gendered mating dance. Parenting is gendered, with different expectations for mothers and for fathers, and people of different genders work at different kinds of jobs. The work adults do as mothers and fathers and as low-level workers and high-level bosses, shapes women's and men's life experiences, and these experiences produce different feelings, consciousness, relationships, skills—ways of being that we call feminine or masculine.[3] All of these processes constitute the social construction of gender.

Gendered roles change—today fathers are taking care of little children, girls and boys are wearing unisex clothing and getting the same education, women and men are working at the same jobs. Although many traditional social groups are quite strict about maintaining gender differences, in other social groups they seem to be blurring. Then why the one-year-old's earrings? Why is it still so important to mark a child as a girl or a boy, to make sure she is not taken for a boy or he for a girl? What would happen if they were? They would, quite literally, have changed places in their social world.

To explain why gendering is done from birth, constantly and by everyone, we have to look not only at the way individuals experience gender but at gender as a social institution. As a social institution, gender is one of the major ways that human beings organize their lives. Human society depends on a predictable division of labor, a designated allocation of scarce goods, assigned responsibility for children and others who cannot care for themselves, common values and their systematic transmission to new members, legitimate leadership, music, art, stories, games, and other symbolic productions. One way of choosing people for the different tasks of society is on the basis of their talents, motivations, and competence—their demonstrated achievements. The other way is on the basis of gender, race, ethnicity—ascribed membership in a category of people. Although societies vary in the extent to which they use one or the other of these ways of allocating people to work and to carry out other responsibilities, every society uses gender and age grades. Every society classifies people as "girl and boy children," "girls and boys ready to be married," and "fully adult women and men," constructs similarities among them and differences between them, and assigns them to different roles and responsibilities. Personality characteristics, feelings, motivations, and ambitions flow from these different life experiences so that the members of these different groups become different kinds of people. The process of gendering and its outcome are legitimated by religion, law, science, and the society's entire set of values. . . .

Western society's values legitimate gendering by claiming that it all comes from physiology—female and male procreative differences. But gender and sex are not equivalent, and gender as a social construction does not flow automatically from genitalia and reproductive organs, the main physiological differences of females and males. In the construction of ascribed social statuses, physiological differences such as sex, stage of development, color of skin, and size are crude markers. They are not the source of the social statuses of gender, age grade, and race. Social statuses are carefully constructed through prescribed processes of teaching, learning, emulation, and enforcement. Whatever genes, hormones, and biological evolution contribute to human social institutions is materially as well as qualitatively transformed by social practices. Every social institution has a material base, but culture and social practices transform that base into something with qualitatively different patterns and constraints. The economy is much more than producing food and goods and distributing them to eaters and users; family and kinship are not the equivalent of having sex and procreating; morals and religions cannot be equated with the fears and ecstasies of the brain; language goes far beyond the sounds produced by tongue and larynx. No one eats "money" or "credit"; the concepts of "god" and "angels" are the subjects of theological disquisitions; not only words but objects, such as their flag, "speak" to the citizens of a country.

Similarly, gender cannot be equated with biological and physiological differences between human females and males. The building blocks of gender are *socially constructed statuses*. Western societies have only two genders, "man" and "woman." Some societies have three genders—men, women, and *berdaches* or *hijras* or *xaniths*. Berdaches, hijras, and xaniths are biological males who behave, dress, work, and are treated in most respects as social women; they are therefore not men, nor are they female women; they are, in our language, "male women."[4] There are African and American Indian societies that have a gender status called *manly hearted women*—biological females who work, marry, and parent as men; their social status is "female men" (Amadiume 1987; Blackwood 1984). They do not have to behave or dress as men to have the social responsibilities and prerogatives of husbands and fathers; what makes them men is enough wealth to buy a wife.

Modern Western societies' *transsexuals* and *transvestites* are the nearest equivalent of these crossover genders, but they are not institutionalized as third genders (Bolin 1987). Transsexuals are biological males and females who have sex-change operations to alter their genitalia. They do so in order to bring their physical anatomy in congruence with the way they want to live and with their own sense of gender identity. They do not become a third gender; they change genders. Transvestites are males who live as women and females who live as men but do not intend to have sex-change surgery. Their dress, appearance, and mannerisms fall within the range of what is expected from members of the opposite gender, so that they "pass." They also change genders, sometimes temporarily, some for most of their lives. Transvestite women have fought in wars as men soldiers as recently as the nineteenth century; some married women, and others went back to being women and married men once the war was over.[5] Some were discovered when their wounds were treated; others not until they died. In order to work as a jazz musician, a man's occupation, Billy Tipton, a woman, lived most of her life as a man. She died recently at seventy-four, leaving a wife and three adopted sons for whom she was husband and father, and musicians with whom she had played and traveled, for whom she was "one of the boys" (*New York Times* 1989).[6] There have been many other such occurrences of women passing as men to do more prestigious or lucrative men's work (Matthaei 1982, 192–93).[7]

Genders, therefore, are not attached to a biological substratum. Gender boundaries are breachable, and individual and socially organized shifts from one gender to another call attention to "cultural, social, or aesthetic dissonances" (Garber 1992, 16). These odd or deviant or third genders show us what we ordinarily take for granted—that people have to learn to be women and men. . . .

For Individuals, Gender Means Sameness

Although the possible combinations of genitalia, body shapes, clothing, mannerisms, sexuality, and roles could produce infinite varieties in human beings, the social institution of gender depends on the production and maintenance of a limited number of gender statuses and of making the members of these statuses similar to each other. Individuals are born sexed but not gendered, and they have to be taught to be masculine or feminine.[8] As Simone de Beauvoir said: "One is not born, but rather becomes, a woman . . . ; it is civilization as a whole that produces this creature . . . which is described as feminine" (1952, 267).

Children learn to walk, talk, and gesture the way their social group says girls and boys should. Ray Birdwhistell, in his analysis of body motion as human communication, calls these learned gender displays *tertiary* sex characteristics and argues that they are needed to distinguish genders because humans are a weakly dimorphic species—their only sex markers are genitalia (1970, 39–46). Clothing, paradoxically, often hides the sex but displays the gender.

In early childhood, humans develop gendered personality structures and sexual orientations through their interactions with parents of the same and opposite gender. As adolescents, they conduct their sexual behavior according to gendered scripts. Schools, parents, peers, and the mass media guide young people into gendered work and family roles. As adults, they take on a gendered social status in their society's stratification system. Gender is thus both ascribed and achieved (West and Zimmerman 1987). . . .

Gender norms are inscribed in the way people move, gesture, and even eat. In one African society, men were supposed to eat with their "whole mouth, wholeheartedly, and not, like women, just with the lips, that is halfheartedly, with reservation and restraint" (Bourdieu [1980] 1990, 70). Men and women in this society learned to walk in ways that proclaimed their different positions in the society:

> The manly man . . . stands up straight into the face of the person he approaches, or wishes to welcome. Ever on the alert, because ever threatened, he misses nothing of what happens around him. . . . Conversely, a well brought-up woman . . . is expected to walk with a slight stoop, avoiding every misplaced movement of her body, her head or her arms, looking down, keeping her eyes on the spot where she will next put her foot, especially if she happens to have to walk past the men's assembly. (70)

. . . For human beings there is no essential femaleness or maleness, femininity or masculinity, womanhood or manhood, but once gender is ascribed, the social order constructs and holds individuals to strongly gendered norms and expectations. Individuals may vary on many of the components of gender and may shift genders temporarily or permanently, but they must fit into the limited number of gender statuses their society recognizes. In the process, they re-create their society's version of women and men: "If we do gender appropriately, we simultaneously sustain, reproduce, and render legitimate the institutional arrangements. . . . If we fail to do gender appropriately, we as individuals—not the institutional arrangements—may be called to account (for our character, motives, and predispositions)" (West and Zimmerman 1987, 146).

The gendered practices of everyday life reproduce a society's view of how women and men should act (Bourdieu [1980] 1990). Gendered social arrangements are justified by religion and cultural productions and backed by law, but the most powerful means of sustaining the moral hegemony of the dominant gender ideology is that the process is made invisible; any possible alternatives are virtually unthinkable (Foucault 1972; Gramsci 1971).[9]

For Society, Gender Means Difference

The pervasiveness of gender as a way of structuring social life demands that gender statuses be clearly differentiated. Varied talents, sexual preferences, identities, personalities, interests, and ways of interacting fragment the individual's bodily and social experiences. Nonetheless, these are organized in Western cultures into two and only two socially and legally recognized gender statuses, "man" and "woman."[10] In the social construction of gender, it does not matter what men and women actually do; it does not even matter if they do exactly the same thing. The social institution of gender insists only that what they do is *perceived* as different.

If men and women are doing the same tasks, they are usually spatially segregated to maintain gender separation, and often the tasks are given different job titles as well, such as executive secretary and administrative assistant (Reskin 1988). If the differences between women and men begin to blur, society's "sameness taboo" goes into action (G. Rubin 1975, 178). At a rock and roll dance at West Point in 1976, the year women were admitted to the prestigious military academy for the first time, the school's administrators "were reportedly perturbed by the sight of mirror-image couples dancing in short hair and dress gray trousers," and a rule was established that women cadets could dance at these events only if they wore skirts (Barkalow and Raab 1990, 53).[11] Women recruits in the U.S. Marine Corps are required to wear makeup—at a minimum, lipstick and eye shadow—and they have to take classes in makeup, hair care, poise, and etiquette. This feminization is part of a deliberate policy of making them clearly distinguishable from men Marines. Christine Williams quotes a twenty-five-year-old woman drill instructor as saying: "A lot of the recruits who come here don't wear makeup; they're tomboyish or athletic. A lot of them have the preconceived idea that going into the military means they can still be a tomboy. They don't realize that you are a *Woman* Marine" (1989, 76–77).[12]

If gender differences were genetic, physiological, or hormonal, gender bending and gender ambiguity would occur only in hermaphrodites, who are born with chromosomes and genitalia that are not clearly female or male. Since gender differences are socially constructed, all men and all women can enact the behavior of the other, because they know the other's social script: " 'Man' and 'woman' are at once empty and overflowing categories. Empty because they have no ultimate, transcendental meaning. Overflowing because even when they appear to be fixed, they still contain within them alternative, denied, or suppressed definitions" (J. W. Scott 1988a, 49). . . .

Gender Ranking

For one transsexual man-to-woman, however, the experience of living as a woman changed his/her whole personality. As James, Morris had been a soldier, foreign correspondent, and mountain climber; as Jan, Morris is a successful travel writer. But socially, James was far superior to Jan, and so Jan developed the "learned helplessness" that is supposed to characterize women in Western society:

> We are told that the social gap between the sexes is narrowing, but I can only report that having, in the second half of the twentieth century, experienced life in both roles, there seems to me no aspect of existence, no moment of the day, no contact, no arrangement, no response, which is not different for men and for women. The very tone of voice in which I was now addressed, the very posture of the person next in the queue, the very feel in the air when I entered a room or sat at a restaurant table, constantly emphasized my change of status.
>
> And if other's responses shifted, so did my own. The more I was treated as [a] woman, the more woman I became. I adapted willy-nilly. If I was assumed to be incompetent at reversing cars, or opening bottles, oddly incompetent I found myself becoming. If a case was thought too heavy for me, inexplicably I found it so myself. . . . Women treated me with a frankness which, while it was one of the happiest discoveries of my metamorphosis, did imply membership of a camp, a faction, or at least a school of thought; so I found myself gravitating always towards the female, whether in sharing a railway compartment or supporting a political cause. Men treated me more and more as junior, . . . and so, addressed every day of my life as an inferior, involuntarily, month by month I accepted the condition. I discovered that even now men prefer women to be less informed, less able, less talkative, and certainly less self-centered than they are themselves; so I generally obliged them (1975, 165–66). . . .[13]

Gender as Process, Stratification, and Structure

As a social institution, gender is a process of creating distinguishable social statuses for the assignment of rights and responsibilities. As part of a stratification system that ranks these statuses unequally, gender is a major building block in the social structures built on these unequal statuses.

As a *process*, gender creates the social differences that define "woman" and "man." In social interaction throughout their lives, individuals learn what is expected, see what is expected, act and react in expected ways, and thus simultaneously construct and maintain the gender order: "The very injunction to be a given gender takes place through discursive routes: to be a good mother, to be a heterosexually desirable object, to be a fit worker, in sum, to signify a multiplicity of guarantees in response to a variety of different demands all at once" (J. Butler 1990, 145). Members of a social group neither make up gender as they go along nor exactly replicate in rote fashion what was done before. In almost every encounter, human beings produce gender, behaving in the ways they learned were appropriate for their gender status, or resisting or rebelling against these norms. Resistance and rebellion have altered gender norms, but so far they have rarely eroded the statuses.

Gendered patterns of interaction acquire additional layers of gendered sexuality, parenting, and work behaviors in childhood, adolescence, and adulthood. Gendered norms and expectations are enforced through informal sanctions of gender-inappropriate behavior by peers and by formal punishment or threat of punishment by those in authority should behavior deviate too far from socially imposed standards for women and men. . . .

As part of a *stratification* system, gender ranks men above women of the same race and class. Women and men could be different but equal. In practice, the process of creating difference depends to a great extent on differential evaluation. As Nancy Jay (1981) says: "That which is defined, separated out, isolated from all else is A and pure. Not-A is necessarily impure, a random catchall, to which nothing is external except A and the principle of order that separates it from Not-A" (45). From the individual's point of view, whichever gender is A, the other is Not-A; gender boundaries tell the individual who is like him or her, and all the rest are unlike. From society's point of view, however, one gender is usually the touchstone, the normal, the dominant, and the other is different, deviant, and subordinate. In Western society, "man" is A, "wo-man" is Not-A. (Consider what a society would be like where woman was A and man Not-A.)

The further dichotomization by race and class constructs the gradations of a heterogeneous society's stratification scheme. Thus, in the United States, white is A, African American is Not-A; middle class is A, working class is Not-A, and "African-American women occupy a position whereby the inferior half of a series of these dichotomies converge" (P. H. Collins 1990, 70). The dominant categories are the hegemonic ideals, taken so for granted as the way things should be that white is not ordinarily thought of as a race, middle class as a class, or men as a gender. The characteristics of these categories define the Other as that which lacks the valuable qualities the dominants exhibit.

In a gender-stratified society, what men do is usually valued more highly than what women do because men do it, even when their activities are very similar or the same. In different regions of southern India, for example, harvesting rice is men's work, shared work, or women's work: "Wherever a task is done by women it is considered easy, and where it is done by [men] it is considered difficult" (Mencher 1988, 104). A gathering and hunting society's survival usually depends on the nuts, grubs, and small animals brought in by the women's foraging trips, but when the men's hunt is successful, it is the occasion for a celebration. Conversely, because they are the superior group, white men do not have to do the "dirty work," such as housework; the most inferior group does it, usually poor women of color (Palmer 1989). . . .

Societies vary in the extent of the inequality in social status of their women and men members, but where there is inequality, the status "woman" (and its attendant behavior and role allocations) is usually held in lesser esteem than the status "man." Since gender is also intertwined with a society's other constructed statuses of differential evaluation—race, religion, occupation, class, country of origin, and so on—men and women members of the favored groups command more power, more prestige, and more property than the members of the disfavored groups. Within many social groups, however, men are advantaged over women. The more economic resources, such as education and job opportunities, are available to a group, the more they tend to be monopolized by men. In poorer groups that have few resources (such as working-class African Americans in the United States), women and men are more nearly equal, and the women may even outstrip the men in education and occupational status (Almquist 1987).

As a *structure*, gender divides work in the home and in economic production, legitimates those in authority, and organizes sexuality and emotional life (Connell 1987, 91–142). As primary parents, women significantly influence children's psychological development and emotional attachments, in the process reproducing gender. Emergent sexuality is shaped by heterosexual, homosexual, bisexual, and sadomasochistic patterns that are gendered—different for girls and boys, and for women and men—so that sexual statuses reflect gender statuses.

When gender is a major component of structured inequality, the devalued genders have less power, prestige, and economic rewards than the valued genders. In countries that discourage gender discrimination, many major roles are still gendered; women still do most of the domestic labor and child rearing, even while doing full-time paid work; women and men are segregated on the job and each does work considered "appropriate"; women's work is usually paid less than men's work. Men dominate the positions of authority and leadership in government, the military, and the law; cultural productions, religions, and sports reflect men's interests.

In societies that create the greatest gender difference, such as Saudi Arabia, women are kept out of sight behind walls or veils, have no civil rights, and often create a cultural and emotional world of their own (Bernard 1981). But even in societies with less rigid gender boundaries, women and men spend much of their time with people of their own gender because of the way work and family are organized. This spatial separation of women and men reinforces gendered differentness, identity, and ways of thinking and behaving (Coser 1986).

Gender inequality—the devaluation of "women" and the social domination of "men"—has social functions and a social history. It is not the result of sex, procreation, physiology, anatomy, hormones, or genetic predispositions. It is produced and maintained by identifiable social processes and built into the general social structure and individual identities deliberately and purposefully. The social order as we know it in Western societies is organized around racial ethnic, class, and gender inequality. I contend, therefore, that the continuing purpose of gender as a modern social institution is to construct women as a group to be the subordinates of men as a group. The life of everyone placed in the status "woman" is "night to his day—that has forever been the fantasy. Black to his white. Shut out of his system's space, she is the repressed that ensures the system's functioning" (Cixous and Clément [1975] 1986, 67).

Notes

1. Gender is, in Erving Goffman's words, an aspect of *Felicity's Condition:* "any arrangement which leads us to judge an individual's . . . acts not to be a manifestation of strangeness. Behind Felicity's Condition is our sense of what it is to be sane" (1983, 27). Also see Bern 1993; Frye 1983, 17–40; Goffman 1977.

2. In cases of ambiguity in countries with modern medicine, surgery is usually performed to make the genitalia more clearly male or female.

3. See J. Butler 1990 for an analysis of how doing gender *is* gender identity.

4. On the hijras of India, see Nanda 1990; on the xaniths of Oman, Wikan 1982, 168–86; on the American Indian berdaches, W. L. Williams 1986. Other societies that have similar institutionalized third-gender men are the Koniag of Alaska, the Tanala of Madagascar, the Mesakin of Nuba, and the Chukchee of Siberia (Wikan 1982, 170).

5. Durova 1989; Freeman and Bond 1992; Wheelwright 1989.

6. Gender segregation of work in popular music still has not changed very much, according to Groce and Cooper 1989, despite considerable androgyny in some very popular figures. See Garber 1992 on the androgyny. She discusses Tipton on pp. 67–70.

7. In the nineteenth century, not only did these women get men's wages, but they also "had male privileges and could do all manner of things other women could not: open a bank account, write checks, own property, go anywhere unaccompanied, vote in elections" (Faderman 1991, 44).

8. For an account of how a potential man-to-woman transsexual learned to be feminine, see Garfinkel 1967, 116–85, 285–88. For a gloss on this account that points out how, throughout his encounters with Agnes, Garfinkel failed to see how he himself was constructing his own masculinity, see Rogers 1992.

9. The concepts of moral hegemony, the effects of everyday activities (praxis) on thought and personality, and the necessity of consciousness of these processes before political change can occur are all based on Marx's analysis of class relations.

10. Other societies recognize more than two categories, but usually no more than three or four (Jacobs and Roberts 1989).

11. Carol Barkalow's book has a photograph of eleven first-year West Pointers in a math class, who are dressed in regulation pants, shirts, and sweaters, with short haircuts. The caption challenges the reader to locate the only woman in the room.

12. The taboo on males and females looking alike reflects the U.S. military's homophobia (Bérubé 1989). If you can't tell those with a penis from those with a vagina, how are you going to determine whether their sexual interest is heterosexual or homosexual unless you watch them having sexual relations?

13. See Bolin 1988, 149–50, for transsexual men-to-women's discovery of the dangers of rape and sexual harassment. Devor's "gender blenders" went in the opposite direction. Because they found that it was an advantage to be taken for men, they did not deliberately cross-dress, but they did not feminize themselves either (1989, 126–40).

References

Almquist, Elizabeth M. 1987. Labor market gendered inequality in minority groups. *Gender & Society* 1:400–14.

Amadiume, Ifi. 1987. *Male daughters, female husbands: Gender and sex in an African society*. London: Zed Books.

Barkalow, Carol, with Andrea Raab. 1990. *In the men's house*. New York: Poseidon Press.

Bem, Sandra Lipsitz. 1993. *The lenses of gender: Transforming the debate on sexual inequality*. New Haven: Yale University Press.

Bernard, Jessie. 1981. *The female world*. New York: Free Press.

Bérubé, Allan. 1989. Marching to a different drummer: Gay and lesbian GIs in World War II. In Duberman, Vicinus, and Chauncey.

Birdwhistell, Ray L. 1970. *Kinesics and context: Essays on body motion communication*. Philadelphia: University of Pennsylvania Press.

Blackwood, Evelyn. 1984. Sexuality and gender in certain Native American tribes: The case of cross-gender females. *Signs* 10:27–42.

Bolin, Anne. 1987. Transsexualism and the limits of traditional analysis. *American Behavioral Scientist* 31:41–65.

———. 1988. *In search of Eve: Transsexual rites of passage*. South Hadley, Mass.: Bergin & Garvey.

Bourdieu, Pierre. [1980] 1990. *The logic of practice.* Stanford, Calif.: Stanford University Press.

Butler, Judith. 1990. *Gender trouble: Feminism and the subversion of identity.* New York and London: Routledge.

Cixous, Hélène, and Catherine Clément. [1975] 1986. *The newly born woman,* translated by Betsy Wing. Minneapolis: University of Minnesota Press.

Collins, Patricia Hill. 1989. The social construction of Black feminist thought. *Signs* 14:745–73.

Connell, R.[Robert] W. 1987. *Gender and power: Society, the person, and sexual politics.* Stanford, Calif.: Stanford University Press.

Coser, Rose Laub. 1986. Cognitive structure and the use of social space. *Sociological Forum* 1:1–26.

De Beauvoir, Simone. 1953. *The second sex,* translated by H. M. Parshley, New York: Knopf.

Devor, Holly. 1989. *Gender blending: Confronting the limits of duality.* Bloomington: Indiana University Press.

Durova, Nadezhda. 1989. *The cavalry maiden: Journals of a Russian officer in the Napoleonic Wars,* translated by Mary Fleming Zirin. Bloomington: Indiana University Press.

Faderman, Lillian. 1991. *Odd girls and twilight lovers: A history of lesbian life in twentieth-century America.* New York: Columbia Univeristy Press.

Foucault, Michel. 1972. *The archeology of knowledge and the discourse on language,* translated by A. M. Sheridan Smith. New York: Pantheon.

Freeman, Lucy, and Alma Halbert Bond. 1992. *America's first woman worrior: The courage of Deborah Sampson.* New York: Paragon.

Frye, Marilyn. 1983. *The politics of reality: Essays in feminist theory.* Trumansburg, N.Y.: Crossing Press.

Garber, Marjorie. 1992. *Vested interests: Cross-dressing and cultural anxiety.* New York and London: Routledge.

Garfinkel, Harold. 1967. *Studies in ethnomethodology.* Englewood Cliffs, N.J.: Prentice-Hall.

Goffman, Erving. 1977. The arrangement between the sexes. *Thoery and Society* 4:301–33.

Gramsci, Antonio. 1971. *Selections from the prison notebooks,* translated and edited by Quintin Hoare and Geoffrey Nowell Smith. New York: International Publishers.

Jacobs, Sue-Ellen, and Christine Roberts. 1989. Sex, sexuality, gender, and gender variance. In *Gender and anthropology,* edited by Sandra Morgen. Washington, D.C.: American Anthropological Association.

Jay, Nancy. 1981. Gender and dichotomy. *Feminist Studies* 7:38–56.

Matthaei, Julie A. 1982. *An economic history of women's work in America.* New York: Schocken.

Mencher, Joan. 1988. Women's work and poverty: Women's contribution to household maintenance in South India. In Dwyer and Bruce.

Morris, Jan. 1975. *Conundrum.* New York: Signet.

Nanda, Serena. 1990. *Neither man nor woman: The hijiras of India.* Belmont, Calif.: Wadsworth.

New York Times. 1989a. Musician's death at 74 reveals he was a woman. 2 February.

Palmer, Phyllis. 1989. *Domesticity and dirt: Housewives and domestic servants in the United States, 1920–1945.* Philadelphia: Temple University Press.

Reskin, Barbara F. 1988. Bringing the men back in: Sex differentiation and the devaluation of women's work. *Gender & Society* 2:58–81.

Rogers, Mary F. 1992. They were all passing: Agnes, Garfinkel, and company. *Gender & Society* 6:169–91.

Rubin, Gayle. 1975. The traffic in women: Notes on the political economy of sex. In *Toward an anthropology of women*, edited by Rayna R[app] Reiter. New York: Monthly Review Press.

Scott, Joan Wallach. 1988a. *Gender and the politics of history.* New York: Columbia University Press.

West, Candace, and Don Zimmerman. 1987. Doing gender. *Gender & Society* 1:125–51.

Wheelwright, Julie. 1989. *Amazons and military maids: Women who cross-dressed in pursuit of life, liberty and happiness.* London: Pandora Press.

Wikan, Unni. 1982. *Behind the veil in Arabia: Women in Oman.* Baltimore, Md.: Johns Hopkins University Press.

Williams, Christine L. 1989. *Gender differences at work: Women and men in nontraditional occupations.* Berkeley: University of California Press.

Williams, Walter L. 1986. *The spirit and the flesh: Sexual diversity in American Indian culture.* Boston: Beacon Press.

Study Questions

1. What does it mean when Lorber writes "night to his day"? What are the sociological implications of this metaphor?

2. After reading this selection, which includes a great deal of sociological theory, how different do you think men and women really are? List the differences and similarities.

Reading 29

Men as Success Objects and Women as Sex Objects
A Study of Personal Advertisements

Simon Davis

Previous research has indicated that, to a large extent, selection of opposite-sex partners is dictated by traditional sex stereotypes (Urberg, 1979). More specifically, it has been found that men tend to emphasize sexuality and physical attractiveness in a mate to a greater extent than women (e.g., Harrison & Saeed, 1977; Deaux & Hanna, 1984; Nevid, 1984); this distinction has been found across cultures, as in the study by Stiles and colleagues (1987) of American and Icelandic adolescents.

The relatively greater preoccupation with casual sexual encounters demonstrated by men (Hite, 1987, p. 184) may be accounted for by the greater emotional investment that women place in sex; Basow (1986, p. 80) suggests that the "gender differences in this area (different meaning attached to sex) may turn out to be the strongest of all gender differences."

Women, conversely, may tend to emphasize psychological and personality characteristics (Curry & Hock, 1981; Deaux & Hanna, 1984), and to seek longevity and commitment in a relationship to a greater extent (Basow, 1986, p. 213).

Women may also seek financial security more so than men (Harrison & Saeed, 1977). Regarding this last point, Farrell (1986, p. 25) suggests that the tendency to treat men as success objects is reflected in the media, particularly in advertisements in women's magazines. On the other hand, men themselves may reinforce this stereotype in that a number of men still apparently prefer the traditional marriage with working husband and unemployed wife (Basow, 1986, p. 210).

Men have traditionally been more dominant in intellectual matters, and this may be reinforced in the courting process: Braito (1981) found in his study that female coeds feigned intellectual inferiority with their dates on a number of occasions. In the same vein, Hite, in her 1981 survey, found that men were less likely to seek intellectual prowess in their mate (p. 108).

The mate selection process has been characterized in at least two ways. Harrison and Saeed (1977) found evidence for a matching process, where individuals seeking particular characteristics in a partner were more likely to offer those characteristics in themselves. This is consistent with the observation that "like attracts like" and that husbands and wives tend to resemble one another in various ways (Thiessen & Gregg, 1980). Additionally, an exchange process may be in operation, wherein a trade-off is made with women offering "domestic work and sex for financial support" (Basow, 1986, p. 213).

With respect to sex stereotypes and mate selection, the trend has been for "both sexes to believe that the other sex expects them to live up to the gender stereotype" (Basow, 1986, p. 209).

Theoretical explanations of sex stereotypes in mate selection range from the sociobiological (Symons, 1987) to radical political views (Smith, 1973). Of interest in recent years has been demographic influences, that is, the lesser availability of men because of population shifts and marital patterns (Shaevitz, 1987, p. 40). Age may differentially affect women, particularly when children are desired; this, combined with women's generally lower economic status [particularly when unmarried (Halas, 1981, p. 124)], may mean that the need to "settle down" into a secure, committed relationship becomes relatively more crucial for women.

The present study looks at differential mate selection by men and women as reflected in newspaper companion ads. Using such a forum for the exploration of sex stereotypes is not new; for instance, in the study by Harrison and Saeed (1977) cited earlier, the authors found that in such ads women were more likely to seek financial security and men to seek attractiveness; a later study by Deaux and Hanna (1984) had similar results, along with the finding that women were more likely to seek psychological characteristics, specific personality traits, and to emphasize the quality and longevity of the relationship. The present study may be seen as a follow-up of this earlier research, although on this occasion using a Canadian setting. Of particular interest was the following: Were traditional stereotypes still in operation, that is, women being viewed as sex objects and men as success objects (the latter defined as financial and intellectual accomplishments)?

Method

Personal advertisements were taken from the *Vancouver Sun*, which is the major daily newspaper serving Vancouver, British Columbia. The *Sun* is generally perceived as a conservative, respectable journal—hence it was assumed that people advertising in it represented the "mainstream." It should be noted that people placing the ads must do so in person. For the sake of this study, gay ads were not included. A typical ad would run about 50 words, and included a brief description of the person placing it and a list of the attributes desired in the other party. Only the parts pertaining to the attributes desired in the partner were included for analysis. Attributes that pertained to hobbies or recreations were not included for the purpose of this study.

The ads were sampled as follows: Only Saturday ads were used, since in the *Sun* the convention was for Saturday to be the main day for personal ads, with 40–60 ads per edition—compared to only 2–4 ads per edition on weekdays. Within any one edition *all* the ads were included for analysis. Six editions were randomly sampled, covering the period of September 30, 1988, to September 30, 1989. The attempt to sample through the calendar year was made in an effort to avoid any unspecified seasonal effect. The size of the sample (six editions) was large enough to meet goodness-of-fit requirements for statistical tests.

The attributes listed in the ads were coded as follows:

1. *Attractive:* specified that a partner should be, for example, "pretty" or "handsome."
2. *Physique:* similar to 1; however, this focused not on the face but rather on whether the partner was "fit and trim," "muscular," or had "a good figure." If it was not clear if body or face was being emphasized, this fell into variable (1) by default.
3. *Sex:* specified that the partner should have, for instance, "high sex drive," or should be "sensuous" or "erotic," or if there was a clear message that this was an arrangement for sexual purposes ("lunchtime liaisons—discretion required").
4. *Picture:* specified that the partner should include a photo in his/her reply.
5. *Profession:* specified that the partner should be a professional.

6. *Employed:* specified that the partner should be employed, e.g., "must hold steady job" or "must have steady income."

7. *Financial:* specified that the partner should be, for instance, "financially secure" or "financially independent."

8. *Education:* specified that the partner should be, for instance, "well educated" or "well read," or should be a "college grad."

9. *Intelligence:* specified that the partner should be "intelligent," "intellectual," or "bright."

10. *Honest:* specified, for instance, that the partner should be "honest" or have "integrity."

11. *Humor:* specified "sense of humor" or "cheerfulness."

12. *Commitment:* specified that the relationship was to be "long term" or "lead to marriage," or some other indication of stability and longevity.

13. *Emotion:* specified that the partner should be "warm," "romantic," "emotionally supportive," "emotionally expressive," "sensitive," "loving," "responsive," or similar terms indicating an opposition to being cold and aloof.

In addition to the 13 attribute variables, two other pieces of information were collected: The length of the ad (in lines) and the age of the person placing the ad. Only if age was exactly specified was it included; if age was vague (e.g., "late 40s") this was not counted.

Variables were measured in the following way: Any ad requesting one of the 13 attributes was scored once for that attribute. If not explicitly mentioned, it was not scored. The scoring was thus "all or nothing," e.g., no matter how many times a person in a particular ad stressed that looks were important it was only counted as a single score in the "attractive" column; thus, each single score represented one person. Conceivably, an individual ad could mention all, some, or none of the variables. Comparisons were then made between the sexes on the basis of the variables, using percentages and chi-squares. Chi-square values were derived by cross-tabulating gender (male/female) with attribute (asked for/not asked for). Degrees of freedom in all cases equaled one. Finally, several of the individual variables were collapsed to get an overall sense of the relative importance of (a) physical factors, (b) employment factors, and (c) intellectual factors.

Results

A total of 329 personal ads were contained in the six newspaper editions studied. One ad was discarded in that it specified a gay relationship, leaving a total sample of 328. Of this number, 215 of the ads were placed by men (65.5%) and 113 by women (34.5%).

The mean age of people placing ads was 40.4. One hundred and twenty seven cases (38.7%) counted as missing data in that the age was not specified or was vague. The mean age for the two sexes was similar: 39.4 for women (with 50.4% of cases missing) and 40.7% for men (with 32.6% of cases missing).

Sex differences in desired companion attributes are summarized in Table I. It will be seen that for 10 of the 13 variables a statistically significant difference was detected. The three largest differences were found for attractiveness, professional and financial status. To summarize the table: in the case of attractiveness, physique, sex, and picture (physical attributes) the men were more likely than the women to seek these. In the case of professional status, employment status, financial status, intelligence,

Table I.   Gender Comparison for Attributes Desired in Partner

| | Gender | | |
Variable	Desired by men ($n = 215$)	Desired by women ($n = 113$)	Chi-square
1. Attractive	76 (35.3%)	20 (17.7%)	11.13[a]
2. Physique	81 (37.7%)	27 (23.9%)	6.37[a]
3. Sex	25 (11.6%)	4 (3.5%)	6.03[a]
4. Picture	74 (34.4%)	24 (21.2%)	6.18[a]
5. Profession	6 (2.8%)	19 (16.8%)	20.74[a]
6. Employed	8 (3.7%)	12 (10.6%)	6.12[a]
7. Financial	7 (3.2%)	22 (19.5%)	24.26[a]
8. Education	8 (3.7%)	8 (7.1%)	1.79 (ns)
9. Intelligence	22 (10.2%)	24 (21.2%)	7.46[a]
10. Honest	20 (9.3%)	17 (15.0%)	2.44 (ns)
11. Humor	36 (16.7%)	26 (23.0%)	1.89 (ns)
12. Commitment	38 (17.6%)	31 (27.4%)	4.25[a]
13. Emotion	44 (20.5%)	35 (31.0%)	4.36[a]

[a]Significant at the .05 level.

commitment, and emotion (nonphysical attributes) the women were more likely to seek these. The women were also more likely to specify education, honesty and humor, however not at a statistically significant level.

The data were explored further by collapsing several of the categories: the first 4 variables were collapsed into a "physical" category, Variables 5–7 were collapsed into an "employment" category, and Variables 8 and 9 were collapsed into an "intellectual" category. The assumption was that the collapsed categories were sufficiently similar (within the three new categories) to make the new larger categories conceptually meaningful; conversely, it was felt the remaining variables (10–13) could not be meaningfully collapsed any further.

Sex differences for the three collapsed categories are summarized in Table II. Note that the Table II figures were not derived simply by adding the numbers in the Table I categories: recall that for Variables 1–4 a subject could specify all, one, or none; hence simply adding the Table I figures would be biased by those individuals who were more effusive in specifying various physical traits. Instead, the Table II categories are (like Table I) all or nothing: whether a subject specified one or all four of the physical attributes it would only count once. Thus, each score represented one person.

Table II. Gender Comparison for Physical, Employment, and Intellectual Attributes Desired in Partner

	Gender		
Variable	Desired by men ($n = 215$)	Desired by women ($n = 113$)	Chi-square
Physical (collapsing Variables 1–4)	143 (66.5%)	50 (44.2%)	15.13[a]
Employment (collapsing Variables 5–7)	17 (7.9%)	47 (41.6%)	51.36[a]
Intellectual (collapsing 8 and 9)	29 (13.5%)	31 (27.4%)	9.65[a]

[a]Significant at the .05 level.

In brief, Table II gives similar, although more exaggerated results to Table I. (The exaggeration is the result of only one item of several being needed to score within a collapsed category.) The men were more likely than the women to specify some physical attribute. The women were considerably more likely to specify that the companion be employed, or have a profession, or be in good financial shape. And the women were more likely to emphasize the intellectual abilities of their mate.

One can, incidentally, also note from this table an overall indication of attribute importance by collapsing across sexes, i.e., it is apparent that physical characteristics are the most desired regardless of sex.

Discussion

Sex Differences

This study found that the attitudes of the subjects, in terms of desired companion attributes, were consistent with traditional sex role stereotypes. The men were more likely to emphasize stereotypically desirable feminine traits (appearance) and deemphasize the nonfeminine traits (financial, employment, and intellectual status). One inconsistency was that emotional expressiveness is a feminine trait but was emphasized relatively less by the men. Women, on the other hand, were more likely to emphasize masculine traits such as financial, employment, and intellectual status, and valued commitment in a relationship more highly. One inconsistency detected for the women concerned the fact that although emotional expressiveness is not a masculine trait, the women in this sample asked for it, relatively more than the men, anyway. Regarding this last point, it may be relevant to refer to Basow's (1986, p. 210) conclusion that "women prefer relatively androgynous men, but men, especially traditional ones, prefer relatively sex-typed women."

These findings are similar to results from earlier studies, e.g., Deaux and Hanna (1984), and indicate that at this point in time and in this setting sex role stereotyping is still in operation.

One secondary finding that was of some interest to the author was that considerably more men than women placed personal ads—almost a 2:1 ratio. One can only speculate as to why this was so; however, there are probably at least two (related) contributing factors. One is that social convention dictates that women should be less outgoing in the initiation of relationships: Green and Sandos (1983) found that women who initiated dates were viewed less positively than their male counterparts. Another factor is that whoever places the ad is in a "power position" in that they can check out the other person's letter and photo, and then make a choice, all in anonymity; one could speculate that this need to be in control might be more an issue for the men.

Methodological Issues

Content analysis of newspaper ads has its strengths and weaknesses. By virtue of being an unobtrusive study of variables with face validity, it was felt some reliable measure of gender-related attitudes was being achieved. That the mean age of the men and women placing the ads was similar was taken as support for the assumption that the two sexes in this sample were demographically similar. Further, sex differences in desired companion attributes could not be attributed to differential verbal ability in that it was found that length of ad was similar for both sexes.

On the other hand, there were some limitations. It could be argued that people placing personal ads are not representative of the public in general. For instance, with respect to this study, it was found that the subjects were a somewhat older group—mean age of 40—than might be found in other courting situations. This raises the possibility of age being a confounding variable. Older singles may emphasize certain aspects of a relationship, regardless of sex. On the other hand, there is the possibility that age differentially affects women in the mate selection process, particularly when children are desired. The strategy of controlling for age in the analysis was felt problematic in that the numbers for analysis were fairly small, especially given the missing data, and further, that one cannot assume the missing cases were not systematically different (i.e., older) from those present.

References

Basow, S. (1986). *Gender stereotypes: Traditions and alternatives.* Brooks/Cole Publishing Co.

Braito, R. (1981). The inferiority game: Perceptions and behavior. *Sex Roles, 7,* 65–72.

Curry, T., & Hock, R. (1981). Sex differences in sex role ideals in early adolescence. *Adolescence, 16,* 779–789.

Deaux, K., & Hanna, R. (1984). Courtship in the personals column: The influence of gender and sexual orientation. *Sex Roles, 11,* 363–375.

Farrell, W. (1986). *Why men are the way they are.* New York: Berkley Books.

Green, S., & Sandos, P. (1983). Perceptions of male and female initiators of relationship. *Sex Roles, 9,* 849–852.

Halas, C. (1981). *Why can't a woman be more like a man?* New York: Macmillan Publishing Co.

Harrison, A., & Saeed, L. (1977). Let's make a deal: An analysis of revelations and stipulations in lonely hearts advertisements. *Journal of Personality and Social Psychology, 35,* 257–264.

Hite, S. (1981). *The Hite report on male sexuality.* New York: Alfred A. Knopf.

Hite, S. (1987). *Women and love: A cultural revolution in progress.* New York: Alfred A. Knopf.

Nevid, J. (1984). Sex differences in factors of romantic attraction. *Sex Roles, 11,* 401–411.

Shaevitz, M. (1987). *Sexual static.* Boston: Little, Brown & Co.

Smith, D. (1973). Women, the family and corporate capitalism. In M. Stephenson (Ed.), *Women in Canada.* Toronto: New Press.

Stiles, D., Gibbon, J., Hardardottir, S., & Schnellmann, J. (1987). The ideal man or woman as described by young adolescents in Iceland and the United States. *Sex Roles, 17,* 313–320.

Symons, D. (1987). An evolutionary approach. In J. Geer & W. O'Donohue (Eds.), *Theories of human sexuality.* New York: Plenum Press.

Thiessen, D., & Gregg, B. (1980). Human assortive mating and genetic equilibrium: An evolutionary perspective. *Ethology and Sociobiology, 1,* 111–140.

Urberg, K. (1979). Sex role conceptualization in adolescents and adults. *Developmental Psychology, 15,* 90–92.

Study Questions

1. What does it mean when Davis concludes that men and women are "objectified" by personal ads? Give an example of how you have objectified someone of the other gender and an example of how you have been objectified, too.

2. What conclusions does Davis draw from the two tables printed in the article?

Sexual Harassment and Masculinity

The Power and Meaning of "Girl Watching"

Beth A. Quinn

Confronted with complaints about sexual harassment or accounts in the media, some men claim that women are too sensitive or that they too often misinterpret men's intentions (Bernstein 1994; Buckwald 1993). In contrast, some women note with frustration that men just "don't get it" and lament the seeming inadequacy of sexual harassment policies (Conley 1991; Guccione 1992). Indeed, this ambiguity in defining acts of sexual harassment might be, as Cleveland and Kerst (1993) suggested, the most robust finding in sexual harassment research.

Using in-depth interviews with 43 employed men and women, this article examines a particular social practice—"girl watching"—as a means to understanding one way that these gender differences are produced. This analysis does not address the size or prevalence of these differences, nor does it present a direct comparison of men and women; this information is essential but well covered in the literature.[1] Instead, I follow Cleveland and Kerst's (1993) and Wood's (1998) suggestion that the question may best be unraveled by exploring how the "subject(ivities) of perpetrators, victims, and resistors of sexual harassment" are "discursively produced, reproduced, and altered" (Wood 1998, 28).

This article focuses on the subjectivities of the perpetrators of a disputable form of sexual harassment, "girl watching." The term refers to the act of men's sexually evaluating women, often in the company of other men. It may take the form of a verbal or gestural message of "check it out," boasts of sexual prowess, or explicit comments about a woman's body or imagined sexual acts. The target may be an individual woman or group of women or simply a photograph or other representation. The woman may be a stranger, coworker, supervisor, employee, or client. For the present analysis, girl watching within the workplace is centered.

The analysis is grounded in the work of masculinity scholars such as Connell (1987, 1995) in that it attempts to explain the subject positions of the interviewed men—not the abstract and genderless subjects of patriarchy but the gendered and privileged subjects embedded in this system. Since I am attempting to delineate the gendered worldviews of the interviewed men, I employ the term "girl watching," a phrase that reflects their language ("they watch girls").

I have chosen to center the analysis on girl watching within the workplace for two reasons. First, it appears to be fairly prevalent. For example, a survey of federal civil employees (U.S. Merit Systems Protection Board 1988) found that in the previous 24 months, 28 percent of the women surveyed had experienced "unwanted sexual looks or gestures," and 35 percent had experienced "unwanted sexual teasing, jokes, remarks, or questions." Second, girl watching is still often normalized and trivialized as only play, or "boys will be boys." A man watching girls—even in his workplace—is frequently accepted as a natural and commonplace activity, especially if he is in the presence of other men.[2] Indeed, it may be required (Hearn 1985). Thus, girl watching sits on the blurry edge between fun and harm, joking and harassment. An understanding of the process of identifying behavior as sexual harassment, or of rejecting this label, may be built on this ambiguity. . . .

Previous Research

The question of how behavior is or is not labeled as sexual harassment has been studied primarily through experimental vignettes and surveys.[3] In both methods, participants evaluate either hypothetical scenarios or lists of behaviors, considering whether, for example, the behavior constitutes sexual harassment, which party is most at fault, and what consequences the act might engender. Researchers manipulate factors such as the level of "welcomeness" the target exhibits and the relationship of the actors (supervisor-employee, coworker-coworker).

Both methods consistently show that women are willing to define more acts as sexual harassment (Gutek, Morasch, and Cohen 1983; Padgitt and Padgitt 1986; Powell 1986; York 1989; but see Stockdale and Vaux 1993) and are more likely to see situations as coercive (Garcia, Milano, and Quijano 1989). When asked who is more to blame in a particular scenario, men are more likely to blame, and less likely to empathize with, the victim (Jensen and Gutek 1982; Kenig and Ryan 1986). In terms of actual behaviors like girl watching, the U.S. Merit Systems Protection Board (1988) survey found that 81 percent of the women surveyed considered "uninvited sexually suggestive looks or gestures" from a supervisor to be sexual harassment. While the majority of men (68 percent) also defined it as such, significantly more men were willing to dismiss such behavior. Similarly, while 40 percent of the men would not consider the same behavior from a coworker to be harassing, more than three-quarters of the women would.

The most common explanation offered for these differences is gender role socialization. This conclusion is supported by the consistent finding that the more men and women adhere to traditional gender roles, the more likely they are to deny the harm in sexual harassment and to consider the behavior acceptable or at least normal (Gutek and Koss 1993; Malovich and Stake 1990; Murrell and Dietz-Uhler 1993; Popovich et al. 1992; Pryor 1987; Tagri and Hayes 1997). Men who hold predatory ideas about sexuality, who are more likely to believe rape myths, and who are more likely to self-report that they would rape under certain circumstances are less likely to see behaviors as harassing (Murrell and Dietz-Uhler 1993; Pryor 1987; Reilly et al. 1992). . . .

Method

I conducted 43 semistructured interviews with currently employed men and women between June 1994 and March 1995. . . . The interviews ranged in length from one to three hours. With one exception, interviews were audiotaped and transcribed in full. . . .

The interviews began with general questions about friendships and work relationships and progressed to specific questions about gender relations, sexual harassment, and the policies that seek to address it.[4] Since the main aim of the project was to explore how workplace events are framed as sexual harassment (and as legally bounded or not), the term "sexual harassment" was not introduced by the interviewer until late in the interview. . . .

Several related themes emerged and are discussed in the subsequent analysis. First, girl watching appears to function as a form of gendered play among men. This play is productive of masculine identities and premised on a studied lack of empathy with the feminine other. Second, men understand the targeted woman to be an object rather than a player in the game, and she is most often not the intended audience. This obfuscation of a woman's subjectivity, and men's refusal to consider the effects of their behavior, means men are likely to be confused when a woman complains. Thus, the production of masculinity though girl watching, and its compulsory disempathy, may be one factor in gender differences in the labeling of harassment.

Findings: Girl Watching as "Hommo-Sexuality"

> [They] had a button on the computer that you pushed if there was a girl who came to the front counter. . . . It was a code and it said "BAFC"—Babe at Front Counter. . . . If the guy in the back looked up and saw a cute girl come in the station, he would hit this button for the other dispatcher to [come] see the cute girl.
>
> *—Paula, police officer*

In its most serious form, girl watching operates as a targeted tactic of power. The men seem to want everyone—the targeted woman as well as coworkers, clients, and superiors—to know they are looking. The gaze demonstrates their right, as men, to sexually evaluate women. Through the gaze, the targeted woman is reduced to a sexual object, contradicting her other identities, such as that of competent worker or leader. . . .

But when they ogle, gawk, whistle and point, are men always so directly motivated to disempower their women colleagues? Is the target of the gaze also the intended audience? Consider, for example, this account told by Ed, a white, 29-year-old instrument technician.

> When a group of guys goes to a bar or a nightclub and they try to be manly. . . . A few of us always found [it] funny [when] a woman would walk by and a guy would be like, "I can have her." [pause] "Yeah. OK, we want to see it!" [laugh]

In his account—a fairly common one in men's discussions—the passing woman is simply a visual cue for their play. It seems clear that it is a game played by men for men; the woman's participation and awareness of her role seem fairly unimportant.

As Thorne (1993) reminded us, we should not be too quick to dismiss games as "only play." In her study of gender relations in elementary schools, Thorne found play to be a powerful form of gendered social action. One of its "clusters of meaning" most relevant here is that of "dramatic performance." In this, play functions as both a source of fun and a mechanism by which gendered identities, group boundaries, and power relations are (re)produced. . . .

Producing Masculinity

I suggest that girl watching in this form functions simultaneously as a form of play and as a potentially powerful site of gendered social action. Its social significance lies in its power to form identities and relationships based on these common practices for, as Cockburn (1983, 123) has noted, "patriarchy is as much about relations between man and man as it is about relations between men and women." Girl watching works similarly to the sexual joking that Johnson (1988) suggested is a common way for heterosexual men to establish intimacy among themselves.

In particular, girl watching works as a dramatic performance played to other men, a means by which a certain type of masculinity is produced and heterosexual desire displayed. It is a means by which men assert a masculine identity to other men, in an ironic "hommo-sexual" practice of heterosexuality (Butler 1990).[5] As Connell (1995) and others (Butler 1990; West and Zimmerman 1987) have aptly noted, masculinity is not a static identity but rather one that must constantly be reclaimed. The content of any performance—and there are multiple forms—is influenced by a hegemonic notion of masculinity. When asked what "being a man" entailed, many of the men and women I interviewed triangulated toward notions of strength (if not in muscle, then in character and job performance), dominance, and a marked sexuality, overflowing and uncontrollable to some degree and natural to the male "species." Heterosexuality is required, for just as the label "girl" questions a man's claim to masculine power, so does the label "fag" (Hopkins 1992; Pronger 1992). I asked Karl, for example, if he would consider his sons "good men" if they were gay. His response was laced with ambivalence; he noted only that the question was "a tough one."

The practice of girl watching is just that—a practice—one rehearsed and performed in everyday settings. This aspect of rehearsal was evident in my interview with Mike, a self-employed house painter who used to work construction. In locating himself as a born-again Christian, Mike recounted the girl watching of his fellow construction workers with contempt. Mike was particularly disturbed by a man who brought his young son to the job site one day. The boy was explicitly taught to catcall, a practice that included identifying the proper targets: women and effeminate men.

Girl watching, however, can be somewhat tenuous as a masculine practice. In their acknowledgment (to other men) of their supposed desire lies the possibility that in being too interested in women the players will be seen as mere schoolboys giggling in the playground. Taken too far, the practice undermines rather than supports a masculine performance. In Karl's discussion of girl watching, for example, he continually came back to the problem of men's not being careful about getting caught. He referred to a particular group of men who, though "their wives are [pause] very attractive—very much so," still "gawk like schoolboys." Likewise, Stephan explained that men who are obvious, who "undress [women] with their eyes" probably do so "because they don't get enough women in their lives. Supposedly." A man must be interested in women, but not too interested; they must show their (hetero)sexual interest, but not overly so, for this would be to admit that women have power over them. . . .

The Problem with Getting Caught

But are women really the untroubled objects that girl watching—viewed through the eyes of men—suggests? Obviously not; the game may be premised on a denial of a woman's subjectivity, but an actual erasure is beyond men's power! It is in this multiplicity of subjectivities, as Butler (1990, ix) noted, where "trouble" lurks, provoked by "the unanticipated agency of a female 'object' who inexplicably returns the glance, reverses the gaze, and contests the place and authority of the masculine position." To face a returned gaze is to get caught, an act that has the power to undermine the logic of girl watching as simply a game among men. Karl, for example, noted that when caught, men are often flustered, a reaction suggesting that the boundaries of usual play have been disturbed.[6]

When a woman looks back, when she asks, "What are you looking at?" she speaks as a subject, and her status as mere object is disturbed. When the game is played as a form of hommo-sexuality, the confronted man may be baffled by her response. When she catches them looking, when she complains, the targeted woman speaks as a subject. The men, however, understand her primarily as an object, and objects do not object. . . .

Reactions to Anti-Sexual Harassment Training Programs

The role that objectification and disempathy play in men's girl watching has important implications for sexual harassment training. Consider the following account of a sexual harassment training session given in Cindy's workplace. Cindy, an Italian American woman in her early 20s, worked as a recruiter for a small telemarketing company in Southern California.

> [The trainer] just really laid down the ground rules, um, she had some scenarios. Saying, "OK, would you consider this sexual harassment?" "Would you . . . " this, this, this? "What level?" Da-da-da. So, um, they just gave us some real numbers as to lawsuits and cases. Just that "you guys better be careful" type of a thing.

From Cindy's description, this training is fairly typical in that it focuses on teaching participants definitions of sexual harassment and the legal ramifications of accusations. The trainer used the common strategy of presenting videos of potentially harassing situations and asking the participants how they would judge them. Cindy's description of the men's responses to these videos reveals the limitation of this approach.

> We were watching [the TV] and it was [like] a studio audience. And [men] were getting up in the studio audience making comments like "Oh well, look at her! I wouldn't want to do that to her either!" "Well, you're darn straight, look at her!"

Interestingly, the men successfully used the training session videos as an opportunity for girl watching through their public sexual evaluations of the women depicted. In this, the intent of the training session was doubly subverted. The men interpreted scenarios that Cindy found plainly harassing into mere instances of girl watching and sexual (dis)interest. . . .

Conclusions

In this analysis, I have sought to unravel the social logic of girl watching and its relationship to the question of gender differences in the interpretation of sexual harassment. In the form analyzed here, girl watching functions simultaneously as only play and as a potent site where power is played. Through the objectification on which it is premised and in the nonempathetic masculinity it supports, this form of girl watching simultaneously produces both the harassment and the barriers to men's acknowledgment of its potential harm.

The implications these findings have for anti-sexual harassment training are profound. If we understand harassment to be the result of a simple lack of knowledge (of ignorance), then straightforward informational sexual harassment training may be effective. The present analysis suggests, however, that the etiology of some harassment lies elsewhere. While they might have quarreled with it, most of the men I interviewed had fairly good abstract understandings of the behaviors their companies' sexual harassment policies prohibited. At the same time, in relating stories of social relations in their workplaces, most failed to identify specific behaviors as sexual harassment when they matched the abstract definition. As I have argued, the source of this contradiction lies not so much in ignorance but in acts of ignoring. Traditional sexual harassment training programs address the former rather than the later. As such, their effectiveness against sexually harassing behaviors born out of social practices of masculinity like girl watching is questionable.

Ultimately, the project of challenging sexual harassment will be frustrated and our understanding distorted unless we interrogate hegemonic, patriarchal forms of masculinity and the practices by which they are (re)produced. We must continue to research the processes by which sexual harassment is produced and the gendered identities and subjectivities on which it poaches (Wood 1998). My study provides a first step toward a more process-oriented understanding of sexual harassment, the ways the social meanings of harassment are constructed, and ultimately, the potential success of antiharassment training programs.

Notes

1. See Welsh (1999) for a review of this literature.
2. For example, Maria, an administrative assistant I interviewed, simultaneously echoed and critiqued this understanding when she complained about her boss's girl watching in her presence: "If he wants to do that in front of other men . . . you know, that's what men do."
3. Recently, more researchers have turned to qualitative studies as a means to understand the process of labeling behavior as harassment. Of note are Collinson and Collinson (1996), Giuffre and Williams (1994), Quinn (2000), and Rogers and Henson (1997).
4. Acme employees were interviewed at work in an office off the main lobby. Students and referred participants were interviewed at sites convenient to them (e.g., an office, the library).
5. "Hommo" is a play on the French word for man, *homme.*
6. Men are not always concerned with getting caught, as the behavior of catcalling construction workers amply illustrates; that a woman hears is part of the thrill (Gardner 1995). The difference between the workplace and the street is the level of anonymity the men have vis-à-vis the woman and the complexity of social rules and the diversity of power sources an individual has at his or her disposal.

References

Bernstein, R. 1994. Guilty if charged. *New York Review of Books*, 13 January.

Buckwald, A. 1993. Compliment a woman, go to court. *Los Angeles Times*, 28 October.

Butler, J. 1990. *Gender trouble: Feminism and the subversion of identity.* New York: Routledge.

Cleveland, J. N., and M. E. Kerst. 1993. Sexual harassment and perceptions of power: An underarticulated relationship. *Journal of Vocational Behavior* 42 (1): 49–67.

Cockburn, C. 1983. *Brothers: Male dominance and technological change.* London: Pluto Press.

Conley, F. K. 1991. Why I'm leaving Stanford: I wanted my dignity back. *Los Angeles Times*, 9 June.

Connell, R. W. 1987. *Gender and power.* Stanford, CA: Stanford University Press.

———. 1995. *Masculinities.* Berkeley: University of California Press.

Garcia, L., L. Milano, and A. Quijano. 1989. Perceptions of coercive sexual behavior by males and females. *Sex Roles* 21 (9/10): 569–77.

Gardner, C. B. 1995. *Passing by: Gender and public harassment.* Berkeley: University of California Press.

Giuffre, P., and C. Williams. 1994. Boundary lines: Labeling sexual harassment in restaurants. *Gender & Society* 8:378–401.

Guccione, J. 1992. Women judges still fighting harassment. *Daily Journal*, 13 October, 1.

Gutek, B. A., and M. P. Koss. 1993. Changed women and changed organizations: Consequences of and coping with sexual harassment. *Journal of Vocational Behavior* 42 (1): 28–48.

Gutek, B. A., B. Morasch, and A. G. Cohen. 1983. Interpreting social-sexual behavior in a work setting. *Journal of Vocational Behavior* 22 (1): 30–48.

Hearn, J. 1985. Men's sexuality at work. In *The sexuality of men*, edited by A. Metcalf and M. Humphries. London: Pluto Press.

Hopkins, P. 1992. Gender treachery: Homophobia, masculinity, and threatened identities. In *Rethinking masculinity: Philosophical explorations in light of feminism*, edited by L. May and R. Strikwerda. Lanham, MD: Littlefield, Adams.

Jensen, I. W., and B. A. Gutek. 1982. Attributions and assignment of responsibility in sexual harassment. *Journal of Social Issues* 38 (4): 121–36.

Johnson, M. 1988. *Strong mothers, weak wives*. Berkeley: University of California Press.

Kenig, S., and J. Ryan. 1986. Sex differences in levels of tolerance and attribution of blame for sexual harassment on a university campus. *Sex Roles* 15 (9/10): 535–49.

Malovich, N. J., and J. E. Stake. 1990. Sexual harassment on campus: Individual differences in attitudes and beliefs. *Psychology of Women Quarterly* 14 (1): 63–81.

Murrell, A. J., and B. L. Dietz-Uhler. 1993. Gender identity and adversarial sexual beliefs as predictors of attitudes toward sexual harassment. *Psychology of Women Quarterly* 17 (2): 169–75.

Padgitt, S. C., and J. S. Padgitt. 1986. Cognitive structure of sexual harassment: Implications for university policy. *Journal of College Student Personnel* 27:34–39.

Popovich, P. M., D. N. Gehlauf, J. A. Jolton, J. M. Somers, and R. M. Godinho. 1992. Perceptions of sexual harassment as a function of sex of rater and incident form and consequent. *Sex Roles* 27 (11/12): 609–25.

Powell, G. N. 1986. Effects of sex-role identity and sex on definitions of sexual harassment. *Sex Roles* 14:9–19.

Pronger, B. 1992. Gay jocks: A phenomenology of gay men in athletics. In *Rethinking masculinity: Philosophical explorations in light of feminism*, edited by L. May and R. Strikwerda. Lanham, MD: Littlefield Adams.

Pryor, J. B. 1987. Sexual harassment proclivities in men. *Sex Roles* 17 (5/6): 269–90.

Quinn, B. A. 2000. The paradox of complaining: Law, humor, and harassment in the everyday work world. *Law and Social Inquiry* 25 (4): 1151–83.

Reilly, M. E., B. Lott, D. Caldwell, and L. DeLuca. 1992. Tolerance for sexual harassment related to self-reported sexual victimization. *Gender & Society* 6:122–38.

Rogers. J. K., and K. D. Henson. 1997. "Hey, why don't you wear a shorter skirt?" Structural vulnerability and the organization of sexual harassment in temporary clerical employment. *Gender & Society* 11:215–38.

Stockdale, M. S., and A. Vaux.1993. What sexual harassment experiences lead respondents to acknowledge being sexually harassed? A secondary analysis of a university survey. *Journal of Vocational Behavior* 43 (2): 221–34.

Tagri, S., and S. M. Hayes. 1997. Theories of sexual harassment. In *Sexual harassment: Theory, research and treatment*, edited by W. O'Donohue. New York: Allyn & Bacon.

Thorne, B. 1993. *Gender play: Girls and boys in school*. Buckingham, UK: Open University Press.

U.S. Merit Systems Protection Board. 1988. *Sexual harassment in the federal government: An update*. Washington, DC: Government Printing Office.

Welsh, S. 1999. Gender and sexual harassment. *Annual Review of Sociology*:169–90.

West, C., and D. H. Zimmerman. 1987. Doing gender. *Gender & Society* 1:125–51.

Wood, J. T. 1998. Saying makes it so: The discursive construction of sexual harassment. In *Conceptualizing sexual harassment as discursive practice*, edited by S. G. Bingham. Westport, CT: Praeger.

York, K. M. 1989. Defining sexual harassment in workplaces: A policy-capturing approach. *Academy of Management Journal* 32:830–50.

Study Questions

1. What methods were used in this research and why were they chosen for this topic?
2. What ways do men and women define "girl watching" differently? Is it harmless fun or sexual harassment?

PART FOUR

Social Institutions

Topic 11
Family

One of the most popular subjects in sociology is the study of the family. The family is a common experience for nearly every person in society. We might idealize the family to be something that nurtures us and out of which we are launched into life—a source of affection and encouragement. It is also true that the family is a place of violence and pain for many people. Families, as a part of society, have many different roles to play in the lives of people who inhabit them. There is an economic role the family plays, an emotional role, a role to socialize children, to parent them, and it is also a place where married couples play out their relational lives. Family is central to our existence as social beings. Family is an institutional pattern, a social structure that focuses social life into a home where busy lives of work, school, and activities must be integrated into some semblance of order. This organizing principle of the family is fraught with pitfalls and potential problems. It is not easy for all these goals to be met, and it is not easy for all persons involved to feel as though they receive what is due them as members of families.

People fall in love, may marry, and often have children. These children will grow up and fall in love and likely marry and have children of their own. These generational patterns create any number of subjects for sociology to study. Dating, courtship, marriage, parenting styles, divorce, dual-earner and dual-career families, grandparents, and many more areas of study arise out of the family. Many of us who study sociology find our own lives represented in these "sociological snapshots" of family life, and we can become interested in how it is that people select a partner or what class and ethnicity differences there are in child rearing. We could wonder how the divorce our own parents might have experienced will affect choices we make about marrying and whether their divorce will affect our own chances for divorce. These and many other topics enliven the pages of sociology texts and research journals.

The intimate relationships that occur inside families are among the most important in our lives. The love and support of a partner, as well as the close connections we experience between parents and children and between siblings, will last for decades and bring us a sense of importance and belonging. Alternately, intimate family relationships are

full of a history that can be negative. Negative history in family relations burdens them with "baggage" and resentments where we might
find ourselves struggling to grow through the problems we inherit as a
result of family life. Positive and negative, families are crucibles of intense feelings and strong allegiances. Learning about the family allows
us to bring closure on much of our own childhood while understanding
that we are caught in and creating patterns for the next generation
as well.

Families, the bedrock of any society, are changing. As society
changes, families must adapt to the new structures and processes
resulting from this change. Families are the nexus of activities that include employment, parenting, and leisure. As the roles of U.S. women
have changed through increased employment and the emancipation
from household labor, this has put additional pressures on the family
to adapt to dual-earner households, higher divorce rates, and the
need for child care. In the personal lives of many, these changes have
become significant political and economic issues.

Article selections in Topic 11, Family, focus on cohabitation,
"peer marriages," and what makes for successful marriages. First,
Susan Brown gives us a look at relationship quality among cohabiting
couples. Cohabiting is one of the fastest growing trends in U.S. families, and understanding the variables that affect the outcomes of
cohabitating is the insight in this quantitative research. Second,
Pepper Schwartz takes us inside the marriages of people who are
more friends than lovers. Peer marriages illustrate equity and equality,
but they have their own, unique problems as well. Third, John Gottman and Nan Silver present many years of research in the "love lab" at
the University of Washington. This work is especially valuable to those
of us who would like to know the specific behaviors that make marriage successful.

Reading 31

Relationship Quality Dynamics of Cohabiting Unions

Susan L. Brown

Cohabitation is now a common feature in the life course. In 1970, there were 500,000 cohabiting couples, whereas today more than 4.2 million couples cohabit (U.S. Bureau of the Census, 1999). A majority of marriages today are preceded by cohabitation (Bumpass & Sweet, 1989). Most of the decline in the first marriage rate and all of the decline in the remarriage rate are offset by corresponding increases in cohabitation (Bumpass, Sweet, & Cherlin, 1991). The rapid increase in cohabitation has led researchers to explore its linkages to other important life events, such as divorce (Bennett, Blanc, & Bloom, 1988; Booth & Johnson, 1988; DeMaris & MacDonald, 1993; DeMaris & Rao, 1992; Lillard, Brien, & Waite, 1995; Schoen, 1992) and nonmarital childbearing (Bachrach, 1987; Landale & Fennelly, 1992; Loomis & Landale, 1994; Manning, 1993, 1995; Manning & Landale, 1996). Essentially, researchers have treated cohabitation as a measure of a premarital event that may influence the likelihood of subsequent events.

But is this how cohabitation ought to be conceptualized? Researchers continue to debate the answer to this question. Cohabiting unions are typically so short (averaging less than 2 years in duration) that we often think of them as transitory in nature. Indeed, research indicates that for most groups, cohabitation serves largely as a stepping-stone to marriage (e.g., Manning, 1993, 1995). For some segments of the population, however, cohabitation appears to be a long-term substitute for marriage (e.g., Puerto Rican women; Landale & Fennelly, 1992). Some researchers have argued that cohabitation is similar to being single (Rindfuss & Vanden-Heuvel, 1990), whereas others have maintained that cohabitation is very much like marriage (Brown & Booth, 1996) and ought to be treated as a family status (Bumpass et al., 1991).

To resolve this debate, we need to move beyond research whose interest in cohabitation lies solely in its relationship to other life events (e.g., childbearing and divorce) and begin to explore the nature of the cohabiting relationship itself. In fact, understanding the nature of co-habiting relationships will help us to decipher those links between co-habitation and other important life events.

Relationship Quality among Cohabitors

Cross-sectional studies demonstrate that on average, cohabitors are involved in unions that are of poorer quality than marriages (Brown & Booth, 1996; Nock, 1995). Cohabitors report more frequent disagreements, less fairness and happiness, and greater instability than their married counterparts. However, a comparison of marrieds to cohabitors who plan to marry their partner (75% of cohabitors plan to formalize their union) reveals that the relationship quality of the two groups does not differ. Cohabitors without plans to marry their partner have especially poor relationship quality and are also in unions of longer duration than their counterparts with marriage plans, suggesting that duration and relationship quality are negatively related. Indeed, relationship duration has a greater negative effect on the relationship quality of cohabitors than of marrieds (Brown & Booth, 1996).

Marriage improves some aspects of cohabitors' relationship quality. For instance, cohabitors are less likely to use violence to solve relationship disputes after they marry (Brown, in press). Marriage also increases cohabiting women's happiness with their relationship. And marriage seems to ameliorate the negative consequences long unions have on perceptions of relationship fairness and happiness. Nevertheless, the strongest predictor of relationship quality at a later point in time is relationship quality at an earlier point in time; cohabitors' relationship quality appears stable. . . .

Taken together, studies of cohabitors' relationship quality and the literature on marital quality suggest potential similarities in union quality patterns for the two groups. For both marrieds and cohabitors, duration is negatively associated with relationship quality, yet relationship quality remains stable over time (Brown & Booth, 1996; Johnson et al., 1992). Consequently, it can be expected that relationship duration will have similar effects on the relationship quality of both cohabitors and marrieds. The present analysis evaluates whether the dynamics of co-habitors' relationship quality exhibit a pattern analogous to that found for marital quality. . . .

Data and Measures

Data come from the fast wave of the NSFH. The NSFH is a multistage probability sample of 13,007 persons who were interviewed during 1987 to 1988. These data are arguably the best available for studying the cohabiting population because cohabitors were oversampled ($N = 678$), and extensive information was gathered about the quality of their unions. More than 6,800 respondents were married at first interview. Fewer than 5% of cohabiting unions last more than 10 years (Bumpass & Sweet, 1989). To maximize comparability with marriages, analyses are restricted to those respondents in cohabiting or marital unions of no more than 10 years' duration.[1] This strategy has been employed in other research on NSFH cohabitors (Brown, 2000; DeMaris & MacDonald, 1993; Nock, 1995; Thomson & Colella, 1992). Also, only Blacks and Whites are examined here due to the small numbers of Hispanic, Asian, and other race cohabitors. These restrictions result in 646 cohabitors and 3,086 marrieds for analysis.[2]

Dependent Variables

Three measures of relationship quality are examined. The relationship happiness variable refers to the respondent's response to the question "Taking all things together, how happy are you with your relationship?" Responses range from 1 = *very unhappy* to 7 = *very happy*. Relationship interaction, a six-category variable, measures the amount of time the respondent spent alone with his or her partner during the past month. . . . Finally, the relationship instability variable gauges the respondent's estimation (on a 5-point scale) of the chance that the relationship will dissolve.

Independent Variables

Relationship duration is measured in months in the NSFH, but for ease of interpretation, this measure has been multiplied by 12 to yield a measure in which the unit is 1 year. The presence of children in the household, prior marital experience, and prior cohabiting experience are all indicator variables. Plans to many among cohabitors is also a dichotomous measure; it is coded 1 if the respondent either reports definite plans to marry or thinks that she or he eventually will marry the current cohabiting partner, and 0 otherwise.

Control Variables

Variables associated with cohabitation and relationship quality are included as control variables. A control for race is included in all models because prior research (e.g., Adelmann et al., 1996) demonstrates that Blacks report poorer marital quality than Whites and because there are considerable racial differences in union formation rates (Raley, 1996). Gender, coded 1 for female, is included as a control variable both because women and men typically report unique views of marital quality (Thompson & Walker, 1989) and because cohabitation is more common among women (Bumpass & Sweet, 1989; Thornton, 1988). Both education and age are associated with cohabitation and relationship quality (Brown & Booth, 1996; Bumpass & Sweet, 1989; Glenn, 1990; Nock, 1995) and thus are included as controls. Education measures the number of years of school completed. Age is coded in years. . . .

Results

Table 1, which shows the means and standard deviations of all variables used in the analyses, reveals that although cohabitors report significantly more interaction with their partners than do marrieds, cohabitors are also significantly less happy with their relationships and believe their relationships are more unstable than do their married counterparts. The average duration of a cohabiting relationship is slightly less than 3 years, whereas among marrieds, average marital duration is a little more than 5 years. Marrieds are significantly more likely to have children than are cohabitors (66% vs. 41%, respectively). Although cohabitors are more likely to have prior marital experience, they are less likely to have prior cohabiting experience than marrieds, perhaps because a majority of cohabitors quickly transform their unions into marriages (Bumpass & Sweet, 1989). And as expected, about 72% of cohabitors report plans to marry their current partners. . . .

Cohabitors' happiness with their relationships, patterns of interaction, and perceived instability are all duration dependent. . . . Figure 1 graphically depicts [the] regression results. . . . With the passage of time,

Table 1 Weighted Means and Standard Deviations of Variables Used in the Analyses

Variable	Cohabiting M (SD)	Married M (SD)
Dependent variables		
Relationship interaction	5.09 (1.29)	4.78 (1.44)
Relationship happiness	5.77 (1.33)	5.95 (1.32)
Relationship instability	2.00 (1.06)	1.46 (0.79)
Independent variables		
Duration	2.80 (2.24)	5.16 (2.78)
Children	0.41 (0.50)	0.66 (0.48)
Previously married	0.44 (0.50)	0.32 (0.47)
Previously cohabited	0.22 (0.42)	0.46 (0.50)
Plans to marry	0.72 (0.45)	
Control variables		
Black	0.18 (0.39)	0.10 (0.33)
Female	0.50 (0.50)	0.50 (0.50)
Education	12.36 (2.70)	13.23 (2.71)
Age	30.49 (9.45)	32.97 (10.22)

Source: National Survey of Families and Households.
Note: Mean values on all variables—except female—significantly differ for cohabitators and marrieds at the $p = .001$ level.

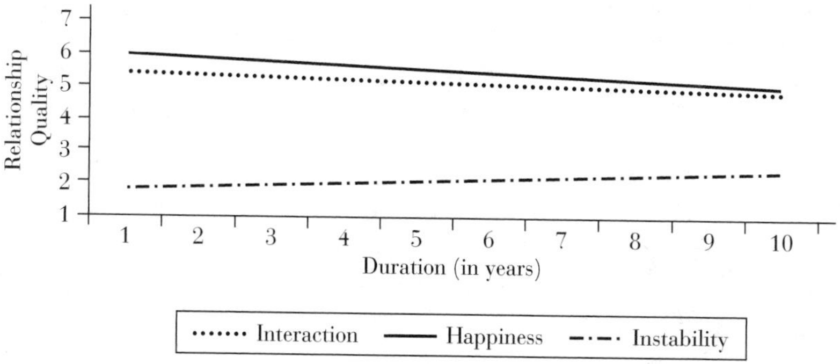

Figure 1 Cohabitors' Predicted Relationship Quality

happiness and interaction decrease, whereas instability increases. Similar to Glenn's (1998) analysis of marital quality, these results demonstrate that cohabitors also experience a linear decline in relationship quality during the first decade. . . .

In Figure 2, the pattern of interaction across duration is essentially the same for cohabitors and marrieds. Average levels of happiness appear slightly higher among marrieds than cohabitors, but happiness declines linearly with the passage of time for both groups. Instability exhibits unique patterns for marrieds and cohabitors. Although cohabitors experience a steady increase in relationship instability over time, marrieds' levels of instability are not related to duration. Rather, marital instability appears static across the first decade of marriage. These findings support the assertion by Johnson et al. (1992) that positive dimensions of marital quality tend to decline with time, whereas negative dimensions, such as instability, remain stable. Among marrieds, race is significantly associated with marital interaction, happiness, and instability. Blacks report lower levels of interaction and happiness and higher levels of instability than Whites, confirming findings from recent research (Adelmann et al., 1996) on racial differences in marital quality. Note that there are no significant racial differences in relationship quality among cohabitors.

Children

The presence of children tends to worsen cohabitors' relationship quality but does not explain the negative association between duration and relationship quality. Children decrease interaction and relationship happiness among cohabitors but do not alter perceptions of the stability of the relationship. Similar effects are observed for marrieds. Additional analyses (results not shown) reveal that differentiating stepchildren from

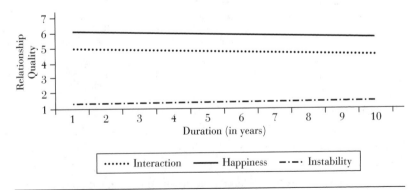

Figure 2　Marrieds' Predicted Relationship Quality

biological children does not alter the pattern of effects. Also, the presence of adult children (i.e., children who are at least 18 years of age) has no significant effects on the three dimensions of relationship quality. Among cohabitors, children and duration negatively interact in their effects on relationship interaction and happiness (results not shown). In long cohabiting unions, children are associated with especially low levels of interaction and happiness, perhaps because nearly half of these unions involve children from prior unions. Among marrieds, children do not modify the effect of duration on marital quality. Children have similar effects on relationship happiness and instability for both cohabitors and marrieds, but the negative effect of children on interaction is somewhat weaker for cohabitors than for marrieds (results not shown).

Prior Union Experience

Prior union experience has significant consequences for the relationship quality of cohabitors and marrieds, but these effects are independent of duration. Among cohabitors, prior cohabitation experience decreases partner interaction and happiness with the current relationship and increases perceived instability. Among marrieds, prior cohabitation experience decreases relationship interaction and happiness and increases instability. There are no significant effects of prior marital unions. Union type does not modify the effects of prior cohabitation experience on relationship quality, nor does duration (results not shown), meaning that the adverse effects of earlier cohabiting unions persist throughout the duration of the current union.

Plans to Marry

Cohabitors with plans to marry their partner report higher relationship quality, on average, than those without such plans. . . . The plans-to-marry variable modifies the effect of duration on instability such that among those in unions of relatively short duration, plans to marry is associated with lower levels of relationship instability; whereas among those in relatively long unions, the plans-to-marry variable is actually associated with higher levels of instability (results not shown). This finding implies that cohabitors with marriage plans expect that their unions will be transformed quickly into marriages. When these expectations are not met, cohabitors perceive greater instability. In contrast, couples who do not desire marriage gain confidence over time that their relationship will remain intact. Hence, the effect of duration on relationship instability is conditioned by the cohabitor's marital intentions. . . .

Discussion

Cohabiting unions are experienced by a majority of young people today (Bumpass & Sweet, 1989). Although researchers (e.g., Brown & Booth, 1996; Nock, 1995) have compared the relationship quality of cohabitors and marrieds, little attention has been paid to the dynamics of cohabitors' relationship quality. Does the quality of cohabiting unions vary according to union duration? If so, how similar is the pattern for cohabiting unions to that observed for marriages?

The present study examines the duration dependence of relationship quality for cohabitors and marrieds and evaluates whether the presence of children or prior union experience account for or moderate the effect of duration. Cohabitors and marrieds experience similar declines in interaction with their partners during the first decade of their unions. Both groups also experience lower levels of happiness across time, although happiness is consistently higher among marrieds than cohabitors. Relationship instability increases considerably with the passage of time among cohabitors, but remains stable among marrieds. For cohabitors, long union duration has particularly devastating consequences for levels of happiness and instability. Both the presence of children and prior cohabitation experience are significantly associated with lower levels of relationship quality. The effect of duration on cohabitors' relationship quality is modified by the presence of children. Cohabitors in long unions with children report especially low levels of relationship interaction and happiness, possibly because nearly one half of such unions involve children from previous cohabitations or marriages.

There are important differences among cohabitors in the effects of duration on relationship quality. Among cohabitors without marriage plans, duration has no significant effect on the three dimensions of relationship quality. Among cohabitors with plans to marry, the effects of duration are similar to those observed for marrieds. For both groups, longer unions are associated with poorer relationship quality (except that marrieds experience no significant duration-related changes in instability).

Cohabiting unions are of relatively short duration, yet the dynamics of relationship quality parallel that of marriages in many regards. An important difference in the duration/relationship quality association for cohabitations and marriages is that the instability of cohabiting unions increases over time, whereas among marriages, reported instability does not vary with duration. This difference is probably due to the role of cohabitation in the life course. For most cohabitors, cohabitation is a transitory stage, typically a step in the courtship process. Most people enter cohabitation not expecting a long-term union but rather a short-term substitute for marriage. Not surprisingly, half of all cohabiting unions are formalized through marriage or dissolve within 2 years, and more than 90% end within 5 years (Bumpass & Sweet, 1989). Hence, the longer a cohabiting union persists, the greater the perceived instability, because cohabiting unions that are not formalized through marriage are likely to soon end in separation. Less than 10% of cohabiting unions are maintained for an extended (i.e., 5 or more years) period of time.

The present study demonstrates that despite their short length, the quality of cohabiting unions varies with time. Cohabitors experience declines in relationship interaction and happiness that are similar to those experienced by marrieds. But unlike marriages, the stability of cohabiting unions is related to duration. This unique effect is indicative of the meaning of cohabitation as well as its role in the family life course. The higher levels of instability characterizing long cohabitations probably result from unrealized marital intentions. Most cohabitors expect to marry their partners, and provided that they do so within a few years of initiating the cohabiting union, perceived instability remains low. Instability levels are extremely high for cohabitors in relatively long unions who intend to marry their partner. The longer cohabitors' intentions remain unmet, the less confident they are that the relationship will remain intact. Factors hindering marriage entry may include relationship stressors such as children or prior union experience, but ultimately, at least one partner is hesitant to marry. Without a commitment to marriage, the union is likely to fail. Thus, these analyses suggest that cohabitations serving as a prelude to marriage are characterized by low levels of instability, whereas cohabitations that are not readily transformed into marriages are hindered not only by high levels of instability but also especially low levels of relationship interaction and happiness.

Notes

1. There is the potential for bias in the estimates of duration effects using cross-sectional models, but this potential is minimized by restricting the analyses to individuals in unions of no more than 10 years' duration.
2. A very small number of cases have missing data on some variables. For respondents with missing data on independent and control variables, the overall mean was substituted. However, for respondents with missing data on the dependent variables (i.e., the three dimensions of relationship quality), mean substitutions were not made. Consequently, the sample sizes used in each of the relationship quality models vary slightly.

References

Adelmann, P. K., Chadwick, K., & Baerger, D. R. (1996). Marital quality of Black and White adults over the life course. *Journal of Social and Personal Relationships, 13,* 361–384.

Bachrach, C. (1987). Cohabitation and reproductive behavior in the U.S. *Demography, 24,* 623–647.

Bennett, N. G., Blanc, A. K., & Bloom, D. E. (1988). Commitment and the modern union: Assessing the link between premarital cohabitation and subsequent marital stability. *American Sociological Review, 53,* 127–138.

Booth, A., & Johnson, D. R. (1988). Premarital cohabitation and marital success. *Journal of Family Issues, 9,* 255–272.

Brown, S. L. (in press). Moving from cohabitation to marriage. Effects on relationship quality. *Social Science Research.*

Brown, S. L. (2000). The effect of union type on psychological well-being: Depression among cohabitors versus marrieds. *Journal of Health and Social Behavior, 41,* 241–255.

Brown, S. L., & Booth, A. (1996). Cohabitation versus marriage: A comparison of relationship quality. *Journal of Marriage and the Family, 58,* 668–678.

Bumpass, L. L., & Sweet, J. A. (1989). National estimates of cohabitation. *Demography, 26,* 615–625.

Bumpass, L. L., Sweet, J. A., & Cherlin, A. J. (1991). The role of cohabitation in declining rates of marriage. *Journal of Marriage and the Family, 53,* 913–927.

DeMaris, A., & MacDonald, W. (1993). Premarital cohabitation and marital instability: A test of the unconventionality hypothesis. *Journal of Marriage and the Family, 55,* 399–407.

DeMaris, A., & Rao, K. V. (1992). Premarital cohabitation and subsequent marital stability in the United States: A reassessment. *Journal of Marriage and the Family, 54,* 178–190.

Glenn, N. D. (1990). Quantitative research on marital quality in the 1980s. *Journal of Marriage and the Family, 52,* 818–831.

Glenn, N. D. (1998). The course of marital success and failure in five American ten-year marriage cohorts. *Journal of Marriage and the Family, 60,* 569–576.

Johnson, D. R., Amoloza, T. O., & Booth, A. (1992). Stability and developmental change in marital quality: A three-wave panel analysis. *Journal of Marriage and the Family, 54,* 582–594.

Landale, N. S., & Fennelly, K. (1992). Informal unions among mainland Puerto Ricans: Cohabitation or an alternative to legal marriage? *Journal of Marriage and the Family, 54,* 269–280.

Lillard, L. A., Brien, M., & Waite, L. J. (1995). Premarital cohabitation and subsequent marital dissolution: Is it self-selection? *Demography, 32,* 437–458.

Loomis. L. S., & Landale, N. S. (1994). Nonmarital cohabitation and childbearing among Black and White American women. *Journal of Marriage and the Family, 56,* 949–962.

Manning, W. D. (1993). Marriage and cohabitation following premarital conception. *Journal of Marriage and the Family, 55,* 839–850.

Manning, W. D. (1995). Cohabitation, marriage, and entry into motherhood. *Journal of Marriage and the Family, 57,* 191–200.

Manning, W. D., & Landale, N. S. (1996). Racial and ethnic differences in the role of cohabitation in premarital childbearing. *Journal of Marriage and the Family, 58,* 63–77.

Nock, S. L. (1995). A comparison of marriages and cohabiting relationships. *Journal of Family Issues, 16,* 53–76.

Raley, R. K. (1996). A shortage of marriageable men? A note on the role of cohabitation in Black-White differences in marriage rates. *American Sociological Review, 61,* 973–983.

Rindfuss, R. R., & VandenHeuvel, A. (1990). Cohabitation: A precursor to marriage or an alternative to being single? *Population and Development Review, 16,* 703–726.

Schoen, R. (1992). First unions and the stability of first marriages. *Journal of Marriage and the Family, 54,* 281–284.

Thompson, L., & Walker, A. J. (1989). Gender in families: Women and men in marriage, work, and parenthood. *Journal of Marriage and the Family, 51,* 845–871.

Thomson, E., & Colella, U. (1992). Cohabitation and marital stability: Quality or commitment? *Journal of Marriage and the Family, 54,* 259–267.

Thornton, A. (1988). Cohabitation and marriage in the 1980s. *Demography, 25,* 497–508.

U.S. Bureau of the Census. (1999). *Unmarried-couple households, by presence of children: 1960 to present, AD-2.* Retrieved June 13, 2000, from http://www.census.gov/population/socdemo/ms-la/tabad-2.txt

Study Questions

1. What are the differences between cohabiting and married couples as the author discusses them?
2. What are the main variables, as presented in Brown's study, that affect the quality of the cohabiting union?

Reading 32

Peer Marriage
How Love Between
Equals Really Works

Pepper Schwartz

In 1983 Philip Blumstein and I published the results of a large study on the nature of American relationships; it was called *American Couples.* The study, which received an enormous amount of notice from the press and the public, was composed of over 12,000 questionnaires and 600 interviews from married, cohabiting, lesbian, and gay members of couples.[1] During the course of what turned out to be a decade-long effort, I noticed that there were many same-sex couples with an egalitarian relationship but very few such heterosexual couples. Because the homosexual couples did not have to surmount the traditions of sex differences, they more often worked out relationships that both partners felt were fair and supportive to each other. My curiosity about their success at this aspect of their relationship, plus my admiration for the few egalitarian heterosexual couples in the study, made me want to know more about how married couples could get past traditions of gender and construct a relationship built on equality. Previous sociological studies on marriage made chances for egalitarian marriage seem grim, but since my own marriage was successfully egalitarian, I had both scientific and personal motivation to see why some couples reconstructed gender roles and others did not. To that end, I reexamined some of the egalitarian marriages in the *American Couples* study, used them as an archetype, and then sought more of these couples to talk to and learn from.

The couples, I discovered, based their marriages on a mix of equity (each person gives in proportion to what he or she receives) and equality (each person has equal status and is equally responsible for emotional, economic, and household duties). But these couples were distinguished by more than their dedication to fairness and collaboration; the most happy and durable among them also had refocused their relationship on *intense companionship.* To be sure, they shared child raising, chores, and decision making more or less equally and almost always equitably, but for most of them, this was just part of a plan for a true companionship marriage. The point of the marriage was not to share everything fifty-fifty. Rather, the shared decisions, responsibility, and household labor were in the service of an intimate and deeply collaborative marriage. I call this kind of marriage peer marriage; it is a marriage of equal companions, a collaboration of love and labor in order to produce profound intimacy and mutual respect.

The people in peer marriage for the most part are not ideologues. They construct and maintain a peer marriage because they find it rewarding. If they are without the means to hire the services of a homemaker, they seek work that allows both spouses to share child care and housework. These couples do not strike acquaintances as odd; they look just like their friends and co-workers, except that they have vigilantly preserved their commitment to equality. Additionally, they see peer marriage as salvation from instability. Many of them have witnessed the deterioration of their own previous marriage, or that of friends, and they believe that the only way to maintain a lifetime together is to create an irreplaceable, and interdependent, union of equals. . . .

In general, four characteristics of peer couples emerged. First, the partners did not generally have more than a sixty-forty traditional split of household duties and child raising. (An exception was made for the early periods of infancy, and even then, there had to be significant paternal involvement.) Second, each partner believed that each person in the couple had equal influence over important and disputed decisions. Third, partners felt that they had equal control over the family economy and reasonably equal access to discretionary funds. Most research has indicated that money confers power and relative income influences decision making.[2] These couples either had to earn similar amounts, or share power over family resources (such as having similar ability to undertake nonmonitored private spending). Fourth, each person's work was given equal weight in the couple's life plans. The person with the less glamorous and remunerative job could not always be the person with the most housework or child care. The requirement of sharing money, influence, decision making, child care and homemaking applied even for couples in which one person had a salaried job and the other stayed home. Among older couples, a history of traditional role division that no longer existed was allowable as long as it had not been true for the previous three years. The point was not to define these characteristics as the only way to reach a just, rewarding, and durable relationship but to use them to define the new, and spreading, phenomenon of marriages in which traditional roles were absent and there was no hidden hierarchy. . . .

My snowball sample (the term sociologists use for a sample whereby one person recommends the next) makes any statistical conclusions about peer couples seriously suspect. Nonetheless, certain attributes appeared again and again and are at least worth mentioning, if only as a guide for future research. These couples tended to be dual income; only three couples contained women who did not work at all. They were in their late twenties to mid-forties. There was only one much older couple (in their mid-sixties) and only a few in their mid-fifties. The age similarity was partially an artifact of the snowball sample but also probably a cohort effect. It was the baby boom generation who came of age at a time when feminist ideology was having its rebirth. This generation, born between 1945 and 1957, and its younger followers had to evaluate whether to embrace the new tenets and criticisms of marriage, or opt for the traditional model. The baby boom and post-baby boom women who endorsed feminist philosophy—or at least wanted to shuck old gender roles and constraints—have had to consider consciously the role of marriage in determining their life. Some had to think about *if* they wanted to be married, and all have examined *how* they wanted to be married. More of these women might be expected to want a relationship that gives them equal standing in marriage. Oddly, younger women among this group sometimes assumed a certain amount of equality and equity and thereby unconsciously settled for less.

This cohort explanation may also explain why almost half of these marriages contain a previously divorced partner. People in this age group have a higher divorce rate than the cohorts ahead of them. Also, the older women of the baby boom generation were more likely to have started marriage under one set of norms and reexamined it under a new, more feminist consciousness. Most of these women who were previously divorced said they left their first marriage because of inequitable treatment. Peer men were far more likely to recite a great number of reasons for the breakup of their marriage but were also likely to say it was either the end of their marriage or the difficult period after the marriage was over, a devastating period of fighting over property and support, that made them seek a peer relationship. Accusations of betrayal or continued emotional and financial dependence of the ex-spouse made these men much more interested in a different kind of marriage the next time: an independent, working spouse who could hold her own in a partnership.

The last, and rather unexpected, commonality among the peer couples was that they tended to be more middle class than working or upper middle class. As we shall see, egalitarian couples seem more likely when male income is not so grand that it encourages a nonworking wife or makes the wife's income unimportant. When a peer marriage had a high-earning male, it was likely there was also a high-earning female (or, as in a couple of cases, a female with a prestigious job such as an elected politician or a successful artist). But generally, most male occupations were *not* high pressure and high profile. It seems to be easier to create an egalitarian relationship if the man has a job (or creates one) that has some flexibility and controllable hours, and if both partners make similar amounts of money (for example, if both partners are teachers). Still, these kinds of background data do not provide the answers to the most intriguing commonalities of all: How did these people come to be in an egalitarian marriage? Why did they want to be peers? . . .

Why Peer Marriage?

To any woman who was or is part of the women's movement, the answer to this question is clear. Women in the recent history of the United States, Canada, and most of Western European have experienced a rise in personal freedom that can be expected to extend to their family and personal life. This is particularly true for the women of the baby boom generation who grew up indulged by a kind economy and relatively permissive parents and who, along with the males in their cohort, rebelled against traditional social expectations: what it meant to be a woman, a man, a partner, a spouse.

Their critique of traditional marriage included the perception that it was unacceptably anti-individualistic. Traditionally, marriage is a corporate entity in which the self is supposed to be transformed to fulfill, depending on one's gender, the demands of supporter and provider, or father and mother. Both men and women, but especially a number of women, defied that loss of individuality and rigid description of duties. Women, for example, decided, either rationally or de facto, that virginity was no longer required in order to be a desirable spouse or a good wife. The institutionalization of premarital sex was just part of the questioning of gender requirements. Young people proclaimed that individual happiness was more important than familial duty. There was a general rejection of capitulation to traditional expectations. A number of women wrote about new ways to be female. Theories of male oppression and patriarchal culture flourished. And although the number of women who directly participated in these forums may have been statistically small, the reach of their thoughts and feelings was deep and broad. Women left marriage—or were left—in extraordinary numbers, the divorce rate has more than doubled since the early 1960s. Both women who stayed in marriages and women who left them learned a new language of anger and inequity. The appetite for equality and equity grew nationally and internationally, and even those who held on to traditional values about roles and relationships found themselves more aware and critical of some of the bargains of male and female relations. . . .

Of course, even if we wanted to, we could not erase all the differences between men and women that make them attracted and attached to each other, emotionally, erotically, and pragmatically. But now that we offer a real possibility of equality, many people get cold feet. They do not seek true equality because they are scared that all they will get is trouble for their effort. In some ways, the most dangerous impact of well-meaning books like *The Second Shift* is that they confirm readers' worst fears about the changing nature of male and female roles: that liberated women will only be liberated for more work, less love, less protection, and more exploitation. Men and women are worried about who they will have to be if they give up their traditional gender territories and remap their personal and family life. They are worried as well that the opening up of roles to personal choice rather than by sex will obliterate sexual differences and the interdependence of the sexes. Men and women know how to enjoy gender and marriage by the old ways, they feel lost when it comes to egalitarian marriage, have trouble believing the rewards of peer marriage would be worth the sacrifice it takes to get there, and they feel they are good enough where they are, having made significant strides from their parents' marriages and moving as close to egalitarian as they will ever get. They don't believe they can take the next step, so they stop short of it. They have a false sense of how far they have come and how far it is possible to go, they do not realize that the path they are on is not actually leading them to the place they want to go.

Then why peer marriage? Why have some couples moved through this considerable gauntlet to create an egalitarian partnership? Most simply, it is because they want to love each other as much as possible. They want a marriage that has intensity and partnership and does not create the distance between men and women that is inevitable between people of unequal status and power. These men and women looked at the lack of intimacy, and even at the anger and resentment between their parents or in previous relationships of their own, and wanted to avoid replication. Women who were consciously feminist did not want to be angry about inequity; men in love did not want to have an accusatory and resentful partner. Men and women who began as friends became deeply committed to maintaining that friendship, and took steps to preserve the relationship from the impact of traditional marriage. The common theme among these peer couples is the preservation of intimacy, the desire to be neither oppressor nor oppressed, the commitment to a relationship that creates a shared universe rather than parallel lives. When they designed their relationship to ensure those goals, the rewards of peer marriage became self-reinforcing.

But Who Would Be a Peer Man?

The common perception is that men do not want a peer marriage. Why should they give up all the privileges conferred by traditional marriage? And even if we can imagine that a man would like to share the burden of supporting a family or would like a career woman with whom to share his life, we know that most men have been loath to take on the burdens that women carry. It is hard to imagine as well that men who have the opportunity for high earnings and a prestigious job would sacrifice either for a more participatory family life. Because of these and similar observations, many women feel that peer men are born, not made, and so few of them exist that they are not worth looking for.

That is a misconception. Peer men often *are* made, *not* born. Many men came to peer values after they tried a fairly traditional relationship and found it didn't work for them. They enjoyed having service, support and household management from a traditional wife or a girlfriend—up to a point. Then they reported being either bored or overwhelmed with responsibility. Some fell in love with a "new woman"—an independent peer who was exactly the sort of woman they avoided or felt insecure around when they were younger. Many of the first wives of these men were furious at losing husbands after they had fulfilled the contract they both had signed. And when these women dated or remarried, they no longer presented themselves as they had as younger, more traditional women.

Others of these men had had traditional relationships that they liked just the way they were, until they went sour for a variety of reasons. It was the aftermath of the separation, divorce, custody, and alimony battles that changed their mind about what they wanted in their next relationship. Many of these men were very attached to their children and vowed never again to be the minor parent. Others had ex-wives who were lost without them, and the responsibility and guilt of that situation made them look for someone stronger.

Nevertheless, some of these men *were* "born peer." They came from homes where they got along with and respected an impressive mother or sister. Some had grown up doing their fair share of chores and babysitting. Quite a few of them were men who never felt comfortable with macho standards of masculinity. They liked female company; they liked to talk; they liked being in a family environment. One common distinguishing factor is that they liked children, looked forward to having their own, and wanted to be involved in the day-to-day upbringing of their family.

Some of these men were ambitious in their work; others were clear from the beginning that their work would come second to their marriage and family. But what they usually shared in common was the idea that they wanted an in-depth personal relationship that would not be sacrificed to work. They wanted a best friend.

It was this goal of deeper friendship that helped to "make" peer men. Much of what evolved between these men and women happened because of their strong desire to stay emotionally connected to one another. They saw each other as individuals rather than as roles and wanted the same things for each other that they sought for themselves. More often than not, the women in these relationships were good communicators and were clear about how they wanted and needed to be treated; they had a strong sense of what was a fair deal. The men had the ability to understand and support their partner's wishes. Most of these couples had to negotiate early in the relationship—and keep negotiating throughout it—to keep it a partnership rather than watching it slip into more traditional roles. One of the interesting things about peer men, is that they too had an investment in keeping that from happening. They were looking for an equal, a partner and a friend. They didn't want to lose that person to pressures to live a more conventional relationship. . . .

Rewards of Peer Marriage

Primacy of the Relationship

Egalitarian couples give priority to their relationship over their work and over all other relationships—with friends, extended family, even their children. Their mutual friendship is the most satisfying part of their lives. The point of equality and equity in these relationships is to create a marriage that makes each partner feel secure in the other person's regard and support.

Intimacy

Peer couples experience much more of each other's lives than do traditional or near peers. Because they share housework, children, and economic responsibility, they empathize as well as sympathize. They experience the world in a more similar way, understand the other partner's personality more accurately, and communicate better because they know each other and each other's world better and because equal power in the relationship changes interaction style. They negotiate more than other couples, they share conversational time, and they are less often high-handed, dismissive, or disrespectful than other couples. They choose to spend a lot of time together.

Commitment

These couples are more likely than traditional couples to find each other irreplaceable. They are likely to describe their relationship as "unique." Their interdependence becomes so deep (unlike near-peer dual-career couples) and so utterly customized that the costs of splitting up become prohibitive.

Costs of Peer Marriage

So if the rewards are so great, how come there are near peers? Why would anyone who believed in equality back off? The following problems will be discussed throughout the chapters.

Treason Against Tradition

One of the costs of defining gender and marriage differently is that many people feel that the nature and purpose of marriage and sex roles have been betrayed. Far from enabling a man to stay home with his children or a woman to take her role as equally responsible breadwinner seriously, co-workers and managers and friends will often question the couple's philosophy and deny modifications of work or schedules that could help the couple share family life more easily. Parents of the man may feel he has been emasculated; parents of the woman may feel she is setting herself up for a fall. Validation and support are rare and have to be consciously sought.

Career Costs

Peer couples need jobs that allow them to coparent. Sometimes they wait long enough to get enough clout in their careers to be able to modify their schedules so that they can share parenting. But more often they have to be lucky enough to be in jobs that naturally support child raising (for example, both working at home work stations), or they have to modify their career ambitions in favor of their family aspirations. This means avoiding or changing jobs that require extensive travel, changing venues in quick succession, and jobs that are all consuming (for example, a high-powered litigator in lengthy trials). Many couples have experienced one or both partners' having to forgo career opportunities. Sometimes it is painful to watch others who have dedicated themselves more singlemindedly to careers do financially better or achieve more prestigious positions.

Identity Costs

By downplaying work and emphasizing family, peer couples go against the prevailing standards of male and female role success. Marriages have traditionally defined themselves as a success if the man made money and created a good life-style for the family and the wife created good children and a satisfied husband. Peer couples have to define success differently. Except for "power couples" who can afford the help that allows them to have high-voltage careers and family time, economic success may have to be modified. Neither sex can assess their success according to traditional roles. It is hard to know how to evaluate oneself.

Sexual Dynamism

Peer partners get so close that some complain that an "incest taboo" sets in. They are each other's best friends, and if they aren't careful, that is exactly what they will start acting like in bed. Many find ways to get around this overfamiliarization problem, but the fact is that their absolute integration in each other's lives has to be leavened with some artifice to put romance back into the relationship.

Exclusion of Others

These couples become each other's best friend, and that can make everyone else feel a bit excluded. Kin and close friends stop getting the kind of attention they used to have and may be resentful. Although these couples tend to be child centered and have in fact organized their lives so that they can parent better, they are also dedicated to their adult relationship. This means they have to be careful not to make their own children feel excluded.

Calibrating the Right Mix of Equity and Equality

It is not always clear how to maintain a peer relationship. Sometimes it requires *equality*, with both partners supporting each other in the home and with the children. This prevents the relationship from being divided into low and high prestige worlds, and undermining deep friendship. But other times the best answer is *equity*. Each partner can and should give in different coin, and that is the best way to be loving and collaborative and supportive to the marriage. Figuring out the right thing to do all the time is tiring and inexact. Sometimes couples just want to retreat to doing the "boy thing" and the "girl thing"—not because it works—but because it is much clearer what each person should do to do his or her part for the relationship.

The Balance of Costs and Rewards

In spite of the costs, the peer couples described in this book believe that they have created an extremely rewarding marriage and family. Many of the costs I have outlined are not costs they feel they have suffered—or if they have, they feel those costs are a manageable part of an otherwise terrific arrangement. Many of them have varied and effective coping strategies that they believe solve or minimize these issues in their relationship.

Notes

1. Philip Blumstein and Pepper Schwartz, *American Couples* (New York: William Morrow, 1983).
2. Philip Blumstein and Pepper Schwartz, *American Couples.* See also Philip Blumstein and Pepper Schwartz, "Money and Ideology: Their Impact on Power and the Division of Household Labor," and Judith Treas, "The Common Pot or Separate Purses? A Transactional Analysis," both in Rae Lesser Blumber, Ed., *Gender, Family and Economy* (Newbury Park, Calif.: Sage, 1991).

Study Questions

1. What are the positive and negative attributes of peer marriages? Would you ever want to be in this sort of marriage? Why or why not?
2. Please answer the question raised in the article, "But who would be a peer man?" If a man becomes a "peer," what does he give up?

Reading 33
Why Marriages Succeed or Fail

John Gottman with Nan Silver

Demystifying the Marriage Crisis

If you are worried about the future of your marriage you have plenty of company. There's no denying that this is a frightening time for American couples. More than half of all first marriages end in divorce. Second marriages do worse, failing at a rate of about 60 percent. . . .

Of course, not all couples ought to stay married. But I do think it's disturbing that the majority of people marrying today will be unsuccessful at nurturing and holding onto their most precious relationship—all the more disturbing because, I believe, an accurate diagnosis of the fault lines in a marriage can help any couple build a stronger union.

On your wedding day you had hopes for a happy, blissful union, and I believe that despite the rising divorce rate you can still fulfill that dream—even if your marriage has started to show signs of trouble. Although our research is far from complete, our current findings offer the most accurate picture available of why some marriages succeed and others fail—and what you can do to improve your own chances of ending up on the positive side of the odds. . . .

Marriage Styles

One important way we identify what type of marriage a couple has is by how they fight. Although there are other dimensions that are telling about a union, the intensity of argument seems to bring out a marriage's true colors. To classify a marriage, we look at the frequency of fights, the facial expressions and physiological responses (such as pulse rate and amount of sweating) of both partners during the confrontation, as well as what they say to each other and their tone of voice. Using these observations as our guideposts, we have named the three types of stable marriages based on their style of combat: validating, volatile, or avoidant. . . .

Betty and Bert: Validating

There are good reasons why Bert and Betty are close to a marriage counselor's ideal: they are virtuosos at communication. Even when discussing a hot topic, they display a lot of ease and calm. Most of all they have a keen ability to listen to and understand the other's point of view and emotions. That's why I call couples like Betty and Bert *validators:* in the midst of disagreement they still let their partner know that they consider his or her opinions and emotions valid, even if they don't agree with them. . . .

This expression of mutual respect tends to limit the number of arguments couples need to have. Validator couples, we've found, tend to pick their battles carefully. Those flare-ups that do occur end up sounding more like a problem-solving discussion than a hostile call to arms. . . .

Of course, validating couples don't necessarily have marriages made in heaven. Even happy unions have their share of problems. I suspect the risk for validating couples is that they may turn their marriage into a passionless arrangement in which romance and selfhood are sacrificed for friendship and togetherness. In such a scenario they may end up forgoing personal development in favor of keeping their bond strong. . . .

Still, a validating marriage appears likely to be a solid one. And that probably shouldn't be surprising. After all, when both partners feel their grievances get a sympathetic hearing, compromise is a lot easier.

Max and Anita: Volatile

. . . Anita and Max certainly take a different approach to squabbling than do Bert and Betty. If you were a fly on the wall of their house, you would hear a lot of *Coke* vs. *Pepsi* bickering: Who is a better cook? Is the drive from New York to Boston four hours or five? Whose mother is a bigger snoop? The content of their arguments is so minor, it's hard to imagine a couple like Bert and Betty wasting time on it. How can people like Max and Anita who seem to thrive on skirmishes live happily together? The truth is that not every couple who fights this frequently has a stable marriage. But we call those who do *volatile.* Such couples fight on a grand scale and have an even grander time making up. An uninvolved or withdrawn partner does not exist in a volatile marriage. These relationships are marked by a high level of engagement during discussions. . . .

Joe and Sheila: Avoidant

Moving from a volatile to an avoidant style marriage is like leaving the tumult of a hurricane for the placid waters of a summer lake. Not much seems to happen between husband and wife in this type of marriage. A more accurate name for them is probably *conflict minimizers* because they make light of their differences rather than resolving them. Like Joe and Sheila, these couples will claim that they have disagreements, but when you actually explore what they mean by *conflict* you realize that they conspire to dodge and hedge. We've seen that validators listen to each other's point of view before trying to persuade, while volatile couples jump right in, advocating for their opinion. But when avoidant couples air their differences very little gets settled. The phrase that comes up time and again when you speak with these couples about their marriage is that they end their friction by "agreeing to disagree." By this they usually mean that they avoid discussions they know will result in a deadlock.

Consider Sheila and Joe. In my view, their major conflict was a common—and potentially calamitous—one for a marriage. Namely, he wanted to have sex far more frequently than she did. She didn't enjoy sex with him, she said, because he was not as affectionate as she wanted at other times. He agreed that this was a problem and attributed it to his stress at work. Over time, she responded by becoming detached when they made love. It's not hard to imagine a conflict of this magnitude having serious consequences for a marriage. . . .

Rather than resolve conflicts, avoidant couples appeal to their basic shared philosophy of marriage. They reaffirm what they love and value in the marriage, accentuate the positive, and accept the rest. In this way, they often end an unresolved discussion still feeling good about one another. . . .

One potentially problematic quality of the avoidant style, however, is that it leaves husband and wife very unschooled in how to address a conflict should they someday be forced to do so. . . .

Another hazard of this type of marriage is that it can become lonely. These marriages are marked by a low degree of introspection or psychological sophistication. As a consequence, husband and/or wife may eventually feel that the other doesn't really know or understand them. . . .

The three types of stable couples will each say that they discuss feelings fully in their marriage and resolve issues. But they differ vastly on these dimensions and on what feels like a satisfying resolution. What is far more important than actually solving the issue or problem is feeling good about the interaction itself, and each of these types of couples has its own way to do that. . . .

The Magic Ratio

By now you may be wondering how these three very different types of marriages can be equally successful, or how couples with such clear difficulties, differences, or apparent inadequacies can stay happily together. The answer is that happiness isn't found in a particular style of fighting or making up. Rather, our research suggests that what really separates contented couples from those in deep marital misery is a healthy balance between their positive and negative feelings and actions toward each other. For example, I mentioned that volatile couples stick together by *balancing* their frequent arguments with a lot of love and passion. But by balance I do not mean a fifty-fifty equilibrium. As part of our research we carefully charted the amount of time couples spent fighting versus interacting positively—touching, smiling, paying compliments, laughing, etc. Across the board we found there was a very specific ratio that exists between the amount of positivity and negativity in a stable marriage, whether it is marked by validation, volatility, or conflict avoidance.

That magic ratio is *5 to 1*. In other words, as long as there is five times as much positive feeling and interaction between husband and wife as there is negative, we found the marriage was likely to be stable. It was based on this ratio that we were able to predict whether couples were likely to divorce: in very unhappy couples, there tended to be more negative than positive interaction. . . .

The three successful styles of marriage are equally successful adaptations that allow very different kinds of couples to maintain this crucial ratio over time. In other words, these three styles may be universal ways of preserving this important balance (or rather, *im*balance in favor of the positive scale). Whether a couple settles into a validating, volatile, or avoidant marriage may depend on their particular temperaments, backgrounds, and personalities. . . .

What was even more striking was the many ways, large and small, that stable couples showed their positivity. It translates into a useful list of ways to put more weight on the positive side of the equation in your marriage. . . .

Show interest. Be actively interested in what your partner is saying. . . .

Be affectionate. You can show affection in low-key, subtle ways simply through quiet acts of tenderness: touching or holding hands while you watch TV, intertwining your feet while you read the Sunday paper together. . . .

Show you care. Small acts of thoughtfulness are a powerful way to boost the positivity in your marriage. Some examples: You are shopping and you pass a florist; you buy your wife some flowers she'd like. Or you're in the grocery store and you think of getting your husband's favorite ice cream. Or you just take a few minutes during your busy day and think about what your partner is facing today; for example, "Right now she is about to run a meeting about staff conflicts and she is real worried about how it will go because of that domineering person on her staff." And you call up to check in, wish her well, see how things are going.

Be appreciative. You put positive energy into the marriage simply through appreciating it—thinking about and remembering positive moments from your past, thinking fondly about your partner, and so on. . . .

Show your concern. Whenever your partner tells you about something distressing or troubling, express your concern. Be supportive when your partner is blue or worried. . . .

Be empathic. Empathy, showing your partner an emotional resonance, is a potent form of affection. You can show that you really understand and feel what your partner is feeling just through an expression on your face that matches your partner's. . . .

Be accepting. Even if your partner is saying something you don't agree with let your partner know what he or she is saying makes sense and is important—that you respect it. . . .

Joke around. Playful teasing, wittiness, silliness, and just having an uproarious time together is especially nourishing. If you, like most couples, have private jokes that only you share, such joking is a way not only to have fun but is also a statement of the intimate and exclusive bond between you. . . .

Share your joy. When you're feeling delighted, excited, or just having a really good time, let your partner know it. . . .

Basic Marital Nutrients: Love and Respect

In our study of long-term marriages we recruited couples from a wide range of backgrounds who had been married twenty to forty years to the same partner. Despite the wide differences in occupations, lifestyles, and the details of their day-to-day lives, I sense a remarkable similarity in the tone of their conversations. No matter what style of marriage they have adopted, their discussions, for the most part, are carried along by a strong undercurrent of two basic ingredients: love and respect.

These are the direct opposite of—and antidote for—contempt, perhaps the most corrosive force in marriage. But all the ways partners show each other love and respect also ensure that the positive-to-negative ratio of a marriage will be heavily tilted to the positive side.

The abundance of love and respect in these long-term marriages is evident everywhere. . . .

Tumbling Down the Marital Rapids

. . . If you are in the middle of a troubled marriage it can seem that your predicament is not only unique but nearly impossible to sort out. But in fact unhappy marriages do resemble each other in important ways. True, each has its own personality and idiosyncrasies, but they share one overriding similarity: they followed the same, *specific*, downward spiral before coming to a sad end. This spiral includes a distinct cascade of interactions, emotions, and attitudes that, step by step, brought these couples close to separation, divorce, or an unhappy, lonely life together. Rather than settling into one of the three stable marital styles, their relationships went into a freefall as they were consumed by negativity. . . .

The first cascade a couple hits as they tumble down the marital rapids is comprised of "The Four Horsemen of the Apocalypse," my name for four disastrous ways of interacting that sabotage your attempts to communicate with your partner. In order of least to most dangerous, they are *criticism, contempt, defensiveness*, and *stonewalling*. As these behaviors become more and more entrenched, husband and wife focus increasingly on the escalating sense of negativity and tension in their marriage. Eventually they may become deaf to each other's efforts at peacemaking. As each horseman arrives, he paves the way for the next. Here is how the horsemen can slowly, insidiously override a marriage that started out full of promise.

The First Horseman: Criticism

. . . On the surface, there may not seem to be much difference between complaining and criticizing. But criticism involves *attacking someone's personality or character—rather than a specific behavior—usually with blame.* . . .

Since few couples can completely avoid criticizing each other now and then, the first horseman often takes up long-term residence even in relatively healthy marriages. One reason is that criticizing someone is just a short hop beyond complaining, which is actually one of the *healthiest* activities that can occur in a marriage. Expressing anger and disagreement—airing a complaint—though rarely pleasant, makes the marriage stronger in the long run than suppressing the complaint. . . .

The Second Horseman: Contempt

. . . What separates *contempt* from criticism is the *intention to insult* and *psychologically abuse* your partner. With your words and body language, you're lobbing insults right into the heart of your partner's sense of self. Fueling these contemptuous actions are negative thoughts about the partner—he or she is stupid, disgusting, incompetent, a fool. In direct or subtle fashion, that message gets across along with the criticism. . . .

In brief, the best way to neutralize your contempt is to stop seeing arguments with your spouse as a way to retaliate or exhibit your superior moral stance. Rather, your relationship will improve if you approach your spouse with precise complaints (rather than attacking your partner's character) and express a healthy dose of admiration—the opposite of contempt—for your spouse. . . .

The Third Horseman: Defensiveness

. . . The fact that defensiveness is an understandable reaction to feeling besieged is one reason it is so destructive—the "victim" doesn't see anything wrong with being defensive. But defensive phrases, and the attitude they express, tend to escalate a conflict rather than resolve anything. If you are being defensive (even if you feel completely righteous in your stance), you are adding to your marital troubles. . . .

If you or your spouse frequently exhibit any of the following defensive behaviors, the third horseman has settled into your relationship. Remember that however it is expressed, defensiveness is fundamentally an attempt to protect yourself and ward off a perceived attack. . . .

Denying Responsibility. No matter what your partner charges, you insist in no uncertain terms that you are not to blame. . . .

Making Excuses. In this defensive maneuver you claim that external circumstances beyond your control forced you to act in a certain way. . . .

Disagreeing with Negative Mind Reading. Sometimes, your spouse will make assumptions about your private feelings, behavior, or motives. When this "mind reading" is delivered in a negative manner, it may trigger defensiveness in you. . . .

The Fourth Horseman: Stonewalling

Stonewalling often happens while a couple is talking. The stonewaller just removes himself by turning into a stone wall. Usually someone who is listening reacts to what the speaker is saying, looks at the speaker, and says things like "Uh huh" or "Hmmm" to let the speaker know that he is tracking. But the stonewaller abandons these messages, replacing them with stony silence.

When we've interviewed stonewallers they often claim that they are trying to be "neutral" and not make things worse. They do not seem to realize that stonewalling itself is a very powerful act: it conveys disapproval, icy distance, and smugness. It is very upsetting to speak to a stonewalling listener. This is especially true when a man stonewalls a woman, and much less true when a woman stonewalls a man. Most men don't seem to get physiologically aroused when their wives stonewall them, but wives' heart rates go up dramatically when their husbands stonewall them. Furthermore, most stonewallers (about 85 percent of them) are men! So this is mainly a problem women have with their men. . . .

The fourth horseman need not mark the end of a relationship. But if your interactions have deteriorated to this extent you are at great risk of caterwauling even farther down the marital cascade—becoming so overwhelmed by the negativity in your relationship that you end up divorced, separated, or living lonely, parallel lives in the same home. Once the fourth horseman becomes a regular resident, it takes a good deal of hard work and soul searching to save the marriage. . . .

What makes the four horsemen so deadly to a marriage is not so much their unpleasantness but the intensive way they interfere with a couple's communication. They create a continuing cycle of discord and negativity that's hard to break through if you don't understand what is happening. . . .

Clearly, "The Four Horsemen of the Apocalypse" are so dangerous to your marriage because they sabotage your attempts to keep negativity from overwhelming your relationship. By unsettling a marriage's healthy ecology—that 5-to-1 ratio in favor of positive interaction—the horsemen can throw a happy couple into a disastrous tailspin. . . .

Four Simple Things You Can Do

By now it's probably clear to you that I believe some conflict and disagreement are crucial for a marriage's long-term success. The idea that conflict is healthy may sound like a cruel joke if you're feeling overwhelmed by the negativity in your relationship. But in a sense a marriage lives and dies by what you might loosely call its arguments, by how well disagreements and grievances are aired. The key is *how* you argue—whether your style escalates tension or leads to a feeling of resolution.

You may assume that learning a healthy disagreement style is a complex, virtually impossible task. Far from it. Although many marriage manuals offer long lists of communication techniques you can follow, I think that most couples (even those in the most miserable marriages) don't really need an intricate, step-by-step program. After all, the same couples who are unable to communicate at home easily do so with their neighbors or at work. Sometimes a marital discussion that is going nowhere will be interrupted by a telephone call and it's amazing to see how capable a communicator the same person is with someone else. Then it's back to the identical frustrating discussion after the phone call, and back to the same old reactions that don't work in the marriage.

Obviously, the problem isn't a lack of skill. It's that their ability to communicate with their loved one is stymied by the negativity that's enveloping their marriage. It's all too easy to let simple disagreements become knock-down, drag-out fights that leave one or both of you wondering if this marriage can be saved. The real problem is a lack of strategy—in other words, losing sight of when to apply the skills you already have.

In fact, I believe there are only four crucial strategies that you need to utilize in order to break through most of the negativity. If you can put them to use, your marriage is almost certain to improve dramatically— all your natural communication and conflict-resolving abilities will come to the fore. Of course, it won't always be easy to put these essentials to work. It will take courage, strength, and trust to use them when you're feeling hurt, angry, and victimized. The key is not only to understand these strategies intellectually but to use them so often that they become second nature and are available to you *even when you are feeling very upset*—the moments you'll need them most. I call this *overlearning* and it is the one principle you need to adopt for my program to work at all.

Master these fundamentals and I think you'll be at least 75 percent of the way toward maximizing your marital happiness. . . .

The major goal is to break the cycle of negativity. You'll learn (1) how to *calm yourself* so that flooding doesn't block your communication; (2) how to *speak and listen nondefensively* so that your discussions or disagreements will be more productive; (3) how to *validate each other* as well as your relationship even (or especially) when the going gets tough; (4) how to *overlearn these principles* so that your new skills become almost second nature. . . .

Strategy #1: Calm Down

The first step is learning to calm down. This is a specific remedy for several problems, most related to flooding. It eases the need to be defensive and to stonewall, undercuts the physical feelings that sustain distress-maintaining thoughts, and is the antidote to flooding. . . .

Strategy #2: Speak Nondefensively

Listening or speaking without being defensive helps counter several destructive habits. Nondefensive *listening* is especially helpful to ease defensiveness. If you are a nondefensive listener, it will make the cycle of negativity less likely. And a nondefensive attitude also helps defuse flooding and the need to stonewall, particularly for men. But defensiveness is a two-way street; if you start *speaking* nondefensively, you will lessen your partner's need to be defensive. . . .

Strategy #3: Validation

. . . Validation is simply putting yourself in your partner's shoes and imagining his or her emotional state. It is then a simple matter to let your mate know that you understand those feelings and consider them valid, even if you don't share them. Validation is an amazingly effective technique. It's as if you opened the door to welcome your partner. When your partner feels validated, he or she will feel much more comfortable confiding in you, and much more open to hearing your perspective as well. . . .

Strategy #4: Overlearning—Try and Try Again

When you've had one successful fight using these techniques, you may think you've mastered the strategies. I'm afraid there's more work involved. In fact, the worst thing you could do is to read this chapter once and never look at it again. It's not enough to have an intellectual understanding of "fighting smart." These lessons have to be practiced *often*. So often, in fact, that they become almost automatic. . . .

If you practice, practice, practice these skills you will have gone a very long way toward improving your marriage. It has been my experience that these four principles—*calming down, communicating nondefensively, validating,* and *overlearning*—are all that most marriages need in order to get back on track. I believe this is even true of marriages that have been almost completely subsumed by negativity. I don't mean to imply that you will see changes overnight, or that transforming your marriage will be easy. But if you are motivated, work hard, and don't let every setback discourage you, over time you will find your marriage a far happier place to be.

Study Questions

1. Please list the "four horsemen" and write your understanding of each. What are some things to look out for in relationships, if we don't want to end in divorce or separation?

2. After a 10-year marriage, what would a couple have to do to keep the 5:1 ratio?

Topic 12
Education and Religion

Along with the family, two of the most important institutions in society are education and religion. For many, formal education in schools is a focal point of early life, and the formal and informal aspects of education continue for many years into adulthood. Often we are educated and trained on the job. Clearly, much of our life is encompassed by the educational institution. Religion is a central part of U.S. life, and often a significant part of individual and family life. The United States is a very religious country as measured by the proportion of believers and attendees. Who can doubt the impact of religion in the unfolding of U.S. history, from the Puritans to the followers of Sun Yung Moon or Krishna Consciousness? Even the politics of U.S. life is laced with religious references, often to the point that sociologists talk of a "civil religion." Education and religion reach into everyone's lives, sometimes personally and sometimes in more distant ways. As social institutions, education and religion house much of our lives, and create focal points that may last a lifetime.

The educational institution in society is seen as being coercive. Just like prisons, schools often control and indoctrinate and they do so in bell-ringing, punctual ways. As young persons, we are often forced to be there by law until the age of 16, and too many absences may result in referral to juvenile court. Some sociologists question whether schools are the optimal way to educate the populace, but schools are a critical part of learning, credentialing, and success in society. Who among us will forget the social cultures in middle and high schools? Remember the intense feelings associated with belonging or not belonging? Remember how important relationships could become? Remember how a single day or a single hour might hold the greatest joy and greatest pain of our young lives? Understanding schools, and the behavior of children in them, has become a national priority, as has improving achievement at all levels.

Religion is a social institution that creates connections between people, a sense of community and social integration, and answers sacred questions about life, death, faith, and catastrophes. As the belief in something that transcends everyday experiences, religion is able to create understanding and acceptance where science or other explanations might fail. How would parents explain the death of their child, or how would a victim explain a rape or the onset of a terminal disease? The history of religion, and indeed the history of the world, is dominated by secularization or the increasing importance of everyday (profane) life and the decreasing importance of religion (sacred). Even religious organizations have secularized their activities and might spend more time and money on new buildings than on the spiritual life of members. In the western world, particularly, we have seen the separation of church and state. Even early in the twenty-first century, this debate rages daily in the press and courts as it is decided when and where we pray, about the placement of the Ten Commandments in public buildings, and whether it is a good idea for political leaders to invoke support from gods and prophets.

The three selections for Topic 12: Education and Religion examine some of the more questionable aspects of social institutions. This representation reminds us that even social institutions are "dysfunctional" at times, and that the personal and structural effects of these social patterns are not always positive. Don Merten examines the "meanness" of a group of high status, popular girls. Violence in our schools has brought sociology and the entire nation to focus on more in-depth understanding of the dynamics that are precursors to such violence. Girls are not strangers to this type of "violence" in junior high schools. Mary Crow Dog and Richard Erdoes autobiographically recount the historical practice of taking Native American children from their families and raising them in boarding schools on the reservation as a way to "civilize" them. This separation from the family and culture and the mistreatment in the schools would have a lasting impact on the lives of the children. Theresa Krebs uses a structural analysis to bring understanding to scandals within the Catholic Church. This research teaches us a valuable lesson about how the culture of religious organizations can go awry, just as they can in businesses and governments.

Reading 34

The Meaning of Meanness

Popularity, Competition, and Conflict among Junior High School Girls

Don E. Merten

The sociocultural construction of meanness among a clique of popular girls in junior high school is the focal point of this article. The term *sociocultural* is used here to designate the interplay of social and cultural phenomena in the construction of meanness (Berger and Luckmann 1967; Geertz 1973; Searle 1995). In the context of the research presented here, the construction was explored primarily by examining how the social relationships, and their meanings, of junior high school girls were shaped by the broader contours of mainstream American culture. Therefore, it considered how meanness acquired meaning through (1) its relationship to other related concepts, such as "niceness"; (2) the meaning of competition and conflict for girls; and (3) the tension between hierarchy and equality. Thus, the construction of meanness involved both social interaction and cultural meaning—the latter often tacit.

For the clique of popular girls whose actions are the focus of this article, meanness became an essential feature of their competition for, and conflict over, popularity. The relationship among competition, conflict, and meanness was far from simple. Sometimes, meanness was a byproduct of competition and conflict, but at other times, girls used meanness instrumentally to gain a competitive advantage in pursuit or protection of popularity. Yet it was not obvious why being mean seemed reasonable to these girls—much less why they took meanness to the point of being considered the meanest girls in school. . . .

Method and Context

The data for this article are from a three-year longitudinal study of junior high school students. The first year was spent observing and interviewing students in the junior high school. Data from the initial observations and interviews (precohort) were used to orient research for the study of the student cohort that entered junior high school the following year. All students who wanted to participate and who had signed informed-consent letters (270 students, 127 boys and 143 girls, 80 percent of the eligible students) formed the study cohort. During the seventh and eighth grades, two school ethnographers observed and interviewed the cohort students at school. A third ethnographer interviewed the parents and adults in the community. . . .

The community in which the junior high school was located was a middle- to upper-middle-class suburb that was overwhelmingly White but was ethnically relatively diverse. It was a community with a heavy emphasis on mobility, both geographic and economic. The adults in the community were also aware that it was not getting any easier to succeed and that children would have to work hard to do as well as their parents—much less surpass them. Community and family resources were expended to create an educational and activity environment that provided students with opportunities that prepared them for future success. The local high school sent many graduates to college, and both the adults and students perceived the two years in junior high school as an important stop in this educational journey. . . .

The Clique: Popular and Mean

Our first encounter with members of the clique came when the community ethnographer spent a day with each of the sixth-grade classes that sent cohort students to the junior high school. Because the elementary school from which the clique came had four sixth-grade classrooms, the ethnographer spent four days there and recorded the following in her notes:

> A clique of 8 to 10 girls dominate the 6th grade, as opposed to Edison [another elementary school] where the dominant group was boys. These girls are considered "cool," "popular," and "mean." They are a combination of cute, talented, affluent, conceited, and powerful. Their presence as a group is much more obvious during noon hour than when they are separated in classrooms.

The core membership of the clique (Megan, Gretchen, Sara, Brenda, Melissa, Sherry, Beth, Gloria, and Alice) came together in sixth grade. In addition, a number of other girls were, from time to time, included and excluded; the clique usually had 10 to 12 members.

Brenda characterized the clique in terms similar to those noted by the ethnographer: "Well, everybody liked us. Everybody thought highly of everyone in the group. A lot of kids were scared of us. Scared that we were going to beat them up or that we wouldn't be friends with them." Even though the clique's members did not physically attack other girls, they intimidated peers with threats to do so. The clique's reputation as being mean and powerful meant that they were able to get their way without resorting to physical violence. Yet as Brenda noted, the clique was highly regarded and popular. Many girls tried desperately to become members and to share the other girls' popularity.

Popularity and Its Management

In junior high school, popularity had two different but interrelated referents. When a girl said someone was popular, she meant first, that the student was widely *known or recognized* by classmates and second, that he or she was *sought after* as a friend. In the best of all worlds, a student enjoyed widespread recognition *and* was sought out by many peers. Two well-traveled routes to popularity were to attract the interest of high-status boys (those who were especially athletic or handsome) by being physically attractive and/or participating in high-prestige activities. For example, cheerleading placed girls in front of their peers by performing at school sports events, and cheerleaders were able to wear their uniforms in class on days they performed, which further enhanced their recognition. Even though attractiveness to boys is important in elementary school (Adler et al. 1992), it became an especially prominent source of popularity during this transition from childhood to adolescence, since dating is a quintessential feature of adolescence. Because cheerleading positions and high-status boys were scarce, acquiring popularity via these routes was a highly competitive undertaking. Whereas being widely recognized enhanced a girl's chances to be sought after as a friend, it also helped if she was friendly or nice. . . .

The clique's popularity made it attractive, and many girls sought to associate with the members, but the members only allowed certain girls to do so. Girls with the potential to be popular or those who were especially nice were sometimes allowed in. However, inclusion in the clique, as Melissa pointed out, sometimes transformed nice girls:

> Once she got into the group she started getting real stuck-up and like she was the big one and the hot shot and everything. And she started going out with

boys that they [the members] liked, and they started getting jealous. They would tell her that she was acting real hot and they didn't like the way she was acting. Then she would get upset.

The exhilaration of popularity was not easy for some girls to contain as they tried to take advantage of their high status. However, the established members of the clique were not looking for competitors. They were willing to accept girls who were grateful for the opportunity to associate with them, but did not hesitate to be aggressive in putting them in their place if they overreached their acceptance.

An often unrealized ideal was that popular girls would also be nice. Being nice, however, carried more weight in interpersonal interaction than with regard to schoolwide recognition. Nevertheless, niceness remained an important interpersonal ideal and was part of female gender construction that emphasizes nurturance and giving (Beauvior, 1957). Junior high school girls used the terms *nice* and *mean* as general evaluative characterizations for peers and their actions. Sherry described what it meant to be nice: "Someone who cares about people's feelings and is real nice to them. Nice to everybody and treats everybody equal and stuff like that. Talk to them, comfort them, ask them to be your partner and stuff like that." Treating peers as equals and caring about their feelings reduced the social distance between individuals and made interaction more comfortable.

Sara also emphasized "caring" for people as an aspect of niceness when she talked about her nonclique friend Missy. She described what made Missy "nicer" than her friends in the clique:

'Cause she is better than even they [the clique members] are. She treats me better. Not that they treat me bad, but she is always there when I need her. She is always understanding. She always knows what to say. She is never off with someone else when you need to talk to her. That is why she is nicer.

Junior High School

The transition to junior high school brought about two, somewhat countervailing, changes. On the one hand, as seventh graders, the clique was at the bottom of the school hierarchy; eighth graders were on top. On the other hand, the junior high school had many more organized activities than did the elementary school from which they came (Merten 1996). In keeping with Eder, Evans and Parker's (1995) observation that extracurricular activities may contribute to the preoccupation with popularity found in American schools, these activities were resources of variable prestige value (Adler and Adler 1994). For girls, the two most valuable activities were cheerleading and pom-pom (the performance of choreographed routines set to music while shaking pom-poms). Compared to these activities, any other was a distant third in popularity. All eight of the seventh-grade cheerleaders were members of the clique, and two other members were on the pom-pom squad. Thus, the activity structure of junior high school enhanced and, more important, publicly validated, the clique's popularity. In other words, the clique's success in *monopolizing* the most prestigious activity in junior high school allowed the members to consolidate and enact their popularity publicly in ways that had not been possible in elementary school.

With their entry into junior high school, the clique's members acknowledged their previous meanness, but saw themselves now as less mean. As Megan observed: "We thought we were really hot. I have cooled down a little this year because of the eighth graders. We just thought that we were the greatest." Megan associated the clique's decreased meanness with their diminished social status now that they were *below* the eighth graders. However, the clique did not "cool" down as much as Megan suggested, nor did their meanness subside much; it simply turned inward. The reality was that the clique had "cornered" most of the popularity available in the seventh grade. This fact, along with the constraining effect that the eighth graders' dominance had on the clique, contributed to the clique's members becoming mean toward each other.

Self-Promotion and Paybacks

As the members directed their meanness toward each other, Sherry became the target of intense meanness. Because her account is not always easy to follow, it is helpful to start with an excerpt from the notes of a fieldworker whom Sherry and her (nonclique) friend Wellsley stopped in the hall:

> Sherry was absolutely in tears. It was like she was starting to hyperventilate; she could not talk through her tears. I asked what was the matter, and Sherry looked at Wellsley and [said] "You tell her; I can't talk." Wellsley, in her real quiet little voice, started to tell me that Rick Castleton has broken up with Missy and that everybody in that group [clique] is blaming Sherry for the breakup.

The fieldworker interviewed Sherry several days later. Sherry began by talking about how she was invited into the clique, "a really mean group," as she described them, in the sixth grade. Then she described the foregoing incident:

> Gretchen was starting to get really mad at me. I talked to her about it and I asked her what was wrong. She just said, "Oh, I heard something that you said about me." But I didn't say anything about her. Sara was mad at me, I don't know why. She started being mad at me and then she started making up things that [she said] I said. Sara told Brenda and Gretchen so that they would get mad at me, too. So now I guess Gretchen has made up something and told Wellsley. They are all mad at me and laughing and everything.

. . . Because most of the meanness occurred outside the classroom (in the hall, the library, and the lunchroom), teachers seldom observed it. The social organization of junior high school—moving from classroom to classroom and teacher to teacher—provided opportunities for surreptitious meanness. Furthermore, some teachers found it difficult to believe that girls who were good students and otherwise popular could be so mean to a friend. Other teachers thought this situation was the sort of peer conflict that students had to learn to handle themselves; for example, one teacher walked away from Sherry and refused to listen as she tried to explain her plight. Sherry's father told of how the principal said he would do whatever he could to make the situation better, *but* if Sherry retaliated, she, too, would be punished. Even more frustrating to Sherry's father were his conversations with the parents of the other girls in the clique. Regarding one mother, he had the following to say:

> One mother's attitude that we talked to is "girls are going to be girls." She said that this type of behavior in preadolescent girls is typical, and it is nothing to be worried about. It is a phase that girls go through, and it will pass. "You are making a mountain out of a molehill. What are you getting so upset about?"

Parents' and teachers' responses were shaped by their interpretation of girls' conflicts as developmental and therefore "natural." First, by considering meanness developmentally "normal," they minimized its seriousness. Second, the school philosophy, which emphasized the need for students to be more independent and self-reliant, dictated that these girls should take care of such conflicts without adult intervention. Thus, a junior high school with a social organization that diffused adult responsibility and with an ideology that demanded students to be self-reliant facilitated meanness. . . .

Contested Status Change

At the beginning of junior high school, popularity was dynamic, and the increased popularity of some of the clique's middle-level members threatened to surpass the popularity of those at the top. Moreover, popularity, and the status it helped determine, was often experienced as schismogenic (Bateson 1958); that is, as the popularity of one girl increased, the popularity of another decreased. Since those at the top of the clique had the most to lose, they were concerned with the other members' successes. Megan, the least physically attractive of the top clique members, was especially vulnerable as attractiveness to boys became an increasingly important source of popularity. Melissa, a seventh-grade cheerleader, found herself more and more attractive to high-status boys; yet her popularity threatened to be short-lived. She described her situation as follows:

> At the beginning of the year when I got into cheerleading, everything was fun. But after Christmas vacation, people started thinking that I was stuck-up. . . . They started writing on the walls, "Melissa Martin is stuck-up." That got me pretty upset.

Melissa never learned who had written these messages, but her friendships in the clique were not going well:

> I thought that my friends were the people in my class like Sara and Megan. After Christmas vacation, they started not to like me. They thought I was stuck-up, too. . . . After Christmas, Megan had a party, and I couldn't go to it because Brenda and I already had skiing arrangements. So I guess that is the time they all got mad at me.

Melissa viewed her situation as one in which her increased popularity was followed by being characterized as stuck-up, and then her closest friends stopped liking her. . . .

Melissa's concern with her friends' meanness toward her extended to such things as family vacations because absence from interaction with the clique often resulted in meanness toward the absent member. Melissa described her predicament as follows:

> I was so afraid that when I came back to school that all of them wouldn't like me. I didn't want to go at first. We were going to go on spring vacation [but] I was afraid my friends wouldn't like me. That is like when they were getting

mad at me all of the time. That was after Christmas vacation when they thought they had a whole lot of power over me. And they were just getting mad at me all of the time for all dumb reasons. They were trying to make me look real bad. Like I would come home from the games and be really upset.

Melissa was so desirous of remaining in the clique that even though she knew the reasons offered for being mad at her, what she called "dumb reasons," were not the real ones, she was in no position to complain. Making her look bad in cheerleading was another way to undermine her popularity. . . .

Because most of the clique's meanness was directed toward its own members, most outsiders continued to think of the members as individuals with whom it would be nice to have a relationship. Thus, the internal focus of meanness generally had the effect of protecting the clique's popularity within the wider social system. . . .

Discussion

Competition-conflict to gain or preserve popularity was an ever-present undercurrent in the interpersonal relationships of the clique and thereby constituted an important condition for meanness. Yet to understand the meaning of meanness, it is necessary to go beyond the competition-conflict with which meanness was often associated. Because competition-conflict between females is frequently mediated in other contexts, one has to ask why competition-conflict around popularity vitiated the norm of mediation. In other words, was there an advantage to being mean when one was trying to be or to remain popular? . . .

Hierarchy and Meanness

. . . To gain a greater understanding of the relationship between hierarchy and meanness, it is necessary to consider how hierarchy was viewed in this community. Hierarchy was perceived as being significantly *truncated*; that is, rather than perceiving many gradations of status, students thought of their own status as essentially dichotomous—either high or low, winners or losers (Merten, 1994). Thus, minor losses in relative popularity were frequently experienced as significant losses in status. . . .

One's position in the clique was important, because it both symbolized one's popularity and was salient in protecting it. That is, hierarchical position was an essential factor for the successful use of meanness in the sense that a girl's effectiveness in being mean depended on her status in the clique. Melissa observed that those members who had more status than she could be mean to her, but she could not effectively be mean to them because they simply became angry and mobilized *her* friends against her. The other side of the hierarchical meaning of meanness was that high status protected girls from the meanness of members with less social status and thus demonstrated their superiority. . . .

The Cultural Logic of Meanness

The larger question, What led these girls to express their concerns with popularity and hierarchy in terms of meanness? requires an examination of the cultural logic by which doing so made sense. To understand how meanness was constructed and what it meant in the context of this junior high school, it is necessary to consider what other possibilities existed. Perhaps the one thing that popular girls dreaded most was losing their popularity by being labeled stuck-up. Loss of popularity in this manner was especially disconcerting in that being labeled stuck-up used the "force" (to use a judo metaphor) of a girl's popularity against her to invert her status. Therefore, it was precisely when a girl enjoyed popularity (as a cheerleader, for example) that she was most vulnerable to being labeled stuck-up. The problem was how to express and enjoy popularity and still manage to keep it. Expressing one's sense of one's own popularity could be as little as projecting a self-confident demeanor or as much as refusing to acknowledge or to associate with anyone who was less popular. Any action that suggested that a girl considered herself popular, however, *could* be taken as an indication that she thought she was superior and hence was stuck-up. Yet to be popular and be unable to express it, and thereby not enjoy it, was less than satisfying. Thus, these girls faced a cultural dilemma that is common for women: They were being implicitly asked to encompass both aspects of a cultural dichotomy—to seek popularity, but when they were successful, to pretend they were not popular. This dilemma is similar to girls being called on, in another context, to be "seductive virgins" (Schwartz and Merten 1980). . . .

To put this rather complex relationship between popularity and meanness another way: Both meanness and popularity had hierarchical aspects and implications. Popularity was an expression and a source of hierarchical position. Furthermore, popularity could be transformed into power, which was also hierarchical. Like popularity, meanness could also be transformed into power. Hence, power was a common denominator between popularity and meanness. In this respect, meanness could be expressed in terms of popularity, and popularity could be expressed in terms of meanness, with power mediating the transition from one to the other. Just as "the language of social inequality is one of vertical imagery" (Schwartz 1981:125), so was the language of meanness. Thus, meanness was, in a fundamental sense, discourse about hierarchical position, popularity, and invulnerability (Gergen 1984).

Conclusion

Why a clique of girls that was popular and socially sophisticated was also renowned for its meanness was the question with which this article began. Yet in this junior high school, where acting like everyone else was important and acting superior to peers was discouraged, popularity was as problematic as it was desired. When something highly valued cannot be openly expressed, alternative forms of expression are often invoked. At this level, it can be said that meanness resulted from the failure of the culture to allow hierarchy to be explicitly celebrated (Merten 1996). That is, the cultural logic that allowed meanness to make sense to these junior high school girls was grounded in broader cultural tensions between hierarchy and equality. As Shweder (1991:108) noted about American society, "We do not know how to justify status obligations and hierarchical relationships, but we live them." Thus, meanness, in a context in which equality was a paramount value and myth, was an action that awkwardly attempted to express and preserve popularity, despite its hierarchical implications.

For women in mainstream American culture, the tension between hierarchy and equality is further exacerbated by the taboo on *open* competition—especially among friends (Tracy 1991). If well-educated, successful women find it difficult to mediate the opposition between solidarity with friends and competition for individual success (Keller and Moglen 1987), then it is little wonder that junior high school girls found it difficult to do so.

References

Adler, Patricia and Peter Adler. 1994. "Social Reproduction and the Corporate Other: Institutionalization of Afterschool Activities." *Sociological Quarterly* 35:309–28.

Adler, Patricia, Steven Kless, and Peter Adler. 1992. "Socialization to Gender Roles: Popularity among Elementary School Boys and Girls." *Sociology of Education* 65:169–87.

Beauvoir, Simone de. 1957. *The Second Sex*. New York: Alfred A. Knopf.

Berger, Peter and Thomas Luckmann. 1967. *The Social Construction of Reality: A Treatise in the Sociology of Knowledge*. Garden City, NY: Doubleday Anchor Books.

Eder, Donna with Catherine Collins Evans and Stephen Parker. 1995. *School Talk: Gender and Adolescent Culture*. New Brunswick, NJ: Rutgers University Press.

Geertz, Clifford. 1973. *The Interpretation of Cultures*. New York: Basic Books.

Gergen, Kenneth. 1984. "Aggression as Discourse." Pp. 51–68 in *Social Pyschology of Aggression: From Individual Behavior to Social Interaction*, edited by Amelie Mummendey. New York: Springer-Verlag.

Keller, Evelyn and Helene Moglen. 1987. "Competition: A Problem for Academic Women." Pp. 21–37 in *Competition: A Feminist Taboo?* edited by Valerie Miner and Helen E. Longino. New York: Feminist Press.

Merten, Don E. 1994. "The Cultural Context of Aggression: The Transition to Junior High School." *Anthropology and Education Quarterly* 25:29–43.

———. 1996. "Burnout as Cheerleader: The Cultural Basis for Prestige and Privilege in Junior High School." *Anthropology and Education Quarterly*, 27:51–70.

Schwartz, Barry. 1981. *Vertical Classification: A Study in Structuralism and the Sociology of Knowledge*. Chicago: University of Chicago Press.

Schwartz, Gary and Don Merten. 1980. *Love and Commitment*. Beverly Hills, CA: Sage.

Searle, John. 1995. *The Construction of Social Reality*. New York: Free Press.

Shweder, Richard. 1991. "Cultural Psychology: What Is It?" Pp. 73–110 in *Thinking Through Cultures: Expeditions in Cultural Psychology*. Cambridge, MA: Harvard University Press.

Tracy, Laura. 1991. *The Secret Between Us: Competition Among Women*. Boston: Little, Brown.

Study Questions

1. Very popular girls are "mean" to one another. What social value comes from being mean?

2. Popularity is a very tricky issue among these girls. How would you explain this issue and "being popular" to one of your friends?

Reading 35
Civilize Them with a Stick

Mary Dog Crow and Richard Erdoes

. . . Gathered from the cabin, the wickiup, and the tepee,
partly by cajolery and partly by threats;
partly by bribery and partly by force,
they are induced to leave their kindred
to enter these schools and take upon themselves
the outward appearance of civilized life.

—Annual report of the Department of Interior, 1901

It is almost impossible to explain to a sympathetic white person what a typical old Indian boarding school was like; how it affected the Indian child suddenly dumped into it like a small creature from another world, helpless, defenseless, bewildered, trying desperately and instinctively to survive and sometimes not surviving at all. I think such children were like the victims of Nazi concentration camps trying to tell average, middle-class Americans what their experience had been like. Even now, when these schools are much improved, when the buildings are new, all gleaming steel and glass, the food tolerable, the teachers well trained and well-intentioned, even trained in child psychology—unfortunately the psychology of white children, which is different from ours—the shock to the child upon arrival is still tremendous. Some just seem to shrivel up, don't speak for days on end, and have an empty look in their eyes. I know of an eleven-year-old on another reservation who hanged herself, and in our school, while I was there, a girl jumped out of the window, trying to kill herself to escape an unbearable situation. That first shock is always there.

Although the old tiyospaye has been destroyed, in the traditional Sioux families, especially in those where there is no drinking, the child is never left alone. It is always surrounded by relatives, carried around, enveloped in warmth. It is treated with the respect due to any human being, even a small one. It is seldom forced to do anything against its will, seldom screamed at, and never beaten. That much, at least, is left of the old family group among full-bloods. And then suddenly a bus or car arrives, full of strangers, usually white strangers, who yank the child out of the arms of those who love it, taking it screaming to the boarding school. The only word I can think of for what is done to these children is kidnapping.

Even now, in a good school, there is impersonality instead of close human contact; a sterile, cold atmosphere, an unfamiliar routine, language problems, and above all the maza-skan-skan, that damn clock—white man's time as opposed to Indian time, which is natural time. Like eating when you are hungry and sleeping when you are tired, not when that damn clock says you must. But I was not taken to one of the better, modern schools. I was taken to the old-fashioned mission school at St. Francis, run by the nuns and Catholic fathers, built sometime around the turn of the century and not improved a bit when I arrived, not improved as far as the buildings, the food, the teachers, or their methods were concerned.

In the old days, nature was our people's only school and they needed no other. Girls had their toy tipis and dolls, boys their toy bows and arrows. Both rode and swam and played the rough Indian games together. Kids watched their peers and elders and naturally grew from children into adults. Life in the tipi circle was harmonious—until the whiskey peddlers arrived with their wagons and barrels of "Injun whiskey." I often wished I could have grown up in the old, before-whiskey days.

Oddly enough, we owed our unspeakable boarding schools to the do-gooders, the white Indian-lovers. The schools were intended as an alternative to the outright extermination seriously advocated by generals Sherman and Sheridan, as well as by most settlers and prospectors over-running our land. "You don't have to kill those poor benighted heathen," the do-gooders said, "in order to solve the Indian Problem. Just give us a chance to turn them into useful farmhands, laborers, and chamber-maids who will break their backs for you at low wages." In that way the boarding schools were born. The kids were taken away from their villages and pueblos, in their blankets and moccasins, kept completely isolated from their families—sometimes for as long as ten years—suddenly coming back, their short hair slick with pomade, their necks raw from stiff, high collars, their thick jackets always short in the sleeves and pinching under the arms, their tight patent leather shoes giving them corns, the girls in starched white blouses and clumsy, high-buttoned boots—caricatures of white people. When they found out—and they found out quickly—that they were neither wanted by whites nor by Indians, they got good and drunk, many of them staying drunk for the rest of their lives. I still have a poster I found among my grandfather's stuff, given to him by the missionaries to tack up on his wall. It reads:

1. Let Jesus save you.
2. Come out of your blanket, cut your hair, and dress like a white man.
3. Have a Christian family with one wife for life only.
4. Live in a house like your white brother. Work hard and wash often.
5. Learn the value of a hard-earned dollar. Do not waste your money on giveaways. Be punctual.
6. Believe that property and wealth are signs of divine approval.
7. Keep away from saloons and strong spirits.
8. Speak the language of your white brother. Send your children to school to do likewise.
9. Go to church often and regularly.
10. Do not go to Indian dances or to the medicine men.

The people who were stuck upon "solving the Indian Problem" by making us into whites retreated from this position only step by step in the wake of Indian protests.

The mission school at St. Francis was a curse for our family for generations. My grandmother went there, then my mother, then my sisters and I. At one time or other every one of us tried to run away. Grandma told me once about the bad times she had experienced at St. Francis. In those days they let students go home only for one week every year. Two days were used up for transportation, which meant spending just five days out of three hundred and sixty-five with her family. And that was an improvement. Before grandma's time, on many reservations they did not let the students go home at all until they had finished school. Anybody who disobeyed the nuns was severely punished. The building in which my grandmother stayed had three floors, for girls only. Way up in the attic were little cells, about five by five by ten feet. One time she was in church and instead of praying she was playing jacks. As punishment they took her to one of those little cubicles where she stayed in darkness because the windows had been boarded up. They left her there for a whole week with only bread and water for nourishment. After she came out she promptly ran away, together with three other girls. They were found and brought back. The nuns stripped them naked and whipped them. They used a horse buggy whip on my grandmother. Then she was put back into the attic—for two weeks.

My mother had much the same experiences but never wanted to talk about them, and then there I was, in the same place. The school is now run by the BIA—the Bureau of Indian Affairs—but only since about fifteen years ago. When I was there, during the 1960s, it was still run by the Church. The Jesuit fathers ran the boys' wing and the Sisters of the Sacred Heart ran us—with the help of the strap. Nothing had changed since my grandmother's days. I have been told recently that even in the '70s they were still beating children at that school. All I got out of school was being taught how to pray. I learned quickly that I would be beaten if I failed in my devotions or, God forbid, prayed the wrong way, especially prayed in Indian to Wakan Tanka, the Indian Creator.

The girls' wing was built like an F and was run like a penal institution. Every morning at five o'clock the sisters would come into our large dormitory to wake us up, and immediately we had to kneel down at the sides of our beds and recite the prayers. At six o'clock we were herded into the church for more of the same. I did not take kindly to the discipline and to marching by the clock, left-right, left-right. I was never one to like being forced to do something. I do something because I feel like doing it. I felt this way always, as far as I can remember, and my sister Barbara felt the same way. An old medicine man once told me: "Us Lakotas are not like dogs who can be trained, who can be beaten and keep on wagging their tails, licking the hand that whipped them. We are like cats, little cats, big cats, wildcats, bobcats, mountain lions. It doesn't matter what kind, but cats who can't be tamed, who scratch if you step on their tails." But I was only a kitten and my claws were still small.

Barbara was still in the school when I arrived and during my first year or two she could still protect me a little bit. When Barb was a seventh-grader she ran away together with five other girls, early in the morning before sunrise. They brought them back in the evening. The girls had to wait for two hours in front of the mother superior's office. They were hungry and cold, frozen through. It was wintertime and they had been running the whole day without food, trying to make good their escape. The mother superior asked each girl, "Would you do this again?" She told them that as punishment they would not be allowed to visit home for a month and that she'd keep them busy on work details until the skin on their knees and elbows had worn off. At the end of her speech she told each girl, "Get up from this chair and lean over it." She then lifted the girls' skirts and pulled down their underpants. Not little girls either, but teenagers. She had a leather strap about a foot long and four inches wide fastened to a stick, and beat the girls, one after another, until they cried. Barb did not give her that satisfaction but just clenched her teeth. There was one girl, Barb told me, the nun kept on beating and beating until her arm got tired.

I did not escape my share of the strap. Once, when I was thirteen years old, I refused to go to Mass. I did not want to go to church because I did not feel well. A nun grabbed me by the hair, dragged me upstairs, made me stoop over, pulled my dress up (we were not allowed at the time to wear jeans), pulled my panties down, and gave me what they called "swats"—twenty-five swats with a board around which Scotch tape had been wound. She hurt me badly.

My classroom was right next to the principal's office and almost every day I could hear him swatting the boys. Beating was the common punishment for not doing one's homework, or for being late to school. It had such a bad effect upon me that I hated and mistrusted every white person on sight, because I met only one kind. It was not until much later that I met sincere white people I could relate to and be friends with. Racism breeds racism in reverse.

The routine at St. Francis was dreary. Six A.M., kneeling in church for an hour or so; seven o'clock, breakfast; eight o'clock, scrub the floor, peel spuds, make classes. We had to mop the dining room twice every day and scrub the tables. If you were caught taking a rest, doodling on the bench with a fingernail or knife, or just rapping, the nun would come up with a dish towel and just slap it across your face, saying, "You're not supposed to be talking, you're supposed to be working!" Monday mornings we had cornmeal mush, Tuesday oatmeal, Wednesday rice and raisins, Thursday cornflakes, and Friday all the leftovers mixed together or sometimes fish. Frequently the food had bugs or rocks in it. We were eating hot dogs that were weeks old, while the nuns were dining on ham, whipped potatoes, sweet peas, and cranberry sauce. In winter our dorm was icy cold while the nuns' rooms were always warm.

I have seen little girls arrive at the school, first-graders, just fresh from home and totally unprepared for what awaited them, little girls with pretty braids, and the first thing the nuns did was chop their hair off and tie up what was left behind their ears. Next they would dump the children into tubs of alcohol, a sort of rubbing alcohol, "to get the germs off." Many of the nuns were German immigrants, some from Bavaria, so that we sometimes speculated whether Bavaria was some sort of Dracula country inhabited by monsters. For the sake of objectivity I ought to mention that two of the German fathers were great linguists and that the only Lakota-English dictionaries and grammars which are worth anything were put together by them.

At night some of the girls would huddle in bed together for comfort and reassurance. Then the nun in charge of the dorm would come in and say, "What are the two of you doing in bed together? I smell evil in this room. You girls are evil incarnate. You are sinning. You are going to hell and burn forever. You can act that way in the devil's frying pan." She would get them out of bed in the middle of the night, making them kneel and pray until morning. We had not the slightest idea what it was all about. At home we slept two and three in a bed for animal warmth and a feeling of security.

The nuns and the girls in the two top grades were constantly battling it out physically with fists, nails, and hair-pulling. I myself was growing from a kitten into an undersized cat. My claws were getting bigger and were itching for action. About 1969 or 1970 a strange young white girl appeared on the reservation. She looked about eighteen or twenty years old. She was pretty and had long, blond hair down to her waist, patched jeans, boots, and a backpack. She was different from any other white person we had met before. I think her name was Wise. I do not know how she managed to overcome our reluctance and distrust, getting us into a corner, making us listen to her, asking us how we were treated. She told us that she was from New York. She was the first real hippie or Yippie we had come across. She told us of people called the Black Panthers, Young Lords, and Weathermen. She said, "Black people are getting it on. Indians are getting it on in St. Paul and California. How about you?" She also said, "Why don't you put out an underground paper, mimeograph it. It's easy. Tell it like it is. Let it all hang out." She spoke a strange lingo but we caught on fast.

Charlene Left Hand Bull and Gina One Star were two full-blood girls I used to hang out with. We did everything together. They were willing to join me in a Sioux uprising. We put together a newspaper which we called the *Red Panther*. In it we wrote how bad the school was, what kind of slop we had to eat—slimy, rotten, blackened potatoes for two weeks—the way we were beaten. I think I was the one who wrote the worst article about our principal of the moment, Father Keeler. I put all my anger and venom into it. I called him a goddam wasičun son of a bitch. I wrote that he knew nothing about Indians and should go back to where he came from, teaching white children whom he could relate to. I wrote that we knew which priests slept with which nuns and that all they ever could think about was filling their bellies and buying a new car. It was the kind of writing which foamed at the mouth, but which also lifted a great deal of weight from one's soul.

On Saint Patrick's Day, when everybody was at the big powwow, we distributed our newspapers. We put them on windshields and bulletin boards, in desks and pews, in dorms and toilets. But someone saw us and snitched on us. The shit hit the fan. The three of us were taken before a board meeting. Our parents, in my case my mother, had to come. They were told that ours was a most serious matter, the worst thing that had ever happened in the school's long history. One of the nuns told my mother, "Your daughter really needs to be talked to." "What's wrong with my daughter?" my mother asked. She was given one of our *Red Panther* newspapers. The nun pointed out its name to her and then my piece, waiting for mom's reaction. After a while she asked, "Well, what have you got to say to this? What do you think?"

My mother said, "Well, when I went to school here, some years back, I was treated a lot worse than these kids are. I really can't see how they can have any complaints, because we was treated a lot stricter. We could not even wear skirts halfway up our knees. These girls have it made. But you should forgive them because they are young. And it's supposed to be a free country, free speech and all that. I don't believe what they done is wrong." So all I got out of it was scrubbing six flights of stairs on my hands and knees, every day. And no boy-side privileges.

The boys and girls were still pretty much separated. The only time one could meet a member of the opposite sex was during free time, between four and five-thirty, in the study hall or on benches or the volleyball court outside, and that was strictly supervised. One day Charlene and I went over to the boys' side. We were on the ball team and they had to let us practice. We played three extra minutes, only three minutes more than we were supposed to. Here was the nuns' opportunity for revenge. We got twenty-five swats. I told Charlene, "We are getting too old to have our bare asses whipped that way. We are old enough to have babies. Enough of this shit. Next time we fight back." Charlene only said, "Hoka-hay!"

We had to take showers every evening. One little girl did not want to take her panties off and one of the nuns told her, "You take those underpants off—or else!" But the child was ashamed to do it. The nun was getting her swat to threaten the girl. I went up to the sister, pushed her veil off, and knocked her down. I told her that if she wanted to hit a little girl she should pick on me, pick one her own size. She got herself transferred out of the dorm a week later.

In a school like this there is always a lot of favoritism. At St. Francis it was strongly tinged with racism. Girls who were near-white, who came from what the nuns called "nice families," got preferential treatment. They waited on the faculty and got to eat ham or eggs and bacon in the morning. They got the easy jobs while the skins, who did not have the right kind of background—myself among them—always wound up in the laundry room sorting out ten bushel baskets of dirty boys' socks every day. Or we wound up scrubbing the floors and doing all the dishes. The school therefore fostered fights and antagonism between whites and breeds, and between breeds and skins. At one time Charlene and I had to iron all the robes and vestments the priests wore when saying Mass. We had to fold them up and put them into a chest in the back of the church. In a corner, looking over our shoulders, was a statue of the crucified Savior, all bloody and beaten up. Charlene looked up and said, "Look at that poor Indian. The pigs sure worked him over." That was the closest I ever came to seeing Jesus.

I was held up as a bad example and didn't mind. I was old enough to have a boyfriend and promptly got one. At the school we had an hour and a half for ourselves. Between the boys' and the girls' wings were some benches where one could sit. My boyfriend and I used to go there just to hold hands and talk. The nuns were very uptight about any boy-girl stuff. They had an exaggerated fear of anything having even the faintest connection with sex. One day in religion class, an all-girl class, Sister Bernard singled me out for some remarks, pointing me out as a bad example, an example that should be shown. She said that I was too free with my body. That I was holding hands which meant that I was not a good example to follow. She also said that I wore unchaste dresses, skirts which were too short, too suggestive, shorter than regulations permitted, and for that I would be punished. She dressed me down before the whole class, carrying on and on about my unchastity.

I stood up and told her, "You shouldn't say any of those things, miss. You people are a lot worse than us Indians. I know all about you, because my grandmother and my aunt told me about you. Maybe twelve, thirteen years ago you had a water stoppage here in St. Francis. No water could get through the pipes. There are water lines right under the mission, underground tunnels and passages where in my grandmother's time only the nuns and priests could go, which were off-limits to everybody else. When the water backed up they had to go through all the water lines and clean them out. And in those huge pipes they found the bodies of newborn babies. And they were white babies. They weren't Indian babies. At least when our girls have babies, they don't do away with them that way, like flushing them down the toilet, almost.

"And that priest they sent here from Holy Rosary in Pine Ridge because he molested a little girl. You couldn't think of anything better than dump him on us. All he does is watch young women and girls with that funny smile on his face. Why don't you point him out for an example?"

Charlene and I worked on the school newspaper. After all we had some practice. Every day we went down to Publications. One of the priests acted as the photographer, doing the enlarging and developing. He smelled of chemicals which had stained his hands yellow. One day he invited Charlene into the darkroom. He was going to teach her developing. She was developed already. She was a big girl compared to him, taller too. Charlene was nicely built, not fat, just rounded. No sharp edges anywhere. All of a sudden she rushed out of the darkroom, yelling to me, "Let's get out of here! He's trying to feel me up. That priest is nasty." So there was this too to contend with—sexual harassment. We complained to the student body. The nuns said we just had a dirty mind.

We got a new priest in English. During one of his first classes he asked one of the boys a certain question. The boy was shy. He spoke poor English, but he had the right answer. The priest told him, "You did not say it right. Correct yourself. Say it over again." The boy got flustered and stammered. He could hardly get out a word. But the priest kept after him: "Didn't you hear? I told you to do the whole thing over. Get it right this time." He kept on and on.

I stood up and said, "Father, don't be doing that. If you go into an Indian's home and try to talk Indian, they might laugh at you and say, 'Do it over correctly. Get it right this time!' "

He shouted at me, "Mary, you stay after class. Sit down right now!"

I stayed after class, until after the bell. He told me, "Get over here!" He grabbed me by the arm, pushing me against the blackboard, shouting, "Why are you always mocking us? You have no reason to do this."

I said, "Sure I do. You were making fun of him. You embarrassed him. He needs strengthening, not weakening. You hurt him. I did not hurt you."

He twisted my arm and pushed real hard. I turned around and hit him in the face, giving him a bloody nose. After that I ran out of the room, slamming the door behind me. He and I went to Sister Bernard's office. I told her, "Today I quit school. I'm not taking any more of this, none of this shit anymore. None of this treatment. Better give me my diploma. I can't waste any more time on you people."

Sister Bernard looked at me for a long, long time. She said, "All right, Mary Ellen, go home today. Come back in a few days and get your diploma." And that was that. Oddly enough, that priest turned out okay. He taught a class in grammar, orthography, composition, things like that. I think he wanted more respect in class. He was still young and unsure of himself. But I was in there too long. I didn't feel like hearing it. Later he became a good friend of the Indians, a personal friend of myself and my husband. He stood up for us during Wounded Knee and after. He stood up to his superiors, stuck his neck way out, became a real people's priest. He even learned our language. He died prematurely of cancer. It is not only the good Indians who die young, but the good whites, too. It is the timid ones who know how to take care of themselves who grow old. I am still grateful to that priest for what he did for us later and for the quarrel he picked with me—or did I pick it with him?—because it ended a situation which had become unendurable for me. The day of my fight with him was my last day in school.

Study Questions

1. Mary Crow Dog was mistreated, along with many other generations of Native American children, in reservation schools. What was the theory or explanation that allowed this to happen, and what social effects did it have?

2. What did Mary have to do to be released from the school? Is there a lesson in this for us regarding conformity and rebellion?

Reading 36

When the Clergy
Goes Astray

Pedophilia in the Catholic Church

Theresa Krebs

In 1993 the highest governing official in the Roman Catholic Church revealed his position regarding the sexual abuse of children by clergy and religious in the North American Catholic Church. As reported in the *Edmonton Journal* on June 24, under the headline "Permissive Society to Blame for Abusive Priests—Vatican," the chief Vatican spokesman, Joaquin Navarro-Valls, identified pedophilic clergy in the Roman Catholic Church as a uniquely North American phenomenon: "One would have to ask if the real culprit is not a society that is irresponsibly permissive, hyperinflated with sexuality [that is] capable of creating circumstances that induce even people who have received a solid moral formation to commit grave moral acts."[1]

Navarro-Valls extended the blame to the media for sensationalizing cases of pedophilia when the number of priests implicated in North America amounts to about four hundred, little more than 1 percent. In a further move that denied institutional responsibility for priestly pedophilia, Navarro-Valls pointed out that the percentage of priests involved in pedophilic acts may be less than in other sectors of the general population (see, e.g., Bishop's Administrative Committee 1989, 394). The Vatican's statement demonstrates the Church's protective stance toward pedophilic clergy in its ranks. By continuing to look beyond itself for possible causes, the Church avoids examining how its structure may facilitate pedophilia among some of its personnel.

I argue that pedophilia among Catholic clergy is possible because both longstanding and newly erected structures within the institutional Church facilitate it. The Church's international nature, its organizational hierarchy, and its internal polity allow pedophiles to remain anonymous to all but a few within the Church hierarchy and secular society. It maintains this anonymity through a complex network of archdioceses, dioceses, provinces, and parishes that absorb and protect perpetrators across geographically disparate regions. By acknowledging instances of such behavior and not removing priests from the priesthood (or reporting them to secular officials), the Church hierarchy accords pedophilia a place within its organization.[2]. . .

The Overall Picture

To analyze pedophilia in longstanding structures in the institutional Catholic Church, I build on Anson Shupe's structural conflict model of clergy malfeasance in North American religious organizations. Shupe argues that new structures adopted by the Catholic Church, such as official policies, are positive responses toward effecting change. I, however, offer an alternative interpretation of the Church's remedial response: While no longer denying pedophilia among its ranks, the Church nevertheless continues to deflect institutional responsibility for it. I come to this conclusion with international examples interpreted through Jean-Guy Vaillancourt's study of Vatican control over lay Catholic elites.

Shupe defines clergy malfeasance as "the exploitation and abuse of a religious group's believers by the elites of that religion in whom the former trust" (Shupe 1995, 15). Pedophilia is a subgroup of sexual malfeasance, and it takes place in what he calls hierarchical denominations. A crucial point in understanding a structural relationship between pedophilia and its occurrence in a hierarchical religious group (such as the Catholic Church) is that the local authority of individual clergy is an extension of a bureaucratic authority that legitimizes it (Shupe 1993, 19).

Hierarchical religious organizations exhibit five characteristics of power inequalities that conceptually facilitate pedophilia. First, institutional religion is based on systems of power inequalities termed "hierarchies of unequal power" (Shupe 1993, 10; 1994, 4; 1995, 27–28). The unequal power is spread across several dimensions, such as elites' claims to possess disproportionate spiritual wisdom, experience, or charisma of office as well as their organizational knowledge and insights.

Second, persons occupying elite positions retain a significant capacity for moral persuasion, and in some instances the "theological authority to deny access to privileges of membership, including ultimate spiritual statuses such as salvation," through excommunication or shunning and other forms of ostracization.

Third, unlike their secular counterparts, religious organizations such as the Catholic Church represent what Shupe calls "trusted hierarchies." Individuals in positions of authority explicitly encourage and admonish individuals in lower statuses to trust in their honorable intentions and unselfish motives. More specifically, leaders encourage parents or guardians to socialize children into honoring the intentions and motives of priests by advocating respect and obedience without question.

Fourth, because of their special status as trusted hierarchies, churches provide unique "opportunity structures" or "protected places" that allow leaders to engage in deviance. At a power disadvantage, organization members who do not hold positions of authority are more susceptible to exploitation, abuse, and manipulation.

Finally, in a social structural sense, clergy malfeasance (the elite exploitation of lay members) occurs in trusted hierarchies because they systematically provide opportunities for such behaviors and allow them to continue. Shupe argues that deviance/malfeasance, when occasional, is "normal" to religious hierarchies rather than "the result of psychological pathologies or moral lapses" (Shupe 1995, 31).

An essential dimension of Shupe's typology, and crucial for understanding how established Roman Catholic Church structures facilitate pedophilia, is lay members' ability to gain access to officials in a hierarchically structured religious organization when making claims against pedophilic clergy. He characterizes the locus of control of religious polities by their degree of *permeability*: How receptive is the official hierarchy to complainants' allegations against its administration or its personnel? Traditional authority in hierarchical religious polities is least responsive to complaints against personnel and slowest to implement resolution and remedies.

One reason for this unresponsiveness is that hierarchical religious organizations consciously employ strategies of "neutralization" to protect their personnel or the Church community (Shupe 1995, 80). Moreover, engaging in these neutralization strategies perpetuates the good reputation of the organization and diffuses public perception and awareness of malfeasance. The institutional Catholic Church's neutralizing allegations of pedophilia against its personnel gives perpetrators tacit approval from their superiors to continue engaging in such behavior.

Although Shupe (1995, 81) proposes that hierarchical religious groups "are more likely to develop policies addressing clergy malfeasance" than are local autonomous congregational groups, new structures such as official policies and parish study groups often appear to be responses to public pressure or legal proceedings—in fact, the Church sometimes ignores them. Documented evidence shows that even with sensitive, well-formulated policies in place, as well as uniform plans of action for responding to allegations of pedophilia, some members of the Catholic Church hierarchy continue to neutralize complainants by offering monetary settlements on condition of secrecy.

Yet, the dynamics of secrecy within Catholicism reveal how the Church continues to deflect institutional responsibility for the pedophilic crimes of some of its personnel. In his study of Vatican control over Catholic elites, Vaillancourt (1980, 286) indicates that one of the most ironic aspects of secrecy is that officials "often hide themselves behind an ideology of dialogue, communication, and participation. The leadership remains bureaucratic and secretive, while it veils its manipulation behind a screen of words." Interestingly, the majority of members do not leave the Church when knowledge about pedophilic clergy becomes public. In some respects, membership is even strengthened, because the hierarchy actively solicits lay involvement under the guise of implementing organizational reform while retaining the right to make final decisions.

According to Vaillancourt, therefore, clerical appeals for official policies and open discussion further neutralize critics. Engaging public awareness of policy and encouraging parishioner participation in study groups and workshops are evidence of further neutralization strategies on the Church's part. Combining the observations of both Shupe and Vaillancourt, I argue that newly erected structures further facilitate opportunities for pedophilia for some Catholic priests and religious.

Longstanding Structures That Facilitate Pedophilia

Within the Roman Catholic Church, three longstanding structures facilitate pedophilia among some clergy: the international institution itself, its hierarchical organization, and its government or polity.

The International Roman Catholic Church

The North American Roman Catholic Church engaged in an institutional cover-up of clerical pedophilia for decades. Indeed, the magnitude of the scandal facing the Church today demonstrates its international dimensions. At the same time that Church officials denied that clergy or lay religious leaders engaged in sexual activities with children, they privately assured complainants that the "problem" would be investigated and resolved immediately. In actuality, the Church began to transfer perpetrators either to active ministry in other parishes or to church-affiliated treatment centers. The international scope of the Catholic Church allowed the official hierarchy to relocate offending individuals to distant geographical locations (Isely and Isely 1990, 92–93). For Church officials, such moves solved the problem.

For example, the diocese of Northampton, England, transferred British priest Anton Mowat to Atlanta, Georgia, without informing the Archdiocese of Atlanta about Mowat's "known predilection for young boys." When Georgia police investigated allegations against Mowat of child sexual abuse in 1990, he fled the United States for a monastery in Turin, Italy. Although U.S. authorities repeatedly appealed to his home diocese in Northampton for information regarding Mowat's whereabouts, Church officials denied having any knowledge (Burkett and Bruni 1993, 33). Indeed, if Mowat's home diocese knew where he was, by denying that knowledge it tacitly approved his actions. Moreover, the Church in three separate countries (England, the United States, and Italy) played host to Mowat. By refusing to disclose his hiding place to authorities and by transferring him to another country, the international Church facilitated Mowat's inclination to pedophilic activity.

Earlier, during the 1960s, dozens of priests accused of pedophilia were on assignment in the United States from England, Mexico, Ireland, Sri Lanka, and Italy (Burkett and Bruni 1993, 41). These assignments had already concerned John Salazar, a consulting psychologist for the Servants of the Paraclete treatment facility in New Mexico. In February 1967, Salazar met with the archbishop of Santa Fe, Robert Sanchez, to explain the dangers in allowing pedophilic priests and lay religious "brought from all over the world" to return to working with children at their former, or any, parishes (Burkett and Bruni 1993, 168). Archbishop Sanchez, however, was less than proactive on the issue, perhaps because (as it became known) he himself maintained sexual relationships with young women—as many as five during the 1980s and others before then (Shupe 1995, 3). Sanchez eventually resigned the priesthood in disgrace.[3]

An alternative to transferring alleged pedophilic clergy to distant parishes is transferring them to treatment centers in other countries. Father Canice Connor, former executive director of Southdown Treatment Centre for clergy and religious near Toronto, Ontario, is president and chief executive officer of St. Luke's Institute in Suitland, Maryland. (In 1990, priest and psychiatrist Michael Peterson founded St. Luke's to treat the psychiatric problems of clergy, which include the suffering caused by depression, alcoholism, and other addictions.) In 1983, St. Luke's broadened its treatment to include priests who sexually abuse children. Connor told the *Washington Post* that St. Luke's patient lists include Roman Catholic priests from South Africa and Australia (Miller 1993). On July 16, 1994, Mary Jane Boland reported in the *New Zealand Herald* under the headline "Church Unveils Its Shame" that before that year, the New Zealand Catholic Church responded to allegations of priestly pedophilia by sending priests to treatment centers "overseas"— facilities probably in the United States. (Before it closed, House of Affirmation in Missouri described itself on its letterhead as the "International Therapeutic Center for Clergy and Religious.")[4]. . .

Hierarchical Organization of the Church

The bishop holds the highest authority in an archdiocese or diocese, and is answerable only to the Supreme Pontiff. His hierarchical roles include teacher of doctrine, priest of worship, and minister of government. As the highest governing official in a diocese, a bishop has executive power to apply the universal laws of the Church, to exercise legislative and judicial power, and to enforce civil law in a diocese. The bishop himself is subject to canon law and, as a citizen, to the civil and criminal laws of the country in which he serves. According to Church and civil laws, the bishop's power, therefore, is limited and not arbitrary. Answerable within the Church only to the pope, bishops nevertheless also possess the potential for considerable power in their dioceses (Archdiocesan Commission of Enquiry [ACE] 1990, 1:69–70).

Former Archbishop Alphonsus Penney's management of pedophilic clergy in Newfoundland is a particularly telling example of the Church hierarchy's ability to manipulate public perception while denying claimants' allegations. Evidence from as early as 1979 suggests that when Penney assumed the bishopric in the archdiocese in St. John's, he knew that priests and Christian Brothers in Newfoundland were committing pedophilic acts with young members of the Church and wards of the Mount Cashel Orphanage. As the representative official of the Archdiocese of St. John's, Newfoundland, and according to Church law, he was responsible for all juridic affairs, including allegations of pedophilic crimes against Church personnel (Paulson 1988, 103). Therefore, by both canon and civil law, Penney ought to have acted on his knowledge and reported the crimes to Church and civil authorities.

A sex scandal of enormous proportions swirled around Penney's mitre while he followed a tragic course of denial, covering his inaction by transferring or counseling perpetrators rather than indicting them under canon and civil criminal law. Moreover, secular authorities investigating suspected and named abusers met with little cooperation from Church and affiliated institutional officials.

As the highest governing official in a diocese, a bishop is responsible for the physical and spiritual well-being of all Church personnel. Alphonsus Penney reportedly advised priests struggling with their sexual predilections to avail themselves of professional counseling services that he retained for their use. One year after he assumed the office of bishop in the Archdiocese of St. John's, Alphonsus Penney established the Ministry to Priests Program (MPP) to address problems of morale associated with restrictions and requirements of the priesthood, another indication that he knew some clergy were engaged in sexual activities proscribed by their vows of celibacy.

The program, however, served another purpose than that intended. Former members testified that its greatest value lay in the opportunity for socializing with peers. Most clergy, however, avoided associating with the group within the MPP known to have a homosexual orientation. The majority of allegations against and convictions of pedophilic priests were of members belonging to that segment of the MPP (ACE 1990, 1:96–99).

The MPP represents one example of the way the Church hierarchy facilitates pedophilia by following a course of denial and diffusion rather than by reporting offenses to appropriate secular authorities. As pastor to the priests in his archdiocese, Penney did take steps to address the problem of pedophilia among them. He ignored his obligations to civil law, however, by providing a forum that facilitated rather than eliminated their illegal sexual practices. . . .

Jason Berry, author of *Lead Us Not into Temptation*, followed the pedophilic priest scandal in the U.S. Catholic Church from Louisiana to Washington, seat of the U.S. papal nunciature, investigating Father Gilbert Gauthe, from the Diocese of Lafayette in Louisiana, who managed to commit pedophilic crimes for many years, apparently undetected. Berry blames the complicity between Church personnel and the official Church hierarchy for perpetuating the problem. "The crisis in the Catholic Church lies not with the fraction of priests who molest youngsters but in an ecclesiastical power structure that harbors pedophiles, conceals other sexual behavior patterns among its clerics, and uses strategies of duplicity and counterattack against the victims" (Berry 1992, xx). . . .

Internal Polity

Shupe characterizes the internal polities of religious organizations by the extent of their permeability and of their neutralization. He measures permeability by the extent to which administrators and leaders in the hierarchy, first, are authentically open to receiving complaints against the organization by lay members and, second, act to eliminate a problem from recurring (Shupe 1995, 118–119). Shupe assesses organizational neutralization by the degree to which administrators and leaders in the hierarchy blame victims, dismiss grievances, or intimidate, bribe, or threaten to ensure the silence and secrecy of complainants. Taking any neutralizing action means that the problem can recur.

The internal polity of the Catholic Church employs numerous methods to neutralize attempts to require accountability or restitution from the Church. Unfortunately, the relationship between parishioners and the Church hierarchy does not encourage, or even allow, demands for institutional accountability. The hierarchy camouflages abuse and abusers against public perception. Relying on their perceived authority, Church officials intimidate claimants, downplay the effects of the acts, or ensure silence from victims by stating that what occurred is an isolated incident. The hierarchy treats each set of allegations in confidence, rather than collaborating and compiling records on named abusers in order to explore behavior patterns. Bishops speak to victims privately, victimizing them further by planting doubts in their minds about possibly having encouraged the attention of the sexual deviant, having enjoyed the attention, and so forth. Bishops also neglect to inform law enforcement officials of sexual abuse. By insulating perpetrators from outside authorities, internal polities of the Catholic Church also promote aspects of pedophilia. . . .

Almost invariably, the Church's internal polity insists that officials maintain secrecy regarding claimants' allegations of sexual abuse against priests or other religious leaders. Often secrecy can be negotiated. In Gauthe's case, mentioned earlier, the Church paid an average of $450,000 to each of nine families. Those settlements, however, came with conditions: Accepting payment required signing an agreement of no liability on the part of the Church. Furthermore, the Gauthe case remains sealed, which decreases the Church's risk of media and public exposure (Berry 1992, 6–25).

In the Gauthe case, as in others researched, the hierarchy sought to protect itself and its priests from public exposure by neutralizing claims. Neutralizing claims, however, ultimately deferred scandals only for a short time (Burkett and Bruni, 1993: 60–62). Documented accounts demonstrate that the pedophiles continued to accumulate victims.

Notes

1. Former Benedictine monk A. W. Richard Sipe estimates that approximately 2 percent of North American priests are sexually fixated on young children and that an additional 4 percent find older youths sexually appealing. Church officials challenge these figures, but Fr. Thomas Doyle, canon lawyer and former advisor to North American bishops regarding sexual abuse by clergy, estimates that three thousand American priests "may be so inclined" (which supports Sipe's estimates). Jason Berry calls disputes over percentage estimates further examples of "concealment strategies" by which Church officials attempt to deny or diffuse the problem of pedophilia among their personnel. The logic runs, "If there are no numbers, [then] it cannot be true" (cited in Berry 1992: xx–xxi).

2. Part of the reason the Church continues to harbor perpetrators rather than dismiss them may be the aging and declining clerical population in North America caused, in part, by resignations and fewer ordinations. The complex canonical process involved in laicizing clergy also may help to explain why the Church excuses pedophilic clergy within its ranks. See, for example, Gilmour 1992, B6; Schoenherr and Young 1990, 463–481; Schoenherr, Young, and Vilarino 1988, 499–523.

3. Perhaps not so ironically, Archbishop Robert Sanchez's March 19, 1993, letter to the Pope requested permission to resign from his position. CBS-TV's *60 Minutes* segment "The Archbishop," aired March 21. 1993, investigated the New Mexico archdiocese where Sanchez faced accusations of "sexual improprieties." The program suggested that as a result of his own sexual proclivities Sanchez was lenient toward other priests who engaged in sexual activity with children. See Sanchez 1993, 722–724.

4. Private correspondence from House of Affirmation, in possession of the author.

References

Archdiocesan Commission of Enquiry into the Sexual Abuse of Children by Members of the Clergy [ACE]. 1990. *The Report of the Archdiocesan Commission of Enquiry into the Sexual Abuse of Children by Members of the Clergy.* 2 vols. St. John's, Newfoundland: Archdiocese of St. John's.

Berry, Jason. 1992. *Lead Us Not into Temptation: Catholic Priests and the Sexual Abuse of Children.* New York: Doubleday.

Burkett, Elinor, and Frank Bruni. 1993. *A Gospel of Shame: Children, Sexual Abuse, and the Catholic Church.* New York: Viking.

Isely, Paul J., and Peter Isley. 1990. "The Sexual Abuse of Male Children by Church Personnel: Intervention and Prevention." *Pastoral Psychology* 39 (2): 85–99.

Miller, Jeanne. 1993. "Update." *Missing Link* (newsletter of The Linkup, Inc.) 1 (4): 2.

Paulson, Jerome E., 1988. "The Clinical and Canonical Considerations in Cases of Pedophilia: The Bishop's Role." *Studia Canonica* 22 (1): 77–124.

Shupe, Anson. 1995. *In the Name of All That's Holy: A Theory of Clergy Malfeasance.* Westport, Conn.: Praeger.

———. 1994. "Authenticity Lost: When Victims of Clergy Abuse Confront Betrayed Trust." Paper presented at the annual meeting of the Association for the Sociology of Religion, Los Angeles.

———. 1993. "Opportunity Structures, Trusted Hierarchies, and Religious Deviance: A Conflict Theory Approach." Paper presented at the annual meeting of the Society for the Scientific Study of Religion, Raleigh, North Carolina.

Vaillancourt, Jean-Guy. 1980. *Papal Power: A Study of Vatican Control over Lay Catholic Elites.* Berkeley: University of California Press.

Study Questions

1. What are the organizational structures that permitted the protection of priests when they victimized the children?
2. What similarities does the Catholic Church, as an organization, have with big businesses like Enron and Wall Street brokerage firms?

Topic 13
Politics and the Economy

The two remaining institutions to discuss in Part 4: Social Institutions are politics and the economy. The sociological view of these two institutions is that they are closely connected, and any of us can recognize the reciprocal impact of the economy and politics. How does politics respond to the demands of big business, the wealthy, political action committees, or lobbies like the National Rifle Association? How is the economy affected by political action in the form of tax refunds, changing interest rates, prosecution of business and investment companies, or tax breaks to corporations (corporate welfare)? Politics creates and oversees the rule of law in society, and as some have said, is really about "who gets what." The economy affects each family and person in society. Having a job, or not, puts people in dramatically different circumstances. In U.S. society where capitalism reigns, the economy regularly moves through "boom and bust" cycles. Full employment and a growing economy make for good times personally and politically. High unemployment and a weak economy have the opposite effect. Many of us have felt the impact of such a changeable economy.

Politics, more than any other institution, is about power and authority. These two ideas illuminate the difference between getting your way through force and coercion (power), and legitimately exercising power such that the decisions made are supported by those who are affected (authority). Inside of politics there is a broad range of views, from the most reactionary to the most radical. Reactionaries wish that there was a way to return to the "good old days" where government did influence everyday life and people could settle their problems the old-fashioned way. Reactionaries, like militia groups, might resort to violence to make their views known. Radicals, who want to change society and social institutions in dramatic ways, may also have violence as part of their political approach. In either case, most U.S. citizens reject such extremes and see themselves as "conservative" or "liberal." These are the more moderate positions on the political continuum, and rarely do we experience decades like the sixties, where radicals pushed social unrest, or the eighties, where reactionaries were making their views felt with violence. Having a political consciousness, an understanding of the micro and macro influences of governmental decisions, is very much a part of the sociological imagination.

The economic institution in society is often the most mysterious. Although many of us have our lives and livelihood driven by the economy, we may be least able to see it and understand its impact. Somehow this lumbering giant of activity, from the most personal pay raise or promotion to the nation's gross national product, escapes our notice. Different societies have different economies; capitalism and socialism are two examples. Along with the economics of socialism, where prices and wages are monitored so that economic change is more controlled, comes less possibility for rapid expansion and longer periods of a "languishing" economy. In capitalism, where a free market economy and competition drive the dynamics, there is the possibility of making great sums of money (profit), with the likelihood that soon there will be a "bust" in the cycle and many people out of work. In the margins between such economic systems, issues like health care make interesting political issues, such as who should bear the cost of health services for the poor or elderly. Many of us will have careers of more than forty years and understanding the dynamics of this enormous presence in our lives will certainly make it more pleasant.

The first article is by C. Wright Mills (sociological imagination) and we are given a theoretical examination of "the power elite" in U.S. politics. Here, business, government, and the military are seen in their collective impact on both politics and the economy. Second, the loss of jobs, "corporate downsizing," is qualitatively researched by Charles Koeber. What is the process by which persons who have been the victims of economic downturns make sense of and cope with their experiences? Finally, Michael Burawoy, a master sociologist who makes the connection between the micro and macro social worlds, takes us on an eloquent biographical journey through factory employment in the United States and Europe. We are treated to the interpersonal dynamics of the shop floor and their connection to the theories of political economy.

Reading 37
The Power Elite

C. Wright Mills

Except for the unsuccessful Civil War, changes in the power system of the United States have not involved important challenges to its basic legitimations. Even when they have been decisive enough to be called 'revolutions,' they have not involved the 'resort to the guns of a cruiser, the dispersal of an elected assembly by bayonets, or the mechanisms of a police state.'[1] Nor have they involved, in any decisive way, any ideological struggle to control masses. Changes in the American structure of power have generally come about by institutional shifts in the relative positions of the political, the economic, and the military orders. From this point of view, and broadly speaking, the American power elite has gone through four epochs, and is now well into a fifth. . . .

. . . We study history, it has been said, to rid ourselves of it, and the history of the power elite is a clear case for which this maxim is correct. Like the tempo of American life in general, the long-term trends of the power structure have been greatly speeded up since World War II, and certain newer trends within and between the dominant institutions have also set the shape of the power elite. . . .

I. In so far as the structural clue to the power elite today lies in the political order, that clue is the decline of politics as genuine and public debate of alternative decisions—with nationally responsible and policy-coherent parties and with autonomous organizations connecting the lower and middle levels of power with the top levels of decision. America is now in considerable part more a formal political democracy than a democratic social structure, and even the formal political mechanics are weak.

The long-time tendency of business and government to become more intricately and deeply involved with each other has, in the fifth epoch, reached a new point of explicitness. The two cannot now be seen clearly as two distinct worlds. It is in terms of the executive agencies of the state that the rapprochement has proceeded most decisively. The growth of the executive branch of the government, with its agencies that patrol the complex economy, does not mean merely the 'enlargement of government' as some sort of autonomous bureaucracy: it has meant the ascendancy of the corporation's man as a political eminence. . . .

II. In so far as the structural clue to the power elite today lies in the enlarged and military state, that clue becomes evident in the military ascendancy. The warloards have gained decisive political relevance, and the military structure of America is now in considerable part a political structure. The seemingly permanent military threat places a premium on the military and upon their control of men, materiel, money, and power; virtually all political and economic actions are now judged in terms of military definitions of reality: the higher warlords have ascended to a firm position within the power elite of the fifth epoch. . . .

III. In so far as the structural clue to the power elite today lies in the economic order, that clue is the fact that the economy is at once a permanent-war economy and a private-corporation economy. American capitalism is now in considerable part a military capitalism, and the most important relation of the big corporation to the state rests on the coincidence of interests between military and corporate needs, as defined by warlords and corporate rich. Within the elite as a whole, this coincidence of interest between the high military and the corporate chieftains strengthens both of them and further subordinates the role of the merely political men. Not politicians, but corporate executives, sit with the military and plan the organization of war effort. . . .

The power elite is composed of political, economic, and military men, but this instituted elite is frequently in some tension: it comes together only on certain coinciding points and only on certain occasions of 'crisis.' In the long peace of the nineteenth century, the military were not in the high councils of state, not of the political directorate, and neither were the economic men—they made raids upon the state but they did not join its directorate. During the 'thirties, the political man was ascendant. Now the military and the corporate men are in top positions.

Of the three types of circle that compose the power elite today, it is the military that has benefited the most in its enhanced power, although the corporate circles have also become more explicitly intrenched in the more public decision-making circles. It is the professional politician that has lost the most, so much that in examining the events and decisions, one is tempted to speak of a political vacuum in which the corporate rich and the high warlord, in their coinciding interests, rule.

It should not be said that the three 'take turns' in carrying the initiative, for the mechanics of the power elite are not often as deliberate as that would imply. At times, of course, it is—as when political men, thinking they can borrow the prestige of generals, find that they must pay for it, or, as when during big slumps, economic men feel the need of a politician at once safe and possessing vote appeal. Today all three are involved in virtually all widely ramifying decisions. Which of the three types seems to lead depends upon 'the tasks of the period' as they, the elite, define them. Just now, these tasks center upon 'defense' and international affairs. Accordingly, as we have seen, the military are ascendant in two senses: as personnel and as justifying ideology. That is why, just now, we can most easily specify the unity and the shape of the power elite in terms of the military ascendancy.

But we must always be historically specific and open to complexities. The simple Marxian view makes the big economic man the *real* holder of power; the simple liberal view makes the big political man the chief of the power system; and there are some who would view the warlords as virtual dictators. Each of these is an oversimplified view. It is to avoid them that we use the term 'power elite' rather than, for example, 'ruling class.'

In so far as the power elite has come to wide public attention, it has done so in terms of the 'military clique.' The power elite does, in fact, take its current shape from the decisive entrance into it of the military. Their presence and their ideology are its major legitimations, whenever the power elite feels the need to provide any. But what is called the 'Washington military clique' is not composed merely of military men, and it does not prevail merely in Washington. Its members exist all over the country, and it is a coalition of generals in the roles of corporation executives, of politicians masquerading as admirals, of corporation executives acting like politicians, of civil servants who become majors, of vice-admirals who are also the assistants to a cabinet officer, who is himself, by the way, really a member of the managerial elite.

Neither the idea of a 'ruling class' nor of a simple monolithic rise of 'bureaucratic politicians' nor of a 'military clique' is adequate. The power elite today involves the often uneasy coincidence of economic, military, and political power. . . .

Despite their social similarity and psychological affinities, the members of the power elite do not constitute a club having a permanent membership with fixed and formal boundaries. It is of the nature of the power elite that within it there is a good deal of shifting about, and that it thus does not consist of one small set of the same men in the same positions in the same hierarchies. Because men know each other personally does not mean that among them there is a unity of policy; and because they do not know each other personally does not mean that among them there is a disunity. The conception of the power elite does not rest, as I have repeatedly said, primarily upon personal friendship.

As the requirements of the top places in each of the major hierarchies become similar, the types of men occupying these roles at the top—by selection and by training in the jobs—become similar. This is no mere deduction from structure to personnel. That it is a fact is revealed by the heavy traffic that has been going on between the three structures, often in very intricate patterns. The chief executives, the warlords, and selected politicians came into contact with one another in an intimate, working way during World War II; after that war ended, they continued their associations, out of common beliefs, social congeniality, and coinciding interests. Noticeable proportions of top men from the military, the economic, and the political worlds have during the last fifteen years occupied positions in one or both of the other worlds: between these higher circles there is an interchangeability of position, based formally upon the supposed transferability of 'executive ability,' based in substance upon the co-optation by cliques of insiders. As members of a power elite, many of those busy in this traffic have come to look upon 'the government' as an umbrella under whose authority they do their work.

As the business between the big three increases in volume and importance, so does the traffic in personnel. The very criteria for selecting men who will rise come to embody this fact. The corporate commissar, dealing with the state and its military, is wiser to choose a young man who has experienced the state and its military than one who has not. The political director, often dependent for his own political success upon corporate decisions and corporations, is also wiser to choose a man with corporate experience. Thus, by virtue of the very criterion of success, the interchange of Personnel and the unity of the power elite is increased.

Given the formal similarity of the three hierarchies in which the several members of the elite spend their working lives, given the ramifications of the decisions made in each upon the others, given the coincidence of interest that prevails among them at many points, and given the administrative vacuum of the American civilian state along with its enlargement of tasks—given these trends of structure, and adding to them the psychological affinities we have noted—we should indeed be surprised were we to find that men said to be skilled in administrative contacts and full of organizing ability would fail to do more than get in touch with one another. They have, of course, done much more than that: increasingly, they assume positions in one another's domains.

The unity revealed by the interchangeability of top roles rests upon the parallel development of the top jobs in each of the big three domains. The interchange occurs most frequently at the points of their coinciding interest, as between regulatory agency and the regulated industry; contracting agency and contractor. And, as we shall see, it leads to co-ordinations that are more explicit, and even formal.

The inner core of the power elite consists, first, of those who interchange commanding roles at the top of one dominant institutional order with those in another: the admiral who is also a banker and a lawyer and who heads up an important federal commission; the corporation executive whose company was one of the two or three leading war materiel producers who is now the Secretary of Defense; the wartime general who dons civilian clothes to sit on the political directorate and then becomes a member of the board of directors of a leading economic corporation.

Although the executive who becomes a general, the general who becomes a statesman, the statesman who becomes a banker, see much more than ordinary men in their ordinary environments, still the perspectives of even such men often remain tied to their dominant locales. In their very career, however, they interchange roles within the big three and thus readily transcend the particularity of interest in any one of these institutional milieux. By their very careers and activities, they lace the three types of milieux together. They are, accordingly, the core members of the power elite.

These men are not necessarily familiar with every major arena of power. We refer to one man who moves in and between perhaps two circles—say the industrial and the military—and to another man who moves in the military and the political, and to a third who moves in the political as well as among opinion-makers. These in-between types most closely display our image of the power elite's structure and operation, even of behind-the-scenes operations. To the extent that there is any 'invisible elite,' these advisory and liaison types are its core. Even if—as I believe to be very likely—many of them are, at least in the first part of their careers, 'agents' of the various elites rather than themselves elite, it is they who are most active in organizing the several top milieux into a structure of power and maintaining it. . . .

The outermost fringes of the power elite—which change more than its core—consist of 'those who count' even though they may not be 'in' on given decisions of consequence nor in their career move between the hierarchies. Each member of the power elite need not be a man who personally decides every decision that is to be ascribed to the power elite. Each member, in the decisions that he does make, takes the others seriously into account. They not only make decisions in the several major areas of war and peace; they are the men who, in decisions in which they take no direct part, are taken into decisive account by those who are directly in charge.

On the fringes and below them, somewhat to the side of the lower echelons, the power elite fades off into the middle levels of power, into the rank and file of the Congress, the pressure groups that are not vested in the power elite itself, as well as a multiplicity of regional and state and local interests. If all the men on the middle levels are not among those who count, they sometimes must be taken into account, handled, cajoled, broken or raised to higher circles. . . .

The conception of the power elite and of its unity rests upon the corresponding developments and the coincidence of interests among economic, political, and military organizations. It also rests upon the similarity of origin and outlook, and the social and personal intermingling of the top circles from each of these dominant hierarchies. This conjunction of institutional and psychological forces, in turn, is revealed by the heavy personnel traffic within and between the big three institutional orders, as well as by the rise of go-betweens as in the high-level lobbying. The conception of the power elite, accordingly, does *not* rest upon the assumption that American history since the origins of World War II must be understood as a secret plot, or as a great and co-ordinated conspiracy of the members of this elite. The conception rests upon quite impersonal grounds.

There is, however, little doubt that the American power elite—which contains, we are told, some of 'the greatest organizers in the world'—has also planned and has plotted. The rise of the elite, as we have already made clear, was not and could not have been caused by a plot; and the tenability of the conception does not rest upon the existence of any secret or any publicly known organization. But, once the conjunction of structural trend and of the personal will to utilize it gave rise to the power elite, then plans and programs did occur to its members and indeed it is not possible to interpret many events and official policies of the fifth epoch without reference to the power elite. 'There is a great difference,' Richard Hofstadter has remarked, 'between locating conspiracies *in* history and saying that history *is*, in effect, a conspiracy . . . [2]

The structural trends of institutions become defined as opportunities by those who occupy their command posts. Once such opportunities are recognized, men may avail themselves of them. Certain types of men from each of the dominant institutional areas, more far-sighted than others, have actively promoted the liaison before it took its truly modern shape. They have often done so for reasons not shared by their partners, although not objected to by them either; and often the outcome of their liaison has had consequences which none of them foresaw, much less shaped, and which only later in the course of development came under explicit control. Only after it was well under way did most of its members find themselves part of it and become gladdened, although sometimes also worried, by this fact. But once the co-ordination is a going concern, new men come readily into it and assume its existence without question.

So far as explicit organization—conspiratorial or not—is concerned, the power elite, by its very nature, is more likely to use existing organizations, working within and between them, than to set up explicit organizations whose membership is strictly limited to its own members. But if there is no machinery in existence to ensure, for example, that military and political factors will be balanced in decisions made, they will invent such machinery and use it, as with the National Security Council. Moreover, in a formally democratic polity, the aims and the powers of the various elements of this elite are further supported by an aspect of the permanent war economy: the assumption that the security of the nation supposedly rests upon great secrecy of plan and intent. Many higher events that would reveal the working of the power elite can be withheld from public knowledge under the guise of secrecy. With the wide secrecy covering their operations and decisions, the power elite can mask their intentions, operations, and further consolidation. Any secrecy that is imposed upon those in positions to observe high decision-makers clearly works for and not against the operations of the power elite.

There is accordingly reason to suspect—but by the nature of the case, no proof—that the power elite is not altogether 'surfaced.' There is nothing hidden about it, although its activities are not publicized. As an elite, it is not organized, although its members often know one another, seem quite naturally to work together and share many organizations in common. There is nothing conspiratorial about it, although its decisions are often publicly unknown and its mode of operation manipulative rather than explicit. . . .

The idea of the power elite rests upon and enables us to make sense of (1) the decisive institutional trends that characterize the structure of our epoch, in particular, the military ascendancy in a privately incorporated economy, and more broadly, the several coincidences of objective interests between economic, military and political institutions; (2) the social similarities and the psychological affinities of the men who occupy the command posts of these structures, in particular the increased interchangeability of the top positions in each of them and the increased traffic between these orders in the careers of men of power; (3) the ramifications to the point of virtual totality, of the kind of decisions that are made at the top, and the rise to power of a set of men who, by training and bent, are professional organizers of considerable force and who are unrestrained by democratic party training.

Negatively, the formation of the power elite rests upon (1) the relegation of the professional party politician to the middle levels of power, (2) the semi-organized stalemate of the interests of sovereign localities into which the legislative function has fallen, (3) the virtually complete absence of a civil service that constitutes a politically neutral, but politically relevant, depository of brainpower and executive skill, and (4) the increased official secrecy behind which great decisions are made without benefit of public or even Congressional debate.

As a result, the political directorate, the corporate rich, and the ascendant military have come together as the power elite, and the expanded and centralized hierarchies which they head have encroached upon the old balances and have now relegated them to the middle levels of power. Now the balancing society is a conception that pertains accurately to the middle levels, and on that level the balance has become more often an affair of intrenched provincial and nationally irresponsible forces and demands than a center of power and national decision.

Notes

1. Cf. Elmer Davis, *But We Were Born Free* (Indianapolis: Bobbs-Merrill, 1953), p. 187.
2. Richard Hofstadter, *The Age of Reform* (New York: Knopf, 1955), pp. 71–2.

Study Questions

1. What parts of society make up the "power elite" discussed by Mills? What practices allow this concentration of power?

2. Is the "power elite" an accident or a conspiracy? Defend your answer with information from the article.

Reading 38

Corporate Restructuring, Downsizing, and the Middle Class
The Process and Meaning of Worker Displacement in the "New" Economy

Charles Koeber

Introduction

The term "downsizing" refers to the large-scale and systematic displacement of workers by typically corporate employers. Although the term is arguably a euphemism, its recent and common usage indicates the pervasiveness of the corporate job-cutting trend. This trend has not only resulted in mass job loss, but has contributed to the transformation of the post-World War II model of employment (Rubin 1996), altered the prevailing structure of labor markets (Osterman 1999), and significantly affected the American class structure (Perrucci and Wysong 1999).

During the 1970s and 1980s, plant closings and displacement of manufacturing workers were largely *reactive* measures that occurred as a response to economic recessions, drops in product demand, and the failure of U.S. companies to compete globally (Bluestone and Harrison 1982). However, during the 1990s, the downsizing of not only manufacturing workers, but also service, managerial, and professional workers became a *proactive* measure, a management strategy that companies in a variety of industries used in attempts to be more competitive and profitable or to increase their stock market value (Downs 1995). Downsizing thus became a defining feature of the new capitalism under which *all* types and classes of workers were at risk of losing their jobs (Smith 2001; Budros 1998; Sennett 1998).[1]

Paradoxically, the job cuts of the mid and late 1990s were not accompanied by or did not result in high levels of national unemployment. Unlike previous waves of layoffs in the twentieth century during periods of economic contraction, these layoffs occurred during an economic recovery and expansion in which many new jobs were created and unemployment rates hovered at or near record lows. Thus, two seemingly contradictory realities characterized part of the U.S. economic environment at the end of the twentieth century: high numbers of job cuts and low unemployment.

The dual reality of high numbers of job cuts alongside low rates of unemployment suggests that studies of worker displacement should focus not merely on aggregate job losses or job loss as an event. Rather, it appears that for many Americans, work has increasingly become a *transitional and transformational process* of "serial employment." Due in part to corporate restructuring and downsizing that occur in the context of a rapidly changing global economy, many workers lose their jobs (Baldoz et al. 2001). When employment levels are sufficiently high, most displaced workers find new jobs and experience an accompanying change in the conditions and relations of their work. This perspective suggests that research concerning downsizing and worker displacement should focus on the complex relationship between the changing work experiences and mobility of displaced workers and changes in the structure of the economy, organizations, and labor markets (Kraft 1999).

Research Methods

The project employed qualitative case study methods as the basis for collecting and analyzing information. The methods of this study yield at least three main advantages. First, the case study approach helps to break down the larger research population of displaced workers into manageable units (White 1992, p. 83), enabling an account of the complex experiences of a specific group of displaced workers. Second, case study techniques provide the subjects with the opportunity to have a "voice" and to tell their "story" (Ragin and Becker 1992, p. 43). The third and most important advantage is that case study procedures encourage and facilitate the development of "grounded theory" (Glaser and Strauss 1967; Strauss and Corbin 1990). In this study I develop grounded theoretical concepts related to work and employment change of displaced workers.

The study draws upon thirty interviews with workers. It is difficult to sample displaced workers, as firms do not publicize the names of workers they displace and often provide limited information about workforce reductions to the public. Since it was not possible to develop a complete sampling frame of displaced workers, I relied on a variation of "snowball" sampling. This sampling procedure is appropriate when studying hard to access populations (Babbie 2001). Initial contacts occurred through personal acquaintances I sought out as a resident of the Binghamton area. These contacts provided me with telephone numbers of additional respondents who in turn provided me with further references. . . .

The occupational composition of the sample fell into mostly white-collar and professional positions and included eight engineers, seven administrative workers, four managers, three programmers, three designers, two technicians, one salesperson, one materials handler and one training instructor. All but one of the respondents were employed full time in the jobs that they lost. In terms of demographic characteristics, all respondents were white. Twenty-one were males and nine, females. The mean age of respondents was 46, but the males in the sample were older than the females. The mean job tenure of respondents in the lost job was 20 years. . . .

I used retrospective interviews to order events and occurrences. According to Schutt, retrospective interviewing is appropriate when longitudinal data are not available and the researcher believes respondents can provide reliable information about their histories (1996, p. 131). The interviews allowed for analysis of work histories and comparison of objective characteristics of respondents' work and employment—such as wages, hours, types of tasks, and types of work relations—before and after job loss. The interviews also explored displaced workers' subjective experiences with downsizing, displacement, and employment change.

Although most of the data for the study came from interviews with displaced workers, I used data from the Department of Labor to examine work and employment conditions in the Binghamton metropolitan statistical area (MSA). This information was useful in approximating the quantity of workforce reductions at IBM and Link and for describing the structural context of the job search and labor market encounters of respondents. The combination of multiple methods and sources of information (or triangulation) in this study is consistent with suggestions in the literature concerning use of multiple research techniques to enhance social science findings (Chen 1998).

The Process of Displacement

The subjects of this study underwent a process by which they experienced work and employment change and by which they became separated and detached from prior conditions, relations, and meanings of work. As noted earlier, I conceptualize this pattern of experiences as the "displacement process." Interviews with workers suggest this process occurred in three main stages, which are summarized in Table 1. The first *stage* of the displacement process began before job loss and occurred in two distinct *phases*. In phase 1A workers experienced a transformation of work relations as the firms began reorganizing and reducing their workforces. During phase 1B, participants lost their jobs. The second stage occurred following job loss, when respondents faced difficulty in the labor market; it was comprised of three phases. Phase 2A consisted of making work-related decisions about the future. Phase 2B involved re-education and/or retraining for most of the subjects. Phase 2C entailed a job search. Stage three of the displacement process covers the re-employment experience. This stage consisted of two phases. Phase 3A involved a period of transitional employment and/or "job hopping" during which time respondents worked in jobs mainly as a means to support themselves while looking or waiting for more favorable work. Phase 3B involved employment resettlement. . . .

Description of Stage One: Employment and Job Loss

Restructuring and downsizing had several related, overlapping and often contradictory effects on the work environments at IBM and Link. Workers' experiences and comments suggested these effects could be divided into four related outcomes: 1) fear of job loss; 2) decline of work effort and enthusiasm; 3) workplace conflict; and 4) diminished work expectations. . . .

Table 1   Stages and Phases of the Displacement Process

Stage 1 Employment and job loss		Stage 2 Unemployment			Stage 3 Re-employment	
Phase 1A	*Phase 1B*	*Phase 2A*	*Phase 2B*	*Phase 2C*	*Phase 3A*	*Phase 3B*
Working in a downsizing firm	Losing or leaving one's job	Decision making	Additional education or training	Job Searching	Job hopping in transitional employment	Resettling into new employment

Not surprisingly, many workers reacted emotionally to their job loss. They expressed feelings of shock, anger, fear, and unpleasant surprise. These emotions were expressed not only as a reaction to job loss per se, but as a reaction to the abandonment of longstanding familial relations and the job security that had previously characterized the two companies. The following IBM worker articulates a common sentiment found among the sample:

> [It was] very discouraging and depressing. You felt a sense of betrayal. It was almost like your wife divorcing you, because you had a strong sense of family. In fact, that was one of IBM's big things, a big happy family. And they did at least try to propagate that feeling through their employees . . . So I felt betrayed, basically. I trusted the organization and it betrayed me. I was doing the best that I knew how to do what I was supposed to be doing. Then they slap you around saying you're worthless and then they show you the door, or you show yourself the door before they do (26).

More surprisingly, some workers did express favorable reactions to their displacement, describing feelings of happiness and relief. While job loss was an unfortunate occurrence, as the following two respondents indicated, it also represented an exit from unsatisfactory conditions and relations of work or a sense of closure to the open-ended possibility of job loss:

> I had a real problem—this is like when I sat down with my second-level manager and we started talking about (early) retirement—I had a real hard time keeping a grin off my face and shaking his hand and saying, "Thank you!" Because the pressure was off; I didn't have to worry any longer what was gonna happen (18).

> As I was walking down, a guy says, "What happened to you? You look like you are happier than hell." [I said], "I'm laid off!" A couple guys said, "I'll trade you." That was the atmosphere: people were looking to get out of there (16).

Description of Stage Two: Unemployment

As noted by the model, stage two of the displacement process involved a period of unemployment consisting of three phases. The first, phase 2A, entailed making difficult decisions about one's work and employment. A major issue in this phase concerned workers' decisions regarding physical relocation options and choices related to job opportunities. Respondents in this sample chose to remain in the Binghamton area. Although some respondents indicated that they chose to remain because they did not think they would be able to sell their homes (and/or sell them at a reasonable price), the most often cited reason for staying among the sample was the preference to remain near family:

> My family's here. I'm an only child. His [her husband] family's here and he is very important in his family. His father is passed away, so he's [her husband] looked upon [sic]. We weren't gonna leave (9).

Following relocation decisions, workers were confronted with the issue of whether to obtain additional education or training (phase 2B). The benefits of education and training for respondents were limited. Although respondents indicated that additional education and training helped them to secure a job, education or training did not necessarily result in higher earnings. There was little difference in the amount of earnings or earnings loss for those in the sample who received re-education/retraining versus those who did not. The mean annual gross earnings of both groups were similar before job loss (approximately $40,000) and after job loss (approximately $30,000) with both groups losing approximately $10,000 per year.

Additionally, having more education in general did not immunize respondents from earnings loss. Although those who possessed education beyond high school did not experience as much earnings loss as those with only a high school diploma, the categories of those with either a high school diploma, an associate's degree, or a bachelor's degree all experienced in subsequent employment yearly gross earnings losses that ranged from an average of $9,000 to $12,000 approximately.

For most workers, the re-education/retraining experience led to a difficult job search. The difficulties were compounded if the participants were searching for employment with pay and benefit levels comparable to their former jobs. In phase 2C participants searched extensively—looking for openings in the newspaper and on the Internet, networking, sending out dozens of resumes—taking many steps in their attempts to secure a job. For these respondents the consequences of corporate downsizing included not only the loss of their jobs, but also difficulties of finding new ones in the Binghamton area. Even professional jobs that one might expect to be in high demand were seemingly in scarce supply in Binghamton. As two respondents commented:

It was kind of a rude awakening. I honestly thought that there would be no problem, you know, getting back into industry in the engineering field. So I started filling out resumes and mailed 'em out to a few places around town, and nothing. No response. It kind of shocked me a little (13).

With IBM downsizing, Link downsizing, it didn't leave a lot of opportunity to find corporations that would be hiring finance people. The number of jobs were few and the number of people looking for jobs was many (23).

Description of Stage Three: Re-employment

For most workers in the study, re-employment occurred in two distinct phases. Workers first experienced a transition in their employment, moving from one job to another, attempting to find satisfactory work (phase 3A). After averaging twenty years of tenure in their prior jobs, at the time of the study respondents had been separated from IBM or Link for an average of four years, during which time they had an average of more than two jobs.

Sometimes transitional employment entailed nonstandard job experiences in which respondents were employed as "contingent" or "alternative/indirect" workers. Some even returned as contingent workers to the same sites from which they were displaced. For instance, as part of an arrangement in which IBM outsourced its customer service functions, an IBM contractor leased a vacant portion of the IBM facility. Several displaced IBM respondents worked part time for the contractor as telephone customer service representatives, trouble-shooting problems with clients' IBM products. Other respondents at both IBM and Link were called back to perform the same jobs from which they were displaced, albeit on a temporary basis. And, in a few cases, some returned to their old workplaces as temporary employees to perform jobs they occupied earlier in their careers. One respondent tersely summed up the main source of discontent that he experienced under this arrangement: "I'm doing the same job I did five years ago for probably a quarter—not even a quarter—of the pay!" (15).

Job hopping also occurred for respondents outside of the Link and IBM organizational context. Some worked for temporary help agencies, bouncing from job to job. Others experimented with various types of sales jobs, working for commission. In the absence of full-time employment opportunities, some respondents worked part-time in service and retail jobs, in restaurants and department stores, as waitresses and clerks.

While nearly half the sample continued to encounter employment transition at the time of interview, the other half indicated that they had entered phase 3B, resettling in a job in which they planned to remain. Re-employment outcomes in this sample corresponded with differences in gender and age. Men under age 50 more often settled in comparable positions whereas women and those age 50 and over were more likely to continue to job hop or to settle in lower paying jobs. The differences between these three gender/age groups were evident in not only the comparison of annual earnings change but also in occupational change and change in the number of hours worked per week. . . .

Younger men, while experiencing formidable challenges of a competitive labor market, were not subject to the same disadvantages that confronted women and older men. Several of these men—mainly engineers and programmers—eventually secured employment at other large high-tech firms in the region. However, even for this group, the process of displacement was arduous. For some, losing a job was particularly hard on their self-esteem, given self-perceptions as breadwinners in the prime of their lives. Some lost income in transition; many worked contingent/alternative jobs before finding comparable work. One relocated and left his family for a year before returning to find work in the Binghamton area. Another commuted an hour each way to and from work. Over half of the respondents in this group reported they were less satisfied with their present employment than with their job at IBM or Link. As a former Link worker explains, the displacement process typically involved drawbacks, even for those who eventually found comparable paying jobs:

Well, obviously the decrease in salary was one of the things. I had to tighten my belt somewhat until I had gone through the training period because I was on a fixed amount of money, which was $9,000 less than I was making before. So obviously I had to cut some corners for probably a good six to eight months. So that was an impact. Getting into the type of [job] situation where my time really wasn't my time, it was my client's time. Obviously to be successful in this type of business you have to pay a price, you have to sacrifice something else to be successful . . . A lot of times I don't get out of here until 5:30 or 6:00 and I may have an appointment with somebody (later in the evening) so this job's the sacrifice. Now my style of managing my time is important, more so now than it was then. It was regimented there. Now I have to manage it. And because of that managing I have to try to reduce the time away from the family as much as I can. I don't have as much time. So I try to structure my day in such a way that is less impacted to the family life because that is obviously just as important or more important than your work life. So it's more of a juggling act now. That can have stress on a marriage . . . To be successful in anything you have to pay a price and in some cases that price will be your family. So going into this business I knew I'd have to give up something. It wasn't going to be all hunky-dory. If I wanted to succeed in this business I would have to pay a price, a price I didn't have to pay over there (22).

Conclusion

Given recent developments in national and global economic and employment trends, some researchers have called for more social science research on work and employment issues in this "era of flexibility." In a recent review essay, Smith notes: "We need a deeper understanding of personal experience, subjective interests, and of how aspirations are sustained or crushed as the opportunity structure undergoes changes that appear to be permanent and radical" (1997, p. 335). This study is an example of one approach to the issue raised by Smith and others. By addressing the ramifications of corporate downsizing in the 1990s, it provides insights into how workers, especially those of a roughly middle-class character, experience this abstract concept.

The experiences of workers before, during, and after job loss suggest that we need to expand the conventional meaning of worker displacement. They also highlight a number of work and employment problems, issues, and new questions concerning the downsizing phenomenon. To be displaced means to be separated or detached. Participants in this study became separated or detached in many ways, and not merely because they lost their jobs. The displacement model illustrates how this patterned process occurred for many workers. As we saw, the meanings of displacement were shaped by workers' prior history of paternalistic work relations at IBM and Link as well as by subsequent restructuring and workforce reductions. Following job loss, the meaning of displacement continued to be shaped by changes at IBM and Link, as workforce reductions transformed the structure of the labor market from one characteristic of a thriving company town to one characteristic of a de-industrialized area. For half the sample, displacement led to contingent employment. This finding raises several interesting questions about the relationship between downsizing and contingent work that may be addressed by future research. For many participants, re-employment was marked by a continuation of severance from more favorable work conditions and relations as they lost careers and became downwardly mobile. Finally, we saw that outcomes of the displacement process varied by age and gender. This suggests a need for more research of the causal mechanisms of gender and age differences among displaced workers and their experiences with downsizing, displacement and employment change.

The generalizability of this case study of displaced workers in the Binghamton, New York area is limited. However, national-level data indicate that the phenomenon of corporate downsizing has been far from limited to Binghamton, New York. Thus, it is likely that hundreds of thousands or even millions of workers have experienced or will experience the displacement process in terms similar to the model presented in this study.

Politically, popular solutions to employment problems of displaced workers, such as education or retraining, imply that workers must adapt to new and inexorable economic realities. As we have seen, this adaptation may involve moving through stages and phases in an arduous process. In one scenario, the displaced worker experiences little in the way of material hardship, but nonetheless suffers a temporary disruption in her or his working life and is forced to redefine expectations and attitudes about work and working. Another less attractive but frequent outcome is that the process of displacement leads many workers through experiences of job instability, downward mobility, and the permanent loss of previously favorable conditions, relations, and meanings of work. The evidence in this study as well as in some larger studies indicates that many workers do not fare well. As we saw, this is not only the case for displaced blue-collar workers; many white-collar and middle-class workers lose their jobs and become downwardly mobile (Newman 1988; Rubin 1994). Even those who do appear to overcome job losses on favorable terms have no guarantee they will not again be displaced. No matter how adaptable the worker, no job is secure. As we move deeper into the twenty-first century, this emerging reality confronts the American workforce and raises issues that will require attention by workers, policy makers, academics, and all interested citizens.

Notes

1. At the end of the twentieth century, many business organizations made frequent and large numbers of job cuts. According to Challenger, Gray and Christmas, a consulting firm that tracks corporate workforce reductions, 1998 was a record setting year for the number of job cut announcements (677,795), breaking the previous record set in 1993

(615,186) by ten percent (Laabs 1999, p. 21). Near record-high numbers of job cut announcements (675,123) were present in 1999 (*The Detroit News* 2000, p. M1). As I write in October of 2001, layoffs and layoff announcements have substantially increased following the events of September 11th and as the economy has slowed down.

References

Babbie, E. (2001). *The practice of social research, ninth edition.* Belmont, CA: Wadsworth/ Thomson Learning.

Baldoz, R., Koeber C., & Kraft, P. (2001). *The critical study of work: Labor, technology, and global production.* Philadelphia: Temple University Press.

Bluestone, B., & Harrison, B. (1982). *The deindustrialization of America: Plant closings, community abandonment, and the dismantling of basic industry.* New York: Basic Books.

Budros, A. (1998). The new capitalism and organizational rationality: The adoption of downsizing programs, 1979–1994. *Social Forces, 76,* 229–250.

Chen, S. (1998). *Mastering research: A guide to the methods of social and behavioral science.* Chicago: Nelson-Hall Publishers.

Downs, A. (1995). *Corporate executions: The ugly truth about layoffs—how corporate greed is shattering lives, companies, and communities.* New York: American Management Association.

Glaser, B. G., & Strauss, A. A. (1967). *The discovery of grounded theory.* Chicago: Aldine.

Kraft, P. (1999). To control and inspire: U.S. management in the age of computer information systems and global production. In M. Wardell, T. L. Steiger, & P. Meiksins (Eds.), *Rethinking the labor process.* Albany: State University of New York Press.

Newman, K. S. (1988). *Falling from grace.* New York: Free Press.

Osterman, P. (1999). *Securing prosperity: The American labor market: How has it changed and what to do about it.* Princeton: Princeton University Press.

Perrucci, R., & Wysong, E. (1999). *The new class society.* Lanham, MD: Rowman and Littlefield.

Ragin, C. C., & Becker, H. S. (1992). *What is a case: Exploring the foundations of social inquiry.* New York: Vintage Books.

Rubin, B. A. (1996). *Shifts in the social contract: Understanding change in American society.* Thousand Oaks, CA: Pine Forge Press.

Rubin, L. (1994). *Families on the fault line: America's working class speaks about the family, the economy, race and ethnicity.* New York: Harper Perennial.

Schutt, R. K. (1996). *Investigating the social world: The process and practice of research.* Thousand Oaks, CA: Pine Forge Press.

Sennett, R. (1998). *The corrosion of character: The personal consequences of work in the new capitalism.* New York: W. W. Norton & Company.

Smith, V. (1997). New forms of work organization. In J. Hagan & K. S. Cook (Eds.), *Annual review of sociology* (pp. 315–339). Palo Alto: Annual Reviews Inc.

Smith, V. (2001). *Crossing the great divide: Worker risk and opportunity in the new economy.* Ithaca: ILR Press.

Strauss, A., & Corbin, J. (1990). *Basics of qualitative research: Grounded theory procedures and techniques.* Newbury Park, CA: Sage.

White, H. (1992). Cases are for identity, for explanation or for control. In C. Ragin & H. Becker (Eds.), *What is a case: Exploring the foundations of social inquiry* (pp. 83–104). New York: Cambridge University Press.

Study Questions

1. What are the stages in the process of adjustment to losing one's job? How would you feel if this happened to you?
2. Many of these "displaced workers" had college degrees and advanced training. Was it easier or more difficult for them to get jobs because of this?

Reading 39

Dwelling in Capitalism, Traveling Through Socialism

Michael Burawoy

My own work took up the challenge of studying both these tracks—the experience of the worker and its relation to class formation—but from the subjective side. *First, how do managers elicit the cooperation of workers in the production of surplus value?* Why should workers offer capitalists more than was required for their own reproduction? . . .

This analysis fed directly into the second question: *what is the role of production in working-class formation?* I found it puzzling that in studying class for itself, class as an actor, so much attention was devoted to the realm of superstructures—education, political parties, ideology, and above all the state. This was putting the cart before the horse. If production was not the crucible of class formation, then the significance of superstructures must be seen in a very different light. They no longer exist to counteract political challenges rising from the bowels of the economy. . . .

Important though such speculation might be, the projection of a utopian vision of socialism based on the inversion of capitalism was unsatisfactory. It entailed the false comparison of the reality of one regime with an idealization of another. It was false in two senses. First, in confining oneself to capitalism, one could not appreciate what was specific to capitalism and what might be the ineluctable imperatives of industrialism. Second, it was dangerous to dismiss capitalism in the name of an unspecified, unelaborated utopia without examining whether the latter was either viable (i.e., self-sustaining) or feasible (i.e., reachable). I instead decided, therefore, to study actually existing socialism, or what I called *state socialism.* How might such research help us comprehend what was intrinsically capitalist about work and its regulation, and what, in turn, might this tell us about the possibilities of a democratic socialism, a socialism in which producers governed their own lives? . . .

Beginning with my research in Africa, my preferred technique had always been participant observation. I had then found a job in a South

Chicago plant, where I worked for a year (1974–75) as a machine operator. From this experience emerged the concept of *hegemonic production regime*, which I contrasted with a *despotic regime*, a notion I derived from my reinterpretation of Donald Roy's (1952) earlier ethnography of the same plant. Like so much of the Marxism of the 1970s, my focus was on the durability of capitalism—how it withstands threats to its own demise, how it overcomes its own internal contradictions. I speculated that regimes under state socialism might produce a more volatile working class. Since we knew so little about production regimes in Eastern Europe and the Soviet Union, and what we did know was so heavily refracted through ideology and counterideology, it was even more imperative that I pursue my ethnographic propensities there. Thus between 1983 and 1985 I found jobs in a Hungarian champagne factory, spinning factory, and autoplant. During the next three years I worked intermittently for about a year *in toto* as a furnaceman in Hungary's largest steel plant. I was so focused on the distinguishing traits of socialist production that I didn't pay much attention to the disintegration of the wider political regime. When that time arrived, I didn't hang around to watch socialism's denouement but jumped ship for the Soviet Union, which was then opening up to foreign researchers. In 1991 Kathryn Hendley and I studied a rubber plant in Moscow, and later that year I found a job in a furniture factory in the northern Republic of Komi. The storm from the paradise that we call capitalism seemed to follow me everywhere. Therefore, I decided to stay put, abandoning the holy grail of a democratic socialism to study the tyranny of an unfettered market. Since 1991 I have been following the destruction—what I call the *involution*—of Komi's timber, coal, and construction industries.

In the essay that follows I recapitulate how my trajectory over the last twenty years was driven by abiding Marxist concerns, and how migration from country to country, from workplace to workplace, reshaped the theory I carried with me and thus also my comprehension of the trail I left behind. I investigate the durability of advanced capitalism, the fragility of state socialism, and the peculiarities of emergent postsocialism—all through the eye of an itinerant worker-academic. Finally, I shall show how this dialectic of experience and interpretation, of practice and theory, was itself reconfigured by profound changes in national and global political economies, crystallized in the Polish Solidarity movement (1980–81), the collapse of communism first in Eastern Europe (1989) and then in the Soviet Union (1991), and the concomitant worldwide ascendancy of neoliberal policies and ideologies.

. . . The theoretical puzzle was born not just out of theory but also out of practice. From July 12, 1974, the day I began work in Allied's South Chicago machine shop, I was struck by how hard my fellow machine operators worked. Advisedly I say "they" since it took me quite a few months before I could even begin to keep up with them. There seemed no good reason for all this effort. Certainly, as my day man would say, "No one pushes you around here. You are on your own." The piece rate system, moreover, guaranteed everyone a minimum wage. Promotion and transfers were decided by a bidding system that favored experience and seniority rather than diligence. So why did everyone stretch and strain to produce those extra pieces that only marginally increased income?

When I asked my fellow workers why they worked so hard, they either looked at me in blank incomprehension or responded indignantly that they were not working hard at all and demonstrated the point by goofing off. They would admit to no such sin. They seemed happier to endorse the managerial view that workers would try to get away with anything than to believe that they were hard workers. I wondered how it was that workers so freely concurred with management's image of them. How was it that management not only exercised domination over workers but won their active consent? My answer borrowed from contemporary analyses of the state, and I showed how similar mechanisms were at work in production (Burawoy 1979).[1]

Management elicited consent to its own domination by allowing work to be organized as a game. To survive in the factory eight hours a day, five days a week, doing monotonous, exhausting, and often dangerous work, laborers turn their work into a game of making out with carefully elaborated rules, sanctioned by shop floor management. Sometimes you made the rate from the job, sometimes you didn't, but always your reputation and self-esteem were on the line. As long as there was work to do, the day sped by. Work as game was framed by two other institutions. One, the *internal labor market*, constituted workers as individuals with rights to job mobility within plant, based on seniority and experience. The longer employees remained at Allied, therefore, the greater their interest in staying with the firm, and the greater their interest in its profitability. The second, the *internal state*, regulated relations between workers and managers. On the one hand collective bargaining forged a common interest between management and union, embodied in the collective contract. . . .

A Comparative History of Despotism

If it was a fluke that I had stumbled into the same South Chicago factory that Donald Roy had studied, it was no less fateful to discover Miklos Haraszti's (1977) depiction of his trials and tribulations in Hungary's Red Star Tractor Factory. While I was marveling at the effort of my fellow machine operators in South Chicago, Haraszti—an intellectual who had been banished to the factory—had scaled unimaginable heights of work intensity in Budapest. His piece rates were based on running two machines at once. His descriptions violated all the stereotypes of socialist production—socialist workers as slackers, noted only for their indolence, who had retained only one right, the right not to work hard. If Roy's work had forced me to theorize the despotic regime under capitalism, Haraszti's *A Worker in a Worker's State* called for theorization of the despotic regime under state socialism.

The secret of all factory despotism lies in the dependence of workers' material survival outside work on their performance at work. It is this dependence that gives managers their coercive whip. But it can assume different forms. Under early capitalism workers were subject to the whim of their overseer or managers who could hire and fire at will. They had no welfare system to fall back on in the case of unemployment. Under state socialism job guarantees came with wage uncertainty. Where at Allied I was guaranteed a minimum wage regardless of what I produced, at Red Star Haraszti had to work for every forint. To earn a living he had to run his two machines, butter up his supervisor to get a continuous flow of work, and grapple with piece rates that he could not make. His supervisor became his tormenter and the almighty norm his dictator. Far from restraining managerial despotism, the state was always on his back, surveilling, calculating, punishing. The party controlled promotions and transfers, the trade union denied workers their rights, and managers bullied workers into submission with their discretion over every petty reward and penalty. Party, trade union, and management conspired to extract the maximum effort from workers. Instead of market despotism, he was held prisoner to *bureaucratic despotism* (Burawoy 1985, 156–208). . . .

Socialism Too Can Be Efficient

Solidarity erupted in Gdansk, Poland, in August 1980. Not even my wildest theorizing of bureaucratic despotism had prepared me for such an epochal event—the first sustained, nationwide revolt of a working class. But before I could pack my bags and search for work in Poland, General Wajciech Jaruzelski had declared marital law on December 13, 1981. Instead I eventually wormed my way into Hungarian factories in the fall of 1983. I began where it looked most feasible, that is in the rural areas, working first in the champagne factory of a state farm and then in various auxiliary workshops on a cooperative farm.

Wherever I went the gender division of labor was startling—women were driven by the relentless pace of a bottling line or enslaved by piece rates to spinning bobbins while the men loafed around as inspectors, mechanics, supervisors, and the like. For the men, as I soon discovered, work was often a place to rest while their true labors took place in the more entrepreneurial second economy, rearing pigs and poultry, growing vegetables, building new houses. It seemed to be bureaucratic despotism for women and self-organization for men.

This was the case in the rural areas, but what about the industrial plants of the towns? It seemed that working-class life was one of socialism's best-kept secrets. It was difficult enough to set foot inside a real socialist factory, let alone work in one. Only the organizational genius of my friend János Lukács made it possible. We first visited the factory of Bánki in November 1983, at the end of my first extended field trip to Hungary. I returned in the summer of 1984 to work there for two months as a radial drill operator. I couldn't believe my luck until I found myself holding down steel flanges with one bare hand, while trying to control an immense, shaking drill with the other. They had been waiting for a sucker like me (see Burawoy and Lukács 1992, 35–58).

Still this was not Haraszti working on two parallel mills. I was in a machine shop like his, but my experience was very different. Comparing our situations, I began to understand the peculiar context that created his isolation, alienation, and intense work under bureaucratic despotism. First, I quickly found myself at the center of attention. Who, after all, had worked with an American professor, even if he was incompetent? On the shop floor I was protected by Anna, Klára, and Ági of the Dobó Katica Brigade, and outside I occasionally joined my workmates in their wine cellars. . . .

Second, just as I was delivered to the worst job in the shop, with the most difficult piece rates and conditions, so the same would be true of any newcomer, Haraszti included. More generally, it is often the case that socialist production divides into a core of key workers, usually male, skilled, and experienced, who bargain their way to comfort but at the expense of peripheral workers, unskilled, inexperienced, often women, shackled by impossible piece rates and subject to despotic rule. . . .

Third, there is an historical component to the difference between Red Star and Bánki that accounts for the overall diminution of the despotism and its continuation in particular for women. With the economic reforms of the late sixties came the opening of a second economy, which gave many workers, particularly skilled workers, access to alternative sources of livelihood and therefore greater bargaining strength on the shop floor. Self-organized cooperatives were introduced within the factory in an attempt to halt the drain of key workers into the cooperative sector. This further complicated and diminished despotism. Women, however, were usually excluded from both external and internal second economies, and so they remained as vulnerable as ever.

Fourth, and finally, Bánki was part of a relatively successful concern that produced buses and other heavy vehicles that were often exported. By contrast, Red Star Tractor Factory had been one of the first large enterprises to be subject to the economic reforms in the late 1960s, and when Haraszti arrived it was in deep trouble, soon to be liquidated. He thus experienced the pressure of working in a factory that had lost favor with the state. . . .

Painting Socialism: The Ritual Enactment of Class

As I made my way from Budapest to the medieval town of Egér, where Bánki was located, I had to pass through Hungary's second biggest city, Miskolc, the capital of its eastern industrial heartland. There, sprawling along the valley, lay the giant Lenin Steelworks, employing fifteen thousand workers and marking the pulse of the city. The soul of the socialist proletariat lay here—capable of heroic feats of endurance, celebrated in posters of the Stalinist past, carriers of that radiant future that was to be communism. To join the army of workers that swarmed through the gates three times a day was my secret dream. Miraculously, János Lukács arranged it, and I won a place at the heart of the steelworks as a furnaceman, tending the state-of-the-art German basic oxygen furnace. I'd finally graduated from an individualistic machine operator to a team worker. I joined the October Revolution Socialist Brigade for about the year over the period 1985–88. . . .

Slowly I began to assimilate the steelworkers' socialist "culture of critical discourse," to play back their cynicism to them. They were steeped in socialist imagery expressed in endless jokes about socialist irrationality, relentlessly drawing attention to the gap between ideology and reality. For them reality appeared to be more the inversion of ideology than its realization. I made much, perhaps too much, of the rituals that workers had to perform in celebration of the wonders of socialism, which included political and production meetings; the circus organized for visiting dignitaries; the badges, flags, and medals that we'd win for outstanding performance. In their joking their cynicism was much in evidence, but in their outbursts of anger I detected a continuing commitment to socialist ideals.

Still vividly etched in my memory was the visit of the prime minister. We had to volunteer a "communist" shift to paint the slag drawer a bright yellow. My fellow October Revolutionaries got out their paintbrushes, but I could only find one with black paint and so I proceeded to paint our shovels black. Along came the superintendent, wanting to know what the hell I was doing. I told him, as innocently as I could, that I was helping to build socialism. ET, the brigade's wit, turned to me and said, "Misi, Misi, you are not building socialism, you are painting socialism, and black at that." All of us roared with laughter, except the superintendent, who stalked off.

It was true: workers had to paint socialism as efficient, egalitarian, and just, while all around them was waste, class privilege, and favoritism. They criticized the socialist regime, the party, the system for failing to realize its promises. They turned the ideology against the regime it was supposed to legitimate. Workers developed a strong sense of class hostility to the red directors and their managerial lackeys, exuding a socialist consciousness at the very same time that they rejected actually existing socialism (Burawoy and Lukács 1992, 111–114). . . .

While I was busy working out why Solidarity occurred in the east and not the west, in Poland and not Hungary, the regime was crumbling from above. I was riveted to my search for socialist symbols and rituals. With my limited historical perspective, I did not recognize—or did not want to recognize—just how attenuated they had become. As I scraped away the dust from the slogans of yesteryear, I didn't appreciate that workers were holding a ruling elite accountable to an ideology in which it no longer believed. The *nomenclatura* was getting ready to cast off the trappings of socialism. When the appropriate moment arrived in 1989, there was surprisingly little resistance to emancipating the economy, at least from the atrophying socialist *ideology*.

There were those like Jancsi, our devoted shop steward, who now saw the chance to create a real trade union. For three years I had chided him for selling his soul to a bankrupt company union. When communism disintegrated, he was one of the first to become active in the burgeoning factory council movement—a throwback to 1956. He promised to build a real union. But in the end these were lone voices. Socialist ideology had been so pummeled, distorted, and deployed against the working class that it could awaken few people's imagination. . . .

The theoretical lesson is that state socialism rests on the central appropriation and redistribution of surplus. Domination and exploitation are transparent and therefore require *legitimation*. Transparency calls for an ideology that presents the party state as all-knowing and embracing the universal interest embodied in the plan.[2] Legitimation based on a radiant future, rather than immemorial tradition, however, invites criticism on its own terms—a criticism that demands that the party state live up to its promises. . . .

Capitalism, by contrast, is blessed with flexible patterns of accumulation and the invisibility of exploitation so that legitimation plays second fiddle to *hegemony*—the coordination of material interests of all classes with the general interest of the dominant class. . . .

On the Cusp Between Perestroika and Privatization

. . . I began the exploration of Soviet enterprises with Kathryn Hendley at the beginning of 1991. For two months we spent every day at Rezina, a famous rubber plant in the center of Moscow. Through the enterprise trade union she had managed to gain unlimited access in exchange for a couple of computers for their kindergartens. We were promised that Rezina was a "drop of water" through which we could study the turbulent seas of perestroika. We were not disappointed (Burawoy and Hendley 1992).

Rezina was a dreadful place, an apparition arisen from the last century. It was just as I imagined those Victorian satanic mills to be, with workers, mainly women, toiling in dark, dank dungeons without ventilation or light, suffering respiratory diseases from the fumes of resin and paid a pittance for the privilege. Whenever we wanted to talk to workers, we were accompanied by managers, and the conversation quickly fell into a sullen silence. Even if they could speak freely, what was there to say to a couple of foreigners? Their humiliation and degradation were palpable.

We managed to inveigle ourselves into the morning planning meetings attended by all the managers and shop chiefs. It was quite a scene to behold, with insults and innuendo thrown from one end of the table to the other, managers fulminating at each other for this failure or that. Usually the manager for supplies bore the brunt of verbal abuse. He had the unenviable task of begging, cajoling, bribing, coercing suppliers from all over the Soviet Union. But that was only half the job. He then had to wave his magic wand over truck drivers and railroad officials to transport the materials. He would never reveal to us the secret of his trade. . . .

I'd seen it all before in Hungary in 1988 and 1989, when managers at the Lenin Steelworks had made themselves (in cooperation with foreigners) share owners of limited companies that they had created from the potentially profitable parts of the enterprise. The state continued to own the company shell and was billed for overheads and the escalating losses, while the limited companies and their shareholders pocketed handsome profits. No wonder workers were cynical about so-called privatization, or what was euphemistically called "spontaneous privatization.". . .

Industrial Involution: Russia's Descent into Capitalism

Syktyvkar, with a population of 250,000, is the capital of the Komi Republic, lying to the west of the Urals in the far north of European Russia. Sparsely populated, it is rich in natural resources—coal, bauxite, oil, and gas—and covered in a rich forest, much of it still inaccessible. Komi has always been a land of exiles from the period of Catherine the Great. Under communism it was an integral part of the gulag, with labor camps feeding the timber and coal industries. The area had long been essentially closed to foreigners, but in the spring of 1991 it was already possible to migrate there to continue my peripatetic vocation as an incompetent factory worker. With the help of a local sociologist, Pavel Krotov, I obtained a job drilling holes at Polar Furniture, the city's model furniture factory (Burawoy and Krotov 1992). . . .

Polar's charmed existence gave its general director the self-assurance to hire me, when every other place had closed their doors. On the shop floor, however, it was a different matter. There the lack of enthusiasm toward me was palpable, and I was shunned from most collective activities. I speculated at the time that I was too much of an oddity for people to accept—an American professor who wanted to work on the shop floor. My work mates had never met an American, let alone one as strange as I. My Russian was still embryonic, and my mechanical ineptitude put me at the very bottom of the status hierarchy. To add insult to injury I was paid more or less the same as everyone else in the brigade. Still, under not too different conditions, Hungarian workers had embraced me. At the time, I speculated that cultural factors must be at work—the legacy of Stalinist suspicion as well as the solidarity of the labor collective. Later I learned the reason was simpler: management, in particular my shop floor supervisors, were using me to discipline the workforce. Sveta, my "master," would say, "Hey, lads, get to work. There's an American watching us!". . .

Flexible Capitalism, Fragile Socialism, and the Aftermath

Braverman captured the rhythm of capitalist expansion, its capacity to reconstitute itself through the recomposition of work in a dialectic of deskilling, reskilling, and further deskilling. But he didn't capture the source of capitalism's political and ideological sustainability, which, I argue, lay first in its despotic and then in its hegemonic apparatuses of production. Capitalism has proved to be as durable as socialism has been fragile. As I scampered away from under Gulliver's feet, migrating from Hungary to Russia, from Moscow to Syktyvkar to Vorkuta, everywhere capitalism caught up with me. Why did socialism keel over, for the most part without even a murmur or a gasp? Too much has been said about the flexibility of capitalism and not enough of the fragility of socialism. . . .

From the standpoint of my own odyssey from capitalism to socialism, I see the political and the economic as inextricable. The hegemonic regimes of advanced capitalism work through the coordination of interests, operating at all levels of society, and not least in production. The bureaucratic regimes of socialism work through the legitimation of a transparent exploitation and domination. Hegemony organizes and isolates struggles on its own terms, while legitimacy invites critique that challenges its own order. To speak of a legitimation crisis in advanced capitalism or a hegemonic crisis of state socialism is to confound their distinctiveness. But understanding the economic foundations of political crisis and continuity is more complicated than simply pinning hegemony to one regime and legitimacy to the other. Each system can only exist when complemented by the other. Capitalism calls on states to compensate for the irrationality of its economy. The fragility of capitalism, therefore, lies with its weakest link, the state, which politicizes its own regulation. Equally, socialism requires an elaborate private sphere, coordinated by market-type relations, to compensate for the malfunctioning of the administered economy. In this complementary world of real socialism, interests can be organized and coordinated, and hegemony can be constituted to bolster legitimacy. This was developed furthest in Hungary and is the mainstay of the Chinese order. Private, market-like coordination may be necessary to sustain socialism, but it may be labeled antithetical to socialism, so deepening the crisis of legitimacy. This was the case in Russia. In short, each system incubates its opposite, which can in turn either reinforce or undermine the dominant order.

Notes

1. This book was heavily influenced by Antonio Gramsci and by the French structuralist Marxism of Louis Althusser and Nicos Poulantzas.
2. Here I am indebted to George Konrád and Iván Szelényi's classic *The Intellectuals on the Road to Class Power* (1979).

References

Burawoy, Michael. 1979. *Manufacturing Consent: Changes in the Labor Process Under Monopoly Capitalism*. Chicago: University of Chicago Press.

———. 1985. *The Politics of Production: Factory Regimes Under Capitalism and Socialism*. London: Verso.

Burawoy, Michael, and János Lukács. 1992. *The Radiant Past: Ideology and Reality in Hungary's Road to Capitalism*. Chicago: University of Chicago Press.

Burawoy, Michael, and Kathryn Hendley. 1992. "Between Perestroika and Privatization: Divided Strategies and Political Crisis in a Soviet Enterprise." *Soviet Studies*, 44: 371–402.

Burawoy, Michael, and Pavel Krotov. 1992. "The Soviet Transition from Socialism to Capitalism: Worker Control and Economic Bargaining in the Wood Industry." *American Sociological Review*, 57(2): 16–38.

Harastzi, Miklos. 1977. *A Worker in a Worker's State.* New York: Penguin Books.
Konrád, George, and Iván Szélenyi. 1979. *The Intellectuals on the Road to Class Power.* New York: Harcourt Brace Jovanovich.
Roy, Donald. 1952. "Restriction of Output in a Piecework Machine Shop." Ph.D. dissertation, University of Chicago.

Study Questions

1. What are the similarities and differences between "socialist" and "capitalist" economies?
2. Using this article and any other resources you have, how would you define "political economy"?

PART FIVE

Social Change
in a Modern World

Topic 14
Population and Ecology

The future of the planet, and our lives, are tied to the macro-social effects of population and the distribution of population in emerging and developed nations. The social and environmental ecology of urban areas brings focus to the sociological forces which will write the future of entire continents and ultimately the world. Although it is true that the dramatic world population growth of the 1960s and 1970s has slowed, what will twelve billion living persons mean to urban areas already impossibly choked by poor living conditions, widespread illness, and environmental pollution? Urbanization is now just as important as population alone, with its own tremendous impact on the environment.

The population of the world passed six billion living inhabitants a few years ago. Even with a slowing growth rate, it is estimated that somewhere in the next century we will almost double the population again. As developed nations reach zero-population growth or have negative growth rates, will the demand for certain types of labor and requirements in their economies mean greater immigration from growing developing nations where the economies cannot find jobs for residents? Examples of these events can be found in Europe and North America already. Such events may result in even greater diversity in receiving countries and help to ease the crises in poorer nations. As Malthus's "dismal thesis" regarding the population's ability to outstrip subsistence (food and resources) fades into insignificance, how will the enormous economic disparity between the world's countries influence the future?

Cities, regions, entire nations, and even the world must contend with changes in the environment. Ecological disaster can come from social, economic, and natural phenomena and thereby change life for small and large numbers of people. Contaminated water supplies from agricultural runoff might mean serious health problems for an area. Deforestation in the rain forests could result in worldwide changes in the climate. Global warming, as evidence mounts for its existence, may change the water level in the oceans, just as acid rain from upwind polluters destroys natural habitat for more circumscribed populations. The world has been made "smaller" with the dynamics of transportation, communication, and globalization. We begin to realize that oceans, mountains, and international borders are less important than in the past, and all of us live in a vast web of interconnections often determined by macro-level events that have examples in our own backyards.

Population and ecology are part and parcel of a key future determinate of life: the politics of consumption. In the world of nations, there are a few very rich, a few in the middle, and many at the bottom of the global stratification system. How will we decide who is to give, who is to support, who is to repay, and who is to have autonomy? Are we on the verge of a "new world order"? Because of the extreme inequalities, where people in many countries live on less than $200 a year and a few countries have per capita incomes 100 times that much, the political processes in the near future must address population, world government, consumption, and economic inequality for the entire planet. This is a monumental task when individual nations can rarely find the ability to do such things for themselves.

The three selections in Topic 14: Population and Ecology present, first, a structural look at international problems with population and urbanization; second, a micro look at the social ecology of an urban skid row; and third, a specific example of the largest environmental disaster in U.S. history. In "Planetary Overload," Anthony McMichael examines the health issues present in urban environments around the globe. John Bardo, Jeff Riemer, Ron Matson, and Bob Knapp enrich our understanding of "social ecology" as they map the interrelated dimensions of skid row. Thomas Beamish, in "Silent Spill," documents the slowly unfolding catastrophe in the middle of California that took decades to recognize.

Reading 40

Planetary Overload

Anthony J. McMichael

*The world . . . is faced both by the massive degradation of the natural envi-
ronment and by the accelerating decline in the quality of life of many of those
who live in the built environment of cities. The two crises are related. The
consequences of urbanization make a major contribution to the global environmental changes that threaten the very existence of life in the future, while
changes in the biosphere increasingly affect health and social conditions in
the cities.*

—WHO, 1991[1]

Introduction

. . . The growth of cities . . . has great ecological significance for at
least three reasons. First, in poor countries, the crowded makeshift
fringes of cities testify to the population pressures on overloaded rural
economies. Second, the artificial ecological setting of high-density city
life alters the profile of health hazards—e.g. more "crowd infections" and
physical (industrial and traffic) injuries. Third, the existence of cities has
adverse impacts on ecosystems, both directly by pollution and by en-
croaching on farmland, wetland and coast, and indirectly by distancing
and disengaging humans from the rhythms of nature. This separation,
this psychological detachment of humans from unpaved nature, helps
confirm those social values and priorities that we in the First World have
acquired and amplified since early in the industrial revolution. Urbanisation is thus both a consequence and a cause of global environmental
change.

The Rise of Cities

Cities have long been the star performers in human culture. Historically, towns and then cities formed when settled farming communities
generated enough surplus food to support an urban population. Archae-
ologists have traced the first remnants of this evolution from peasant village to trading town in the Palestine–Syria–Anatolia region, dating back
to around 9,000–8,000 BC. Subsequently, as wealth and power accrued
at the centre, cities evolved. Aristocrats, academics, artisans and artists

live in cities, which have thus become the seat of learning, religion, scientific discovery, culture, commerce and government. While cities have poured forth a stream of literature, music and fine arts, there are also darker sides—poverty, squalor, high crime rates, and exposure to infectious diseases, accidents and antisocial behaviours.

Cities attest to the unique capacity of humans to superimpose the complexities of culture upon basic biological destiny. Living in cities distances us from nature; this reduces some risks to health, but creates others. As cities grow, and crowds multiply, so many of these risks are amplified. Historically, early towns and cities lived in some sort of balanced reciprocity with their surrounding countryside. Skills and money were exchanged for food. While urban populations have generally had the upper hand, and have tended to be parasitic upon rural populations,[2] there have been redeeming reciprocal benefits. In today's world, however, as populations surge, as economies become internationalised, and as rural production in the Third World becomes hostage to international debt, so the historic localised urban–rural relationship is breaking down. So too is the fabric of much of urban life around the world. The implications for human health are great.

An increasing proportion of the world's burgeoning population lives in cities—that is urban settlements (towns or cities) of over 10,000 people. In 1800, only 5% of the world population lived in cities—i.e. around 40 million people. In 1900, the figure was around 250 million, or 15%. By 2000, half of the world's six billion people will be urban-dwellers, and, by early next century, *Homo sapiens* will have become a predominantly urban species. (At the same time, the proportion of the world's population aged over 65 years will have increased by around 40% between now and 2020.) While this dramatic shift in where people live has occurred in both rich and poor countries, the proportional rate of growth is now several times greater in less developed than in more developed countries. Although the level of urbanisation is low in sub-Saharan Africa, the *rate* of urbanisation in many African cities is very high (up to 10% per year), as the displaced rural poor migrate to the cities. (The word "urbanisation," as used by demographers, refers to an increase in the proportion of the national population living in cities.) Rapid urbanisation represents a profound transformation of human ecology—a transformation that is generally outstripping social and political responses.

The most dramatic evidence of accelerating urbanisation has been in the growth of very large cities, with populations greater than five million. In 1950 there were seven such cities, by 1970 there were twenty, and by the year 2000 there will be around sixty—three-quarters of them in developing countries. The four largest cities, in 1990, were Tokyo-Yokohama (29 million) and Mexico City, New York and Sao Paulo (each of 16–19 million).[3] On current trends, the population of greater Mexico City will exceed 25 million by the end of this century, while Sao Paulo, Dacca, Bombay, Calcutta, Delhi, Shanghai, Cairo and others will reach 15–20 million. The urban population of the developing world will then be double that of the developed countries; by 2025 the differential could be as great as four-fold. Environmental refugees, already numbered in millions, will add further to these bulging numbers, and will gather precariously at the socially fragile fringes of urban populations.[4] Nearly all the world's rapidly-growing cities are in poor countries, and approximately half of this Third World urban population lives in conditions of extreme deprivation.[5] In some cities, like Ibadan in Nigeria and Calcutta in India, around 70% of the population live in degraded shanty towns or slums; in Addis Ababa in starving, war-exhausted Ethiopia the figure is 80–90%.[6] WHO warns: "Nations must face the devastating facts that this deprived sector of the urban population is not only at greatest risk of disease, injury and starvation in the city environment, but by the end of this century the extreme poor in the cities of the world could represent a quarter of the global population."[7] One-half of these urban poor will be in Asia, while Latin America and Africa, with their smaller populations, will each account for around one-quarter.

The current surging growth of many large Third World cities resembles that of industrialising Europe last century—but on a much larger scale. Within many poor countries, displaced rural workers are moving to cities, supplementing the already-high fertility within those impoverished urban-fringe communities. Their move reflects a mix of influences, including the need for paid work, the search for food and shelter, and displacement from rural life by environmental deterioration or overcrowding. Much of this enforced ("push") migration differs from the dominant prosperity-driven "pull" of economic and lifestyle attraction to city life that, this century, has underlain the prolonged growth of cities in rich countries. It is misleading, however, to envisage the urban poor as politically or economically marginal. Many squatter settlements are stable, with spontaneous forms of social organisation and support networks and with long-term dwellers who are well integrated as cheap labour in industry or as participants in the "informal sector" of the economy.[8] This largely self-employed "informal" sector is, in many ways, complementary and functional in relation to the formal economy. In sub-Saharan Africa the informal sector—called the *jua kali* ("hot sun") economy in Kenya— accounts for as much economic activity as the formal economy and, in the estimation of the UN's International Labor Organization, employs 59% of the urban workforce.

Urban migration is also occurring *between* countries. Most of the people who migrate between countries move to larger cities in more affluent countries. Many of these migrants are poor or displaced, seeking a new life in a new country. Consequently, the new urban underclass of cities like London, Paris, Berlin, Stockholm and New York is dominated by immigrants from hot poor countries—such as Pakistan, Bangladesh, India, northern Africa, Turkey and Puerto Rico.

Not all of the world's population movement, however, is in the direction of the city. In many rich countries, much residential and industrial development is now occurring outside, but near, major cities. These developments draw on the high-quality infrastructure and services available from them: piped water, sewers, telephones, television, garbage collection, paved roads and public transport. Indeed, this "suburbanisation" has been evident around various of Europe's larger cities throughout this century.[8] In recent decades a more clearcut "counter-urbanisation" has developed, with development reorienting to smaller towns and rural areas. This has been facilitated by extended and improved roads and by workers having faster cars and higher incomes. Meanwhile, many of the once dominant industrial cities are going into decline as the wealthiest countries move towards post-industrialism; examples include Cleveland, Detroit and Pittsburgh in the USA, Liverpool and Belfast in the UK, Lille and St. Etienne in France, Dortmund, Essen and Duisburg in Germany, Rotterdam in the Netherlands, Bilbao in Spain and Genoa in Italy.

Although urbanisation strains social and political infrastructures, physical facilities and local ecosystems, it often confers benefits on national economies. The World Bank estimates that, in recent years, the one-third of the population of developing countries living in cities has produced nearly two-thirds of their national "wealth." While, in conventional economic terms, that may vindicate urbanisation, this calculus ignores the externalised costs of urban-industrial activity to the environment and to the health of the workforce. Besides, urban economic performance is very vulnerable to receding economic tides. Poor urban populations therefore have insecure prospects, but, for many, it beats being landless, hungry and exploited in the countryside. . . .

The Urban Health Profile

Many health indices, particularly in rich countries, suggest that the *average* level of health is better in large cities than in the countryside. These statistics often mislead, however, because measures of urban health are heavily weighted by the superior health experience of the affluent segment of city-dwellers. In the Netherlands, for example, while the life expectancy for the urban poor is five years less than for the well-to-do, the overall figure is close to that of me latter majority group.[1] In reality, the poorer segments of urban communities often have much worse health status than the rural poor.[9] However, the poorest of the urban poor are often statistically elusive: they may be illegal immigrants, they may be transitory, and their health and vital statistics are usually not recorded. In Third World countries, further bias results from the selective tendency for the more severely disabled and sick to stay with their rural community and not migrate into the non-supportive urban milieu.

WHO estimates that 600 million urban-dwellers in developing countries live or work in "life and health threatening environments." For many poor urban residents, the main daily struggle is for food. Their typical intake is around 60% of the city average, while the intake of various key micronutrients such as vitamin A is usually proportionately much less. Severe malnutrition is common in slum children, and the health and nutritional status of their mothers—poorly educated, struggling to breastfeed and care for a succession of young children and subjected to discriminatory social practices—is particularly vulnerable. In many urban slums, a malnourished child, lacking safe water and sanitation, is 40–50 times more likely to die before reaching five years of age than is a child in a rich country.[10] The dominant causes of illness and death in young children are diarrhoeal diseases, respiratory infections, vaccine-preventable diseases (especially measles) and nutritional deficiencies; all are strongly associated with poverty, overcrowding and poor environmental conditions.

Many epidemiological studies have described gradients in health, particularly child health, between urban and rural populations and between different segments of urban populations.[1,11,12] The following are examples of the former comparison. The rates of leprosy are lower in urban than in rural populations in many African countries; in the UK, lung disorders are more prevalent in cities than in countryside; and in Spain, there is a higher prevalence of mental retardation in rural areas than in cities. Studies *within* cities show consistent health deficits among the poor. The infant death rates from diarrhoea are correlated with lack of piped water in urban populations of southern Brazil. In Quito, the capital of Ecuador, the infant death rate has been 20–30 times higher in squatter settlements than in upper-class districts.[12] In the slums of Haiti's capital, Port-au-Prince, the infant death rate is three times that of the rural area and many times greater than in the richer areas of the city, while in Manila, capital of the Philippines, the infant death rate in squatter communities has been three times higher than for the rest of the city.[10] Various studies have shown consistently higher levels of intestinal parasitic infestations (especially *Ascaris* and *Trichuris*) in the poorer areas of the cities and a variety of nutritional deficiencies among those socioeconomically disadvantaged groups.[8] It is clear from these and a great many other studies that there is a strong link between poverty and generally poor health—although some care is needed in the interpretation of such statistics since their quality may vary between the compared subpopulations.

Some of these studies have sought also to identify the actual environmental factors or circumstances that are the immediate cause of poor health. For example, a study of infant diarrhoeal deaths in Pelotas, Brazil, showed that households sharing taps or using public stand pipes were at higher risk than those with in-house piped water.[13] Readers familiar with the history of epidemiological research will hear echoes of John Snow's seminal studies in cholera-afflicted London 140 years ago. Presumably we will go on documenting this deadly relationship for so long as there is persistence of the underlying poverty that leaves communities without safe drinking water. Lack of clean water and adequate sanitation is widespread in Third World cities and remains a major killer. The previous Director-General of WHO, Halfdan Mahler, claimed that the number of water taps per thousand persons is a better indicator of health than is the number of hospital beds.

Today, about 80% of the world's city-dwellers are supplied with safe water, either by in-house connections or public stand-pipes, and about 65% have sanitation via sewer connections, septic tanks or latrines. The corresponding figures are lower in rural populations. Most of those without are in the Third World, where the general lack of maintenance further erodes these statistics. Up to one-half of the piped water is lost or unavailable because of leakages, broken water mains, or malfunctioning stand-pipes. Some of the official statistics are hardly credible anyway—for example, Nigeria and Liberia reported in the mid-1980s that 100% of their urban populations had access to safe water. (Presumably the word "access" encourages creative statistics.)

Poor sanitation is an even more widespread problem. In many large cities, particularly in Africa and Asia, there is no sewerage system, and so much of the human excreta and household wastes end up, entirely untreated, in rivers, stream, canals, gullies and ditches.[14] People largely depend on backyard pit toilets, while, in the worst slum areas, open defaecation in lanes and alleyways helps to spread hookworm, other intestinal worms, typhoid, dysentery and diarrhoeal diseases.[15] One-seventh of the world's population is infested with hookworm, resulting in 50,000 deaths annually This parasite enters via the skin, usually of the feet, and makes its way via the blood stream to the intestine. There it attaches to the intestinal lining, where it grows (thus depriving the host individual of scarce nutrients), and sheds eggs. These are transferred, via faecally contaminated groundwater and soil, to the next pair of unsuspecting passing feet. Other widespread intestinal worms, such as round-worms, whipworms and others, have similar life cycles. They all spread readily in urban environments where poor sanitation creates special ecological opportunities. In Mexico City, for example, cysticercosis (a tapeworm that is usually transmitted in contaminated pork) is now spread more widely via sewage-contaminated vegetable gardens.

In addition to unsafe water and lack of sanitation, urban populations in poor countries are prone to other causes of disease and death—including malnutrition, inadequate housing, lack of facilities for solid waste disposal, narrow and dangerous roadways and overcrowding. Some of these health hazards are clearcut, and their effects are hardly contentious. For example, the accumulation of solid wastes in, or next to, urban slums encourages the spread of parasitic diseases such as leptospirosis, primarily because of the garbage-associated proliferation of insect and rodent vectors. Physical injuries frequently result from unsafe buildings, which often collapse, and from children playing on dangerous unplanned roads. Cities also pose social–environmental health problems, especially to young people. In Third World countries, approximately half of all urban children under age fifteen live in conditions of extreme poverty. About one-fifth of these children are "street children" with minimal or no family support. They work at odd jobs, scavenge or beg for food and often have to seek out shelter. They are exposed to great physical, emotional and sexual hazards. The problem is severe in Latin America, where there are an estimated 20 million homeless "street children.". . .

Sexually Transmitted Diseases

By the middle of this century, in rich countries, the long decline in most of the age-old infectious diseases—especially those that killed young children—had finally been capped by the advent of modern antibiotics and vaccinations. Infectious disease seemed no longer to be a serious public health problem in those countries. However, the 1980s have reminded us of the ever-present hazards of infectious diseases: microbes, the tiniest members of our ecosystems, are always with us. Their genetic profile changes restlessly as, in effect, they probe for new ecological niches in which to multiply, or for defences against human anti-microbial factors (such as antibiotic drugs).

During the past decade there has been a widespread outbreak of sexually transmitted diseases (STD)—"wide" both in the number of infectious agents and in the range of human populations affected. The attack has come predominantly from four bacteria: those responsible for syphilis, gonorrhoea, chancroid and chlamydia; and from four viruses: the herpes simplex virus, human papilloma virus, hepatitis B virus (HBV) and human immunodeficiency virus (HIV—i.e. the AIDS virus). These sexually transmitted diseases are particularly associated with urban poverty and with the disintegration of traditional forms of social and family organisation. In developed countries, and particularly in the USA, the rates of most STDs are highest among the urban poor. These are primarily diseases of teenage years and young adulthood, and the age profile of much of the world's urban poor renders those populations susceptible. Not only is the age-profile loaded towards risk of infection from sexual activity, but, in the case of HBV and HIV, intravenous drug abuse compounds the risk.

AIDS was first identified in 1981, in the USA, and has subsequently been widely reported from around the world. The circumstances in which the virus first entered the human species remain uncertain and controversial; there may have been undetected cases of AIDS in the 1960s, or even earlier. Speculation about its origins has encompassed the possibilities of contamination of early polio vaccine grown on monkey kidney tissue, transfer of infected primate blood to volunteers during laboratory studies of malaria transmission, and localised African ritual contact with monkey blood. Validity aside, these possibilities remind us again that changes in human demography, culture and technological practice create ecological opportunities for microbes. In late 1992, WHO estimated that 10–15 million men, women and children had been infected worldwide. Of these, 1.5 million had progressed to clinical AIDS. The HIV pandemic continues to grow and has now also become widely established in the big cities of India and Southeast Asia (particularly Thailand) and Latin America.

By 2000, an estimated 40–50 million people will have become infected with HIV—perhaps more according to less conservative estimates. If so, around one-tenth of the world's annual tally of deaths would be attributable to AIDS by early next century. Most new HIV infections during the 1990s will occur in poor countries, particularly in urban populations, and including 5–10 million children. In Africa, the infection is approximately equally distributed between men and women and is being passed on to an increasing proportion of new-born children. By the late 1990s, there will be around 10 million uninfected African children orphaned by the death of both parents from AIDS. Some demographers now think that AIDS will cause the worst-affected parts of sub-Saharan Africa to experience a reversal in population growth. Meanwhile, in developed countries, HIV infection has been much more closely associated with male homosexuality and intravenous drug abuse than in Africa or Asia. Heterosexual transmission, while still only a minor contributor in developed countries, appears to be gradually increasing. . . .

Optimal Size and Form of Cities?

. . . In the early 1970s, *A Blueprint for Survival* proposed the decentralisation of urban populations into small village-like settlements of about 500 people, aggregated into larger communities of around 50,000.[17] In this way, "human-scale" communities would replace the social and ecological problem of the modern, ever-expanding, megalopolis. They would have their own internal sense of identity, with a sense of shared responsibility and cooperation. Critics argued that such small and self-contained settlements would breed social pressures and moral coercion, thus infringing the freedom of action and the opportunity for independence and anonymity of city life. They predicted the recreation of the pettiness, rigidity and tedium of life in small villages. Others objected to the intellectual and cultural constraints that would apply, arguing that modern massive cities are, like mediaeval cathedrals, an expression of human creativity, spirituality and striving. Clearly, in the debate about the optimal size of human settlements, there are romantics on both sides of the fence.

Related to size, but distinguishable from it, is the consideration of patterns of social contact. Peter Wilmott, an English researcher, argues that even superficial interactions between local residents, if regular, encourage some sense of attachment to the locality. Regular residents, he says, "get to know each other by sight. . . . Recognising and being recognised by others creates a sense of belonging."[18] However, the creation of small and cohesive "communities of attachment"—whether in the post-industrial rich world where people will live, work and play predominantly in and around their homes, or in the urbanised populations of poorer countries where, in coming decades, activities will be simpler and more traditional—needs to be balanced against considerations of efficiencies of scale for the provision of services.

Other commentators argue that humans have a basic need for contact with nature and its spontaneous forms. Modern Japanese techno-cities, with their over-designed and chaos-free environments, along with social isolation of non-working spouses, have acquired a reputation for depressive illness and high suicide rates—the so-called "Tsukuba Syndrome."[19] The colour green, say psychologists, is the most soothing to the human psyche. In some of the heavily concreted high-rise housing estates of big cities, the only blades of grass visible are those that penetrate the cracks in the concourse. Cities that sprawl unrelentingly to the horizon, that lack parks and gardens, that do not plant street trees, and that provide no ready public transport for the poor are environments in which nature is neither much known about nor experienced. In such environments children think that apples grow in supermarkets. For such reasons, there is increasing advocacy for planting "edible landscapes" in cities. This has been done in the city of Davis, California, where market gardens and vineyards within housing developments and fruit trees within the adjoining public spaces now produce more food than when those areas were plain farmland. In many large African cities, the slums and shanty towns are being "greened" as people recreate, on slivers of land, microcosms of village agriculture. Around the world, the ancient urge to garden, to grow food and to get dirt under the finger-nails still finds many and varied outlets for city-dwellers. That urge would be (partially) met by restoring greenery and localised food-production to city life.

Urban Villages

There is a growing consensus among city planners that an ecologically sound approach to urban planning will require greater population density, clearer community identity, green areas, and better transit, biking and walking areas. Car dependence increases sharply as population density decreases below around 30 people per hectare of urban land. There are other positive reasons for increasing the density in urban areas, including the fact that sprawl is very costly and that, as an area ages, its older people need options for smaller, closer housing.

One very productive way of achieving density increases is by building semi-detached "urban villages," each with integrated high-density mixed land use. This enhances sustainability because it facilitates greater local self-sufficiency, and thus shorter trips with more walking and biking. Research in Australia has shown that if urban villages became the basis for city development then at least a 20% per-person reduction in greenhouse gases could be achieved by 2021, saving $5.5 billion in infrastructure costs for the government, with extensive light-rail and traffic calming paid for out of reallocated road funds. Additional savings would be achieved in reduced road accidents, noise and smog costs.[20]

The urban village concept has so far largely been confined to European city-planning, but it is now increasingly on the social agenda in car-based cities in North America and Australia. Existing examples may not yet be very radical, but they provide something that is more integrated, less car-dependent and more oriented to the "urban commons" than standard low-density, privatised suburbia. Says Newman: "They reach back to the roots of how cities first began with a mutual co-operation and sharing that enables diversity to be achieved in human activity. They provide a model for us in cities that have lost their way ecologically and socially because of a total orientation towards optimising life for private needs and neglecting the public good or urban commons."[16]

Summary

Villages, towns and cities are a natural expression of human sociability, skills, hopes and fears. Over thousands of years, they have played the pivotal political and cultural role in agrarian and industrial populations. However, cities have become the locus of a new generation of ecological, demographic and political problems. An increasing proportion of the world's expanding population, particularly in poor countries, is living in cities. Fertility rates in the Third World urban poor are high. Much of the in-migration reflects the decline of rural life; ecological disruption and environmental disasters are likely to increase the move to the cities. By the year 2000, half of the world's population will live in cities. By early next century, various large cities in India, Latin America and elsewhere will contain 20–30 million people.

Three-quarters of the cities that contain more than 5 million people are in developing countries. In these cities there are an estimated 100 million homeless adults and perhaps as many as 80 million homeless and, in many cases, abandoned children. Although the *average* level of health has usually been better in cities than in rural areas, there are stark contrasts in health within those expanding urban populations, many of which are now seriously outstripping the urban infrastructural capacity. Overall, one in four people in these Third World cities lack safe water and over one-third of city-dwellers lack access to sanitation. The figures are much higher in the slums, where diarrhoeal disease is consequently rife— and continues to kill vast numbers of young children. In many of these cities, air pollution has now become a much graver public health problem than it is in rich countries.

Very large cities are a recent, unplanned experiment in human ecology. The sheer scale, rapidity of growth, and the dimensions of poverty, misery and poor health now evident in many Third World cities raise basic questions about the sustainable healthy forms of urban social organisation. The fact that infectious diseases thrive on urban populations has been underscored by recent surges in cholera, tuberculosis (the world's major killer infectious disease), AIDS and other sexually transmitted diseases. In addition to their immediate physical influences upon population health, cities distance urban-dwellers from the rhythms of nature, potentiate industrial expansion and encroach on and violate local ecosystems. Humans have never before tried living in cities with populations of several tens of millions of people. Such cities are rapidly becoming a spectacular, but formidable, social and ecological experiment.

References

1. WHO. Environmental Health in Urban Development. WHO Technical Report Series, No. 807. Geneva: WHO, 1991.
2. McNeill WH. *Plagues and Peoples.* Anchor Doubleday: New York, 1976.
3. UN Department of International Economic and Social Affairs. *World Urbanization Prospects 1990.* New York: United Nations, 1991.
4. Despite the dramatic megacity statistics mentioned above, most of the urban-dwellers of Africa, Latin America and Asia live in smaller cities—many of them less than 100,000 persons. (Large cities require a powerful economy to sustain them, and in some poor countries, lacking export income, there has been little urbanisation.) Meanwhile, the most common type of human settlement is the rural village, with between 10 and 10,000 people. In India, in 1980, 98% of all settlements were villages with less than 5,000 inhabitants.
5. WHO. Urbanization and health in developing countries. The urban crisis. *World Health Statistics Quarterly* 1991; 44: 189–97.
6. Jensen L. Developing countries begin grappling with urban woes. *World Development* 1988; 1(4): 4–8.
7. Report of Urbanization Panel, WHO Commission on Health and Environment. WCHE/URB/2/8. Geneva: WHO, 1992.
8. Harpham T, Stephens C. Urbanization and health in developing countries. *World Health Statistics Quarterly* 1991; 44: 62–9.
9. Tabibzadeh I, Rossi-Espagnet A, Maxwell R. *Spotlight on the Cities: Improving Urban Health in Developing Countries.* Geneva: WHO, 1989.
10. WHO. *Urbanization and its Implications for Child Health: Potential for Action.* Geneva: WHO, 1988.
11. Williams BT. Assessing the health impact of urbanization. *World Health Statistics Quarterly.* 1990; 43: 145–52.
12. Harpham T, Lusty T, Vaughan P (eds). *In the Shadow of the City: Community Health and the Urban Poor.* Oxford: Oxford University Press, 1988.
13. Victoria CG *et al.* Water supply, sanitation and housing in relation to the risk of infant mortality from diarrhoea. *International Journal of Epidemiology* 1988; 17: 651–4.
14. WHO Commission on Health and Environment. *Our Planet, Our Health.* Geneva: WHO, 1992.
15. In 1991 I visited Banjul, the capital of The Gambia in West Africa, on the edge of the Sahel. Ten years earlier, at the beginning of the UN's Water and Sanitation Decade (see chapter 8), the government had torn up the old sealed roads in order to put in a sewer system. The installation is still proceeding, at a very West African pace. Meanwhile, the pit latrines and open drains dominate the olefactory landscape—and the dry read dust, liberated from beneath the old roadway bitumen, blows everywhere.

16. Newman PWG. *Sustainable cities: International and Australian progress.* Proceedings of EcoCity Conference, Adelaide, April 1992.
17. Goldsmith E *et al.* (eds). *A Blueprint for Survival.* Boston: Houghton Mifflin, 1972.
18. Wilmott P. *Community Initiatives, Patterns and Prospects.* London: Policy Studies Institute, 1989.
19. Sonoda K. *Health and Illness in Changing Japanese Society.* Tokyo: University of Tokyo Press, 1988.
20. McGlynn G, Newman PWG, Kenworthy JR. *Towards Better Cities: Reurbanisation and Transport Energy Scenarios.* Melbourne: Australian Commission for the Future, 1991.

Study Questions

1. What is the structural relationship between urbanization and health? Give some specific examples of this connection.

2. How does being a rich or poor nation affect things like health, urbanization, and the environment? Be specific.

Reading 41
The Social Ecology of Skid Row

John W. Bardo
Jeffrey W. Riemer
Ronald R. Matson
Robert K. Knapp

Introduction

Since the early days of the Chicago School, human ecologists, urban sociologists, and deviance specialists have emphasized social structures and life-styles of inhabitants in the "zone in transition," or "moral zone" located near U.S. central business districts. Classic studies such as Zorbaugh's *Gold Coast and the Slum* (1929), Reckless' "Distribution of Commercialized Vice in Chicago" (1926), Thrasher's *The Gang* (1929), Anderson's *The Hobo* (1923), and Cressey's *The Taxi Dancehall* (1932) all portray the deviant aspects of life in the run-down central city slums. More recent studies, such as Suttles' *Social Order of the Slum* (1967), Rainwater's *Behind Ghetto Walls* (1970), Gans' *The Urban Villagers* (1962), and Liebow's *Tally's Corner* (1967), have stressed the significance of slum life as an adaptation to social structural conditions. The poor and other inhabitants of central city slums are seen not within a perjorative, deviance framework but more in relation to their adaptations to such situations as economic and social marginality, discrimination, and harassment by legal authorities such as the justice system or urban renewal.

This paper reports the results of an application of a sociological-ecological approach to a study of an urban skid row area. Specifically a sociocultural ecological model is applied to the problem of possibly relocating homeless men who inhabit a blighted area immediately adjacent to a mid-western city's central business district.

Defining Skid Row

Sociological studies have generally employed one of two orientations in defining the concept of skid row: it is seen either as a natural area, in the ecological sense, or as a style of life, without geographic boundaries, typical of certain deviant groups.

Ecologically, skid row areas have been typically portrayed as bounded neighborhoods that provide needed institutional services and facilities to inhabitants. Bahr (1973) suggests that cheap hotels and lodging houses, gospel missions, and bars are three necessary elements that "when they appear in close proximity, indelibly mark a neighborhood as a skid row" (p. 123). Other supplementary institutions mentioned by Bahr include the following:

> restaurants, liquor stores, secondhand stores and thrift shops, pawnshops, junk yards, public parks, barber colleges, all night movies, public libraries, banks . . . hospitals, . . . and small grocery stores. (p. 148)

When agents of social control concern themselves with a skid row area they typically focus on these facilities and their run-down condition. Wiseman (1970) offers a listing of common terms used by professionals to describe the condition of these facilities: "below code," "deteriorated property," "dilapidated structures," "blighted zone," "detrimental land use," and "firetraps" (p. 5).

These unattractive physical conditions are easily linked to the essential character of the inhabitants. According to Wiseman (1970),

> studies that speak of stench, degrading social conditions, and urban blight also describe . . . the residents as depressed, down and out, apathetic, mentally and physically ill, the dregs of society, having a dependency problem, lacking in religious belief, needing counseling and psychic support, needing rehabilitation, requiring institutional care, discouraged and frustrated. (p. 6)

Culturally, skid row has been portrayed as a unique urban subcommunity. Wallace (1965) defines skid row as "an isolated and deviant subcultural community expressing the features of a distinct and recognizable way of life" (p. 96). The proponents of the approach suggest that skid row members are trapped in their life-style by virtue of being stigmatized by outsiders (and themselves) as undesirable. To use Goffman's (1963) term they are a "discredited" community.

Blumberg, Shipley, and Moor (1971) suggest that urban areas not referred to as skid row also harbor persons with the same social characteristics. They suggest that skid row is really a human condition and not a place. Similarly, Spradley (1970) argues that "the institutions which seek to control and punish these men for living as urban nomads actually draw them into this world and keep them there" (p. 253). Bahr (1973) also argues this way when he suggests that

> the primary problem of the skid row man is not alcoholism. Nor is it advanced age, physical disability and moral inferiority. Instead, the primary problem is that the combined weight of stigmatization which accompanies many different kinds of human defectiveness is focused upon a few men in a distinctive neighborhood. (p. 287)

In both of these definitions it is clear that the residents of skid row are considered deviant. In the former skid row is a locale; in the latter it is a way of life. In this study skid row is defined as the nexus of these two traditional positions: a geographical area, a natural area where the residents exhibit a life-style that is defined as deviant by the dominant society. What is highlighted in the literature on skid row renewal is a perception of skid row members as objectionable persons who need to be rehabilitated (Vander Kooi, 1973).

Methods

This research was conducted in a middle-sized midwestern city, with a population of approximately 250,000. Skid row in this city is located immediately east of the downtown along a three-block section of the major east-west thoroughfare. The city's urban renewal agency and the local downtown development corporation had decided to rehabilitate this section by upgrading the businesses and buildings on the north side of the street and constructing a park, a convention center, and major hotel on the south side. In addition, an old hotel, which at the time housed transients, was to be upgraded as a support facility for the convention center. (At the time these data were collected only the park had been constructed, and a building previously used by the Salvation Army had been acquired.)

A team of sociologists was hired by the urban renewal agency to determine (1) the nature of the population on skid row, (2) where skid row members might be relocated, (3) probable areas to which skid row residents would gravitate in the event of nonrelocation, and (4) ways in which this relocation could be implemented. The research design used to determine probable outcomes of renovation of this area included both fieldwork and ecological analyses.

Life-style data were generated using standard field research techniques including informal semistructured interviews and observation. Interview schedules were devised and committed to memory by field interviewers. Respondents interviewed included a number of transients, Salvation Army employees, residents, shopkeepers, and police, as well as public and private social service workers. Field notes were not usually taken during the interview in an effort to minimize expected difficulties in obtaining responses but were completed immediately following each interview period. Observations were conducted in and around the skid row area to determine space utilization and locational structure and to obtain a feel for the geist (spirit) of the area. Observational data were also noted immediately following observation periods.

Observations and interviews centered on the following:

1. the life patterns of the various groups living around the skid row area;
2. the services needed by and the services provided to these groups;
3. the locational needs of the individuals based on their own life-styles;
4. the responses of these persons to dislocation;
5. the likely ways in which successful relocation of the target population might be conducted; and
6. an estimation of the size of the target population in the skid row area.

Most observations were made in the early spring, and it is therefore probable that perceptions of the size of the population may have been affected by the recency of the winter months. Additionally, it had been a hard winter so movement of the population may have been suppressed.

As a means of testing the validity of the field research design several teams of researchers collected data independently. On completion of the fieldwork, each team was debriefed and their conclusions compared for consistency. Results obtained revealed no major inconsistencies or issues of conflict, so results were accepted as valid.

The ecological analysis portion of this research involved close examination of land use patterns (Firey, 1937; Jonassen, 1949; Michelson, 1976; Seeley, 1956; Jacobs, 1961; Young and Willmott, 1957; Gans, 1962, 1967) in the central area of the city; this area covered approximately 20 square miles.

Individual plot maps were obtained for the targeted area and were analyzed for specific land use patterns and location relative to significant ecological structures typifying the skid row area. All locations not possessing ecological characteristics similar to the skid row area were eliminated; remaining locations were retained for further analysis as potential sites for skid row relocation.

Using the plot maps of the skid row area, the ecological territory of the local transient group was mapped according to location of significant institutions. Remaining areas were then compared by apparent structure, by plot, and by site visit to determine possible alternative locations. Finally, areas were analyzed according to sociodemographic and ecological structure-specific variables to ensure comparability.

Findings

Data generated during field research revealed that skid row is the habitat for many significant groups and organizations, and each group plays a significant role in skid row's functioning. The most important of these identifiable clusters of people and organizations are merchants, police, service organizations, and the skid row residents.

Merchants

Merchants (operators of pawnshops, taverns, liquor stores, clothing stores, restaurants, hotels, etc.) on skid row do a limited business with persons in the skid row population. The liquor store, secondhand clothing stores, and taverns in the area do the most business. In general, the merchants expressed a tolerant acceptance of the members of the local population saying that "they don't cause much trouble." Any trouble is easily handled by a call to the police.

Merchants' estimations of the skid row population's size range from 10 to 200. Most merchants believed renewal of the area would encourage the local population to stay and increase the likelihood that more like them would come to the city. One merchant, when asked if the transients were leaving the area, responded, "Why should they? Urban renewal came in and built them nice benches to lie on. They built a beautiful park for them to sleep in."

Merchants in the area were also concerned about the new, period, old-fashioned street lamps, which provide far less light than the modern, high-intensity ones that they replaced. One merchant had his front window broken and merchandise stolen the first night the new lights were used.

In general, the merchants were tolerant of the skid row residents, were skeptical of the consequences urban renewal would have on the area, and did not think that the skid row members would relocate or that their numbers would decline.

Police

The police officers who worked the skid row area were tolerant of the local population. Police tended to view the members more as an eyesore than a real problem. Keeping the peace rather than enforcing the law appeared to be their approach (see Bittner, 1967).

The police gave estimates of the total population on the street (about 100) similar to those given by the merchants. They also thought it unlikely that the skid row residents would move and thought that they needed very little to survive on the street. The police were not aware of any movement by residents to other parts of the city because of changes in the area.

All the officers contended that young people are more of a problem in the area than the residents. (Teenagers tend to use this area for their local weekend "dragging" and drinking sprees.) The police expect that as the area becomes renovated there will be more trouble and more calls to make. Calls in the area made by the police were usually of the nuisance type or involved only minor problems. One officer thought that any attempt to improve the area would achieve only cosmetic results and not involve any real change in social structure.

Service Organizations

The main organizations in the skid row area that provide some service to transients include the mission, the detoxification center, and a day labor personnel recruitment office.

The mission does not cater to the hard-core problem drinkers. Rather it provides clothing, food, shelter, and religious education to persons passing through the city and to a few poor men in need of food at the end of each month who have overextended their social security or other pension checks. On average, about 15 persons sleep in the mission each night.

The detoxification center provides food and shelter for problem drinkers, and it is the major service facility for the hard-core members of the skid row area. The center handles between 18 and 25 persons a night with highest attendance during the last two weeks of the month.

The personnel office offers temporary work opportunities to the residents. Day labor provides an opportunity for residents to quickly obtain a small amount of money; current policy allows a worker to draw $8 at the end of the day against his paycheck thus allowing some money for a drink, a little food, and possibly a room. Hard-core skid row residents rarely use the personnel office; it is mainly used by transients who also make their homes on skid row for the short period they are in town.

In general, the various service organizations in the skid row area believed that the skid row population was not going to relocate because of urban renewal efforts and portrayed the residents as a collection of various diverse subgroups.

A Taxonomy of the Skid Row Population

Our research suggests that the population of this skid row area is composed of two major groupings: locals and true transients. The local group, however, can be divided into several significant subcategories.

Locals

The locals were the more stable members of the area. The size of the total group varied with the time of year, available work, and the extent of their individual life problems. This group is best understood by focusing on the four major subgroups making up the larger group.

Young Locals

The young locals numbered approximately 70–100 persons at any one time. They ranged in age from 20 to 40 years, typically had drinking problems, worked intermittently, lived in cheap housing in the area, and would, given prevailing circumstances, either become more or less a part of the skid row subculture. Their age gave them some flexibility to control their fate. However, it is this group that would eventually become the hard-core local group.

Old Hard-Core Locals

This was the focal group in the skid row area. Many of the members had lived in this area for most of their lives and some had relatives in the city or nearby towns. They numbered only 10–15 persons but were highly visible because they lived on the street. All had serious drinking problems. In addition, they were ill, extremely poor, and old. Most were older than 60, and some were in their 70s.

Intermittent Older Locals

This group strayed in and out of the core local population. Although older, some members were still mobile and traveled around the country usually by riding freight trains or hitch hiking. They still considered this skid row area their home territory and had strong friendships with the hard-core locals. (Some even wrote letters in care of general delivery when traveling.) This subgroup numbered from 15 to 20 persons. They were characterized by serious drinking problems and poor health. These men received some money from social security and pensions, and they became highly visible through living on the street when in town.

Intermittent Locals

This group fell in between the local and transient. They spent more than a few days in the city, and some would try to set down roots. Numbering from 20 to 40, they usually had drinking problems, lived in cheap housing, were poor and relatively young, but were also relatively mobile.

Transients

This group lived only a short time in the city; they were just "passing through." They would avail themselves of the local facilities for a short period and then leave. This group often included families (husband and wife with children). Transients were usually poor but also included some of the middle-class youth who were hitchhiking and backpacking across the country. This was the least stable of the groups in skid row.

Salvation Army Resident Center

Although the Salvation Army had been relocated to an area several miles away on the northern edge of the city it had played an important role in skid row life. At the time of the study the center provided long-term housing and meals for persons who conformed to the program. To fit into the program was to stay sober and typically to work for the Salvation Army in some capacity. A common job was to work on the trucks or on the material docks. The level of group solidarity was quite high, and the residents clearly distinguished between themselves and the derelicts, as well as between themselves and transients. Transients were persons in transit, whose stay at the center was usually very brief.

The SA bus took residents to their job sites each morning and returned them to the center in time for the evening meal. The returning bus might also bring transients to the center. The number of such transients fluctuated, peaking during bad weather, with minor peaks occurring on weekends. During midweek in good weather, only one transient might be among the returning residents; on a chilly Friday, as many as 15 transients might come to the center. Clearly, the transient group (an entity distinct from the skid row derelicts) represented a minority among center residents, a group as large as 50 persons. The center was not highly regimented, so no one seemed to know exactly how many beds were occupied at any given time. There was also an outflow from the center, again depending on weather, job availability, and idiosyncratic factors.

In sum, the center met the needs of a fairly large and diverse group of persons for whom it was home. There was a certain pride in being a member of the center family. This pride stemmed in part from the resident's awareness of fitting the program. (To get drunk was to risk expulsion from the program.) There were complaints expressed by some, but no one problem was severe enough to produce flight from the center. These persons might have disaffiliated from contemporary society, but most had clearly (and somewhat contentedly) affiliated with the Salvation Army program. So, although previous relationship to skid row was altered by urban renewal, the Salvation Army program relocated its constituent population and maintained its major functions.

Ecological Structure of Skid Row

The primary territory inhabited by the skid row residents spanned a six-block area adjacent to the central business district and along a major east-west thoroughfare. The most significant characteristics of this area included (1) a liquor store on a corner of the main street, (2) a detoxification center on the northern edge of the area, (3) alleys honeycombing the area, (4) a "drinking tree" at a railroad overpass and main street, and (5) an alley on the south side of the main street and a large hotel.

Locals spent most of their time near the main street in the alleys, on the park benches, and by the drinking tree. Those people, many of whom did not have rooms, slept in doorways, alleys, behind buildings, under loading docks, or in abandoned warehouses. The remainder of the territory was traversed to reach the detoxification center and a local food store.

For the locals, skid row was a relatively compact area encompassing only a few square blocks. It provided shelter, liquor, access to food, and, the very important factor, easy access to downtown. For the transients who inhabited the skid row area, its territory was not so circumscribed. Transients found skid row a convenient place to find cheap lodging, and it also provided easy access to day labor in the center city. Ecologically, it was the caliber of the hotels in the area and the nearness to the center city that were significant. Use of space other than hotels and center city did not appear as consistent for transients as for locals. This resulted from two conditions: (1) transients' life-styles did not permit them to be as committed to a particular area and (2) location in skid row was more a matter of convenience than design. Because transients resided in the city for only a short time they did not establish the ties to the skid row manifested by locals. Transients sought out skid row because its location provided them with access to the center city, which supported their life-style, and low-cost lodging.

Discussion

The data presented above suggest that life-style diversity and differences in territoriality among skid row residents would result in several diverse movements of people if urban renewal were to occur as planned. First, upgrading or demolition of cheap accommodations in skid row would probably remove most transients from the area. They would either leave the city or seek lodging in another location. (Other transients moving through the city after renewal would also have to seek lodging elsewhere in low-cost accommodation.) Locals, conversely, because of their ties to the locale and because of their use of specific facilities in skid row (e.g. the liquor store, a specific food market, detoxification center, the drinking tree, the park benches, and the railroad overpass) were found to more likely hold on to the skid row locale.

We find that a socioculture ecological model can provide important insights into the probable effects of urban renewal of a skid row area. Applying this model to a particular skid row has shown a possible explanation for apparently conflicting findings in previous research on skid row renewal. Vander Kooi (1973) argues that skid row renewal results in the dispersion of the population; Bloomberg and co-workers (1978) show that it is possible for skid row to relocate. What this current study suggests is that the probable outcomes of skid row renewal depend on several factors including (1) the nature of the renewal project, (2) its location relative to the territory defined and used by skid row residents, (3) the types of people who inhabit skid row and the diversity of their life-styles and territorial definitions, and (4) the availability of areas likely to become skid rows in other parts of the city.

It would be expected, for instance, that if most skid row residents consisted of a diverse and amorphous grouping of transients with little affinity for the specific territory they occupied, renewal would result in their dispersion to other low-rent areas. On the other hand, local populations who are tied to the skid row neighborhood would probably not relocate or would move only a short distance depending upon the degree to which urban renewal disrupted their territory. Only if their entire territory were renewed and no new skid row areas existed, would it be likely for locals to scatter rather than relocate. Because their use of space can be seen as being governed both by the location of institutions and sentimental attachment to a local area and certain people, dispersion would not be a likely outcome.

References

Anderson, Nels
    1923   The Hobo. Chicago: University of Chicago Press.
Bahr, Howard M.
    1973   Skid Row. New York: Oxford University Press.
Bittner, Egon
    1967   "The police on skid row: A study of peace keeping." American Sociological Review 32 (October):699–715.
Blumberg, Leonard U., Thomas Shipley, Jr., and Joseph Moor, Jr.
    1971   "The skid row man and the skid row status community." Quarterly Journal of Studies on Alcohol 32 (December):909–929.
Blumberg, Leonard U., Thomas E. Shipley, Jr., and Stephen F. Barsky
    1978   Liquor and Poverty: Skid Row as a Human Condition. New Brunswick, N.J.: Rutgers Center of Alcohol Studies.
Cressey, Paul G.
    1932   The Taxi Dancehall. Chicago: University of Chicago Press.

Firey, Walter
    1937   Land Use in Central Boston. Cambridge, Mass.: Harvard University Press.
Gans, Herbert
    1962   The Urban Villagers. New York: Free Press.
    1967   The Levittowners. New York: Pantheon Books.
Goffman, Erving
    1963   Stigma. Englewood Cliffs, N.J.: Prentice-Hall.
Jacobs, Jane
    1961   The Life and Death of Great American Cities. New York: Random House.
Jonassen, Christen T.
    1949   "Cultural variables in the ecology of an ethnic group." American Sociological
            Review 14:32–41.
Liebow, Elliot
    1967   Tally's Corner. Boston: Little, Brown and Company.
Michelson, William
    1976   Man and His Urban Environment. Reading, MA: Addison Wesley.
Rainwater, Lee
    1970   Behind Ghetto Walls. Chicago: Aldine.
Reckless, Walter C.
    1926   "The distribution of commercialized vice in Chicago." Publications of the
            American Sociological Society 20:164–176.
Seeley, John, Alexander Sim, and E. W. Loosley
    1956   Crestwood Heights. New York: Basic Books.
Spradley, James P.
    1970   You Owe Yourself a Drunk. Boston: Little, Brown and Company.
Suttles, Gerald
    1967   The Social Order of the Slum. Chicago: University of Chicago Press.
Thrasher, Frederick
    1929   The Gang. Chicago: University of Chicago Press.
Vander Kooi, Ronald
    1973   "The main stem: Skid row revisited." Society 10:64–71.
Wallace, Samuel E.
    1965   Skid Row as a Way of Life. New York: Harper & Row.
Wiseman, Jacqueline
    1970   Stations of the Lost: The Treatment of Skid Row Alcoholics. Englewood
            Cliffs, N.J.: Prentice-Hall.
Young, Michael, and Peter Willmott
    1957   Family and Kinship in East London. Baltimore: Penguin.
Zorbaugh, Harvey
    1929   Gold Coast and the Slum. Chicago: University of Chicago Press.

Study Questions

1. What do the authors mean by "social ecology"? List some of the
   parts of this ecology.
2. What types of residents live on skid row? Is transience a social problem? Why or why not?

Reading 42
Silent Spill

Thomas D. Beamish

Underneath the Guadalupe Dunes—a windswept piece of wilderness[1] 170 miles north of Los Angeles and 250 miles south of San Francisco—sits the largest petroleum spill in US history. The spill emerged as a local issue in February 1990. Though not acknowledged, it was not unknown to oil workers at the field where it originated, to regulators that often visited the dunes, or to locals who frequented the beach. Until the mid 1980s, neither the oily sheen that often appeared on the beach, on the ocean, and the nearby Santa Maria River nor the strong petroleum odors that regularly emanated from the Unocal Corporation's oil-field operations raised much concern. Recognition, as in the frog parable, was slow to manifest. The result of leaks and spills that accumulated slowly and chronically over 38 years, the Guadalupe Dunes spill became troubling when local residents, government regulators, and a whistleblower who worked the field no longer viewed the periodic sight and smell of petroleum as normal.

The specific intent of this book is to relate how the change in perception took place, why it took nearly 40 years for the spill to become an agenda item (Crenson 1971), and why the response was controversial. The premise of the book is that social and institutional preoccupation with the "acute" and the "traumatic" has left us passive and unresponsive to festering problems. I begin with a general description of what locals have dubbed "the silent spill" (Bondy 1994).

I first heard of the Guadalupe spill on local television news in August 1995. (My home was 65 miles from the spill site.) The scene included a sandy beach, enormous earth-moving machinery, a hard-hatted Unocal official, and a reporter, microphone in hand, asking the official how things were proceeding. The interplay of the news coverage and Unocal's official response [was what] caught my attention more than anything else. The representative asserted that Unocal had extracted 500,000 gallons of petroleum from a large excavated pit on the beach just in view of the camera. The newscaster ended the segment by saying (I paraphrase) "It's nice that Unocal is taking responsibility to get things under control." This offhand remark about responsibility set me to thinking about the long-term nature of the spill and about why it had not been stopped sooner, either by Unocal managers or by regulators.

A few months later, a colleague and I drove to the beach. My colleague, a geologist who was familiar with the area, had suggested that we visit the Guadalupe Dunes for their scenic beauty. We walked the beach and the dunes that border the oil field, alert for signs of the massive spill. The pit that Unocal had recently excavated had been filled in. The only hint of the project that remained was a small crew that was driving pilings into the sand to support a steel wall intended to stop hydrocarbon drift (movement of oil on top of groundwater) and the advancing Santa Maria River, which threatened to cut into an underground petroleum plume and send millions more gallons into the ocean.

Unocal security personnel followed along the beach, watching suspiciously as we took pictures. In fact, the spill was so difficult to perceive (only periodically does the beach smell of petroleum and the ocean have rainbow oil stains) that my impressions wavered. Was this really a calamitous event? The whole visit was imbued with the paradox of beauty and travesty.

Under my feet was the largest oil spill in California, and most likely the largest in US history. . . . There is still controversy over just how big this spill really is. . . . The estimates quoted most often by government personnel put the spill at 20 million gallons or more, which would make it the largest petroleum spill ever recorded in the United States.

At first glance, it seems strange that so many individuals and organizations missed the spillage[2] for so many years; "passivity" seems to be the word that best characterizes the personal and institutional mechanisms of identification and amelioration. It is also clear that the Guadalupe spill is very different from the image of petroleum spills that dominates media and policy prescriptions and the public mind: the iconographic spill of crude oil, complete with oiled birds and dying sea creatures.

The Guadalupe Dunes spill is only the largest *discovered* spill. Representing an inestimable number of similar cases, it exemplifies a genre of environmental catastrophe that portends ecological collapse.

Describing his impression of the spill in a 1996 interview, a resident of Orcutt, California, explained why he remained unsurprised by frequent diluent seeps: "When you grow up around it—the smell, the burning eyes while surfing, the slicks on the water—I didn't realize it could be a risk. It was normal to us." In a 1997 interview, a local fish and game warden—one of those initially responsible for the spill's investigation—responded this way to the question "Why did it take so long for the spill to be noticed?": "It is out of sight, it's out of mind. I can't see it from my back yard. It is down there in Guadalupe, I never go to Guadalupe. You know, I may have walked the beach one time, but I never saw anything. It smelled down there. What do you expect when there is an oil field? You know, you drive by an oil production site; you are bound to smell something. You are bound to."

In the days and weeks after my initial visit to the dunes, I wondered why the spill had gained so little notoriety. Beginning my research in earnest, I visited important players, attended meetings, took official tours of the site, and followed the accounts in the media.

What makes the Guadalupe spill so relevant is that it represents a genre—indeed a pandemic—of environmental crises (Glantz 1999). Collectively, problems of this sort—both environmental and non-environmental—exemplify what I term *crescive troubles.* According to the Oxford English Dictionary, "crescive" literally means "in the growing stage" and comes from the Latin root 'crescere', meaning to "to grow." 'Crescive' is used in the applied sciences to denote phenomena that accumulate gradually, becoming well established over time. In cases of such incremental and cumulative phenomena (particularly contamination events), identifying the "cause" of injuries sustained is often difficult if not impossible because of their long duration and the high number of intervening factors.[3] Applied to a more inclusive set of social problems, the idea of crescive troubles also conveys the human tendency to avoid dealing with problems as they accumulate. We often overlook slow-onset, long-term problems until they manifest as acute traumas and/or accidents (Hewitt 1983; Turner 1978).

There are also important political dimensions to the conception of crescive troubles. Molotch (1970), in his analysis of an earlier and more infamous oil spill on the central coast of California (the 1969 Santa Barbara spill), relates a set of points that resonate with my discussion. In that article, Molotch examines how the big oil companies and the Nixon administration "mobilized bias" to diffuse local opposition, disorient dissenters, and limit the political ramifications of the Santa Barbara spill. Two of his ideas have special relevance: that of the *creeping event* and that of the *routinization of evil*. A creeping event is one "arraigned to occur at an inconspicuously gradual and piecemeal pace" that in so doing diffuses consequences that would otherwise "follow from the event if it were to be perceived all at once" (ibid., p. 139). Although Molotch is describing the manipulation of information for political purposes, his account of attention thresholds and of the consequences that the "dribbling out of an event" can have on popular mobilization resonates with both the "real" incident (i.e., the leaks themselves) and the "political" incident (the court case, the media coverage, etc.) that unfolded at the Guadalupe Dunes. Molotch's idea of the routinization of evil pertains to naturalization processes whereby an issue takes on the quality of an expected event and in so doing loses urgency. (What is one more oil leak if oil leakage is the norm?)

Our preoccupation with immediate cause and effect works against recognizing and remedying problems in many ways. It is mirrored in the way society addresses the origin of a problem and in the way powerful institutional actors seek to nullify resistance and diffuse responsibility. The courts and the news media, for instance, often disregard the underlying circumstances that led to many current industrial and environmental predicaments, focusing instead on individual operators who have erred and pinning the blame for accidents on their negligence (Perrow 1984; Vaughan 1996; Calhoun and Hiller 1988). Yet this ignores the systemic reasons why such problems emerge. In short, most if not all of our society's pressing social problems have long histories that predate their acknowledgment but are left to fester because they provide few of the signs that would predict response—for example, the drama associated with social disruption and immiseration.

Specific to pollution scenarios, in California 90 percent of marine oil pollution is attributable to unidentified, small, chronic petroleum releases that are neither investigated nor remedied. According to some experts, these smaller, less dramatic spills are "more severe than catastrophic [spills]" (Elliott 1999, p. 26). What is more, while legislation to stop dramatic tanker spills has halved the incidence of such spills off California, less dramatic spills on land continue unrestrained at 700 times the rate of tanker spills (Dinno 1999). Similarly, in 1980 the federal government officially listed 400,000 previously unacknowledged toxic waste sites across the United States; by 1988 the number had grown to more than 600,000. Of these, the Environmental Protection Agency has designated 888 as highly hazardous and in need of immediate attention; 19,000 others are under review (Edelstein 1988; Hanson 1998; Brown and Mikkelsen 1990; Brown 1980). Recent estimates put the number of US sites with dangerously polluted soil and groundwater alone at more than 300,000 and the annual projected cleanup bill at $9 billion (Gibbs 1999).

Another example may provide some clarity, conceptually connecting instances that at first glance may appear disparate and unrelated. More familiar, but just as crescive and troubling, is the increase in ultraviolet radiation due to deterioration of the ozone layer. This has been "collective knowledge" for some time. Many of us have altered our behavior. More important, however, we have expanded what is normal to us by accommodating this looming threat. Applying sunscreen or avoiding direct sunlight has become routine. This is not, however, a solution; it is a coping strategy.[4] Would many people passively accept ozone depletion if cancer were to manifest in days rather than years?

The inability of our current remedial systems, policy prescriptions, and personal orientations to address a host of pressing long-term environmental threats is frightening. There are, however, numerous examples of disconnected events—seemingly unrelated individual crises recognized after the fact—that have received widespread public attention. Through national media coverage, images of ruptured and rusting barrels of hazardous waste bearing the skull and crossbones have become icons that fill many Americans with dread (Szasz 1994; Erikson 1990, 1994). But these are only the end results of ongoing trends that have been repeated across the country with less dramatic consequences. In view of the startling deterioration of the biosphere, much of which is due to slow and cumulative processes, more attention should be devoted to how such scenarios unfold. That is precisely what I intend to do in this book, in which I reconstruct how the parties involved in the Guadalupe Dunes case understood and responded to the chronic leaks.

Social scientists across the spectrum of interests agree that human action and interpretation can be made meaningful only by relating them to their social contexts. Like more conventional sociological topics, oil spills (Clarke 1990, 1999), toxic contamination (Mazur 1998; Brown and Mikkelsen 1990; Levine 1982; Brown 1980), and conflicts over industrial siting (Couch and Kroll-Smith 1994; Freudenburg and Gramling 1994; Edelstein 1993, 1988) are cases in which the objectives of industry, government, and the community structure the interpretation of the event, the range of solutions entertained, and ultimately the solutions chosen. In a similar vein, I focus on the Guadalupe spill's social causes and social ramifications and on the social responses to it.

My specific intent is to uncover how and why the Guadalupe spill went unrecognized and was not responded to even though it occurred under unexceptional circumstances. The industrial conditions were quite normal, and the regulatory oversight was typical. It would seem that there was nothing out of the ordinary, other than millions of gallons of spilled petroleum. This is, in part, why the spill is so instructive. It represents a perceptual lacuna—a blank spot in our organizational and personal attentions.

My approach stands in marked contrast to conventional environmental assessment, where analysis starts with the "accident" itself (i.e., post hoc) and moves forward in time and where the emphasis is on quantifying the direct impacts a hazard has had or is predicted to have on a localized environment.[5] The Guadalupe spill was not an accident and was a long time in the making. Tracing knowledge of the leaks as they worsened but were overlooked, ignored, and then covered up sheds light on "how contemporary disasters depend upon the way 'normal everyday life turns out to have become abnormal, in a way that affects us all' " (Hewitt 1983, p. 29). To this end, I trace the *career of knowledge* of the spill through its social contexts: the oil field (the origin of the spill), the regulatory institutions, and the local community. In each location, the search is for answers to the pattern of non-response. Why didn't local managers report the seepage, as the law requires? How did field personnel understand their role? How could pollution of such an enormous magnitude be left so long before receiving official recognition and action? Why did the surrounding community take so long to react? . . .

Although sociological analysis of environmental phenomena is many times more widespread today than it once was, it continues to hold a peripheral position in mainstream environmental debates (MacNaghten and Urry 1995, p. 203). This is not to say that sociology or other social science work is unimportant. In fact, environmental concerns are a growing and increasingly important area within the social sciences. It is only to say that, in terms of "resources allocated, . . . the public visibility and acceptance of these works, and perhaps most of all . . . the attachment of this view to more powerful institutions of modern states" (Hewitt 1983, p. 4), the dominant paradigms concerning disaster, industrial crises, and environmentalism more generally lie in the physical sciences.

In a critique of the classical theories of sociology, Anthony Giddens (1990, p. 8) has gone so far as to assert that "ecological concerns do not brook large in the traditions of thought incorporated into sociology."[6] Historically, theorists of industrial societies, and before them theorists of agricultural societies, tacitly assumed the limitlessness of the environment and the limitlessness of human potential.[7] For instance, Marx (at least in his early writings) defined the human condition—particularly psychic health—in terms of man's ability to intentionally transform nature into the object of his desires (Marx 1974; McLellan 1977). Though Marx's insights into the contradictions inherent in capitalist systems of production and consumption are unrivaled, his attention to the industrial juggernaut's potential effects on the global ecological system was less than thorough or sustained. To Marx's credit, his writings, when painstakingly examined, do contain rudiments of what may be called environmental warnings (Dickens 1996; Foster 1999). For example, he developed a basic notion of soil nutrient depletion that he posited in large-scale industrial agricultural practice. Yet Marx and Engels articulated contradictory themes. On the one hand, Marx revealed the inherent contradictions that he felt would lead capitalism to destroy itself, of which agricultural soil depletion was just one manifestation. On the other hand, capitalism's inexorable global expansion meant that nothing in nature remained untouched. Nature, according to Marx, had become humanized. In view of current sentiments, this may seem to indicate that Marx and Engels were sincerely concerned with human domination of and penetration into everything "natural" (Merchant 1980). But that is not so. A strong component of Marx's writings was a theme that posits in the domination of "nature" the emancipation of human beings. Marx expressed the idea that a society that harnessed nature assured its members of freedom from the struggle to survive.

Durkheim touted an industrial age of interdependence and social fulfillment based on industrial expansion and division of labor. (See Durkheim 1984.) Moreover, Durkheim, with his early emphasis on explaining social phenomena exclusively by analyzing social facts by means of other social facts, actively eschewed the use of environmental factors to help explain human behavior. Until quite recently, sociology and social science more generally have, implicitly if not explicitly, advocated the idea that the human transformation of the environment was natural, unthreatening, even preferred. My point here is not to devalue the scholarship of

Marx and Durkheim or to imply that rereading them and applying what one learns from doing so is fruitless; it is only to point out the intellectual "Balkanization of knowledge" and to emphasize the theoretical hole that is only recently beginning to be filled (Buttel 1987).

Mainstream sociology's historical neglect of environmental problems reveals a proclivity to sense only immediate and sudden threats to our well being (social or environmental). Especially in circumstances of slow and incremental change, threatening changes are normalized because actors (corporate and individual) accommodate themselves to gradually evolving signs of crises. This proclivity is not limited to environmental matters. For instance, Diane Vaughan's argument in *The Challenger Launch Decision* (1996) rests largely on the idea of normative drift—i.e., the idea that organizational actors, while working together, developed routines that blinded them to the consequences of their actions. Through their continual iteration, incremental expansion of normative boundaries took place, and unanticipated consequences resulted. This incremental expansion not only habituated social actors to what were in retrospect deviant events; over time it also increased their tolerance for greater levels of deviation. "Small changes . . . gradually become the norm, providing a basis for accepting additional deviance." (ibid., p. 409)

The response a potential threat receives depends largely on its social salience. However, contrary to intuition, salience is not always something obvious or easy to identify. For example, surreptitious forms of contamination such as radiation hold very little tangible and immediate effect; however, they can evoke a great deal of dread and awareness.[8] They provoke as much fear as earthquakes, floods, fires, hurricanes, or tornadoes (Erikson 1994). The defining feature of a threat, then, is its social salience, which captures the perceptual impact of a hazard's biophysical attributes and/or its social construction.

Thus, the salience of a crisis need not be derived only from extrinsic characteristics (e.g., a sudden onset, a dramatic and immediate impact). Salience also derives from less direct mediating social factors—factors in which a nexus of circumstances, both material and ideational, magnify perceived impacts—for instance, when a potential hazard affects many people (or, more important, when it affects politically endowed stakeholders) (Bullard 1990; Hofrichter 1993); when government responds swiftly and unequivocally (Cable and Walsh 1991); when daily routines are disrupted by an event (Flacks 1988); or, perhaps most significant, when the media define a hazard as newsworthy by providing for its widespread dissemination and problematization (Cable and Walsh 1991; Stallings 1990; Molotch and Lester 1975). These are all conditions that contribute to an event's salience. A conjunction of some or all of these factors can give an event notoriety even if it lacks obvious and immediate impact.

Low in immediate and tangible impact but high in public awareness, the events that surrounded the malfunction of a reactor at the Three Mile Island nuclear power plant in Pennsylvania are instructive as an example of political and media construction of social salience in a case where biophysical attributes were almost completely absent. On the morning of March 28, 1979, one of the two reactors at the Three Mile Island facility partially melted down, releasing radioactive steam into the surrounding countryside (Erikson 1994; Cable and Walsh 1991). Urging residents to remain calm, the governor suggested that pregnant women and preschool children evacuate an area within 5 miles of the plant. He also advised pregnant women and preschool children within a 10-mile radius of the plant to stay inside their homes. Unexpectedly, 150,000 men, women, and children—45 times the number of people advised to do so—fled the area. Although the Three Mile Island incident lacked sufficient physical characteristics to impress local residents that something was wrong, it was quickly and unequivocally translated for them by regulators and other government officials. Moreover, extensive coverage in the national press lent it durability and drama that it otherwise may have lacked.[9]

At the other extreme is the 1989 *Exxon Valdez* tanker incident, in which an ocean-going oil tanker ran aground, disgorging as much as 10.8 million gallons of crude oil into Alaska's Prince William Sound. Though that accident occurred in a remote locale, it was sudden, obvious, and pictorially dramatic (Birkland 1998; Slater 1994; Clarke 1990). Its "media fit"—that is, its fulfilling the conventions of contemporary journalism (Gamson and Modigliani 1989; Wilkins 1987; Gans 1980)—also made it an extremely visible event. Virtually every major and minor news service in the nation carried copy and pictures as the story unfolded. And by disrupting the local commercial fishing industry, a crucial means of livelihood for the region, the event mobilized a group whose collective voice was hard for politicians to ignore.[10]

Industrial crises comparable to the *Exxon Valdez* and Three Mile Island debacles have gained widespread attention for similar reasons. The toxic contamination of Love Canal (Fowlkes and Miller 1982; Gibbs 1982; Levine 1982), the poisoning of the drinking water in Woburn (Harr 1995; Brown and Mikkelsen 1990), the abandonment of a dioxin-contaminated office building in Binghamton (Clarke 1989), and beaches turned black with crude oil near Santa Barbara (Molotch and Lester 1975; Easton 1972) are conspicuous examples of health-related crises that have garnered sustained attention from regulators and the public.

But lurking potential problems that currently lack extreme attributes, a convenient location, and an obvious beginning, and which do not lend themselves easily to media coverage, grow insidiously, getting little attention and rarely evoking an outcry. Pollution resulting from sea-bed disturbance, leakage of toxins from dumps, and deterioration of industrial infrastructure often present silent, slow, and creeping effects that accumulate incrementally over months, years, and decades, sometimes surfacing as catastrophes only after a long history of inattention and sometimes left entirely for future generations. Erikson (1991, p. 27) admonishes us to become aware of such phenomena and to act before it is too late:

> Incidents of the kind [toxic contamination] that have concerned us here are really no more than locations of unusual density, moments of unusual publicity, involving perils that are spread out more evenly over all the surface of the earth. An acute disaster offers us a distilled, concentrated look at something more chronic and widespread. . . . Sooner or later, then, the discussion will have to turn to broader concerns—the fact of radioactive wastes, with half-lives measured in thousands of years, will soon be implanted in the very body of the earth; that modern industry sprays toxic matter of the most extraordinary malignancy into the atmosphere; that poisons which cannot be destroyed or even diluted by the technologies responsible for them have become a permanent part of the natural world.

The reality that surrounds crescive circumstances is characterized by polluters who are unlikely to report the pollution they cause, authorities who are unlikely to recognize that there is a problem to be remedied, uninterested media, and researchers who take interest only if (or when) an event holds dramatic consequence.[11] In short, all those who are in positions to address crescive circumstances are disinclined to do so. Forms of degradation that lack direct and immediate impact on humans, dramatic images of dying wildlife, or other archetypal images of disaster tend to be downplayed, overlooked, and even ignored.

The national print media certainly mirrored the propensity to ignore the Guadalupe spill (Hart 1995). Over the period 1990–1996, the national press devoted 504 stories to the *Exxon Valdez* accident and only nine to the Guadalupe spill.[12]. . .

Insofar as the Guadalupe spill goes back 38 years, one is tempted to write off much of it as a vestige of a "pre-environmental" era in which corporations, the government, and individuals were not conscious that dumping and spilling were detrimental,[13] and that similar events will no longer occur because we are now aware of the consequences. Two points of fact contradict such thinking. First, the Guadalupe spill was evident for at least 20 years in a time when popular consciousness concerning environmental issues was high and environmental laws were in place.[14] Second, regulators were concerned with the conditions at the Guadalupe field as early as 1982, and perhaps earlier (Rites 1994; Paddock 1994a; Greene 1993a; Freisen 1993), but did not respond. We should expect similar incremental and cumulative environmental problems to continue to occur, even if environmentalism is rife. To be sure, negligence and criminal misconduct figure in the Guadalupe narrative, especially in the latter years. However, at least as important to the generation of destructive events is the interplay of selective perceptions, limited organizational attentions, personal stakes, and a propensity to accommodate socially and psychically low-intensity and non-extreme events.

Notes

1. The Guadalupe Dunes have been designated a National Natural Landmark. This designation, conferred by the US Secretary of the Interior, acknowledges the national significance of the dunes as a exceptional and rare ecosystem.

2. I use 'spill' to refer to the total accumulation of diluent—the end product. I use 'spillage', 'leaks', and 'leakage' to denote the process by which diluent was chronically lost over time, eventually becoming an enormous spill.

3. For analyses of cases of community contamination and the struggle to seek legal redress, see Calhoun and Hiller 1988; Brown and Mikkelsen 1990; Hawkins 1983.

4. This is also very similar to what the medical establishment refers to as "postponement behavior." As used by medical practitioners, that term refers to patients' resistance to modifying their behavior(s) in the face of incrementally deteriorating health. (Examples include diabetics who will not restrict their eating habits and smokers who continue to smoke.)

5. Both Turner (1978, pp. 81–125) and Hewitt (1983, pp. 3–29) identify this proclivity to ignore what Turner refers to as the "incubation stage" of industrial crises.

6. Giddens has fallen prey to a related critique of his own work. He has been faulted for excessive social-constructionist tendencies. Though he has attended to ecological crises as both a defining feature of "high modernity" as well as a significant problem that confronts us all, he does so almost exclusively from the vantage point of discourse. Giddens goes so far as to claim that nature has ceased to exist as a category external

to human social life. The problem relates to the obvious contradiction that this implies: If nature no longer exists, why then are ecological "ills" a threat, aside from the social anxiety they may produce? It would seem, then, that from Giddens's perspective all we need do is convince ourselves that they are not occurring! (See Dickens 1996, p. 41.)

7. On the entrenchment of the "human exceptionalist paradigm" in the social science and in Western society in general, see Dunlap and Catton 1979 and Dunlap 2000.
8. On "invisible" contaminants and their ability to "traumatize," see Vyner 1988.
9. A Hollywood movie titled *The China Syndrome*, released 2 weeks before the event at Three Mile Island, played a part in popularizing nuclear issues and fears.
10. For instance, on the West Coast the Pacific Coast Federation of Fishermen's Association is a very powerful lobby. This group lobbies state legislatures from California to Alaska, as well as the US Congress, on the behalf of sport fishermen and commercial fishing interests. Another lobby, more local to Alaska, is Cordova District Fishermen United, an influential political player in Alaska resource policy.
11. I am as guilty of this as anyone. I did not become aware of the Guadalupe spill until the local news media reported that 500,000 gallons of petroleum had been recovered by Unocal.
12. For the national search, I used the University of California's MELVYL news database, which looks for words used in headlines. Five leading US newspapers are indexed: the *New York Times*, the *Los Angeles Times*, the *Washington Post*, the *Christian Science Monitor*, and the *Wall Street Journal*. I searched headlines for mentions of "*Exxon Valdez* Spill" and "Guadalupe Spill." Because the search turned up so few Guadalupe Spill articles, I then searched for "Unocal Oil Spills" and "California Oil Spills" (and various synonyms), finding three more stories.
13. Compare Mazur 1998.
14. Especially in a region where oil and environmentalism do not mix.

References

Birkland, T. 1998. "In the Wake of the *Exxon Valdez:* How Environmental Disasters Influence Policy." *Environment* 40, no. 7: 4–9, 27–32.

Bondy, C. 1994. "Guadalupe Isn't the First." *San Luis Obispo New Times*, February 23.

Brown, M. 1980. *Laying Waste: The Poisoning of America by Toxic Chemicals*. Pantheon.

Brown, P., and E. Mikkelsen. 1990. *No Safe Place: Toxic Waste, Leukemia, and Community Action*. University of California Press.

Bullard, R. 1990. *Dumping in Dixie: Race, Class, and Environmental Quality*. Westview.

Buttel, E. 1987. "New Directions for Environmental Sociology." *Annual Review of Sociology* 13: 465–488.

Cable, S., and E. Walsh. 1991. "The Emergence of Environmental Protest: Yellow Creek and TMI Compared." In *Communities at Risk*, ed. S. Couch and S. Kroll-Smith. Lang.

Calhoun, G., and H. Hiller. 1988. "Coping with Insidious Injuries: The Case of Johns-Manville Corporation and Asbestos Exposure." *Social Problems* 35, no. 2: 162–181.

Clarke, L. 1989. *Acceptable Risk? Making Decisions in a Toxic Environment*. University of California Press.

Clarke, L. 1990. "Oil Spill Fantasies." *Atlantic Monthly*, November: 65–77.

Clarke, L. 1999. *Mission Improbable: Using Fantasy Documents to Tame Disaster*. University of Chicago Press.

Couch, S., and S. Kroll-Smith. 1994. "Environmental Controversies, Interactional Resources, and Rural Communities: Sitting versus Exposure Disputes." *Rural Sociology* 59: 25–44.

Crenson, M. 1971. *The Un-Politics of Air Pollution: A Study of Non-Decision Making in the Cities.* Johns Hopkins University Press.

Dickens, P. 1996. *Reconstructing Nature: Alienation, Emancipation, and the Division of Labor.* Routledge.

Dinno, R. 1999. Protecting California's Drinking Water from Inland Oil Spills. Planning and Conservation League, Sacramento.

Durkheim, E. 1984. *The Division of Labor in Society.* Free Press.

Easton, R. 1972. *Black Tide: The Santa Barbara Oil Spill and Its Consequences.* Delacorte.

Edelstein, M. 1988. *Contaminated Communities: The Social and Psychological Impacts of Toxic Exposure.* Westview.

Edelstein, M. 1993. "When the Honeymoon is Over: Environmental Stigma and Distrust in the Siting of a Hazardous Waste Disposal Facility in Niagara Falls, New York." *Research in Social Problems and Public Policy* 5: 75–96.

Elliott, G. 1999. "Shunning the Tarbaby." *California Coast and Ocean* 15, no. 3: 24–31.

Erikson, K. 1990. "Toxic Reckoning: Business Faces a New Kind of Fear." *Harvard Business Review* 90: 118–126.

Erikson, K. 1991. "A New Species of Trouble." In *Communities at Risk*, ed. S. Couch and S. Kroll-Smith. Lang.

Erikson, K. 1994. *A New Species of Trouble: The Human Experience of Modern Disasters.* Norton.

Flacks, R. 1988. *Making History.* Columbia University Press.

Foster, J. 1999. "Marx's Theory of Metabolic Rift: Classical Foundations for Environmental Sociology." *American Journal of Sociology* 105, no. 2: 366–405.

Fowlkes, M., and P. Miller. 1982. *Love Canal: The Social Construction of Disaster.* Federal Emergency Management Agency.

Freudenburg, W., and R. Gramling. 1994. *Oil in Troubled Waters: Perceptions, Politics, and the Battle over Offshore Drilling.* State University of New York Press.

Friesen, T. 1993. "Criminal Charges May Be Eliminated against Unocal." *Five Cities Times-Press-Recorder*, December 7.

Gamson, W., and A. Modigliani. 1989. "Media Discourse and Public Opinion on Nuclear Power: A Constructionist Approach." *American Journal of Sociology* 95: 1–37.

Gans, H. 1980. *Deciding What's News.* Vintage.

Gibbs, L. 1982. *Love Canal: My Story.* State University of New York Press.

Gibbs, W. 1999. "Not Cleaning Up: Faster, Cheaper Ways to Restore Polluted Ground Are Largely Shunned." *Scientific American*, February: 39–41.

Giddens, A. 1990. *The Consequences of Modernity.* Stanford University Press.

Glantz, M., ed. 1999. *Creeping Environmental Problems and Sustainable Development in the Aral Sea Basin.* Cambridge University Press.

Greene, J. 1993. "Unocal Spills May Have Gone Unreported." *Telegram-Tribune*, July 1.

Hanson, D. 1998. *Waste Land: Meditations on a Ravaged Landscape.* Aperture.

Harr, J. 1995. *A Civil Action.* Vintage Books.

Hart, G. 1995. "How Unocal Covered Up a Record-Breaking California Oil Spill." In *The News That Didn't Make the News and Why*, ed. C. Jensen. Four Walls, Eight Windows.

Hewitt, K., ed. 1983. *Interpretations of Calamity: From the Viewpoint of Human Ecology.* Allen & Unwin.

Hofrichter, R. 1993. *Toxic Struggles: The Theory and Practice of Environmental Justice.* New Society.

Levine, A. 1982. *Love Canal: Science, Politics, and People.* Lexington Books.

MacNaghten, P., and J. Urry. 1995. "Towards a Sociology of Nature." *Sociology* 29, no. 2: 203–220.

Marx, K. 1974. *Early Writings.* Vintage.

Mazur, A. 1998. *A Hazardous Inquiry: The Rashomon Effect at Love Canal.* Harvard University Press.

McLellan, David. 1977. *Karl Marx: Selected Writings.* Oxford University Press.

Molotch, H. 1970. "Oil in Santa Barbara and Power in America." *Sociological Inquiry* 40 (Winter): 131–144.

Molotch, H., and M. Lester. 1975. "Accidental News: The Great Oil Spill as Local Occurrence and National Event." *American Journal of Sociology* 81: 235–260.

Paddock, R. 1994. "Setbacks Slow Cleanup of Huge Oil Spill." *Los Angeles Times*, October 11.

Perrow, C. 1984. *Normal Accidents: Living With High Risk Technologies.* Basic Books.

Ritea, S. 1994. "Silent Spill." *San Luis Obispo New Times*, February 23.

Slater, D. 1994. "Dress Rehearsal for Disaster." *Sierra Magazine*, May–June: 53.

Stallings, R. 1990. "Media Discourse and the Social Construction of Risk." *Social Problems* 37, no. 1: 80–95.

Szasz, A. 1994. *Ecopopulism: Toxic Waste and the Movement for Environmental Justice.* University of Minnesota Press.

Wilkins, Le. 1987. "Risk Analysis and the Construction of News." *Journal of Communication* 37, no. 3: 80–92.

Turner, B. 1978. *Man-Made Disasters.* Wykeham.

Vaughan, D. 1996. *The Challenger Launch Decision: Risky Technology, Culture, and Deviance at NASA.* University of Chicago Press.

Study Questions

1. What social factors allowed the Guadalupe Spill to remain so "silent"?

2. What does the author say about balancing the responsibility between big business and the environment?

Topic 15
Technology and Globalization

Much of what sociology understands about social change and the future is tied to such things as "technology" and "globalization." Some would argue that we live in the technological age, that we are experiencing a "biological revolution." Others would mention the effect of the microchip on the world as we swim in a sea of "information" and the "communication revolution" brought on by wireless technology and the Internet. The personal and structural aspects of all these changes remind humans that we are often led by technology into social arrangements with which we have not yet learned to cope. It is true; culture "lags" behind technology. The success of the Human Genome Project has brought about the prospect of human engineering and cloning. The advent of the computer a short half-century ago brings us to the brink of e-mail, e-commerce, and e-communities. Much of the world perches on our visual and intellectual doorstep as a computer monitor. A new reality waits nanoseconds away. How has and how will social life be affected by such rapid change?

Toffler's "future shock" theory warned us that the future is rushing toward us at an ever-increasing pace. If this is true, the mandate for social and personal adaptation seems more real than ever. Perhaps the "post-modern" world is more about pretense than substance, more about TV shows than human relationships and substantive issues. Will technology, computers, movies, and electronic games become reality? If this is so, the shift toward virtual reality will soon affect all our definitions of what is important and meaningful, and social life will have passed into another level that can no longer be understood using the traditional tools of science. Technology, by itself, is neither good nor bad. The Internet is a place of great, expanding possibilities for commerce and learning and, simultaneously, is a place of gross pornography that victimizes women and children while feeding lewd interests among the masses. Will society—indeed, humanity—rise to meet such challenges?

Globalization is the worldwide adoption of similar social and economic patterns. When the entire world watches U.S. TV, the news and shows of the day will be defined, in part, by the filtered content on the screen. This content, in turn, affects individual perceptions and collective cultural values. Social life is leveled to a plane that has more similarity than diversity, and the world proceeds with a "globalized" sense of what is right, just, and true. Is this something that rests in the immediate future? Will the U.S. version of capitalism be exported across the globe and become the standard by which many societies measure themselves? Will democracy become the political preference for many nations? To be sure, McDonald's has arrived on the world scene and most are rejoicing. Even the standardization of computer software, which more and more of us use through much of the day, creates culturally imposed patterns and globalized restrictions on creativity.

In Topic 15, Technology and Globalization, three articles outline some of the important issues raised by this introduction. First, George Ritzer's "McDonaldization of Society" illustrates the underlying rationality of production done to preserve profit at the least expense. With thousands of stores worldwide, and success of storybook proportions, other businesses will adopt the McDonald's approach to hiring, creating, and selling a product. Second, cyberspace centers the technological discussion in Keith Durkin and Clifton Bryant's piece on how pornography and eroticism have been advanced through the increasing availability of "carnal" opportunities. Finally, Stephen Haseler's "The Super-Rich" does point to a new world order, in this case a new world "economic" order. The super-rich billionaires have set the international stage with as yet untold stories of power. When individual people have more money than entire sovereign nations, what will be the economic and political impact on our future?

The McDonaldization of Society

George Ritzer

Ray Kroc, the genius behind the franchising of McDonald's restaurants, was a man with big ideas and grand ambitions. But even Kroc could not have anticipated the astounding impact of his creation. McDonald's is one of the most influential developments in twentieth-century America. Its reverberations extend far beyond the confines of the United States and the fast-food business. It has influenced a wide range of undertakings, indeed the way of life, of a significant portion of the world. And that impact is likely to expand at an accelerating rate.[1]

However, this is *not* a book about McDonald's, or even the fast-food business, although both will be discussed frequently throughout these pages. Rather, McDonald's serves here as the major example, the "paradigm," of a wide-ranging process I call *McDonaldization*, that is,

> the process by which the principles of the fast-food restaurant are coming to dominate more and more sectors of American society as well as of the rest of the world.

As you will see, McDonaldization affects not only the restaurant business, but also education, work, health care, travel, leisure, dieting, politics, the family, and virtually every other aspect of society. McDonaldization has shown every sign of being an inexorable process by sweeping through seemingly impervious institutions and parts of the world.

McDonald's success is apparent: in 1993 its total sales reached $23.6 billion with profits of almost $1.1 billion.[2] The average U.S. outlet has total sales of approximately $1.6 million in a year.[3] Many entrepreneurs envy such sales and profits and seek to emulate McDonald's success. McDonald's, which first began franchising in 1955, opened its 12,000th outlet on March 22, 1991. By the end of 1993, McDonald's had almost 14,000 restaurants worldwide.

The impact of McDonaldization, which McDonald's has played a central role in spawning, has been manifested in many ways:

- The McDonald's model has been adopted not only by other budget-minded hamburger franchises such as Burger King and Wendy's, but also by a wide array of other low-priced fast-food businesses. Subway, begun in 1965 and now with nearly 10,000 outlets, is considered the fastest-growing of these businesses, which include Pizza Hut, Sbarro's, Taco Bell, Popeye's, and Charley Chan's. Sales in so-called "quick service" restaurants in the United States rose to $81 billion by the end of 1993, almost a third of total sales for the entire food-service industry.[4] In 1994, for the first time, sales in fast-food restaurants exceeded those in traditional full-service restaurants, and the gap between them is projected to grow.[5]

- The McDonald's model has also been extended to "casual dining," that is, more "upscale," higher-priced restaurants with fuller menus. For example, Outback Steakhouse and Sizzler sell steaks, Fuddrucker's offers "gourmet" burgers, Chi-Chi's and Chili's sell Mexican food, The Olive Garden proffers Italian food, and Red Lobster purveys . . . you guessed it.

- McDonald's is making increasing inroads around the world.[6] In 1991, for the first time, McDonald's opened more restaurants abroad than in the United States.[7] As we move toward the next century, McDonald's expects to build twice as many restaurants each year overseas than it does in the United States. By the end of 1993, over one-third of McDonald's restaurants were overseas; at the beginning of 1995, about half of McDonald's profits came from its overseas operations. McDonald's has even recently opened a restaurant in Mecca, Saudi Arabia. . . .[8]

- Almost 10% of America's stores are franchises, which currently account for 40% of the nation's retail sales. It is estimated that by the turn of the century, about 25% of the stores in the United States will be chains, by then accounting for a whopping two-thirds of retail businesses.[9] About 80% of McDonald's restaurants are franchises.[10]

McDonald's as "Americana"

McDonald's and its many clones have become ubiquitous and immediately recognizable symbols throughout the United States as well as much of the rest of the world. For example, when plans were afoot to raze Ray Kroc's first McDonald's restaurant, hundreds of letters poured into McDonald's headquarters, including the following:

Please don't tear it down! . . . Your company's name is a household word, not only in the United States of America, but all over the world. To destroy this major artifact of contemporary culture would, indeed, destroy part of the faith the people of the world have in your company.[11]

In the end, the restaurant was not only saved, but turned into a museum! A McDonald's executive explained the move: "McDonald's . . . is really a part of Americana." Similarly, when Pizza Hut opened in Moscow in 1990, a Russian student said, "It's a piece of America."[12] Reflecting on the growth of fast-food restaurants in Brazil, the president of Pepsico (of which Pizza Hut is part) of Brazil said that his nation "is experiencing a passion for things American."[13]

McDonald's truly has come to occupy a central place in popular culture.[14] It can be a big event when a new McDonald's opens in a small town. Said one Maryland high-school student at such an event, "Nothing this exciting ever happens in Dale City."[15] Newspapers avidly cover developments in the fast-food business. Fast-food restaurants also play symbolic roles on television programs and in the movies. A skit on the television show *Saturday Night Live* satirized specialty chains by detailing the hardships of a franchise that sells nothing but Scotch tape. In the movie *Coming to America*, Eddie Murphy plays an African prince whose introduction to America includes a job at "McDowell's," a thinly disguised McDonald's. Michael Douglas, in *Falling Down*, vents his rage against the modern world in a fast-food restaurant dominated by mindless rules designed to frustrate customers. *Moscow on the Hudson* has Robin Williams, newly arrived from Russia, obtain a job at McDonald's. H. G. Wells, a central character in the movie *Time After Time*, finds himself transported to the modern world of a McDonald's, where he tries to order the tea he was accustomed to drinking in Victorian England. In *Sleeper*, Woody Allen awakens in the future only to encounter a McDonald's. Finally, *Tin Men*, ends with the heroes driving off into a future represented by a huge golden arch looming in the distance.

Many people identify strongly with McDonald's; in fact to some it has become a sacred institution.[16] At the opening of the McDonald's in Moscow, one journalist described the franchise as the "ultimate icon of Americana," while a worker spoke of it "as if it were the Cathedral in Chartres . . . a place to experience 'celestial joy.' "[17] Kowinski argues that shopping malls, which almost always encompass fast-food restaurants, are the modern "cathedrals of consumption" to which people go to practice their "consumer religion."[18] Similarly, a visit to another central element of McDonaldized society, Walt Disney World,[19] has been described as "the middle-class hajj, the compulsory visit to the sunbaked holy city."[20]

McDonald's has achieved its exalted position because virtually all Americans, and many others, have passed through its golden arches on innumerable occasions. Furthermore, most of us have been bombarded by commercials extolling McDonald's virtues, commercials that are tailored to different audiences. Some play to young children watching Saturday-morning cartoons. Others solicit young adults watching prime-time programs. Still others coax grandparents to take their grandchildren to McDonald's. In addition, these commercials change as the chain introduces new foods (such as breakfast burritos), creates new contests, and ties its products to things such as new motion pictures. These ever-present commercials, combined with the fact that people cannot drive very far without having a McDonald's pop into view, have served to embed McDonald's deep in popular consciousness. A poll of school-age children showed that 96% of them could identify Ronald McDonald, second only to Santa Claus in name recognition.[21]

Over the years, McDonald's has appealed to people in many ways. The restaurants themselves are depicted as spick-and-span, the food is said to be fresh and nutritious, the employees are shown to be young and eager, the managers appear gentle and caring, and the dining experience itself seems fun-filled. People are even led to believe that they contribute, at least indirectly, to charities such as the Ronald McDonald Houses for sick children.

The Long Arm of McDonaldization

McDonald's has strived to continually extend its reach within American society and beyond. As the company's chairman said, "Our goal: to totally dominate the quick service restaurant industry worldwide. . . . I want McDonald's to be more than a leader. I want McDonald's to dominate."[22]

McDonald's began as a phenomenon of suburbs and medium sized towns, but in recent years it has moved into big cities and smaller towns,[23] in the United States and beyond, that supposedly could not support such a restaurant. You can now find fast-food outlets in New York's Times Square as well as on the Champs Elysees in Paris. Soon after it opened in 1992, the McDonald's in Moscow sold almost 30,000 hamburgers a day and employed a staff of 1,200 young people working two to a cash register.[24] McDonald's plans to open many more restaurants in the former Soviet Union and in the vast new territory in Eastern Europe that has now been laid bare to the invasion of fast-food restaurants. In early 1992, Beijing witnessed the opening of the world's largest McDonald's, with 700 seats, 29 cash registers, and nearly 1,000 employees. On its first day of business, it set a new one-day record for McDonald's by serving about 40,000 customers.[25]

Small satellite, express, or remote outlets, opened in areas that cannot support full-scale fast-food restaurants, are expanding rapidly. They have begun to appear in small store fronts in large cities and in nontraditional settings such as department stores, service stations, and even schools. These satellites typically offer only limited menus and may rely on larger outlets for food storage and preparation.[26] McDonald's is considering opening express outlets in museums, office buildings, and corporate cafeterias.

No longer content to dominate the strips that surround many college campuses, fast-food restaurants have moved onto many of those campuses. The first fast-food restaurant opened at the University of Cincinnati in 1973. Today, college cafeterias often look like shopping-mall food courts. In conjunction with a variety of "branded partners" (for example, Pizza Hut and Subway), Marriott now supplies food to almost 500 colleges and universities.[27] The apparent approval of college administrations puts fast-food restaurants in a position to further influence the younger generation.

More recently, another expansion has occurred: People no longer need to leave the highway to obtain fast food quickly and easily. Fast food is now available at convenient rest stops along the highway. After "refueling," we can proceed with our trip, which is likely to end in another community that has about the same density and mix of fast-food restaurants as the locale we left behind. Fast food is also increasingly available in service stations,[28] hotels,[29] railway stations, airports, and even on the trays for in-flight meals. The following advertisement appeared in the *Washington Post* and the *New York Times* a few years ago: "Where else at 35,000 feet can you get a McDonald's meal like this for your kids? Only on United's Orlando flights." Now, McDonald's so-called "Friendly Skies Meals" are generally available to children on Delta flights. Similarly, in December 1994, Delta began to offer Blimpie sandwiches on its North American flights,[30] and Continental now offers Subway sandwiches. How much longer before McDonaldized meals will be available on all flights everywhere by every carrier? In fact, on an increasing number of flights, prepackaged "snacks" have already replaced hot main courses. . . .

As powerful as it is, McDonald's has not been alone in pressing the fast-food model on American society and the rest of the world. Other fast-food giants, such as Burger King and Kentucky Fried Chicken, have played a key role, as have innumerable other businesses built on the principles of the fast-food restaurant.

Even the derivatives of McDonald's and the fast-food industry in turn exert their own influence. For example, the success of *USA TODAY* has led many newspapers across the nation to adopt, for example, shorter stories and color weather maps. As one *USA TODAY* editor put it, "The same newspaper editors who call us McPaper have been stealing our McNuggets."[31] The influence of *USA TODAY* is blatantly manifested in *The Boca Raton News*, a Knight-Ridder newspaper. This newspaper is described as "a sort of smorgasbord of snippets, a newspaper that slices and dices the news into even smaller portions than does *USA TODAY*, spicing it with color graphics and fun facts and cute features like 'Today's Hero' and 'Critter Watch'.[32] As in *USA TODAY*, stories in *The Boca Raton News* usually do not jump from one page to another; they start and finish on the same page. To meet this need, long, complex stories often have to be reduced to a few paragraphs. Much of a story's context, and much of what the principals have to say, is severely cut back or omitted entirely. With its emphasis on light news and color graphics, the main function of the newspaper seems to be entertainment. Even the *New York Times* has undergone changes (for example, the use of color) as a result of the success of *USA TODAY*.

The expansion deep into the newspaper business suggests that McDonaldization may be inexorable and may therefore come to insinuate itself into every aspect of society and people's private lives. In the movie *Sleeper*, Woody Allen not only created a futuristic world in which McDonald's was an important and highly visible element, but he also envisioned a society in which even sex underwent the process of McDonaldization. The denizens of his future world were able to enter a machine called an "orgasmatron," which allowed them to experience an orgasm without going through the muss and fuss of sexual intercourse.

Sex actually has, like virtually every other sector of society, undergone a process of McDonaldization. "Dial-a-porn" allows people to have intimate, sexually explicit, even obscene conversations with people they have never met and probably never will meet.[33] There is great specialization here: Dialing numbers such as 555-FOXX will lead to a very different phone message than dialing 555-SEXY. Those who answer the phones mindlessly and repetitively follow "scripts" that have them say such things as, "Sorry, tiger, but your Dream Girl has to go . . . Call right back and ask for me."[34] Escort services advertise a wide range of available sex partners. People can see highly specialized pornographic movies (heterosexual, homosexual, sex with children, and sex with animals) at urban multiplexes and can rent them from local video stores for viewing in the comfort of their living rooms. Various technologies (vibrators, for example) enhance the ability of people to have sex on their own without the bother of having to deal with a human partner. In New York City, an official called a three-story pornographic center "the McDonald's of sex" because of its "cookie-cutter cleanliness and compliance with the law."[35] These examples suggest that no aspect of people's lives is immune to McDonaldization.

The Dimensions of McDonaldization

Why has the McDonald's model proven so irresistible? Four alluring dimensions lie at the heart of the success of this model and, more generally, of McDonaldization. In short, McDonald's has succeeded because it offers consumers, workers, and managers efficiency, calculability, predictability, and control.[36]

First, McDonald's offers *efficiency*, or the optimum method for getting from one point to another. For consumers, this means that McDonald's offers the best available way to get from being hungry to being full. (Similarly, Woody Allen's orgasmatron offered an efficient method for getting people from quiescence to sexual gratification.) Other institutions, fashioned on the McDonald's model, offer similar efficiency in losing weight, lubricating cars, getting new glasses or contacts, or completing income-tax forms. In a society where both parents are likely to work, or where there may be only a single parent, efficiently satisfying the hunger and many other needs of people is very attractive. In a society where people rush, usually by car, from one spot to another, the efficiency of a fast-food meal, perhaps even without leaving their cars by wending their way along the drive-through lane, often proves impossible to resist. The fast-food model offers people, or at least appears to offer them, an efficient method for satisfying many needs.

Like their customers, workers in McDonaldized systems function efficiently. They are trained to work this way by managers, who watch over them closely to make sure they do. Organizational rules and regulations also help ensure highly efficient work.

Second, McDonald's offers *calculability*, or an emphasis on the quantitative aspects of products sold (portion size, cost) and service offered (the time it takes to get the product). Quantity has become equivalent to quality; a lot of something, or the quick delivery of it, means it must be good. As two observers of contemporary American culture put it, "As a culture, we tend to believe deeply that in general 'bigger is better.' "[37] Thus, people order the *Quarter Pounder*, the *Big* Mac, the *large* fries. More recently, there is the lure of the "double this" (for instance, Burger King's "Double Whopper With Cheese") and the "triple that." People can quantify these things and feel that they are getting a lot of food for what appears to be a nominal sum of money. This calculation does not take into account an important point: the extraordinary profitability of fast-food outlets and other chains, which indicates that the owners, not the consumers, get the best deal.

People also tend to calculate how much time it will take to drive to McDonald's, be served the food, eat it, and return home; then, they compare that interval to the time required to prepare food at home. They often conclude, rightly or wrongly, that a trip to the fast-food restaurant will take less time than eating at home. This sort of calculation particularly supports home-delivery franchises such as Domino's, as well as other chains that emphasize time saving. A notable example of time saving in another sort of chain is Lens Crafters, which promises people, "Glasses fast, glasses in one hour."

Some McDonaldized institutions combine the emphases on time and money. Domino's promises pizza delivery in half an hour, or the pizza is free. Pizza Hut will serve a personal pan pizza in five minutes, or it, too, will be free.

Workers at McDonaldized systems also tend to emphasize the quantitative rather than the qualitative aspects of their work. Since the quality of the work is allowed to vary little, workers focus on such things as how quickly tasks can be accomplished. In a situation analogous to that of the customer, workers are expected to do a lot of work, very quickly, for low pay.

Third, McDonald's offers *predictability*, the assurance that their products and services will be the same over time and in all locales. The Egg McMuffin in New York will be, for all intents and purposes, identical to those in Chicago and Los Angeles. Also, those eaten next week or next year will be identical to those eaten today. There is great comfort in knowing that McDonald's offers no surprises. People know that the next Egg McMuffin they eat will taste about the same as the others they have eaten; it will not be awful, but it will not be exceptionally delicious, either. The success of the McDonald's model suggests that many people have come to prefer a world in which there are few surprises.

The workers in McDonaldized systems also behave in predictable ways. They follow corporate rules as well as the dictates of their managers. In many cases, not only what they do, but also what they say, is highly predictable. McDonaldized organizations often have scripts that employees are supposed to memorize and follow whenever the occasion arises.[38] This scripted behavior helps create highly predictable interactions between workers and customers. While customers do not follow scripts, they tend to develop simple recipes for dealing with the employees of McDonaldized systems.[39] As Robin Leidner argues,

> McDonald's pioneered the routinization of interactive service work and remains an exemplar of extreme standardization. Innovation is not discouraged . . . at least among managers and franchisees. Ironically, though, 'the object is to look for new, innovative ways to create an experience that is exactly the same no matter what McDonald's you walk into, no matter where it is in the world.'[40]

Fourth, *control*, especially through the *substitution of nonhuman for human technology*, is exerted over the people who enter the world of McDonald's. A *human technology* (a screwdriver, for example) is controlled by people; a *nonhuman technology* (the assembly line, for instance) controls people. The people who eat in fast-food restaurants are controlled, albeit (usually) subtly. Lines, limited menus, few options, and uncomfortable seats all lead diners to do what management wishes them to do—eat quickly and leave. Further, the drive-through (in some cases walk-through) window leads diners to leave before they eat. In the Domino's model, customers never come in the first place.

The people who work in McDonaldized organizations are also controlled to a high degree, usually more blatantly and directly than customers. They are trained to do a limited number of things in precisely the way they are told to do them. The technologies used and the way the organization is set up reinforce this control. Managers and inspectors make sure that workers toe the line.

McDonald's also controls employees by threatening to use, and ultimately using, nonhuman technology to replace human workers. No matter how well they are programmed and controlled, workers can foul up the system's operation. A slow worker can make the preparation and delivery of a Big Mac inefficient. A worker who refuses to follow the rules might leave the pickles or special sauce off a hamburger, thereby making for unpredictability. And a distracted worker can put too few fries in the box, making an order of large fries seem skimpy. For these and other reasons, McDonald's has felt compelled to steadily replace human beings with nonhuman technologies, such as the soft-drink dispenser that shuts itself off when the glass is full, the french-fry machine that rings and lifts itself out of the oil when the fries are crisp, the preprogrammed cash register that eliminates the need for the cashier to calculate prices and amounts and, perhaps at some future time, the robot capable of making hamburgers.[41] This technology increases the corporation's control over workers. Thus, McDonald's can assure customers that their employees and service will be consistent.

The Advantages of McDonaldization

This discussion of four of the fundamental characteristics of McDonaldization makes it clear that there are good, solid reasons why McDonald's has succeeded so phenomenally and why the process of McDonaldization is moving ahead so dramatically. As a result, people such as the economic columnist, Robert Samuelson, strongly support McDonald's. Samuelson confesses to "openly worship McDonald's," and he thinks of it as "the greatest restaurant chain in history." However, even Samuelson recognizes that there are those who "can't stand the food and regard McDonald's as the embodiment of all that is vulgar in American mass culture."[42]

McDonaldization has undoubtedly led to positive changes.[43] Here are a few specific examples:

- There is a far greater availability of goods and services than before; their availability depends less on time or geographic location.
- This wider range of goods and services is available to a much larger portion of the population.
- People are able to get what they want or need almost instantaneously.
- It is far more convenient to get what they want or need.
- Goods and services are of a far more uniform quality; at least some people get even better goods and services than before McDonaldization.
- Far more economical alternatives to high-priced, customized goods and services are widely available; therefore, people can afford things they could not previously afford.
- Fast, efficient goods and services are available to a population that is working longer hours and has fewer hours to spare. . . .

More specifically, McDonald's itself offers many praiseworthy programs, such as its Ronald McDonald Houses, which permit parents to stay with children undergoing treatment for serious medical problems; job-training programs for teenagers; programs to help keep its employees in school; efforts to hire and train the handicapped; the McMasters program, aimed at hiring senior citizens; and an enviable record of hiring and promoting minorities.[44]

A Critique of McDonaldization: The Irrationality of Rationality

Though McDonaldization offers powerful advantages, it has a downside. Efficiency, predictability, calculability, and control through nonhuman technology can be thought of as the basic components of a *rational* system.[45] However, rational systems inevitably spawn irrationalities. The downside of McDonaldization will be dealt with most systematically under the heading of the *irrationality of rationality;* in fact, paradoxically, the irrationality of rationality can be thought of as the fifth dimension of McDonaldization. The basic idea here is that rational systems inevitably spawn irrational consequences. Another way of saying this is that rational systems serve to deny human reason; rational systems are often unreasonable.

For example, McDonaldization has produced a wide array of adverse effects on the environment. Take just one example: the need to grow uniform potatoes to create those predictable french fries that people have come to expect from fast-food restaurants. It turns out that the need to grow such potatoes has adversely affected the ecology of the Pacific Northwest. The huge farms that now produce such potatoes rely on the extensive use of chemicals. The need to produce a perfect fry means that much of the potato is wasted, with the remnants either fed to cattle or used for fertilizer. However, the underground water supply is now showing high levels of nitrates that may be traceable to the fertilizer and animal wastes.[46] There are, of course, many other ecological problems associated with the McDonaldization of society—the forests felled to produce paper, the damage caused by polystyrene and other materials, the enormous amount of food needed to produce feed cattle, and so on.

Another unreasonable effect of the fast-food restaurant is that it is often a dehumanizing setting in which to eat or work. Customers lining up for a burger or waiting in the drive-through line and workers preparing the food often feel as though they are part of an assembly line. Hardly amenable to eating, assembly lines have been shown to be inhuman settings in which to work.

Of course, the criticisms of the irrationality of the fast-food restaurant will be extended to all facets of the McDonaldizing world. For example, at the opening of Euro Disney, a French politician said that it will "bombard France with uprooted creations that are to culture what fast food is to gastronomy."[47] This clearly indicates an abhorrence of McDonaldization, whatever guise it may take.

As you have seen, there *are* great gains to be made from McDonaldization. However, this book [The MacDonaldization of Society] will focus on the great costs and enormous risks of McDonaldization. McDonald's and the other purveyors of the fast-food model spend billions of dollars each year outlining the benefits of their system. However, the critics of the system have few outlets for their ideas. There are, for example, no commercials between Saturday-morning cartoons warning children of the dangers associated with fast-food restaurants.

A legitimate question may be raised about this critique of McDonaldization: Is it animated by a romanticization of the past and an impossible desire to return to a world that no longer exists? Some critics do base their critiques on the idea that there was a time when life was slower and less efficient, and offered more surprises; when people were freer; and when one was more likely to deal with a human being than a robot or a computer.[48] Although they have a point, these critics have undoubtedly exaggerated the positive aspects of a world without McDonald's, and they have certainly tended to forget the liabilities associated with such a world. As an example of the latter, take the following case of a visit to a pizzeria in Havana, Cuba:

> The pizza's not much to rave about—they scrimp on tomato sauce, and the dough is mushy.
> It was about 7:30 P.M., and as usual the place was standing-room-only, with people two deep jostling for a stool to come open and a waiting line spilling out onto the sidewalk.
> The menu is similarly Spartan. . . . To drink, there is tap water. That's it—no toppings, no soda, no beer, no coffee, no salt, no pepper. And no special orders.
> A very few people are eating. Most are waiting. . . . Fingers are drumming, flies are buzzing, the clock is ticking. The waiter wears a watch around his belt loop, but he hardly needs it; time is evidently not his chief concern. After a while, tempers begin to fray.
> But right now, it's 8:45 P.M. at the pizzeria, I've been waiting an hour and a quarter for two small pies.[49]

Few would prefer such irrational systems to the rationalized elements of society. More important, critics who revere the past do not seem to realize that we are not returning to such a world. In fact, fast-food restaurants have begun to appear in Havana.[50] The increase in the number of people, the acceleration of technological change, the increasing pace of life—all this and more make it impossible to go back to the nonrationalized world, if it ever existed, of home-cooked meals, traditional restaurant dinners, high-quality foods, meals loaded with surprises, and restaurants populated only by chefs free to fully express their creativity.

While one basis for a critique of McDonaldization is the past, another is the future.[51] The future in this sense is defined as human potential, unfettered by the constraints of McDonaldized systems. This critique holds that people have the potential to be far more thoughtful, skillful, creative, and well-rounded than they are now. If the world were less McDonaldized, people would be better able to live up to their human potential. This critique is based not on what people were like in the past, but on what they could be like in the future, if only the constraints of McDonaldized systems were eliminated, or at least eased substantially.

Notes

1. For a similar but narrower viewpoint to the one expressed here, see Benjamin R. Barber. "Jihad Vs. McWorld." *The Atlantic Monthly*, March 1992, pp. 53–63.
2. These and other data on McDonald's come from its most recent (1993) annual report, *The Annual*.
3. Cynthia Rigg. "McDonald's Lean Units Beef up NY Presence." *Crain's New York Business*, October 31, 1994, p. 1.
4. The source for this information is Pepsico, Inc.'s 1993 Annual Report, p. 18.
5. Mark Albright. "INSIDE JOB: Fast-Food Chains Serve a Captive Audience." *St. Petersburg Times*, January 15, 1995, p. 1H.
6. Bill McDowall. "The Global Market Challenge." *Restaurants & Institutions*, vol. 104, no. 26, November 1, 1994, pp. 52ff.
7. Eben Shapiro in "Overseas Sizzle for McDonald's." *New York Times*, April 17, 1992, pp. D1, D4.
8. "Investors with Taste for Growth Looking to Golden Arches." *Tampa Tribune*, January 11, 1995, Business and Finance, p. 7.
9. Paul Gruchow. "Unchaining America: Communities Are Finding Ways to Keep Independent Entrepreneurs in Business." *Utne Reader*, January–February 1995, pp. 17–18.
10. McDonald's Corporation Customer and Community Relations.
11. E. R. Shipp. "The McBurger Stand That Started It All." *New York Times*, February 27, 1985, section 3, p. 3.
12. "Wedge of Americana: In Moscow, Pizza Hut Opens 2 Restaurants." *Washington Post*, September 12, 1990, p. B10.
13. Jeb Blount. "Frying Down to Rio." *Washington Post/Business*, May 18, 1994, pp. Fl, F5.
14. Marshall Fishwick, Ed. *Ronald Revisited. The World of Ronald McDonald*. Bowling Green, OH: Bowling Green University Press, 1983.
15. John F Harris. "McMilestone Restaurant Opens Doors in Dale City." *Washington Post*, April 7, 1988, p. DI.
16. Conrad Kottak. "Rituals at McDonald's," in Marshall Fishwick (ed.). *Ronald Revisited: The World of Ronald McDonald*. Bowling Green, OH: Bowling Green University Press, 1983, pp. 52–58.
17. Bill Keller. "Of Famous Arches, Beeg Meks and Rubles." *New York Times*, January 28, 1990, section 1, pp. 1, 12.
18. William Severini Kowinski. *The Malling of America: An Inside Look at the Great Consumer Paradise*. New York: William Morrow, 1985, p. 218.
19. Stephen M. Fjellman. *Vinyl Leaves: Walt Disney World and America*. Boulder, CO: Westview Press, 1992. In another example of other countries creating their own McDonaldized systems and exporting them, Japan's Sega Enterprises is planning to open the first Segaworld indoor urban theme park in London in 1996; see "A Sega Theme Park for Piccadilly Circus." *New York Times*, February 14, 1995, p. D5.
20. Bob Garfield. "How I Spent (and Spent and Spent) My Disney Vacation." *Washington Post*, July 7, 1991, p. B5. See also Margaret J. King. "Empires of Popular Culture: McDonald's and Disney," in Marshall Fishwick (ed.). *Ronald Revisited: The World of*

Ronald McDonald. Bowling Green, OH: Bowling Green University Press, 1983, pp. 106–119.

21. Steven Greenhouse. "The Rise and Rise of McDonald's." *New York Times,* June 8, 1986, section 3, p. 1.
22. Richard L. Papiernik. "Mac Attack?" *Financial World,* April 12, 1994, p. 30.
23. Laura Shapiro. "Ready for McCatfish?" *Newsweek,* October 15, 1990, pp. 76–77; N. R. Kleinfeld. "Fast Food's Changing Landscape." *New York Times,* April 14, 1985, section 3, pp. 1, 6.
24. Louis Uchitelle. "That's Funny, Those Pickles Don't Look Russian." *New York Times,* February 27, 1992, p. A4.
25. Nicholas D. Kristof. " 'Billions Served' (and That Was Without China)." *New York Times,* April 24, 1992, p. A4.
26. Cynthia Rigg. "McDonald's Lean Units Beef up NY Presence." *Crain's New York Business,* October 31, 1994, p. 1.
27. Carole Sugarman. "Dining Out on Campus." *Washington Post/Health* February 14, 1995, p. 20.
28. Gilbert Chan. "Fast Food Chains Pump Profits at Gas Stations." *Fresno Bee,* October 10, 1994, p. F4.
29. Edwin McDowell. "Fast Food Fills Menu for Many Hotel Chains." *New York Times,* January 9, 1992, pp. D1, D6.
30. "Fast-Food Flights." *Phoenix Gazette,* November 25, 1994, p. D1.
31. Peter Prichard. *The Making of McPaper: The Inside Story of USA TODAY.* Kansas City, MO: Andrews, McMeel and Parker, 1987, pp. 232–233.
32. Howard Kurtz. "Slicing, Dicing News to Attract the Young." *Washington Post,* January 6, 1991, p. Al.
33. Nicholas D. Kristof. "Court Test Is Likely on Dial-a-Porn Service Game." *New York Times,* October 15, 1986, section 1, p. 16.
34. Cited in Robin Leidner. *Fast Food, Fast Talk: Service Work and the Routinization of Everyday Life.* Berkeley: University of California Press, 1993, p. 9.
35. Martin Gottlieb. "Pornography's Plight Hits Times Square." *New York Times,* October 5, 1986, section 3, p. 6.
36. Max Weber. *Economy and Society.* Totowa, NJ: Bedminster Press, 1921/1968; Stephen Kalberg. "Max Weber's Types of Rationality: Cornerstones for the Analysis of Rationalization Processes in History." *American Journal of Sociology* 85(1980): 1145–1179.
37. Ian Mitroff and Warren Bennis. *The Unreality Industry: The Deliberate Manufacturing of Falsehood and What It Is Doing to Our Lives.* New York: Birch Lane Press, 1989, p. 142.
38. Robin Leidner has developed the idea of scripts in her book, *Fast Food, Fast Talk: Service Work and the Routinization of Everyday Life.* Berkeley: University of California Press, 1993.
39. The idea of recipes comes from the work of Alfred Schutz. See, for example, *The Phenomenology of the Social World.* Evanston, IL: Northwestern University Press, 1932/1967.
40. Robin Leidner. *Fast Food, Fast Talk: Service Work and the Routinization of Everyday Life.* Berkeley: University of California Press, 1993, p. 82.
41. Experimental robots of this type already exist.
42. Robert J. Samuelson. "In Praise of McDonald's." *Washington Post,* November 1, 1989, p. A25.

43. I would like to thank my colleague, Stan Presser, for suggesting that I enumerate the kinds of advantages listed on these pages.

44. Edwin M. Reingold. "America's Hamburger Helper." *Time*, June 29, 1992, pp. 66–67.

45. It should be pointed out that the words *rational, rationality,* and *rationalization* are being used differently here and throughout the book than they are ordinarily employed. For one thing, people usually think of these terms as being largely positive; something that is rational is usually considered to be good. However, they are used here in a generally negative way. The positive term in this analysis is genuinely human "reason" (for example, the ability to act and work creatively), which is seen as being denied by inhuman, rational systems such as the fast-food restaurant. For another, the term *rationalization* is usually associated with Freudian theory as a way of explaining away some behavior, but here it describes the increasing pervasiveness of rationality throughout society. Thus, in reading this book, you must be careful to interpret the terms in these ways rather than in the ways they are conventionally employed.

46. Timothy Egan. "In Land of French Fry, Study Finds Problems." *New York Times*, February 7, 1994, p. A10.

47. Alan Riding. "Only the French Elite Scorn Mickey's Debut." *New York Times*, April 13, 1992, p. A 13.

48. George Stauth and Bryan S. Turner. "Nostalgia, Postmodernism and the Critique of Mass Culture." *Theory, Culture and Society* 5(1988):509–526; Bryan S. Turner. "A Note on Nostalgia." *Theory, Culture and Society* 4(1987):147–156.

49. Lee Hockstader. "No Service, No Smile, Little Sauce." *Washington Post*, August 5, 1991, p. A12.

50. Douglas Farah. "Cuban Fast Food Joints Are Quick Way for Government to Rally Economy." *Washington Post*, January 24, 1995, p. A14.

51. In this sense, this resembles Marx's critique of capitalism. Marx was not animated by a romanticization of precapitalist society, but rather by the desire to produce a truly human (communist) society on the base provided by capitalism. Despite this specific affinity to Marxist theory, this book is, as you will see, premised far more on the theories of Max Weber.

Study Questions

1. What is the meaning of McDonaldization? How is this related to "globalization"?

2. List other businesses that have become like the McDonald's restaurant. Can you look at places where you go that have become like McDonald's? What similarities do they have with McDonald's?

Reading 44

"Log on to Sex"
Some Notes on the Carnal Computer and Erotic Cyberspace

Keith F. Durkin and Clifton D. Bryant

Technology and Deviant Behavior

Behavioral scientists have long recognized that emerging technology has a powerful influence on human behavior, although frequently there is a delay or lag between the emergency of the technology and the social behavioral adaptation to it (Ogburn 1964).[1] The social response to technology often takes the form of *technicways*, or normative and patterned behavioral configurations (Odum 1937; Bryant 1984).[2] Whereas technicways generally assume functional dimensions, they may also mutate and take on dysfunctional or even deviant parameters. These deviant technicways often encompass sexually proscribed behavior. Furthermore, deviant sexual technicways would appear to divide and multiply in an entropic fashion.

Some examples of technology and sexually deviant adaptation include the automobile, which was intended as a means of transportation but has also proved to be a splendid platform for private assignation and fornication, as well as a major "vehicle" for a wide variety of clandestine sexual misconduct; and Edison's motion picture projector, which was intended for wholesome vicarious entertainment but has also proved to be extremely effective in affording vicarious carnal gratification in the form of pornographic films. The telephone also has served to generate a multitude of opportunities for carnal gratification. Its capacity for anonymous communication has made possible the obscene phone call.[3] It has also afforded the opportunity for the telephone masturbator to use a telephone conversation with a female as the basis for sexual fantasy and carnal stimulation, incorporating the autoerotic activity into the fantasy.[4] The effectiveness of this practice has been exploited in recent years by so-called "dial-a-porn" services,[5] which offer sexually explicit conversation for salacious purposes on a commercial basis. Undoubtedly, in time many others will grasp the deviant efficacy of the telephone and perceive additional innovative uses.

The citizens-band (CB) radio is another case in point. The CB radio initially appealed to persons who sought a convenient and efficient means for communicating in emergencies and in other inopportune circumstances. Truck drivers proved to be an enthusiastic customer group, using the CB radio to contact other truckers. Prostitutes also found truck drivers to be an enthusiastic customer group for their sexual services, and for some prostitutes, using the CB radio, which proved to be an expedient way to contact truckers, became a standard mode of soliciting customers (Klein 1981; Luxenburg and Klein 1983). Like legitimate businesspeople, deviant commercial enterprises are often quick to take advantage of new technology to improve efficiency and maximize profits. For example, rather than the bordello prostitute of times past, the prostitute contacted by telephone—the "call girl"—is now the norm in some locales. Prostitutes in some resort cities, such as Las Vegas, are said to carry beepers, in order to be able to respond quickly to telephone requests for sexual services.

The near explosion of technological advances in recent decades, in such fields as electronics, photography, and communications, to mention but a few, has deluged society with a cornucopia of devices and appliances, compelling in their novelty and application, but ominous in their latent deviant capabilities. Numerous instruments and mechanisms ranging from the Polaroid camera to the camcorder have been shown to have suitable utility for the facilitation of sexual deviance. Of the most recent technological products, the computer promises to open enormous new frontiers of opportunity for the proliferation and enhancement of sexual deviance, to have an applicability for carnal behavior that is socially volatile in both its perversity and import.

The Computer, Cyberspace, and Deviant Information

The computer, although intended primarily as a mechanism for extremely rapid, extraordinarily complex, computational purposes, quickly came to be seen also as a communication device. The computer paired with modern telephone technology has come to serve as a highly efficient means of contacting persons and corporate entities all over the world. On-line bulletin board systems, known as BBSs, are essentially modern-day, high-tech, electronic "party lines," by which users can send and receive messages, engage in conversations, and upload and download files. The electronic entity or domain that encompasses bulletin boards and all of the other communicative potential of computers has become known as "cyberspace" (Gibson, 1989). By linking up with a particular, specialized BBS, one can use a computer to contact individuals with mutual interests anywhere in the world. In 1987, there were 4,000 BBSs; by 1992, there were 44,000. Periodicals such as *Board-watch* or *Computer Shopper* list and describe the array of available BBSs (see *New York Times* 1989, p. 38). On-line services such as CompuServe, Prodigy, America Online, and Delphi offer the computer user immediate access to all sorts of information, such as news, weather, travel services, and stock market quotes, as well as access to all kinds of specialized interest bulletin boards and the means to send and receive private messages. On-line services thus permit people to contact and communicate with persons who share similar interests and avocations, which may involve such disparate topics as cooking, cats, and chess (see *U.S. News and World Report* 1985, p. 59).

Because the on-line services reach an unknown multitude of computer users (inasmuch as institutional computers are used by vast numbers of individuals for purposes not related to their work, the actual number of persons who can access BBSs cannot be accurately calculated), there is the potential for an enormous range of interests to be addressed, including deviant interests. Aware of this market, entrepreneurs of all stripes are rising to the need and offering unique BBSs to satisfy even the most exotic requirements. A relatively superficial exploration of available bulletin boards reveals a diverse array of nonsexual, deviant variants seeking subscribers or interested persons who might like to share information. Included among this genre of BBS is one that collects and distributes all sorts of law-enforcement radio codes, including generic codes and frequencies as well as special codes for specific law enforcement agencies. While these codes are made available ostensibly to help computer users better "enjoy" and understand the radio traffic on a police scanner, it is patently obvious that this master list of police codes could easily find miscreant uses. Additionally, this bulletin board provides a compendium of information concerning plants and substances that have psychotropic properties but are technically not illegal to possess at this time. It also contains relatively detailed information about automatic teller machine (ATM) fraud, which would no doubt be quite instructive to a would-be ATM thief. The same bulletin board gives advice on how to cause vandalistic damages, including lists of useful vandalism tools (wire cutter, BB gun, etc.) and appealing sites to be vandalized, such as the showroom windows of automobile dealerships.

In addition to bulletin boards that deliberately provide deviant information, some bulletin boards are used by individuals seeking technical advice for deviant acts. Several years ago, for example, a 10-year-old youngster in the Midwest placed an ad seeking instructions for making a time bomb on a bulletin board devoted to scientific interests. Someone with the necessary expertise did provide the information, and the boy subsequently blew up a mailbox using a bomb that he had constructed (Jackson 1989, p. 20).

The Carnal Computer and Cybersex

Sometimes the interest being catered to by a bulletin board may be sex, particularly esoteric variations of sex that frequently are deviant and sometimes illegal. This potential use of bulletin boards has not escaped the notice of relevant U.S. governmental agencies. The Attorney General's Commission on Pornography (U.S. Department of justice 1986, p. 1437), for example, has stated:

> The personal home computer provides individuals with an extraordinary new form of communication and information access. Providers of sexually explicit materials have taken advantage of this new technology by making computer subscription services the most recent advance in "sexually explicit communications."

Although the computer can be used to communicate directly with specific individuals in other locales using E-mail and other modes of communication, initial and subsequent contacts involving "erotic entertainment" are often made through intermediate computer networks, in the form of sexually oriented bulletin boards.[6] Because it allows "two users to exchange intimacies in private" (*Time* 1984, p. 83), the computer bulletin board, particularly when used for erotic purposes, can perhaps best be likened to the Valentine box in grammar or middle school into which students could put anonymous Valentine messages to be taken out and read by those to whom they were addressed. The box could also be used to respond privately. The sexually oriented computer bulletin board permits users to trade pseudonymous messages.

The initial anonymity of these bulletin boards may give way to a more intimate and personalized (albeit guarded) form of carnal interaction. One newspaper account (Markoff 1992, p. 5), for example, describes this process:

> One recent evening, users of the America Online network had the opportunity to visit a series of "rooms" offering, for example, "Naughty Girls," "Romance Connection" and a "Gay Room." After meeting electronically in the public room—actually a window in which comments from many users scroll by—new friends adjourned to private rooms for intimate conversations, often using noms de plume or "handles."

Exchanging erotic verbal chit-chat via computer has been labeled as a new form of "erotic entertainment in which consenting computer owners exchange X-rated messages over the telephone lines" (*Time* 1984, p. 83). Allegedly, some couples who meet over the computer and exchange erotic pleasantries sometimes move on to exchange names, telephone numbers, and pictures; they may even arrange dates. Some have gotten married (*Time* 1984, p. 83). Media accounts have even reported a new formalized or institutionalized bond between computer daters that represents a step in commitment that is short of marriage but perhaps more analogous to an engagement. Some computer partners enter into a "cyber-wedding'" an electronic bond that lets the individuals "pledge their love while looking ahead to a future that could include real-life marriage—if they hit it off [when they later meet in person]" (Haight 1994, p. 1).

A few years back, erotic exchange by computer was said to be "mostly lighthearted flirting" (*Time* 1984, p. 83). Recently, however, computer sex has been moving in more intimate and compelling directions. On-line socializing with a member of the opposite sex that has moved beyond lighthearted flirting has been termed "hot chatting" (Tamosaitis 1994, p. 56). The anonymity that computer interaction affords provides self-confidence, allows the individual to assume almost any identity (e.g., become any age, take on any appearance, and affect any persona), and promotes inspiration. A person can interact with a "computer pal," develop a symbolic sexual intimacy, share erotic fantasies, talk "dirty," and in the process, experience a "tonic" for his or her real-life sex. Hot chatting in cyberspace appears to help energize the libido of persons who have a jaded sex relationship with their regular partner. As one 45-year-old attorney was reported to have revealed (Tamosaitis 1994, p. 68):

> I've been married for 15 years and sex with my wife has grown routine. But after I've spent some time in erotic banter with a sensitive female online, I bring new enthusiasm and desire back into my bedroom.

Such an erotic process would seem to be functional, provided the individual does not become unduly preoccupied with his or her cyberspace "lover." Such a preoccupation could conceivably lead to marital friction.

While hot chatting may be a developmental process, with the interaction moving in incremental fashion to more intense levels of salacious conversation, it appears that participants' intentions often are obvious from the outset, as evidenced by the computer names they select. One researcher (Matek 1988, pp. 120–121) has observed, for example, that

> [O]bscene content is not always a part of this chatter, but the names of "handles" chosen by many of these participants divulge a sexual implication: Honey Blonde, Priapus Rex, Wet End, Love for Tender, Bilady Jugs. At times the "conversation" too is suggestive, and occasionally the computer screens read like a pornographic novel, as two or more strangers engage in "computer sex" with each of the participants describing successive steps in their fantasy encounter.

Obviously, some individuals derive carnal enjoyment from the mutual use of sexual words with a person of the opposite sex, and the computer handily affords the opportunity with both convenience and anonymity. . . .

The hazards of *cybersex* do not pertain only to children. Electronic erotica may also come to be a "rival" in a marriage. In another newspaper report (Garreau 1993, p. A-10), the author reveals:

> One woman wrote *The Washington Post* complaining that her husband, who had been in therapy for his sexual problems, found affirmation, acceptance and ultimately physical companionship in the bondage and discipline conference on CompuServe, one of several large switching systems on which subscribers can order merchandise, make airline reservations, check the weather and talk dirty. The pair is now divorcing.

There is yet another danger in cyberspace. Females are more sought after than men for computer talk. As a result, some users resort to "gender bending"—a person of one sex (usually a man) portraying himself as the opposite sex. According to a newspaper report, "male wallflowers have learned, however, that if they sign on as women they are instantly flocked to" (Garreau 1993, p. A-10). Sometimes gender bending can become quite elaborate, and even sinister. One such instance was the case of "Joan," a gregarious computer user who used the handle "Talkin Lady" and became something of an electronic celebrity (see Van Gelder 1985, p. 94). "Joan" claimed to be a New York neuropsychologist in her late 20s who was confined to a wheelchair because of a serious automobile accident that had killed her boyfriend and left her severely disfigured and with multiple physical handicaps. "Joan" had many computer friends and fans. One of her fans, a married woman, developed such affectionate ties to her as a sexual confidant and vicarious "lover" that she almost left her husband. In reality, "Joan" was a prominent New York psychiatrist named Alex in his 50s who made a hobby out of his computer deception. On one occasion, "Joan" introduced a woman "she" met through the computer to the real-life Alex, who went on to have an affair with her. It was traumatic to many of "her" contacts when "Joan's" true identity was revealed.

This type of occurrence, coupled with the reported attempts (sometimes successful) on the part of some individuals to lure juveniles into meetings for sexual purposes, raises the possibility of "gender bending" as a device for developing a misrepresented relationship with a woman via computer and luring her into a meeting for perverse purposes.

The use of cyberspace for criminal intent with a sexual dimension sometimes assumes convoluted parameters. It has been reported, for example, that authorities have uncovered that a "violence-prone organization" called the Aryan Brotherhood Youth Movement had established electronic bulletin boards in three different states in order to compile lists of suspected homosexuals for the intended purpose of assaulting them (Jackson 1989, p. 20).

Computer Guides to Sexual Deviance

Whereas there are numerous bulletin boards that address nonsexual deviancy, a significant number also have a sexual orientation. These are available in great variety. Some are like travel guides, in that they provide information about the sexual services (and prices) available in different cities in the United States, Mexico, various countries in Europe, and so forth. Sometimes, specific establishments are mentioned, and some bulletin boards even provide an estimate of mugging risk in each city or place of business.

Some of these travel guide bulletin boards deal essentially with prostitution services; others provide details about other sexual commodities, including erotic dancing, stripping, table dancing, lap dancing, nude showering on stage, dancers having sex with each other, being able to inspect the genital areas on nude dancers ("some women will give you a view of spots only her gynecologist sees," advises one bulletin board), and being allowed to touch or fondle the performers. Given today's tolerant standards, the on-line travel guides to erotic establishments are relatively tame.

Computer Bulletin Boards and Sexual Deviancy "Menus"

Some on-line bulletin board services make direct appeals for individuals of more perverse appetites. A lengthy exploration of the diversity of bulletin boards available in cyberspace reveals an amazing inventory of sexual interests, carnal activities, and exotic enterprises. A bulletin board can be accessed for almost any sexual appetite or persuasion. The topics discussed on these boards range from erotic enemas to zoophilia and include such singular subject matter as ritual genital mutilation, naming the penis, semen speed at ejaculation, having sex with a tiger, breast size versus IQ, pubic hair removal techniques, and a "pop-up" Kama Sutra book. In fact, there have been recent postings from *ampotemnophiles*, or persons with an "erotic obsession or fetish for amputated limbs or digits" (Money et al. 1977). One of these individuals had a leg amputated some years ago and now wished to have the other leg amputated as well (presumably for erotic reasons). This person was seeking a medical professional to perform the procedure, and also wished to contact others of similar desires.

The Social Meaning of Electronic Erotica

The emergence of computer sex can be interpreted at various functional levels. First, it may be viewed as *intellectual graffiti*. Like some more conventional varieties of graffiti, computer erotica can be an outlet for a person's carnal thoughts or a manifestation of sexuality. It can be a plea for sexual advice (or an attempt to give it), or it may afford a sense of sexual self-assertion or even an expression of hostile sexuality, inasmuch as graffiti blatantly violates the social norms that circumscribe sexual expression while avoiding external social sanction (see Bryant 1982, pp. 116–117, 129). In a similar vein, cybersex may sometimes function as an *electronic aphrodisiac*, helping to energize the libido and reinvigorate a genuine sexual relationship that has been burdened by routine and ennui.

Computer erotica can also be conceptualized as *interactive externalized fantasy*. The isolated sexual deviant with an unusual sexual preference may previously have had to rely on fantasy for carnal fulfillment. Now such fantasies can be operationalized within a social context. In addition to simply facilitating contact with others who have similar inclinations, computer bulletin boards also make it easier for sexual fantasies to be reinforced and fed. A passing erotic interest of perverse stripe that might have withered previously may now be nourished by the knowledge that other persons who harbor similar erotic desires exist and that anonymous interaction through the computer is possible.

Furthermore, the computer would seem to serve as a *catalytic* or *facilitating mechanism*. In the past, technological change has often proved to be the catalyst for dramatic social change, sometimes highly functional and other times highly dysfunctional. Often, the social change has been sufficiently widespread and has had enough social support to constitute a new normative pattern—a technicway. But technological change has often also been a catalyst for new forms of deviant behavior. The computer has proved to be something of a supercatalyst for both functional social change and deviant behavior. In effect, the computer "makes it happen!"

The computer may also be viewed as a *germination* and *distribution mechanism* for sexual deviancy. It possesses the capabilities for creating, imitating, enhancing, and extending deviant sexual behavior. The computer can provide an incredibly rapid communication link with a vast number of people throughout the United States and the world. In this way, the process of diffusion, including the diffusion of criminal and deviant practices, can be expanded and facilitated in an almost exponential fashion. The Tibetan monk writes his prayers on a piece of paper, places the paper in his prayer wheel, and spins the wheel, thereby "multiplying" and "amplifying" his message to the gods. The computer seems to serve much the same function, "multiplying" and "amplifying" the deviant messages to all those who log on.

The computer operates as a *social consolidation mechanism*, inasmuch as it can aggregate large numbers of individuals of similar sexually deviant persuasion with great facility. The individual deviant can easily identify other, similar deviants and subsequently form social coalitions. In doing so, a "critical mass" of persons seeking a social context for their deviant inclinations is achieved. The computer is also a highly effective learning device, and the would-be deviant can readily locate expertise and edification.

Most important, perhaps, the computer can be conceptualized as a *mechanism of metamorphosis*, or a kind of deviant "dream machine." Deviant sexual fantasies that might well have remained simply the distorted musings of an imaginative mind may now be operationalized and implemented. Like the genie in the bottle, the computer can transform deviant sexual reverie into deviant reality by feeding and enriching the individual's fantasies, aiding him or her in identifying others with analogous sexual predilections, assisting in the coalescence of like-minded sexual deviants, and contributing to the constitution of an opportunity structure for the actualization of the fantasied behavior.

Notes

1. All sorts of technological inventions and procedures have had a heavy impact on society. The steam engine, the cotton gin, the telegraph, the telephone, the automobile, the airplane, the still and movie cameras, radio, television, and the computer have all drastically altered the nature of social life. Even simple inventions such as the safety pin, the paper clip, the aerosal spray can, and the safety razor have brought about significant changes in cultural patterns and social behavior. Various behavioral scientists have spoken to the question of technology and social change. William F. Ogburn (1964), for example, advanced the notion of *cultural lag* by suggesting that nonmaterial culture change occurs more slowly than material culture change. In effect, technological change invites adaptation, but the subsequent social change may be slow in occurring.

2. Howard W. Odum (1937) also addressed social change and pointed out that, where new technology is accepted, the response or adaptation to the innovation or new technological process takes the form of *technicways*, or normative behavior patterns. A technicway encompasses more than merely the socially habituated use of a particular technique or tool, however. For Odum, the concept also referred to a more generalized value system stance or ideological posture as an adaptive response to certain technology and innovation. The cause and effect linkages may be somewhat more convoluted than simple innovation-producing behavioral response. For example, after King

Gillette invented the safety razor, home shaving for men became a national grooming pattern. Beyond this, however, social values shifted to the point that the bearded male face was considered objectionable, if not uncouth, certainly among "gentlemen" (at least until the 1960s). In his discussion of Odum's concept, Bryant (1984) suggested that technicways do not always occur as a single swell of normative adaptive response to new technology, but rather, in some instances, the social response may occur in a chain-reaction fashion, assuming the form of *secondary* or even *tertiary* technicways as well as *primary.* The availability of the husband's safety razor in the home led to the grooming pattern of women shaving their legs (a secondary technicway), and, in time, the shaven legs led to the fashion of shorter skirts (a tertiary technicway).

Further reflection on the ripple effect of social adaptation to innovation and new technological processes seems to indicate that technicways may often mutate, as it were, in an aberrant fashion, becoming *deviant* technicways. Such seems to have been the case with numerous innovations, including the computer.

3. The maker of an obscene phone call, relying on anonymity, can telephone a victim and utter obscenities or sexually explicit suggestions, or simply breathe heavily into the receiver, in a real or simulated lustful fashion and derive vicarious carnal gratification in the process (Nadler 1968, pp. 521–526; Mead 1975, pp. 127–128; Matek 1988, pp. 113–130).

4. Other, more elaborative variations on telephone-related sexual deviancy include the telephone masturbator (Brockopp and Lester 1969, pp. 10–13; Lester 1973, pp. 257–260). The male deviant calls a female (often a counselor at an open-line crisis therapy agency) and, sexually stimulated by the sound of the female therapist's voice, engages in masturbation. The telephone masturbator uses the conversation with the unknown female as the basis for sexual fantasy and vicarious carnal stimulation. He can embellish the sexual drama with his own imaginative ability and masturbate as a constituent part of the fantasy, with complete anonymity, thanks to the technology of the telephone.

5. For those of less imaginative bent, the telephone has enabled the offering of "dirty" stories, obscene language, and salacious conversation from a female as part of a commercial service. Alleged to have originated in Japan (Parade 1976, p. 20), the so-called "dial-a-porn" services have become big business in the United States. The individual with a lascivious aural appetite can dial an advertised telephone number and be carnally entertained, either by a conversation with a paid female performer, or by listening to a prerecorded message (see Borna, Chapman, and Menezes 1993; Glascock and LaRose 1993). In either instance, the caller hears sexually explicit talk or sounds and is billed for the time on the line, on his or her monthly telephone bill (U.S. Department of Justice 1986, pp. 1428–1436). (Although primarily used by males, women do use these services.)

6. Both a computer and a modem (a telecommunicational device for computers) are a prerequisite for gaining access to these sexually orientated bulletin boards. To access these services, users dial the bulletin board's inbound phone number. Some of these numbers may be obtained from advertisements in computer or pornographic magazines, others by word-of-mouth. Moreover, once one bulletin board is accessed, information about other boards can readily be obtained from that service. When people initially call one of these bulletin boards, they typically have to complete a registration process. Users normally have to indicate that they are older than 18 or 21, and that they are not an employee of any law enforcement agency. Also, users normally have to pay a registration fee. Although this payment may be made by mail, many services allow users to

make the payment on line by credit card. After this process is complete, users can readily access the sexually explicit services offered.

One notable exception to the aforementioned procedures is USENET. USENET is an international noncommercial information network used by persons at academic institutions, research facilities, and major corporations. This network is made possible by more than 1,600 mainframe computers that act as data transfer stations (Horvitz 1989). Access is free to persons at sponsoring sites. It is estimated that well over 500,000 people have access to USENET (Horvitz 1989). Information on this network is categorized into newsgroups, each of which provides postings on one or more of a multitude of topics. There are hundreds of newsgroups, a few of which are dedicated to topics of a prurient nature. For example, there are newsgroups dedicated to bestiality, sadomasochism, masturbation, and pornographic movies. Several newsgroups contain personal ads from a multitude of sexual deviants, such as, for example, sadomasochists and swingers.

References

Becker, Jay. 1982. "Computer Crime: Career of the Future." *Computer and Society* 12:12–15.

Borna, Shaheen, Joseph Chapman, and Dennis Menezes. 1993. "Deceptive Nature of Dial-a-Porn Commercials and Public Policy Alternatives. *Journal of Business Ethics* 12:503–509.

Brockopp, Gene W., and David Lester. 1969. "The Masturbator." *Crisis Intervention* 1:10–13.

Bryant, Clifton D. 1982. *Sexual Deviancy and Social Proscription.* New York: Human Science Press.

———. 1984. "Odum's Concept of the Technicways: Some Reflections on an Underdeveloped Sociological Nation." *Sociological Spectrum* 4:115–142.

Garreau, Joel. 1993, November 29. "Bawdy Bytes: The Growing World of Cybersex. *The Washington Post.* pp. 1, A10.

Haight, Kathy. 1994, March 7. "Love: Couples Are Meeting, Courting, Getting Married On-Line." *Roanoke Times and World-News* (Extra Section). pp. 1, 3.

Jackson, Robert L. 1989, October 1. "Computer-Crime Sleuths Go Underground." *Los Angeles Times.* p. 20.

Klein, Lloyd. 1981. "Sex Solicitation by Short-Wave Radio. *Creative Sociology* 9:61–68.

Lester, David. 1973. "Telephone Counseling and the Masturbator: A Dilemma." *Clinical Social Work Journal* 1:257–260.

Luxenburg, Joan, and Lloyd Klein. 1984. "CB Radio Prostitution: Technology and the Displacement of Deviance." *Journal of Offender Counseling, Services, and Rehabilitation* 9(Fall/Winter):71–87.

Markoff, John. 1992, March 22. "Sex by Computer: The Latest Technology Fuels the Oldest of Drives. *New York Times.* p. 5.

Matek, Ord. 1988. "Obscene Phone Callers." *Journal of Social Work and Human Sexuality* 7:113–130.

Mead, Beverly F. 1975. "Coping with Obscene Phone Calls." *Medical Aspects of Human Sexuality* 9:127–128.

Money, John, Russell Jobaris, and Gregg Furth. 1977 "Ampotemnophilia: Two Cases of Self-Demand Amputation as a Paraphilia." *Journal of Sex Research* 13:115–125.

Nadler, R. P. 1968. "Approach to Psycho-Analysis of Obscene Telephone Calls. *New York State Journal of Medicine* 68:521–526.

The New York Times. 1989, April 2. "As Computer Bulletin Boards Grow: If It's Out There It's Posted Here." p. B38.

Odum, Howard W. 1937. "Notes on the Technicways in Contemporary Society." *American Sociological Review* 2:336–346.

Ogburn, William E. 1964. *On Culture and Social Change.* Chicago: University of Chicago Press.

Parade. 1976, July 4. "Dirty-Story Time." p. 20.

Tamosaitis, Nancy. 1994. "Modem Sex: Can Online Fantasies Rev Up Your Libido?" *Longevity*:56, 68.

Time. 1984, May 14. "X-Rated: The Joys of Compusex." p. 83.

U.S. Department of Justice. 1986. *The Attorney General's Commission on Pornography, Final Report.* Washington, DC: U.S. Government Printing Office.

U.S. News and World Report. 1985, June 3. "For Every Taste a Bulletin Board." p. 59.

Van Gelder, Lindsey. 1985, October. "The Strange Case of the Electronic Lover." *Ms.* pp. 94, 99, 101–104, 117, 123–124.

Study Questions

1. Can you explain how it is that technology can be both an asset and liability to society? Give some examples that are not found in this study.

2. In thinking beyond this article, but including ideas from other material in this reader and your course, what are the social effects of pornography in general?

Reading 45

The Super-Rich

Stephen Haseler

The Super-Rich

The end of the forty years of Cold War was more than the political triumph of the West over the Soviet Union. It was also more than the victory of freedom and pluralism over command communism. When the Berlin Wall cracked open and the iron curtain fell a new form of capitalism came into its own—global capitalism—and with it new global elite, a new class.

This new class already commands wealth beyond the imagination of ordinary working citizens. It is potentially wealthier than any super-rich class in history (including the robber barons, those 'malefactors of great wealth' criticised by Teddy Roosevelt, and the nineteenth-century capitalists who inspired the opposition of a century of Marxists). The new class of super-rich are also assuming the proportions of overlordship, of an overclass—as powerful, majestic and antidemocratic as the awesome, uncompromising imperial governing classes at the height of the European empires.

The awesome new dimension of today's super-rich—one which separates them sharply from earlier super rich—is that they owe no loyalty to community or nation. The wealthy used to be bounded within their nations and societies—a constraint that kept aggregations of wealth within reason and the rich socially responsible. Now, though, the rich are free: free to move their money around the world. In the new global economy super-rich wealth (capital) can now move their capital to the most productive (or high profit, low cost) haven, and with the end of the Cold War—and the entry into global economy of China, Russia, Eastern Europe and India—these opportunities have multiplied. The super-rich are also free to move themselves. Although still less mobile than their money, they too are becoming less rooted, moving easily between many different locations.

Millionaires

Mobility is made possible by the lack of a need to work—a 'lifestyle' normally fixed in one nation or location for many years at a time. It is this escape from the world of work which effectively defines the super-rich. The lowest-ranking dollar *millionaire* household can, depending upon the interest and inflation rate, secure an *unearned* annual income of, say, $60 000 per year, which is almost double that of the median annual income of American families and four times that of the median income of British households.[1]

These millionaires are by no means lavishly well-off, particularly if they are in three- or four-people families or households. However they are financially independent—as one commentary put it, they can 'maintain their lifestyle for years and years without earning even one month's pay'.[2] It has been estimated that in 1996 there were as many as six million dollar millionaires in the world, up from two million at the end of the Cold War.[3] Over half of these—estimates claim about 3.5—are to be found in the United States.[4]

Multimillionaires

However these dollar millionaires find themselves at the *very* lower reaches of the world of the super-rich. Their homes and pensions are included in the calculations that make them millionaires, they often work—if not for a living, then for extras—and their lifestyles are often not particularly extravagant or sumptuous. They are, in fact, poor cousins in comparison with the more seriously rich families and individuals who are now emerging in the global economy. Official US statistics report that around a million US households—the top 1 per cent of total US households—possess a *minimum* net worth of over $2.4 million each and an average of $7 million each. In Britain the top 1 per cent have an average of around $1.4 million each.

The top half a per cent of US households, about half a million people, are staggeringly rich. This group has a *minimum* net worth of $4.7 million and an *average* of over $10 million each, which could produce an unearned annual income of over $600 000. In Britain the top half a per cent, around 48 000 households, have on average something like $2 million each—a fortune that can produce, again depending on interest and inflation rates, an unearned annual income of around $120 000 before tax and without working.[5]

These households are the truly super-rich, whose net worth, much of it inherited, is the source of considerable economic power and produces an income (mainly unlinked to work) that allows, even by affluent Western standards, extraordinarily sumptuous lifestyles. Estimates vary about the world-wide number of such super-rich families and individuals, but over two million in the plus $2.5 million category and over one million in the over $4.7 million (average $10 million) category would seem reasonable.[6]

Although huge amounts of the money of these multimillionaires are held outside the United States, in Europe, Asia and Latin America, this tells us nothing about the nationality of the holders.[7] In a sense these super-rich multimillionaires are the world's true global citizens—owing loyalty to themselves, their families and their money, rather than to communities and territorial boundaries—but reasonable estimates suggest that over half of them are American, and that most of the rest are European, with—certainly until the 1998 crash in Asia—a growing contingent from Asia.[8]

Their money is highly mobile, and so are they themselves, moving between their various homes around the world—in London, Paris and New York; large houses in the Hamptons in the United States, in the English and French countryside, and in gated communities in sun-belt America, particularly Florida, southern California and Arizona, and for the global super-rich the literal mobility of yachts in tropical paradises not scarred by local poverty.

Mega-Rich and Billionaires

Amongst multimillionaires there is a sharpish distinction to be made between those at the lower end—say the $20 million net worth households—and those at the higher end—say the $500 million plus households. The distinction is one of power, not lifestyle. From most perspectives the income from $20 million (say $1 million)—about 70 000 US households in 1994—can, at least on the face of it, produce the same kind of lifestyle as income from the net worth of the more serious multimillionaires (there is arguably a limit to the number of homes, yachts and cars that can be enjoyed and consumed in a lifetime).[9] $50 million in net worth, however, simply does not command as much economic power—over employment, over small businesses—than do the resources of the big time multimillionaires, much of whose money is tied up in big transnational corporations.

At the very top of this mega-rich world are the dollar billionaires, those who command over $1000 million in net worth, a fortune that can secure an unearned annual income, depending on inflation and interest rates, of $50 million a year before tax—staggeringly well over 1000 times more than the average US income. In 1997 estimates of the number of these ultra-super-rich individuals varied from 358 to 447 world-wide, and the number is growing fast, virtually doubling during the few years of the post Cold War era.[10]

Who Are the Billionaires?

The 400 or so billionaires in the world are a varied lot. In one sense they are like the rest of us (and like those who will read this book). They are overwhelmingly Western, primarily American or European, and male, but they represent no single ethnic group, no single social background, and certainly possess no single business or financial secret for acquiring these awesome fortunes.

Many of the billionaires, though, would not be in the mega-rich category without an inheritance—which remains the most well-trodden route to great multimillion dollar wealth. Of the top 400 wealthiest people in the United States, 39 made the list through inheritance alone and many of the others had some inheritance to help get them started.[11] The British queen, Elizabeth Windsor, is perhaps the most famous example of such massive unearned wealth. In 1997 Phillip Beresford (*The Sunday Times'* 'Rich List', (*Sunday Times* 6 April 1997) put her net worth at a staggering $10.4 thousand million in 1992 (double the 1997 figure for top-listed Joseph Lewis). However, after she took a rival 'rich list' to the Press Complaints Commission over its valuation of her assets, *The Sunday Times'* Wealth Register excluded from its calculations the royal art collection, which, had it been included, would have given her a $16 billion figure, making her the world's wealthiest woman and the second wealthiest person in the world, with half the net worth of the Sultan of Brunei but more than the Walton family.[12]

In contrast to the inheritors, there are some 400 'self-made' mega-rich men (there are no women). Yet even these men of merit have not necessarily made their inordinate fortunes through extraordinary amounts of work and talent—certainly not its continuous application. Many of the self-made mega-rich are certainly talented and creative (and often ruthless), but many of them have become mega-rich through one-off bursts of insight or risk or luck.

William (Bill) Gates is seen as 'self-made', very much the American entrepreneurial hero. His vast resources—*Newsweek* calls him 'the Croesus
of our age'—have been built upon the meritorious image of having run a
successful company which provides a real service, a real addition to human
understanding and communication. His huge net worth—he was listed in
1997 by *Forbes* magazine as the richest American at $36.4 billion—is
based upon the value of his shares in his company Microsoft. It was Gates'
original burst of imagination that created his fortune—the initial stock offering in 1986 of 100 Microsoft shares cost $2100 but by the first trading
day in August 1997 this had risen to 3600 shares at $138.50 each! Gates'
personal share of the company rose from $234 million to $37.8 billion in
the same period.[13] Certainly Gates has managed the company and taken
many crucial decisions. Yet as Microsoft grew he needed the more 'routine'
skills of thousands of major company directors—such as managerial ap-
titude and the ability to stave off competition. As with all established businesses, less and less risk and less and less creativity was needed (and a
junior hospital doctor probably put in more hours).

Paul Raymond is a different type of self-made billionaire. Described
by academic John Hills as Britain's richest man—in 1995 he placed him
ahead of Joseph Lewis—Raymond's fortune is thought to be well over
£1.65 billion. Having founded Raymond's revue bar in the Soho district
of London, with topless dancers, he made his money by investing in soft
pornography and property.[14] Like Gates he had the talent to spot a coming market—albeit one that was less elevating and educational. And also
like Gates, and the other mega-rich, once the original burst of inventive-
ness (perhaps amounting only to the one great insight) was over the rest
of his working life has consisted of simply managing his empire and
watching his money grow. . . .

Comparisons

This group of late twentieth-century billionaires not only dwarf their
'ordinary' super-rich contemporaries but also the earlier race of mega-
rich 'robber barons' who were so identified with the burgeoning capitalism of the early twentieth-century. In terms of resources at their personal
command, in 1997 William Gates, was three times richer than John D.
Rockefeller (Standard Oil) was in 1918, Warren Buffet was over ten
times richer than Andrew Carnegie (Steel) was in 1918, and it was esti-

mated that in 1992 the British queen was ten times richer than Henry Ford (automobiles) was in 1918, although some of these early-twentieth-century super-rich probably commanded a greater percentage of their nations' resources.[15]

The resources at the disposal of these super-rich families—a huge pool of the globe's wealth—are truly astounding, beyond the wildest imaginings of most of the affluent Western middle classes. These high net worth individuals (HNWI's, as they are depicted in the financial services sector that serves them) accounted for almost $17 trillion in assets in 1996.

The power—that is, command over resources—of the world's super-rich is normally expressed in raw monetary figures, but the sheer, egregious extent of these private accumulations of wealth can also be given some meaning by making comparisons. . . . Eighty four of the world' richest people have a combined worth greater than that of China.[16] So the wealth of just one of these super-rich individuals is equal to that of about 12.5 million of his fellow humans.

Just as awe-inspiring is the fact that the total wealth of the world's few hundred billionaires equals the combined income of 45 per cent of the planet's population.[17] It is also somewhat sobering to realise that the *individual* wealth of the world's billionaires can exceed the gross national product of whole nations.[18] The world's ten richest billionaires all individually possess more in wealth than the GNP of many nation-states. The world's richest individual, the Sultan of Brunei, weighing in at over $45 billion, commands more resources than the combined GNP of 40 nation-states. To give his wealth some form of reality, it is larger than the GNP of the Czech republic (population 10.3 million); while William Gates commands more resources than the GNP of Africa's oil-rich giant, Nigeria (with a population of 111.3 million); the Walton family commands over $27.6 billion, more than the GNP of Vietnam (peopled by 73.5 million); Paul Sacher and the Hoffmann family command over $13 billion, more than the GNP of Bulgaria (population 8.4 million); Karl and Theo Albrecht command over $8 billion, more than the GNP of Panama (with its 2.6 million inhabitants); Joseph Lewis, the highest ranking mega-rich British citizen, commands just under $5 billion, which gives him more control over resources than his country of residence, the Bahamas.[19]

Another way of grasping the huge personal agglomerations of wealth in the modern global economy is to compare income levels. On 1997 interest-rate figures, and assuming that all assets are not income producing, the Sultan of Brunei could easily receive from his assets something in the region of $3 billion a year as income—compared with an average of $430 per person in the 49 lowest-income nation-states, $2030 per person in the 40 middle-income nation-states, $4260 in the 16 upper-middle income states and $24 930 in the 25 highest income economies. . . .

Get the world's top three mega-rich (dollar billionaire) people into one room and you would have assembled command over more resources than the GNP of Israel; the top four and you would tie with Poland, the top ten and you would beat Norway and South Africa. Europe's richest 20 families command around $113 billion, a little more than the whole Polish economy; America's richest 10 ($158 billion) and Britain's richest 1000 families ($156 billion) together command more resources than the GNP of the entire Russian Federation.[20]

If the top 200 or so billionaires could ever be assembled together then the command over assets, in that one room, would outrank the GNP of each of Australia, the Netherlands, Belgium, possibly even Brazil; and with 400 or so billionaires the one gathering would outrank Britain and almost overtake France!

It is these kinds of statistic that bring into sharp focus the economic power limitations of elected presidents and prime ministers (and other public sector officials)—who also have to share their economic power with cabinets and parliaments—compared with the economic power of the unelected mega-rich, whose only accountability is to the market. Such economic power was on display when the American media billionaire Ted Turner decided to donate $1 billion to the United Nations and 'to put on notice . . . every rich person in the world . . . that they're going to be hearing from me about giving money'.[21] For a Western politician to move a billion dollars in the direction of the UN would have involved months and months of negotiating and a bruising campaign.

All of our four categories of the world's super-rich (the 'ordinary' millionaires with up to $2.5 million, those with $2.5–5 million, those with $5–1000 million, and the billionaires with over $1000 million) have a combined net worth of $17 trillion, more than double the GNP of the United States.[22]

Just as awe-inspiring is the proportion of national wealth of the Western nations held by their own passport-holding super-rich.[23] In 1995 in the US the amount of wealth (total net worth) held by 90 per cent of

American households—everyone under the top 10 per cent—came to only 31.5 per cent, whereas the top 10 per cent of American households own 69.5 per cent of the US. More striking still, the top 1 per cent of Americans hold 35.1 per cent of US wealth, and the top half a per cent of households (500 000 households), those with a minimum net worth of $4.7 million, own 27.5 per cent of the US.

In Britain too the super-rich also own a huge proportion of the net worth of their country.[24] In 1992 the top 10 per cent of Britons owned half of the country's marketable wealth (for the top US 10 per cent the 1995 figure was a whopping 69.5 per cent). The wealthiest 5 per cent of Britons owned around 37 per cent of Britain's marketable wealth. The top 1000 super-rich families in Britain own about $160 billion worth of wealth, about the same average (0.16 billion each) as the top half a per cent in the US; Britain's top 100 command $89 billion, its top 50 own $69 billion and the top 20 own $42 billion.[25]

Among the 1997 British 'top twenty' Joseph Lewis (finance) was estimated to have a net worth of $4.8 thousand million; Hans Rausing (food packaging) came just behind with $4.72 thousand million; David Sainsbury (retailing) and Garfield Weston and family (food production) third with $4 thousand million each; Richard Branson (airline, retailing and entertainment), Sir Adrian and John Swire (shipping and aviation) and the Duke of Westminster (landownership) all joint fifth with $2.72 thousand million each; Lakshimi and Usha Mittal (steel) eighth with $2.4 thousand million; and Joe and Sir Anthony Bamford (construction equipment) and Viscount Rothermere (newspapers) joint ninth with $1.92 thousand million.

A particular feature of the British super-rich scene is the concentration in very few hands of land ownership. Britain—or rather the land area known as the United Kingdom—is, quite literally, owned by a very small caste; as is the capital city, London. It remains a poignant commentary on wealth concentration that large tracts of London are owned by just a few individuals. The Duke of Westminster, through the Grosvenor Estate, owns around 200 acres of Belgravia and 100 acres of Mayfair—a dynastic inheritance created by the seventeen-century marriage of Cheshire baronet Thomas Grosvenor to Mary Davies, the '12 year old heiress to a London manor that at the time included 200 acres of Pimlico'. Viscount Portman owns 110 acres north of Oxford Street. Lord Howard de Walden's four daughters, through a holding company, own 90 acres of

Marylebone. Elizabeth Windsor, the queen, remains the 'official' owner of 150 acres of 'crown estates' in central London, as the eight crown estates commissioners address their annual report to her. Andrew Lycett has argued that although 'millions of pounds are exchanged every week in leasehold property deals . . . London still has no sizable new landowners' with the exception of the Sultan of Brunei and Paul Raymond.[26]

Richer Still, Yet Richer

And the super rich are getting richer. The former vice chairman of the US Federal Reserve Board said in 1997 that 'I think when historians look back at the last quarter of the twentieth century the shift from labour to capital, the almost unprecedented shift of money and power up the income pyramid, is going to be their number one focus.'[27] The figures are indeed dramatic. In the US the top half a per cent rose from 23 per cent to 27.5 per cent between 1989 and 1995. The next half a per cent rose from 7.3 per cent to 7.6 per cent in same period. However the next 9 per cent fell from 37.1 per cent 33.2 per cent, while the lowest 90 per cent fell from 32.5 per cent to 31.5 per cent. As the most reliable and scholarly analysis put it, the evidence shows 'a statistically significant increase in the share of household net worth held by the wealthiest half a per cent of [US] households from 1992 to 1995'.[28]

There are no figures available for the British top half a per cent, but tax authority figures—which do not include the considerable amounts of offshore money held by the British-passport-holding rich—suggest that whereas the top 1 per cent of the population were losing ground between 1950 and 1980, during the Thatcherite, globalising 1980s and 1990s their share of the wealth of Britain stabilised.[29]

And the assets held by the world-wide super-rich (the HNWIs) are expected to continue to grow. One assessment portrays them as more than doubling (from $7.2 trillion in 1986 to $15.1 trillion in 1995), and they are projected to grow from the 1996 level of $17 trillion to $25 trillion (up by more than 50 per cent) by the new millennium. . . .

An Overclass?

If the new global super-rich do not amount to an old-style ruling class, they are certainly becoming an overclass: the mirror image of the more publicised urban underclass—separated from the rest of us, with distinct interests that differ from those of the mass of the peoples of Western societies.

In a very real sense the new super-rich are becoming removed from their societies. This is happening physically. The higher levels of the super-rich have always lived apart: within their walled estates or in wealthy ghettos in the centre of Manhattan, London and other cities. They have always owned possessions that have singled them out. Today, of course, mere diamonds, helicopters and expensive cars no longer signify the apex of great wealth. Now it is the luxury yacht (normally personally designed by John Banneman), the personal aeroplane—the Sultan of Brunei has a Boeing 747—(normally supplied by Grumanns), and one or two of the highest valued paintings that signify someone has reached the top. . . .

Of course one test of loyalty to a society is a willingness to pay its taxes, particularly if they are not onerous. Yet increasingly the super-rich are dodging the taxes of their countries of origin. In 1997 the *New York Times* reported that

> nearly 2,400 of the Americans with the highest incomes paid no federal taxes in 1993, up from just 85 individuals and couples in 1977. While the number of Americans who make $200,000 or more grew more than 15 fold from 1977 to 1993, the number of people in that category who paid no income taxes grew 28 fold or nearly twice as fast, according to a quarterly statistical bulletin issued by the IRS.[30]

So difficult was it for the US authorities to collect taxes from the super-rich that Congress introduced a new tax altogether—the Alternative Minimum Tax—to catch them.[31] With the American 'middle classes'—the middle income groups—paying a larger percentage of their earnings in taxes (including sales taxes, property taxes and social security payroll taxes), tax evasion and avoidance is becoming a growing cause of economic inequality and social fracture. . . .

'The World Is in the Hands of These Guys'

The emergence of this global overclass not only raises the question of equality—or inequality—but also of power. Supporters of this new 'free market' global capitalism tend to celebrate it as a force for pluralism and freedom; yet so far these egregious aggregations of assets and money have placed in very few hands enormous power and influence over the lives of others. Through this accumulation of assets and money the super-rich control or heavily influence companies and their economic policies, consumer fashions, media mores, political parties and candidates, culture and art.

What is more the resources at the disposal of many of these super-rich individuals and families represent power over resources unattained by even the most influential of the big time state politicians and officials—'the panjamdrums of the corporate state' who populated the earlier, more social democratic era, and who became targets of the new capitalist right's criticism of the abuse of political power.

In the new capitalist dispensation it is the global super-rich who are 'lords of humankind', or 'lords of the Earth' like Sherman McCoy in Tom Wolfe's all too apt social satire on Wall Street, *Bonfire of the Vanities*, weilding power like old-fashioned imperial pro-consuls. The new global super-rich have now got themselves into a position where they not only have a 'free market' at their disposal, and not only is this market now global, but they can also command the support of the world's major governments. . . .

Onward and Upward

The new super-rich global overclass seems to be possessed of one crucial attribute: a sense of ultimate triumph. As globalisation has proceeded all the bulwarks of social democracy that stood in their way, the cultures that acted as a balancing force and succeeded in civilising, and to some extent domesticating, raw capitalism have fallen. The primary casualty has been the nation-state and its associated public sector and regulated markets. The global economy has also helped to remove that other crucial balancing power available in the Western world—trade unions—which for the most part acted to check unbridled business power and ensure some basic rights to employees, often at the expense of rises in short-term money incomes.

Finally, the end of the Cold War was a seminal moment and played a fateful role as midwife. At one fell swoop the end of command communism (in Eastern Europe, in Russia and, in the economic field, in China) made footloose capital both possible and highly attractive by adding a large number of low-cost production and service centres and new markets to the economy. It also removed the need for the Western super-rich to be 'patriotic' (or pro-Western). It also made redundant the instinct of social appeasement held by many Western capitalists and induced by the need, in the age of Soviet communism, to keep Western publics from flirting with an alternative economic model.

The stark truth is that not one of these obstacles—not the public sector, not the trade unions, not an alternative economic and social model—is ever likely to be reerected. In the short to medium term, without a change in the political climate of the Western world there is nothing to stop further globalisation, higher and higher profits, more and more millionaires. For the new overclass it is onward and upward.

Notes

1. The median income of US families was about $37 000 in 1993. US Census Bureau, Income and Poverty, CD-ROM, table 3F (1993). The median income of UK households was about $16 500 (The exchange rate used here is $1.6 to the pound) in 1990 at 1993 prices. See John Hills, *Income and Wealth*, vol. 2 (Joseph Rowntree Foundation, Feb. 1995).
2. Thomas J. Stanley and William D. Danko, *The Millionaire Next Door* (Atlanta, GA: 1997). Some scholars have suggested defining 'the rich' not in terms of millions but rather as those with a family income over nine times the poverty line—in US terms about $95 000 a year in 1987. See S. Danziger, P. Gottschalk and E. Smolensky, 'How The Rich Have Fared, 1973–87', *American Economic Review*, vol. 72, no. 2 (May, 1989), p. 312.
3. The US Finance House Merrill Lynch in conjunction with Gemini Consulting, 'World Wealth Report 1997' (London: Merrill Lynch, 1997).
4. Stanley and Danko, *The Millionaire Next Door*, op. cit., p. 12.
5. US figures for 1995 from Arthur B. Kennickell (board of governors of the Federal Reserve System) and R. Louise Woodburn, 'Consistent Weight Design for the 1989, 1992 and 1995 SCF's and the Distribution of Wealth', revised July, 1997 unpublished. The UK figures are for 1993–4. For the UK figures, which include pensions, see Hills, *Income and Wealth*, op. cit., ch. 7.
6. Merrill Lynch, 'World Wealth Report, 1997', op. cit.
7. The 'World Wealth Report, 1997' (Merrill Lynch, op. cit.) projected, before the late 1997 Asian economic decline, that in 2000 the division of high net worth assets by source region would be Europe 7.1, North America 5.8, Asia 6.1, Latin America 3.8, Middle East 1.2 and Africa 0.4.
8. Of these multimillionaire Americans, families of British (that is English, Scottish, Welsh and Irish) and German descent account for 41.3 per cent of the total.
9. *Newsweek*, 4 Aug. 1997 (source IRS).
10. The UN *Human Development Report* (1996) put the figure at 358, and *Forbes* magazine's 1997 wealth list put the figure at 447, up from 274 in 1991.
11. *Newsweek* 4 Aug. 1997 (source *Forbes*, op. cit.)
12. See also, Phillip Hall, *Royal Fortune: Tax, Money and The Monarchy* (London: 1992) for a systematic account of the mysteries of the royal finances. One fact about the

Queen's money remains: since 1998 she has remained above the law as far as taxation is concerned as she is not treated in exactly the same way—with all tax laws applying to her—as every other British person.

13. See *Newsweek*, 'The New Rich', 4 Aug. 1997.

14. Hills, *Income and Wealth*, op. cit., p. 9. Hills suggests that 'If Britain's richest man, Soho millionaire Paul Raymond, receives a modest 3 per cent net real return on his reported £1.65 billion fortune' his income would be £1 million a week.

15. Figures from *Newsweek*, 4 Aug. 1997, reporting *Forbes* in June 1997. The figures for the Queen were for 1992 (as published in *The Sunday Times'* 'Rich List', 1997), and were subsequently revised downwards following a complaint to the Press Complaints Commission.

16. John Gray, 'Bill Rules the World—And I Don't Mean Clinton', *Daily Express*; 11 Sep. 1998.

17. UN, *Human Development Report*, (1966). Comparing wealth with income is highly problematic, but nonetheless serves to display the enormity of the comparison. These comparisons—between asset net worth and gross national product (GNP) are not of course comparing like with like, but are used in order to show the extent of the egregious financial and economic power of the high net worth individuals. The most reasonable method of comparison would be to compare the net worth of super-rich individuals and groups of super-rich individuals with the total net worth of each country (That is, each individual/family in the country). These figures are not available for more than a handful of countries.

18. 'Billion' here and throughout the book is used in the US sense that is, nine noughts.

19. Wealth figures from *The Sunday Times'*, 1997 'Rich List', op. cit., population figures for 1995 from *World Development Report* (Washington, DC: World Bank, 1997).

20. The US figure is from *Forbes*, June 1977, and the European and British from *The Sunday Times*, 6 April, 1977. For GNP figures see World Bank, *The World Atlas*, op. cit.

21. *Guardian*, 23 Sep. 1997.

22. These estimates are based upon the net worth estimates cited in *Forbes* magazine, June 1977, and in 'The Wealth Register', compiled by Dr Richard Beresford for *The Sunday Times* (extracts published in *The Sunday Times*, 6 April, 1997), who also cites *Forbes* magazine. *The World Atlas*, op. cit.

23. As I argue throughout this book, the super-rich are in reality global; but they all need a passport, and we are talking here about US passport holders.

24. The percentage of net worth of the total marketable net worth of all British passport holders.

25. *The Sunday Times*, 6 April, 1997. This is the British billion, that is, 12 noughts as opposed to the US nine noughts.

26. Andrew Lycett, 'Who Really Owns London?', *The Times*, 17 Sep. 1997.

27. Alan Blinder, former vice chairman of the US Federal Reserve, quoted in *Newsweek*, 23 June 1997.

28. Figures from 'Consistent Weight Design for the 1989, 1992 and 1995 SCF's and the Distribution of Wealth' by Arthur Kennickell (Federal Reserve System) and R. Louise Woodburn (Ernst and Young), revised July 1997 (unpublished). Figures derived from the Survey of Consumer Finances sponsored by the US Federal Reserve System and the Statistics of Income Division of the IRS.

29. See Charles Feinstein, 'The Equalising of Wealth In Britain Since The Second World War', *Oxford Review of Economic Policy*, vol. 12, no. 1 (Spring 1996), p. 96 ff. In British estimates distinctions tend to be made between marketable wealth and total

wealth—marketable wealth excludes state pensions, occupational pensions and tenancy rights.

30. *New York Times*, 18 April, 1997.

31. The US Alternative Minimum Tax is levied on those who have substantial incomes but, because of their use of tax shelters and exemptions, submit a zero tax return.

Study Questions

1. The "super-rich" may be reshaping the global economy. What power do they have and how might they exercise it?

2. What social theory would you use to explain why the "super-rich" have come into existence? Use some sociological concepts to show how this happened.

Credits

Peter Berger, from *An Invitation to Sociology*, copyright © 1963 by Peter L. Berger. Used by permission of Doubleday, a division of Random House, Inc.

C. Wright Mills, from *The Sociological Imagination*, copyright © 1959, 2000 by Oxford University Press, Inc. Used by permission of Oxford University Press, Inc.

W. Richard Stephens, from *Careers in Sociology* (2nd ed.), published by Allyn and Bacon, Boston. Copyright © 1999 by Pearson Education. Reprinted by permission of the publisher.

Paul Colomy, from "Three Sociological Perspectives" in Patricia A. Adler and Peter Adler (Eds.), *Sociological Odyssey*. Belmont, CA: Wadsworth Publishing. Reprinted by permission of the author.

Elliot Liebow, from *Tell Them Who I Am: The Lives of Homeless Women*. Reprinted with the permission of The Free Press, a Division of Simon & Schuster Adult Publishing Group. Copyright © 1993 by Elliot Liebow. All rights reserved.

Howard M. Rebach and John G. Bruhn, from "Theory, Practice, and Sociology" in *Handbook of Clinical Sociology* (2nd ed.). Copyright © 2001. New York: Kluwer. Reprinted by permission.

Barry Glassner, from *The Culture of Fear*. Copyright © 1999 by Barry Glassner. Reprinted by permission of Basic Books, a member of Perseus Books, L.L.C.

Horace Miner, "Body Ritual among the Nacirema." *The American Anthropologist*, 58, June pp. 503–507. Copyright © 1956.

Mitch Albom, from *Tuesdays with Morrie*, copyright © 1997 by Mitch Albom. Used by permission of Doubleday, a division of Random House, Inc.

Madonna G. Constantine and Sha'kema M. Blackmon, "Black Adolescents' Racial Socialization Experiences: Their Relations to Home, School, and Peer Self-Esteem," *Journal of Black Studies* Vol. 32 No. 3, January 2002, pp. 322–335, copyright © 2002 by Sage Publications. Reprinted by permission of Sage Publications.

Kingsley Davis, "Final Note on a Case of Extreme Isolation," *American Journal of Sociology*, 52, pp. 432–447. Copyright © 1947. Reprinted by permission of Marta Seoane.

Joan M. Morris and Michael D. Grimes, "Contradictions in the Childhood Socialization of Sociologists from the Working Class," *Race, Gender, and Class* Vol. 4 No 1, pp. 63–81. Copyright © 1996. Reprinted by permission of Jean Ait Belkhir, Editor.

Emile Durkheim, from *The Rules of Sociological Method*, translated by W. D. Hallis, edited by Steven Lukes. Reprinted with the permission of The Free Press, a Division of Simon & Schuster Adult Publishing Group. Copyright © 1982 by Steven Lukes. Translation copyright © 1982 by Macmillan Publishers Ltd. All rights reserved.

William J. Chambliss, "The Saints and the Roughnecks," *Society* Vol. 11, No. 1, pp. 24–31. Copyright © 1973. Reprinted by permission of Transaction Publishers.

Lillian B. Rubin, "The Approach-Avoidance Dance: Men, Women, and Intimacy." Copyright © 1983 by Lillian B. Rubin. Reprinted by the permission of Dunham Literacy, as agent for the author.

James F. Quinn, from "Angels, Banditos, Outlaws, and Pagans: The Evolution of Organized Crime among the Big Four 1% Motorcycle Clubs," *Deviant Behavior* 22, pp. 379–399. Copyright 2001. Reproduced by permission of Taylor & Francis, Inc., www.routledge-ny.com.

Additional Titles of Interest